Pandeism:
An Anthology of
Worlds Unseen

Pandeism:
An Anthology of Worlds Unseen

Edited by

Knujon Mapson

Pandeism Anthology Press

TABLE OF CONTENTS

v

Dedication

In memory of our fathers.

And our forefathers before them.

Preface

Welcome to the fourth–and final, in this form– volume of the Pandeism Anthology series.

This collection, the culmination of a journey spanning decades, continues what might well at this point be called a tradition: amalgamating into book form essays delineating disparate directions of discourse, seeking many voices and origins, each contributing to a tumescent whole. As with the previous books in this series, we do not demand uniform agreement on any central thesis. We instead celebrate even oppositional diversity of thought, curiosity of inquiry, and profound reflection, as such a concept as Pandeism inspires.

Throughout history, our naked ape forebears grappled with questions of metaphysical entities, the cosmos and our place within it, its meaning and perhaps motive. The idea of a power exceeding our capacity to perceive — a power that may forever elude our full comprehension — has been a common thread uniting various cultures and epochs. And yet, it is the very divergence of our interpretations and depth of our inquiries that reveals the hidden essence of human exploration. For all that we perceive (or think we do), our perception is limited in space and time, scope and scale, and this Anthology seeks to explore the boundaries of these limitations.

Pandeism offers a unique framework, interweaving the logical and defensible elements of Pantheism and Deism. It posits a Creator that became the universe, relinquishing its divine state to experience existence through the myriad forms of life and matter. This perspective not only seeks to answer profound existential questions but to reconcile, as well, the seemingly paradoxical nature of an omnipotent, omniscient entity choosing to become finite and limited.

In this Anthology, you will encounter a wide array of essays, poems, and reflections. Some authors delve deeply into the philosophical underpinnings of Pandeism, meticulously examining its logical structures and implications. Others approach it from more creative angles, offering insights through art, literature, and personal narrative. This diversity of styles and perspectives is intentional, reflecting the broad and inclusive spirit of Pandeism itself.

Our contributors come from various walks of life, bringing with them a wealth of experiences and insights. From seasoned scholars and writers to those making their first foray into published discourse, each voice adds a unique thread to our collective tapestry. Throughout these pages, you will find explorations of Pandeism in relation to other spiritual and philosophical traditions, examinations of contemporary scientific and metaphysical questions, and reflections on the personal and societal implications of such a worldview. Historical pieces, literary excerpts, and poetic interludes further enrich the collection, providing a multifaceted approach to the themes at hand.

It is our hope that this Anthology will not only inform and challenge you but also inspire you to ponder deeply and engage actively and reflectively with the ideas presented. Whether you are a long-time follower of Pandeism or encountering it for the first time, we trust that you will find something within these pages to enlighten, provoke, and perhaps even transform your understanding.

Acknowledgments

We would like to acknowledge the authors and the poets. Your essays, poems, and reflections have brought depth, diversity, and richness to this anthology. Your willingness to share your insights and perspectives has been the cornerstone of our work.

To our readers, thank you for your curiosity, your engagement, and your support over the years. Your interest in Pandeism and your willingness to explore new ideas have been a driving force behind this series. It is our hope that these anthologies have sparked thought, inspired conversation, and perhaps even transformed your perspectives.

We are deeply appreciative of the spiritual and philosophical communities that have welcomed and supported our work. Your open-mindedness and commitment to inquiry have created a fertile ground for the ideas presented in these volumes.

Lastly, we extend our gratitude to the unseen forces that have inspired this journey. Whether you call it creativity, intuition, or divine guidance, we acknowledge the mysterious and profound energies that have guided us and fueled our exploration of the worlds unseen.

As we conclude this series, we reflect on the decade-long journey with a sense of fulfillment and accomplishment. This final volume is not just an end but a testament to the power of collective inquiry and the enduring relevance of Pandeism as a framework for understanding our universe.

Thank you all for joining this historic journey.

Pandeism:
An Anthology of
Worlds Unseen

GoDaemonics - A Scientific Model of Pandeism?

By Anthony Peake

Anthony Peake is a writer who deals with borderline areas of human consciousness. His first book, *Is There Life After Death?* was published in 2006 and since then he has gone on to develop his own ideas together with exploring the latest areas of research in his field. His fourth book, *Making Sense of Near-Death Experiences*, is a collaborative effort with some of the world's leading authorities on the near-death phenomenon. His seventh book, *A Life of Philip K Dick: The Man Who Remembered the Future*, is a departure from his previous works in that it is a mixture of biography, literary criticism and psychological/neurological analysis. His eighth book, *The Immortal Mind: Science and the Continuity of Consciousness Beyond the Brain*, was a joint project with Professor Ervin Laszlo, published in Autumn 2014. His ninth book, *Opening the Doors of Perception*, published on 13 September 2016, takes the work of Aldous Huxley and updates it using the latest information from such seemingly unrelated fields as quantum mechanics, neurochemistry and consciousness studies.

Please note this contains amended sections from a number of my books.

Introduction

There once was a man who said "God
Must think it exceedingly odd
If he finds that this tree
Continues to be
When there's no one about in the Quad."

Dear Sir,

Your astonishment's odd.
I am always about in the Quad.
And that's why the tree
Will continue to be
Since observed by
              Yours faithfully,
                  God

It was exactly 100 years ago, in 1924, that Ronald Arbuthnott Knox, an English Roman Catholic priest published this intriguing limerick in an attempt to explain the existence of unobserved phenomena.

This issue, originally as a development of the extreme Idealism of Irish cleric George Berkeley who had argued that Berkeley holds that there are no such mind-independent things, that, in the famous phrase, **esse est percipi (aut percipere)** — to be is to be perceived (or to perceive).

In his poem Knox attempts to explain how unseen objects continue to exist if there is no observer present. He jokingly states that as God is always "observing" then all of the phenomenal world continues to exist.

It was also in 1924 that French physicist Louis de Broglie proposed that matter behaved as a wave in exactly the way that light did. This was an astonishing suggestion, one later proved by experimentation. But why is this in any way related to Knox's poem other than they shared the same year? Well, it does in that it effectively proved that both Berkeley and Knox were right and, in doing so, also suggest that the concept of Pandeism has a solid scientific foundation.

In this chapter I will attempt to explain exactly why this may be.

The Mystery of Light

We use the term light waves all the time. Received wisdom 'knows' that light is made up of waves. After all Thomas Young proved it in 1800 and school day experiments confirm it. As we all know a wave does not exist in itself. If two people hold a skipping rope between them they can create a wave along the rope by moving their arms up and down. The wave is not the rope or vice versa. In the same way a wave in water consists of water, a sound wave travels in air and so do light waves. So how do light waves travel in outer space? Get ready for a surprise. Scientists have not got a clue what light is for one simple reason; sometimes it acts as a wave, a disturbance spread over a distance in space, but sometimes it acts like a particle, a point located in one specific place. How can one thing be both?

This was discovered by some curious results involving light and an exercise that is known as the 'two slit experiment.' Imagine dropping a pebble into a pond. The waves form a series of ripples moving out from the point where the pebble entered the water. Now imagine what would happen if a barrier was placed across the pond. As the waves hit the barrier, they bounce back in the direction they came. Now we place two holes in the barrier, both much smaller than the wavelength of the ripples. On the other side of the barrier two sets of waves, starting at each hole, spread out as if two new pebbles were dropped in the water at the same place as each hole. As the two new sets of ripples move out, they begin to 'interfere' with each other, disrupting the flow of the two sets of semicircles. In some places the two sets of ripples add up to make extra-large ripples; in other places, the two sets of ripples cancel out leaving little, or no, wave motion in the water.

The same exercise can be done with light. Light is shone through a single hole in a barrier. As the light flows out it encounters a second barrier, this time with two holes. The light acts like a wave in that each hole then starts its own wave pattern the other side of the second barrier. Immediately the two waves start to interfere with each other. A screen is set up after the second barrier. When the light hits this screen, it shows a pattern of light and dark stripes. These stripes are called *interference fringes*. They correspond to where the light waves add together (*constructive interference*) and where the waves cancel each other out (*destructive interference*).

In this way Thomas Young in 1800 proved that light functions as a wave. However, in 1905 Einstein proposed that light was also made up of individual particles. As far as he was concerned it was the only way that a particular puzzle for early 20th century science could be explained. When light was shone on a solid object it seemed to 'kick out' electrons from the surface. This phenomenon, known as the 'photoelectric effect', could not be explained. However, as Einstein said in his 1905 paper, if light is made of particles, then each particle hits the surface and knocks out the electrons. This supposition was supported by experimentation and in recognition of this discovery Einstein was awarded the Nobel Prize for physics. Subsequently these particles of light were given the name "photons", from the Greek word for light, φῶς (*phôs*). One problem solved, many opened. This dual nature of light (wave and particle) was to cause a radical review of our perception of electro-magnetic radiation. If light was also made up of discrete packets how can this be squared with the fact that light is also a wave? We need to re-visit the Young Experiment.

We need to understand what would, or should, happen if photons were sent through the two slits. As an analogy imagine that the two holes were holes in a barn door, the holes being about three times the size of a soccer ball. Now we kick balls against the door. After a few dozen balls are kicked through the holes we stop the exercise. We will then find two piles of balls on the other side of the barn door. We would expect to find the pattern (two piles of footballs) to be exactly the same if, instead of both holes being open at the same time, each hole was open on its own for half the time and then the other hole for the other half. What you would not expect would be a group of balls centred half way between the two holes, right behind the solid door. Footballs, like particles, do not interfere with one another.

Now imagine a single photon being fired at the barrier. The photon, in order to get to the other side, has to go through *one or other* of the two holes. Recording such a small particle of light needs a super sensitive photographic plate and this is set up at the other side of the barrier. Each photon, as it arrives, registers on the photographic plate as a single white spot. As thousands, then millions of photons arrive at the plate a pattern begins to emerge. Common sense would lead you to assume that there would be two circles of white light coinciding with the trajectory of each photon through whichever hole it selected, just like our piles of footballs in our barn door analogy. However, we are dealing with the quantum world where common sense does not exist. In fact, what we do get is the interference pattern again. Now think about this; each particle goes through one hole on its own, however something seems to interfere with it as it goes through to form the unexpected interference pattern. This leaves us with one of only two options, both of which are peculiar in the extreme. The first option is that the photon starts out as a particle, and arrives as a particle, but en route it seems to go through both holes. In doing so it interferes with itself as it comes through the holes, and then works out exactly where to place itself on the photographic plate to ensure that ultimately, and with all its fellow protons, a perfect pattern of light and dark stripes is to be found. The mystery of this first option is how does the photon manage to go through both holes at the same time, and having done that how does it 'know' where to place itself on the photographic plate?

This duality of light is a puzzle but light is strange anyway. It travels at a huge speed (either as a wave or a photon) and seems to be constant at all times. This speed of light (186,000 miles per second) is the fastest anything can possibly travel. According to physics it is impossible to travel any faster. Okay, so what if I am sitting on a train travelling at 100 miles an hour and I switch on my torch in the direction of travel? Surely those light waves (photons) will be travelling at 186,000.0277 miles per second and therefore faster than light? Actually no, they are still travelling at 186,000 miles per second *relative* to you and the train. However *relative* to somebody on the platform of the station you have just travelled through the speed of light has been exceeded by 100 miles per hour. However, and this is another curiosity of modern physics, Einstein argued that even relative to the observer on the station the speed of light was constant. So, what has given? Einstein says that time itself slows down (or speeds up) to accommodate the anomaly. So, for you on the train time was passing more slowly than for those on the platform. At greater speeds the relative time differences become greater until at nearly the speed of light time almost stops.

So light is weird, but at least atoms, however empty they may be, are, in the final analysis, solid and do not suffer the wave-particle schizophrenia of light.

Imagine however if it was shown, in support of De Broglie's 1924 theory that electrons and atoms also hade wave-like properties then the same strange effects will be observed in matter. In 1987 teams from Hitachi research laboratories and Gakushuin University in Tokyo found that electrons do, indeed, have the same duality. Problematic yes, but electrons are still incredibly small and nobody has ever seen or photographed one. Atoms, now they are different. We can photograph the larger types so they are 'solid' in a very real sense. However, at the beginning of the 1990's a team from the University of Konstanz, in Germany proved the impossible; atoms also travel as a wave and arrive as a particle. Your chair is not only made up of vast areas of empty space, but what solidity it has depends upon whether the atoms choose to be solid particles or non-solid waves. The question is what makes them make this choice? The answer is simple but hair raising. The factor that pulls the atom from a non-physical wave to a solid point of matter is your mind. The act of observation by a thinking being brings matter into physical existence!

Indeed, two years after De Broglie made his incredible suggestion, in 1926, another physicist, Max Born, suggested that electrons do not actually exist as individual entities but are merely 'statistics'. By this he meant that a scientist can calculate with great accuracy the behaviour of trillions of electrons but he has no way of predicting the behaviour of any single electron. We only have a statistical chance of finding an electron in a particular place. He termed this the 'Probability Amplitude'. Born then proposed that the 'wave function' of electrons is a statistical wave, similar to a crime wave. As such a crime wave itself has no actual existence. A person cannot be affected by a crime wave but only by an actual crime taking place. Thus, the electron 'wave' only becomes a solid, real, electron when it is measured and found to be in a particular location. Before the measurement takes place, the electron does not exist except as a probability. The act of observation makes the wave function 'collapse' into a solid object, in this case an electron. It is important that this concept is understood. Before an observer detects the quantum particle *it does not exist*. The consciousness brings the object into reality. Without conscious observation, no reality. We create our own universe!

But what constitutes an "observer" and, more importantly, what about a physical system consisting of electrons and atoms and illuminated by photons where there is no "observer"?

So now you will, I hope, understand, the significance of Knox's poem. So, who is the "observer" that maintains the solidity and, indeed, existence of the universe?

Cheating the Ferryman

In 1999 I wrote my first book. Initially this was simply an attempt to understand what is taking place when somebody experiences déjà vu. This is the overwhelming sensation that you are re-living something that you had already experienced in an undefined time in your past. This is an extremely common sensation, and research has suggested that at least 70% of human beings will experience this at least once in their lives. For me it has been a frequent experience and it usually manifests as part of my classic migraine aura (a curious set of visual and aural hallucinations that are perceived just before a migraine headache begins). I therefore had personal reasons for understanding more about this peculiar sensation.

In my research I discovered a paper by Dr Arthur Funkhouser, an American physicist based in Switzerland. In this paper he argued that a déjà vu is actually the memory of the circumstances experienced in a recent, but forgotten, dream that is subsequently perceived in real life. Funkhouser argues that this is why what is taking place feels familiar but without any recognition regarding where the familiarity is sourced. I contacted Dr Funkhouser and discussed with him how his "dream theory of déjà vu" was intriguing but that its central premise – a dream which subsequently comes true – had no basis is science. He agreed, but argued that he had experienced a number of precognitive dreams as had many of his clients (he works now as a Jungian analyst).

This intrigued me and lead me to the writings of an Anglo-Irish aeronautical engineer, John William Dunne. In 1902, while working in South Africa, Dunne had a series of powerful precognitive dreams which inspired him to keep a dream diary by his bedside. Over a number of years Dunne discovered that many of his dreams were precognitive. In 1927 he published a book entitled "An Experiment with Time" that presented irrefutable evidence that the future can be perceived in dreams. This book proved immensely popular and thousands of people across the world started their own dream diaries. Dunne argued in later books that when we dream, we share our consciousness with another element of ourselves he called "Observer Two" (the dreamer themselves being "Observer One"). "Observer Two" exists in a different type of time which, not surprisingly, he called "Time Two". This form of time involves a perception of the contents of Observer One's immediate future, awareness of which is available to Observer Two. In the dream state the knowledge of Observer Two is available to Observer One but is not recalled in waking life. Dunne suggested a wonderful analogy. He asked us to visualise Observer One sitting in a train carriage looking straight out the carriage window at a station platform. As the train draws out of the station the platform moves from our present set of perceptions into the past and our present is then filled with the views of the townscape surrounding the station. Observer Two, meanwhile, is sitting on the roof of the carriage and can see forward to take in the railway lines running off into the distance. In effect, continuing the time analogy, he can see the contents of the future that Observer One, from the confines of the inside of the carriage cannot see.

Here was an analogy of how Funkhouser's Dream Theory may work, but it totally failed to explain the mechanism by which another part of ourselves can know the future. According to modern science, the future has yet to happen and therefore does not exist. So how can Observer Two perceive it? I needed a more scientific explanation and one that was logical and rational.

And it was then that I began researching near-death experiences (NDEs). Through a chance encounter with a business associate who had recently been diagnosed with a neurological illness called Temporal Lobe Epilepsy (TLE) I discovered that there was a direct neurochemical link between TLE and the NDE. Earlier I mentioned my own migraine-related aura states. Individuals who experience TLE have similar pre-seizure auras but they are much more powerful. They involve time dilation, a sensation of leaving the body, elaborate hallucinations, a sensation of somebody sharing their consciousness and, most importantly for me, profound déjà vu perceptions. These perceptions, as was the case with my friend, involved precognitive deja vus in which the contents of the person's immediate future is perceived before it actually happens in reality. I have subsequently witnessed a TLEr announcing a future event while in an aura state, an event that came to pass exactly as she described a few seconds later.

One researching this further I discovered that neurologists have noted many neurochemical similarities between NDEs and TLE. Indeed, in recent years it has also been discovered that a number of psychedelic substances such as ketamine and dimethyltryptamine (DMT) and psilocybin can also create NDE-like experiences.

I decided that it was the NDE that needed to be the central theme of my research. An NDE is exactly what the words describe. Many individuals over the centuries have reported, during close encounters with death, that a series of related perceptions are encountered (for a full review of the NDE, check out my forthcoming book *The Near-Death Experience - The Science, Psychology and Anthropology Behind the Phenomenon* which will be published in November 2024). I discovered that a number of "traits" have been reported in most NDEs and these include out-of-body experiences, travelling towards a light, a tunnel, encounters with an entity known as the "Being of Light", time dilation and, of most significance for me, a "panoramic life-review" (PLR) in which the person's whole life, or snapshots of that life, are experienced.

Indeed, there were three traits that I found of possible significance in my attempt to explain déjà vu. They were the PLR, the being of light and time dilation. By analysing these in detail I was able to create a hypothetical scenario of possible immortality that did not conflict with known or theoretical science and, in effect, explain how precognitive déjà vu experiences can be explained. I called this concept "Cheating the Ferryman" (CTF) and, seven years later, in 2006, my first book explaining this concept was published.

I differentiate between the classic Near-Death Experience and a Real-Death Experience (RDE) and argue that those who survive a close encounter with death perceive a number of the traits in a reduced way in that in an RDE the traits. This involves a dilation of subjective time perception to such an extent that a century of objective time can be experienced in a fraction of a second. In effect the dying person's consciousness falls into Dunne's "Time Two". And stretching the link with the Dunne model, Dunne's "Observer Two" also becomes manifest within the consciousness of "Observer One". Using my own terminology "Time Two" I call the "Bohmian IMAX" and "Observers One and Two" are the "Eidolon" and "Daemon" respectively. But most importantly, it is how the PLR is perceived in an RDE. In an NDE the dying person experiences their life flashing by in a series of snapshots or as if their whole life has been recorded and is perceived as a fast-forwarded video recording. But in an RDE the whole life is experienced second by second. In effect, their life is totally re-lived.

But let me explain my terminology here as it is very important. In his 1992 book "Consciousness Explained" philosopher Daniel Dennett to sarcastically dismiss the long-held belief that the universe comprises two quite distinct types of 'stuff' – matter and spirit. That is, material things that have extension in space and non-physical things that do not. The body is matter, whereas the mind is not. This is known as substance dualism. This idea was discussed extensively by French philosopher René Descartes and so is also referred to as Cartesian dualism. Descartes presented his ideas in his 1641 book Meditations on First Philosophy. For eliminative materialists such as Daniel Dennett, this idea is ludicrous. They argue that if mind is not matter, but some kind of 'ghost in the machine', a term coined by another eliminative materialist philosopher, Gilbert Ryle (Ryle, 1949), how can it physically affect matter in any way? In mechanics, every action is brought about by a force, but spirit, as it is defined, cannot create any force. So how does it influence nerves to bring about muscular contractions? Indeed, Dennett takes this further by suggesting that the idea of a 'ghost in the machine' brings about an infinite regress.

For example, when I perceive the outside world, I imagine a miniature version of myself sitting in a small room inside my head. It has a pair of speakers on either side broadcasting the sound signals from my ears and a stereo TV screen in front of me showing what my eyes are seeing. I sit in a chair that reproduces the nerve sensations from my skin. In this way, all my senses are presented to me. All these are the contents of my consciousness, and 'I' am the audience who experiences them. But there is a problem. If I imagine this little homunculus in my head, then he, in turn, must have a little person in his head sitting in his own little room, and so on and so on. This quickly becomes an infinite regress of eversmaller homunculi. This makes no sense. This inner auditorium is what Dennett calls the 'Cartesian theatre'. This is the place in the brain where consciousness resides and 'observes' the sights and sounds processed by the senses. But for Dennett to believe this is to fall into another version of Cartesian dualism.

My concept of the "Bohmian IMAX" (BIMAX) is a counter-point to Dennett's "Cartesian Theatre". I argue that mind generates reality and that reality is as richer in detail and clarity as is an IMAX cinema in relation to a stage theatre. The word "Bohmian" is in recognition of the work of Anglo-American physicist David Bohm.

Bohm believed that holograms could be used to explain his belief that our perception of separate things is an illusion and that there exists an underlying order of wholeness. He likened this to a flowing stream. He asked us to visualize the surface of this stream. We see an ever-changing pattern of vortices, ripples, waves and splashes. These seem real, but in actual fact, they have no independence from their underlying cause, the continual flowing of the water. They have no autonomy of their own. They cannot exist without this underlying motion. And so, he argued, it is with what we believe to be perceived reality, including human consciousness itself.

From this, Bohm suggested a model whereby the whole universe can be thought of as a kind of giant, flowing hologram, or holomovement, in which a total order is contained, in some implicit sense, in each region of space and time. I called this higher level of reality the Implicate Order. From this our perceptual universe, the Explicate Order, is projected. The apparent stability and solidity of the objects and entities within the Explicate Order are generated and sustained by an ongoing process of enfoldment and unfoldment. We shall return to this later.

Now we turn our attention to "The Daemon" and "The Eidolon". These are terms taken from the Ancient Greek Pre-Socratics which then became central to the Eleusinian mystery cults. It was believed that we all have two components to our personalities: an Eidolon which is the everyday person that exists in the world and has limited knowledge of that world presented through the five senses. The Eidolon is mortal and, after one life, dies. The Daemon on the other hand is immortal and lives multiple lives. The Daemon acts as the protector and spirit guide to the Eidolon. Of great significance is that this belief was to become a central part of many esoteric belief systems and occult practices.

So, to recap, in Cheating the Ferryman I argue that at the point of death human consciousness, which up to that point has been singular, splits into two. In effect the Daemon manifests and becomes self-aware. The Daemon becomes aware of itself and its role in facilitating the next stage of consciousness whereas the dying Eidolon, which can only live one life, is about to cease to exist. The newly self-aware Daemon has certain processes it needs to activate, including the starting of the panoramic life-review (PLR).

However, In an NDE, one that the Eidolon survives, the newly self-aware Daemon realises that death is not about to take place, and realises that the literal minute by minute life-review is not needed and, to use an analogy from modern video technology, metaphorically presses the "fast-forward" on the life-review. This is perceived by the Eidolon as is regularly reported by NDE survivors: "I saw my life flash before my eyes" is the common description.

But if the NDE is actually an RDE, then death is the only outcome for that specific Eidolon and the Daemon continues with the PLR which starts in real-time duration. The previous eidolonic consciousness is snuffed out to be replaced by a new Eidolon which has no memories of its previous life. That Eidolon then goes through a birth process within the PLR and begins a new life experience within the BIMAX. To re-cap, this is a minute-by-minute recreation of the previous life – well it is initially anyway.

CTF suggests that your consciousness enters a timeless location at the point of death, and you are 'reborn' in a new version of your previous life. You are reborn as you, not as somebody else. You are born of the same parents (or possibly any scenario whereby your exact DNA profile is reproduced).

Of course, your birth location and scenario will depend upon a myriad of life decisions made by your parents, your grandparents and, indeed, all your ancestors. Each outcome of every decision is made by a consciousness that can 'collapse a wave function' and therefore creates a reality out of the information field that exists within the macroverse. Your 'rebirth' will involve you downloading an initial information field based very closely on your previous life. This allows for logical and sequential progression whereby the last life's issues can be resolved or unfulfilled scenarios followed through. These alternate realities are created from information, not physical objects (although their amalgamations are perceived as being physical objects).

This is like loading a third-person role-playing computer game. The game's scenario is rendered from digital information that appears as a location and landscape on your PC screen (more accurately, a virtual-reality world as rendered by an Oculus Rift or similar device.

Once you start this new life, all outcomes of all your decisions can be 'collapsed', but once 'collapsed', the scenario becomes physical and cannot be changed. Decision by decision your new life enfolds (to use a David Bohm reference) out of the Implicate Order and into the Explicate Order.

But the Daemon can guide you only as long as it has experienced the decision-outcomes taken in previous lives. When a completely new scenario is encountered, its only advice can be general because it, like the Eidolon, is encountering this set of circumstances for the first time. And here is the big difference between ITLAD and reincarnation. Here, there is development; here, there is a carry-through of life experiences. Here is the opportunity to learn from one's mistakes. Indeed, here is a scenario to right the wrongs and explore other avenues not taken. Over many lives (because at the end of each one, a new one is encountered), 'all roads can be taken', especially with an effective and engaged Daemon.

But what about the other consciousnesses we interact with within the BIMAX? Are the real or simply zombies, just like the non-sentient sprites we encounter in computer games? Well, this is where Pandeism comes into the equation, and where I attempt to answer the question first posited at the start of this chapter. Who is the "observer" that collapses the wave function of seemingly unobserved realities?

Let's return to the central concept of CTF. In this each consciousness, at the point of death, goes back and relives its life. This life is in the same time and culture as the previous life. But this time, the Daemon guides the Eidolon using knowledge gained from the previous life (or lives, as multiple lives are experienced, and with each life, more knowledge is achieved and an individuated evolution takes place). But – and this is a crucial point – this is happening to every other sentient intelligence that the original Eidolon interfaces within each life-iteration. Millions of Daemon-guided singular consciousnesses, embodied as Eidolons, are collectively evolving as an Uber-Eidolon, which is the collective known as society. As this society evolves, it will develop new technologies and medical advances within its own historical time period. This is again important. Each society will, over multiple runs through its collective Bohmian IMAXs, evolve scientifically and culturally, and each individuated Eidolonic consciousness within that BIMAX will be 'reborn' into progressively more sophisticated cultural environments. Scientific and medical advances will be made by those who learn from their multiple lives and iteratively apply this knowledge. Each individual contributes to a collective change. And BIMAX after BIMAX, this will evolve a technological civilization similar and, in some cases, identical, to our own 21st-century world. This means that discoveries will be made which will eradicate diseases and illnesses, people will survive accidents that in earlier BIMAXs would have killed them. This, in turn, will allow these Eidolons to live a full life and, in turn, for them to contribute to society as a whole.

But if time is orthogonal and not linear, these 'earlier' societies exist concurrent to our own. Indeed, how would we know if our society is not one of these earlier ones? Or, more interestingly, that there has only ever been one actual society, and we are in it?

After all, if time is subjective, then why should this not be the case?

So, all human beings, since time immemorial, may be actually still alive and experiencing life now. We are all evolving together. In effect, this is a variation on Pandeism in which we are all really one consciousness experiencing itself subjectively.

CTF, proposes a model of human immortality that makes logical sense. It gives consciousness a reason for being rather than simply a pointless exercise in a nihilism that achieves nothing. We are here to learn and grow towards perfection. But, most importantly, CTF is supported by the science, which other alternative models of survival after death are not.

But what, exactly, is consciousness? Philosopher David Chalmers has argued that how the brain creates referential self-awareness is the greatest problem for modern science, a mystery that we are no nearer solving now than we were a hundred years ago.

I would like to suggest that consciousness is the medium whereby information becomes physical in the sense that it becomes sensual. Indeed, could it be that consciousness and the universe are simply manifestations of a deeper reality, a reality that is actually unitary in nature? Are we all a singular consciousness experiencing itself subjectively?

If we are, then what is the nature of that consciousness? Is this just another variation on Brahman discussed in the section on theology, or is it more? I suspect that we have levels of awareness. This starts with the Eidolon, the consciousness that exists within the simulation and experiences just one life. It is the equivalent of any in-game avatar generated for a singular game-play session within a video game. It exists for one game which ends at its 'death' within the game-play. This is a single life. As we have already discussed, the Eidolon is born, experiences a life and then ceases to exist. When a new game is started, a new Eidolon is created with no memories of the last game (life).

But experiencing every game-play is the game-player who exists outside of the game. This is the Daemon. It remembers all previous games (lives) and uses this knowledge to assist each new Eidolon to advance successfully through the game. How effective it will be on doing this will depend upon various factors. For a full discussion on how this may work, check out my books *The Daemon: A Guide to Your Extraordinary Secret Self (2008)* and *Opening the Doors of Perception: The Key to Cosmic Awareness (2016)* and the book that this section is adapted from, *Cheating the Ferryman: The Revolutionary Science of Life After Death* (2022). We, therefore, have two forms of memory: Eidolonic Memory (EM), which is the recollections of experiences encountered within one run of the game; while Daemonic Memory (DM), on the other hand, is the memories of all the previous games experienced by the Daemon. EM is precisely what the famous Swiss psychiatrist Carl Gustav Jung (1875–1961) called the 'personal unconscious'. DM has an awareness of the events of which each individual EM is cognisant. What is of great importance here is to realize that there will be a point in the game when DM will have no prior knowledge. Although it can guide the Eidolon using its previous experience, its precognitive abilities will have ceased. I have argued in the past that this is why déjà vu experiences are perceived less and less as we age (Adachi, et al., 2003).

But I now believe that there may be another two levels above this 'Daemon-Eidolon Dyad'. These I call the *Uber-Daemon* and the *GoDaemon*. The Uber-Daemon is, in effect, the consciousness that created the game itself. It has full access to all the information contained within David Bohm's Implicate Order that involves humanity. This is identical to Jung's second level of awareness, the 'collective unconscious'. Jung defined this as:

> The collective unconscious as the ancestral heritage of possibilities of representation, is not individual but common to all men, and perhaps even to all animals, and is the true basis of the individual psyche.
>
> Jung, 1998

I would like to argue that the Jungian collective unconscious is the source of two of the experiences that are regularly cited as evidence of survival after death, and are seemingly contradictory to my CTF hypothesis. The first is past-life memories that are either spontaneously recalled or evoked through hypnotic regression. In these, individuals describe in detail elements of another life experienced in the past. These facts are subsequently checked and found to be true. I would like to suggest that what is taking place here is the person is tapping into the collective unconscious of the human species and has randomly attuned into a specific lifetime. This is a memory of a past life, but not their life. This information may be carried through in our DNA or simply be facilitated by attuning into a broader area of Bohm's Implicate Order. The second area that the collective unconscious could explain is clairvoyance and psychic mediums. These individuals attune into the collective unconscious and pick up information created by the expectations of their clients. Furthermore, one could add as an additional explanation that such experiences could be related directly to my 'egregore' model extensively discussed above.

And now we turn to the GoDaemon. By this, I mean the collective consciousness of everything in the multiverse. This is what the Hindus mean when they discuss *Brahman*; Quabbalists when they describe the *Ain Sof*; and the Kashmiri Shaivites concept of *Citi*. In effect, this is pure Advaita, non-dualism, a model of understanding whereby everything is created out of pure consciousness that is information. And it is this greater version of ourselves, the "god within" that we are advised to search for, that manifests the tree in the quad.

And what is the technical term for the idea that God has, as a form of pure consciousness, manifesting as everything that exists? Yes, it is called Pandeism!

The Divine Feminine and Sacred Nature in Pandeism: Embracing Immanence and Re-Imagining Spirituality

By Lisa M. Christie, PhD

Lisa M. Christie, PhD, is a spiritual eco-feminist teacher and author of Reality Unbound: A New Science Exploration of Psychic Experiences and the Conscious World in Which We Live. She received her doctorate in Philosophy and Religion, with a Concentration in Women's Spirituality, from the California Institute of Integral Studies (CIIS), and currently teaches philosophy and religion at that same institution. Known for her investigative research of psycho-spiritual experiences and what they might tell us about the nature of Reality, she has spoken at the American Academy of Religion (AAR), the Association for the Study of Women and Mythology (ASWM), Cherry Hill Seminary, and many other organizations. Her driving passion is to help enable those who have had psychic spiritual experiences to connect with the sacredness of the natural world, live in greater harmony and richness, and share their wisdom with the wider world.

The Goddess in all her manifestations was a symbol of the unity of all life in Nature. Her power was in water and stone, in tomb and cave, in animals and birds, snakes and fish, hills, trees, and flowers. Hence the holistic and mythopoeic perception of the sacredness and mystery of all there is on Earth.

—Marija Gimbutas, *Language of the Goddess*

The masculine pronoun safeguards ... the transcendence of God against the illusion nature is born from God as a mother rather than created.

—Peter Kreeft and Ronald K. Tacelli, *The Handbook of Christian Apologetics*

Pandeists' view of the divine as immanent in the world has implications for the metaphors we use for the divine as well as for theology. For those new to Pandeism, this theological perspective holds that God created the cosmos from Himself through a process of self-transformation. Therefore, God is immanent in the world—which is seen as a living organic whole—and everything that exists is a manifestation of the divine. Here I have used "God" vs. "Goddess" language because (implicitly masculine) "God" language is commonplace in contemporary Western thought, a convention I propose that Pandeism should reconsider for reasons described below.

Since the dawn of humanity, gender has functioned as a primary philosophical and religious symbol that invokes a paradigm or worldview, including the relationship of the divine to the world and hence to us. Theologians and philosophers have described this relationship in terms of *immanence* and *transcendence*. In philosophy, immanence means being within or inherent in something, and transcendence means being outside or beyond something. Throughout the history of Western thought, immanence has been symbolically female, and transcendence, symbolically male. These orientations shape our relationship to other beings and nature, our social structures, our ways of knowing, and our psychology. In this way, our paradigm of reality reinforces itself, making it seem to be "just the way things are."

To illustrate this point, for most of human history, the primary metaphor for the divine was the Great Mother, who gave birth to all beings from Her body. In this view, the cosmos and all beings are manifestations of Her divine essence. Accordingly, humans envisioned the divine in the forms of a Mother Goddess and Her diverse manifestations as nature—expressed in the forms of humans, animals, plants, landscapes, and the Earth.

The metaphor of the Creator as primarily masculine arose only relatively recently, beginning in c. 5000 BCE, in response to specific historical events. Over thousands of years, this view evolved into the classical theological view in which God created the cosmos out of nothing—most definitely not out of Himself. In this view, when God is depicted, it is in the likeness of a human male. Although Christianity describes God as both immanent and transcendent, in a Christian theological context, God's immanence refers to His presence, involvement, and power over the world, not to His being the world or part of the world, which Christian theology explicitly denies. In this sense, God is more like an involved father than a mother.

Although many contemporary religious institutions have moved towards gender-neutral language for the divine, conservative theologians strenuously object to using female metaphors for theological reasons. For example, the prominent Catholic philosopher and theologian Peter Kreeft and priest Ronald K. Tacelli argue for the maleness of God, stating, "the masculine pronoun safeguards the transcendence of God against the illusion that nature is born from God as mother rather than created"[1]—that is, it defends against the view that the divine is immanent in the world.

How did Western religious ideas shift from viewing the divine as immanent, symbolized by female and diverse imagery, to seeing the divine as primarily or fully transcendent, represented by male imagery? To answer this question, we first explore the environmental, social, and psychological factors that influence human ideas about the immanence or transcendence of the divine, and so, the symbolic gender of the divine.

We then examine how these factors have played out over the course of human history to shape Western spiritual and philosophical thought, social structures, and psychology. This historical survey reveals that catastrophic environmental and social events shifted human consciousness, leading to the modern theological view that the divine exists entirely outside of nature, and to the modern secular view that the world consists of inanimate matter.

Expressed as spirit-world and mind-body dualism and as philosophic materialism, these views perpetuate our cultural alienation from the Earth, our own bodies, and each other, leading to environmental degradation, social inequality, institutionalized violence, and the intergenerational perpetuation of trauma.

Pandeism, with its affirmation of divine immanence, can contribute to creating a more connected, equitable, peaceful, and healthy world by embracing the spiritual, environmental, social, and psychological implications of divine immanence, including a wider set of symbols and metaphors for the divine.

Gender Symbolism and Paradigms of Reality

What factors shape our ideas about the divine, particularly regarding its immanence or transcendence? And how do these factors and ideas influence our social structures and psychology? To address these questions, we will first examine anthropologist Peggy Reeves Sanday's global analysis of the environmental and social factors that shape our fundamental worldview, including our concepts of the immanence or transcendence of the divine and its symbolic gender.

Next, we will explore the environmental scientist James DeMeo's study on how harsh ecological conditions can lead to the belief that the Divine is transcendent. DeMeo also examines how these conditions affect our minds and bodies, degrading the quality of our relationships with each other and the environment. Finally, we will review the research of scientist and historian Jared Diamond, who explores the types of events that can lead to the collapse of human cultures and so potentially alter worldviews.

Basic Patterns of Orientation to the World

The gender of a culture's primary deity or deities arises from complex environmental, social, and psychological factors. Having studied over 148 past and present societies using qualitative and statistical analysis, Sanday concluded that the environment is critical in how people perceive the world and gender the divine. She identified two primary cultural orientations, an *inner orientation,* and an *outer orientation* (described below), with cultures falling on a spectrum between the two.[2] In most—but not all—societies, women are symbolically associated with the Earth, due to their ability to create and nurture life from their bodies,[3] and so, as we will see, their spiritual and social status is linked to abundance or harshness of the environment.

On the one hand, when the environment is abundant—when people can easily sustain themselves from the fertile earth, rivers, and sea—they generally develop an inner orientation. In such societies, people usually perceive the sacred as inherent in the natural world and envision the creator deity as female or as a male-female pair.[4] In cultures where the creator deity is female, all beings are believed to have emerged from Her and to partake in Her divinity. In these societies, not only women but also men, non-human animals, plants, and other entities can serve as representations of the divine. As we shall see below, this orientation evolved into the theological concept of immanence.

Inner-oriented cultures tend to be egalitarian, peaceful, and nurturing. Both men and women gather food or practice early forms of agriculture and share in child-rearing responsibilities.[5] Unsurprisingly, such cultures tend to be peaceful with little or no social violence, including against women and children. Such cultures are often *matrilineal* (based on kinship with the mother or mother line) and *matristic* (woman-centered). From a psychological perspective, we might assume that children experience their mother and father figures as close, generally available, and supportive, leading to greater social and spiritual trust. People in these circumstances tend to live more settled lives and feel a closer connection to the land.

On the other hand, when the environmental or social conditions are harsh, societies usually perceive the realm of the sacred to be *out there*, in the sky, and the primary creator to be male. In this case, the creator makes the world not from His body but via His spit, ejaculation, or Word. This *outer orientation* is ultimately expressed in the concept of transcendence: In Judaism and Christianity, God is considered separate from His Creation, creating the world out of nothing (*ex nihilo*) by verbally invoking it into existence rather than out of His substance.

In such cultures, gender roles are highly differentiated.[6] Men are often away in groups to hunt large game, to raid other groups, or to engage in warfare. Consequently, women become the primary or only caretakers of children and continue to engage in food gathering, early agriculture, and animal domestication. In modern societies, this differentiation in gender roles was more evident before the Women's Liberation Movement. According to the then prevailing social model, men worked outside the home while women—especially white women—were more limited to the domestic sphere.[7] Under more severe conditions, such as drought, severe poverty, or warfare, women and children as well as men may become mobile.

Outer-oriented cultures are generally hierarchical, with men dominating women and children (as well as each other). Under these harsh conditions, men tend to see women and children as relatively unproductive mouths to feed, assume dominance, and seek to control women's fertility. Consequently, men tend to become more violent towards women and children. This social system is called *patriarchy* or the "rule of the fathers." In such circumstances, we might expect the dominance and distance of the authoritarian father to condition an understanding of the divine as authoritative and distant. People also tend to become more distant from the land (or Earth).[8]

Because these cultural paradigms influence every aspect of life, they are often seen as natural—"the way things are." Consequently, they tend to be persistent, changing only slowly as conditions evolve; however, they may change more rapidly in response to dramatic events.

Desertification, the Arising of Male Domination, and the Armored Personality

DeMeo's research builds on Sanday's findings by examining the somatic and psychological effects of growing up in outer-oriented versus inner-oriented cultures. With a strong interest in Wilhelm Reich's studies on the development of heavily armored personalities, DeMeo sought to understand the origins of this unhealthy psychological pattern, which often manifests in interpersonal violence. He also connects these cultural patterns to specific geographical regions and environmental conditions.

Reich explains in *Character Analysis*, that abuse and neglect lead to the formation of *character* armor—muscular and emotional defenses that block natural emotional and sexual energy. This armor functions as a "deadening emotional wall"[9] between individuals, reflecting the belief that pleasure, especially sexual pleasure, is bad and that suppressing pleasurable feelings is good.

Such armoring degrades the quality of human relationships and our connection to nature. By impairing emotional connections, it fosters a sense of separation from others, resulting in a lack of trust, empathy, and communication problems. In interactions with others, this armoring results in defensive behaviors like denial, projection, and aggression, which can manifest as violence. Additionally, it creates a sense of disconnection from the natural world, diminishing empathy for other living beings and reducing interest in environmental stewardship.

Reich explains that armoring typically arises within patriarchal cultures. In **The Mass Psychology of Fascism**, he argues that the authoritarian family, as a microcosm of the broader patriarchal society, suppresses natural emotional and sexual expressions. This suppression leads to the development of what he calls the *authoritarian* *character*, which is marked by submissiveness to authority and a tendency toward fascism.[10]

To determine the origins of armoring and systemic human violence, Demo began by undertaking a cross-cultural study of violence. Drawing on large anthropological and ethnographical databases, he discovered that

> cultures with the highest levels of social violence are characterized by the harsh and abusive treatment of babies and children, by the sexual repression of adolescents and the unmarried, by compulsive marriage and deeply hierarchal social structures that push women down, and by religious authoritarianism. Cultures with the lowest levels of violence are opposite to this description in nearly every respect.[11]

More explicitly, cultures with low levels of violence typically do not systematically promote psycho-physical armoring. As a result, they often exhibit more positive social relationships characterized by strong emotional connections to others and high levels of interpersonal trust, as well as trust in the world. People in such cultures, can more easily resolve conflicts in healthy ways and experience a deeper connection with the natural world.[12]

When DeMeo mapped the locations with high concentrations of heavily armored characters based on levels of interpersonal violence, he identified "a startling and clear-cut geographic pattern of human behavior."[13] His World Behavior Map showed, the most armored cultures were patriarchal and found in desert regions:

[These societies were] clustered across the vast ... desert region that encompasses North Africa, the Middle East and Central Asia .... which encompasses the harshest and largest region of uninterrupted desert in the world .... [It is] the most extreme environment on the planet [where life] is exceedingly difficult and often hangs on by its fingernails.[14]

DeMeo referred to this extensive region as *Saharasia*.

DeMeo's research supports Sanday's observation that outer-oriented cultures developed in response to harsh environments. Consistent with Sanday's analysis, we will see that this orientation can also be propagated through harsh social conditions including colonization, invasion, and internal violence. Consequently, during periods of social disruption, an outer orientation can spread to cultures that were previously inner-oriented.

Varieties of Human Catastrophes

The social scientist Jared Diamond expands on DeMeo's analysis of factors that can shift a culture from an inner orientation to an outer orientation. Diamond argues that societies tend to collapse due to climate change, environmental damage, peoples' responses to those changes, war and the threat of war, and the influence of trading partners.[15] Social collapse can lead to a shift towards an outer orientation.

In the next section, we will consider how these factors have evolved over the history of Western thought to give rise to our current mainstream cultural orientation and worldview.

Gendered Symbolism in the Evolution of Western Thought

Although Western culture has considered both the separation of God from the world and male dominance as normal—viewed as the way things have always been—examining how these perspectives developed over time can provide a clearer understanding. The following analysis covers a broad expanse of human history, from the Paleolithic to the Scientific Revolution.[16]

Although parallel developments have taken place on other parts of the planet, I focus this broad-brush review on the regions that have most influenced modern Western thought: Europe, the Near East, and the Mediterranean—especially classical Greece, whose philosophies strongly influenced development of Jewish and Christian theology and modern science. Before proceeding, however, it will be helpful to say a few words about the Paleolithic and Neolithic eras, which are often called *prehistory*.

In line with the view that "things have always been this way," it is commonly assumed that Paleolithic and Neolithic peoples were "warlike, bloodthirsty savages, ruled by Big Men."[17] Additionally, it is believed that these cultures remain largely unknown to us due to the lack of written records. As a result, it is often thought that Western history truly began around 4500 BCE in Sumer, where written language and complex urban societies are believed to have originated.[18]

For this reason, many scholars distinguish between prehistory (encompassing the Paleolithic and the Neolithic Ages), and history (covering the Bronze, Iron, and Modern Ages). This perspective, which makes relatively recent history appear essentially the same as human history in all significant ways, is reinforced by our Gregorian calendar, which aligns our sense of time with the estimated birth of Jesus of Nazareth just 2,000 years ago.

Other scholars disagree with this distinction between history and prehistory, arguing that history encompasses the study of human societies and events, regardless of whether they were recorded in writing that we currently can decipher. Among those holding this view is the renowned historian of religion and philosopher Mircea Eliade.

Eliade reviewed the evidence regarding the *Paleanthropians*—the people of the Paleolithic era, including both humans and our human-like ancestors who lived at least 2 million years ago. He cautions against confusing a lack of technical sophistication with a lack of cultural sophistication: "The very slow progress made in technology does not imply a similar development of intelligence. We know that the extraordinary upsurge in technology during the past two centuries has not found expression in a comparable development of Western man's intelligence."[19] He goes on to argue, on the contrary, "What matters is ... their *works;* and these demonstrate the activity of an intelligence that cannot be defined otherwise than as "human."[20]

Our earliest human-like ancestors, *Homo habilis*, who lived at least 1.75 million years ago, worked with only wood, stone, and other natural materials. Yet, despite these limitations, they shared several traits with us, including larger brains, bipedalism (walking on two feet), toolmaking, and the ritual burial of their dead. These ritual burials suggest both symbolic thought and spiritual beliefs in an afterlife, as will be described below. Additionally, Paleolithic and Neolithic peoples left evidence of counting, calendars, and writing. Although these records are challenging to translate, ongoing scholarly research is gradually making them more comprehensible.[21]

Given the challenges in fully understanding the writing and symbol systems of earlier cultures, scholars studying the Paleolithic and Neolithic periods employ interdisciplinary methods to reconstruct these societies' beliefs, practices, and ways of life. These methods draw from archaeology, anthropology, genetics, linguistics, art history, mythology, and cognitive science. Scholars also compare their findings with those of both earlier and later cultures—especially those with decipherable writings—as well as with contemporary cultures that use similar technologies or symbol systems. While these interpretations are subject to interpretation and debate, they nonetheless provide a clearer picture of these ancient societies.

The following review of the historical development of contemporary Western thought supports Sanday's model of human cultures and validates DeMeo's thesis that Western outer-oriented cultures initially developed in harsh environments. It shows that, for most of human history, people perceived the divine to be within the natural world—a perspective consistent with Pandeism—and that environmental catastrophes contributed to the shift toward an outer orientation and ultimately to the belief that the divine is purely transcendent of the world. It will also illustrate how these inner-oriented and outer-oriented worldviews have been consistently gendered.

Upper Paleolithic – c. 40,000 BCE – 10,000 BCE

The spiritual and philosophical orientation of the peoples of ancient Europe and the Mediterranean during the Upper Paleolithic reflected a deep respect for the Earth and nature. Scholars suggest that this reverence was often expressed through the worship of a Goddess of nature, believed to give birth to all beings and regenerate them in Her earthly womb.[22] Evidence of this practice spans Europe and the Mediterranean, reaching as far as the Mal'ta-Buret culture in Russia. The similar dating and forms of goddess figurines indicate a widespread, shared spiritual system across this vast region.[23] In line with Sanday's thesis, these cultures appear to have been egalitarian, with gender equality. While there are signs of individual violence, there is no evidence of large-scale, organized warfare during this period.[24]

The Paleolithic Goddess was depicted in artifacts, ritual sites, and in stone carvings and paintings. Votive figures—some dating back as far as 25,000 BCE—often feature exaggerated breasts, buttocks, and pubic triangles, reflecting a widespread veneration of fertility and the nurturing aspects of life, embodied as a Great Mother. Many of these figurines have tapered legs and feet, suggesting they were used as ritual objects inserted into the Earth.[25]

Ritual sites, such as the paintings in the great cave sanctuaries of Les Trois Frères, Tuc d'Audoubert, and Lascaux in France also attest to Her worship. Joseph Campbell, a noted expert in comparative mythology and religion, observed that the cave labyrinths of Tuc d'Audoubert and Les Trois Frères were some of the most important religious centers in the ancient world and used for at least 20,000 years.[26]

These caves, which have been interpreted as the metaphorical and literal wombs of the Earth, have walls covered with images of humans, plants, and animals. [27] The depiction of a horned male-animal figure on one of the cave walls has sometimes been interpreted variously as a god of fertility and consort of the goddess, or as a male shaman.[28] Numerous scholars propose that the cave imagery reflects an animistic, shamanic spirituality, highlighting the deep spiritual connection early humans had with the natural world.[29]

A belief in this Goddess of life, death, and regeneration is also suggested by Paleolithic burial practices in which the body of the deceased was placed in a fetal position and covered with red ocher, symbolizing menstrual blood or the blood of life, as though preparing them for rebirth from the womb of the Great Mother.

Consistent with Sanday's thesis, Paleolithic peoples appear to have been socially egalitarian. Living spaces and burials are similar across different individuals, cave paintings show no evidence of social hierarchy, and the prevalence of female figurines indicates a widespread cultural or religious reverence for the feminine, likely reflecting a broader respect for women.

We will see these elements again in greater abundance in the Neolithic Age.

Neolithic – c. 10,000 BCE – 5500 BCE

Copious evidence from the Neolithic shows that Europeans and peoples in the Mediterranean remained inner oriented and primarily worshipped a Goddess or Goddesses, immanent in nature. During this period, these peoples experienced significant lifestyle changes, but remained largely peaceful and egalitarian.

Spirituality

Goddess worship was a central aspect of Neolithic spiritual and cultural life in Europe and the Mediterranean, as attested by figurines, ritual spaces, burial practices, and pottery with spiritual motifs. Archaeologists have found many "Venus" figurines in Neolithic sites like those from the Paleolithic era, reflecting the continued significance of female deities.

Neolithic ritual spaces included large temple complexes, shrines, and caves. The Ġgantija temples in Malta, among the oldest free-standing structures in the world, suggest the worship of a Mother Goddess and featured altars, statues, and other ritual artifacts dedicated to Her. At Çatalhöyük, shrines dedicated to female deities are adorned with wall paintings, reliefs, and installations depicting goddesses or female figures. Caves also continued to serve as centers of worship, with rock carvings and paintings depicting female figures or symbols interpreted as goddesses, often associated with natural elements like animals, plants, or celestial bodies.

Burial practices from the Paleolithic continued into the Neolithic, with the deceased positioned in a fetal pose, covered in red ochre, and oriented towards the east. This practice, along with grave goods related to fertility or the earth, suggests a belief in rebirth from the womb of a nurturing, earth-centered goddess.

Symbols often linked with female divinity, such as spirals, circles, and crescents, which may represent the womb, cycles of life, or the moon, are often found on European and Mediterranean pottery from this era. Vessels used in ritual contexts sometimes bear these symbols, further suggesting their association with goddess worship, and their presence on household pottery indicates that spirituality was integrated with everyday life, possibly including household shrines.

We can see the nature of Neolithic spirituality more clearly in ancient Crete, a Neolithic island civilization whose culture survived into the Bronze Age. The Cretans viewed the natural world as a sacred whole, where humans, animals, plants, and the elements were all interconnected in a pleasurable dance. They worshipped powerful goddesses, sometimes depicted as part human and part animal, surrounded by symbols like snakes, birds, and trees. For example, one cylinder seal shows priestesses honoring a goddess in the form of a tree. The Cretans' respect for nature is evident in their religious practices, which aimed to maintain harmony with nature and ensure the fertility of crops and livestock.

Later Cretan burial practices in *tholos* tombs—rounded structures with a narrow opening—symbolize a path toward rebirth. Consistent with Neolithic customs, bodies were placed in a fetal position, covered in red ochre, and oriented toward the east, the direction of the rising sun, suggesting that the Cretans, too, viewed the dead as being within the womb of the Goddess, awaiting rebirth.

The Cretans' spirituality appears to have been deeply integrated into their daily lives. Their utensils, crafted with great artistry, often depicted divine themes through natural imagery. Their joyful and elegant artwork suggests a love for beauty and a celebration of life.

Lifestyle

The Neolithic period marked a shift from gathering and hunting to a more sedentary lifestyle based on farming and herding. Although the Neolithic peoples still used tools of wood and stone, they created larger settled communities and urban areas, developed advanced agriculture, domesticated animals, and created pottery. Consistent with their inner orientation, they appear to have been egalitarian and generally peaceful. Their settlement patterns, housing structures, and burial practices all suggest an equitable distribution of resources.[30] Additionally, their burial sites reveal minimal variation in the wealth and types of grave goods, reflecting a communal approach to death and burial.[31] The presence of numerous images of goddesses and priestesses further supports the notion of gender equality in these societies.

Several factors indicate the peacefulness of these cultures: the presence of comparatively few fortified structures, fewer depictions of weapons, and a lack of glorification of warfare as compared to later periods. Additionally, skeletal remains show few signs of violent conflict or traumatic injuries linked to war.[32]

That said, in western and northern Europe, we find evidence of fortified settlements, mass graves, and skeletal remains showing traumatic injuries suggestive of violence and warfare.[33] What might explain these findings?

One hypothesis is the Black Sea Flood theory, which posits that around 6600 BCE, a major flood linked to the melting of Ice Age ice caps, dramatically reshaped Europe, turning the UK and Ireland into islands.[34] Geophysicists William Ryan and Walter Pitman propose that this is the great Flood described in the Bible.[35] The massive scale of this flooding would have displaced surrounding populations, who then likely migrated into western and northern Europe, leading to conflict. While eastern and southern Europe and the Mediterranean remained inner-oriented cultures during the Neolithic, disruption in northern and western Europe foreshadowed changes that would continue into the Chalcolithic Age.

Chalcolithic (or Copper) Age – c. 5500 BCE - 3500 BCE

The Chalcolithic Age, named for the copper that was smelted and used for toolmaking in this era, was a transitional period between the Neolithic and the Bronze ages. Spiritually, Europeans and

Mediterranean peoples continued to revere a nature Goddess, symbolized primarily as female and by plants, animals, and insects. In alignment with their inner orientation, they continued to have egalitarian and generally peaceful societies. These cultures also developed complex social structures and economies that included agriculture, animal husbandry, metal working, and the elegant and skilled crafting of pottery and art, which continued to incorporate natural and spiritual motifs. Trade also became more significant.

Beginning in 5,000 BCE to 4000 BCE, however, significant environmental, cultural, and religious changes occurred in central Asia, southern Russia, the Arabian Peninsula, and Northern Africa. These changes would dramatically transform the worldview and culture of the peoples who inhabited these regions and subsequently that of the peoples of Europe, the Mediterranean, and the Near East. These changes include spiritual changes, such as the introduction of primary male deities—especially sky and storm gods—and of material culture, including social inequality, and saliently, evidence of large-scale warfare.

The desertification of these previously fertile areas initiated these transformations, leading to catastrophic and often violent migrations of displaced populations. First, we will examine the desertification of central Asia and southern Russia and the first migration of Proto-Indo-Europeans from this area into Europe. Next, we explore DeMeo's proposal that similar dynamics led to the migration of the Semitic tribes from the Arabian Peninsula into the Near East.

The Proto-Indo-Europeans

Who were the Proto-Indo-Europeans? The term *Proto-Indo-European* refers not to a single group but to various groups based in around the Pontic-Caspian steppe north of the Black Sea that shared a common language and culture.[36] Archaeological evidence indicates that these cultures, like those of Neolithic Europe and the Mediterranean, were originally peaceful and egalitarian.[37] However, over a thousand years or more, their way of life and religious and philosophical views changed dramatically as the ground "literally dried up under the feet of the large (probably matriarchal) populations who lived there."[38]

As desertification set in, the Proto-Indo-Europeans likely initially tried to adjust to changing conditions by creating new settlements where the land could still support agriculture. However, as the drought continued, they increasingly turned to pastoralism.[39]

While pastoralism appears to have worked for a time, continuing desertification and population growth[40] further stressed their economy. By 5000 BCE, having domesticated horses,[41] men relied on them to expand the range of their herds, which brought them into conflict with neighboring groups. Chinese researcher Min Jiayin speculates that the Proto-Indo-Europeans began looting other settlements, rustling cattle, and engaging in warfare to survive.[42] Marija Gimbutas, a renowned archaeologist with a background in linguistics and mythology, coined the term *Kurgans*[43] for these aggressive pastoralists, naming them after their characteristic pit-style graves where the dead were buried in a pit and covered with a mound of stones and dirt.[44]

We can imagine how these devastating environmental changes might have ruptured the spiritual relationship between these peoples and the Earth, profoundly reshaping their religious ideas. Historian Brian Griffin proposes, "Where the earth seemed hostile to humanity, culture grew hostile to the earth."[45] He continues:

> Mother Earth became the dead earth, and only the heavens above still seemed holy.
>
> The desert landscape often seemed animated with hostility towards humanity. The frequent dust devils and storms of sand appeared as an incarnation of malice. So, in the Sahara ... the 'forces of nature' seemed to be primarily forces of death. In the common themes of desert mythology, the earth was a fallen world and an abode of death. It was a place of trial and exile, rather than our good home ....
>
> When desert migrants came into other lands, they brought their views of the world with them.... Religion from the desert became "Western Religion" as we know it."[46]

The Kurgans addressed the conflict created from their view of the Earth as hostile by developing an outer orientation, one of the earliest forms of religious dualism. They projected the realm of the sacred primarily onto the sky, worshiping a sky god as their primary deity.[47] This conflict between earth and sky is expressed in later Indo-European mythology, which often depicts conflicts between sky gods vs. Earth goddesses and gods of order and gods of chaos.[48] Philosophically, this conflict was translated into the conceptual dualisms of the qualities of light versus dark, order versus chaos, and life versus death.[49]

Socially, the Kurgans developed highly differentiated gender roles. Men spent increasingly amounts of time away from home, engaging in herding and later warfare, while women were fully occupied with childcare, the increasingly difficult jobs of fetching water and gathering fuel, and eventually moving camp.[50] Men saw women and children as mouths to feed, and viewed women as "the unproductive sex."[51] Consistent with Sanday's thesis, Kurgan culture became patriarchal.[52]

Children's earliest environment changed in unfavorable ways as well. Men likely became increasingly distant from and likely violent with their families. Women, under increasing stress to survive in a difficult environment, were likely unable to provide a fully nurturing environment for their children. This abuse and neglect combined with the trauma of war and the idealization of warriors, likely led to a generalized psycho-physical armoring of the Kurgan people. Such armoring would have intensified their emotional distance from the environment and each other and led to increased conflict.

Their search for greener pastures ultimately led the Kurgans to migrate into Europe, beginning with south-eastern Europe. Based on the archaeological evidence, anthropological comparisons, and linguistic analysis, Gimbutas posited that the Kurgan's entered Europe and Asia through three waves of major migrations, beginning in 4000 BCE.[53] The migrations are believed to have been violent, as indicated by the destruction of settlements, the appearance of fortified sites, shifts in settlement patterns, the presence of weapons, and skeletal evidence showing injuries consistent with combat. These violent interactions likely facilitated the spread of Indo-European languages, as they overpowered or assimilated existing populations.[54]

Although some scholars have challenged this narrative, studies of ancient DNA, particularly those published in the 2010s, have revealed significant genetic contributions from steppe populations to European gene pools around the time of the proposed Kurgan migrations (c. 4000–2500 BCE).[55] These genetic findings align with Gimbutas' theory by showing a substantial influx of people from the steppe into Europe during the same period. The DNA evidence also supports the idea that these migrations were associated with significant demographic shifts, corroborating Gimbutas's claims of population replacement or assimilation, and validating the violent nature of these movements as suggested by archaeological evidence.

The first wave of Kurgan migration, during the Chalcolithic Era, is generally characterized by conflict and conquest, as the Kurgan people expanded into new territories, often displacing or dominating the existing populations. While at times there may have been some peaceful co-existence, the overall process was likely marked by significant upheaval and cultural transformation.

The Semitic Tribes

DeMeo hypothesizes that the same dynamics that drove the Indo-Europeans from their homelands in southern Russia and central Asia into Europe also drove the Semitic tribes to leave the Arabian Peninsula for the Near East, particularly Mesopotamia and the Levant.[56]

This proposal aligns with archaeological evidence indicating significant population movements from the Arabian Peninsula during the Chalcolithic Age. Artifacts and cultural remnants resembling those from the Arabian Peninsula have been found in the Near East. And Semitic languages emerged in the Near East during this period.[57]

The integration of these newcomers with the indigenous populations of the Near East likely led to religious *syncretism*, or the blending of the religious beliefs, practices, and traditions of the two peoples. This process influenced the development of early civilizations in the Near East, which were later encountered by the Hebrew tribes.

While the exact timing and routes of Semitic tribe's migrations into the Near East remain subjects of ongoing research and debate among scholars, DeMeo's work provides a valuable framework for understanding the movement of Semitic tribes and their impact on the early history of the Near East.[58]

Although the peoples of Europe and the Mediterranean continued to worship their indigenous Goddess and goddesses and maintain an egalitarian social structure, this age marked the emergence of primary male deities and social inequality. As the catastrophic drought and desertification of Indo-European homelands continued to push the patriarchal and warlike Kurgans *en masse* into Europe and the Mediterranean, the Bronze Age would also see a massive clash of worldviews, leading to the religious and social transformation of those regions.

Bronze Age – c. 3500 BCE – 1200 BCE

The Bronze Age, named for the introduction of bronze—an alloy of copper and tin—was marked by tremendous violence, massive migrations, and radical social and religious changes. Beginning around 3500 BCE, the successively larger second and third waves of Kurgan migration led to the Indo-Europeanization of Europe and the Mediterranean.[59] This process introduced the primacy of male sky gods, a dualistic worldview, patriarchy, and a social hierarchy that privileged warriors and Indo-Europeans/Kurgans over the region's original inhabitants.

Reflecting on how the second wave of Kurgan migration may have unfolded, the social historian and philosopher Heide Göttner-Abendroth writes that as the Kurgans first encountered the "highly developed urban cultures"[60] in eastern Europe, "they may have looked upon this abundance and wealth in wonder."[61] Although some of the migrants may have found refuge and arable land, the indigenous Europeans had already largely occupied this land to its fullest capacity to support life, and were likely overwhelmed by the massive migration.

The Kurgans may have seen no option other than to take the land for their own. Since the peaceful Europeans had not known warfare, they were unprepared for what became an invasion.[62] This led to widespread destruction, with nearly 700 major settlements across southeast Europe being destroyed and burned in clashes between the incoming Kurgan groups and the indigenous Europeans. The scale of this devastation was so vast that it was later named the "Burned House Horizon."[63] Where European settlements were not destroyed but instead conquered, the Kurgan strongmen often reduced the indigenous Europeans to a subjugated class and ruled over them.[64]

The third wave of Indo-European migration, around 3000 BCE, expanded into western, northern, and northeastern Europe, as well as Greece. This wave completed the Indo-Europeanization of the continent and significantly altered its ethnic composition.[65]

Much in the same way that Christianity later spread through the absorption of elements of the extant religions of the region, when Indo-Europeans dominated rather than destroyed the indigenous Europeans, we see a *syncretism* of pantheons, in which the Indo-Europeans made European goddesses into brides of powerful sky gods.[66]

The Indo-Europeanization of Europe did not always involve direct conquest. While some groups were invaded, conquered, or destroyed, other Indigenous Europeans resisted the invaders and so were compelled to become militarized themselves.[67] They established their own warrior classes, primarily composed of men. This shift led to a decrease in the status of women and the development of a more patriarchal culture. This is an example of how a culture can shift from an inner orientation to an outer orientation due to social pressures.

The massive social disruption and violence of this era would continue into the Iron Age, ushering in an era of persistent warfare. During this time, religions would emerge within the Semitic empires of Mesopotamia and the Levant that would profoundly influence Western philosophy and theology.

Iron Age – c. 1200 BCE – 500 BCE in the Near East

While the Iron Age is notable for the introduction of iron, which was used to forge weapons among other things, it was also marked by endemic warfare in Europe and the Mediterranean. This period saw increased desertification and conflict in the Near East, as well as the evolution of religious beliefs among the Israelites that would come to significantly influence Western thought.

Yahwehism, the precursor to Judaism, emerged in the early Iron Age from earlier Canaanite religious beliefs and practices. Yahweh was a warrior sky and storm god, embodying the outer orientation of the desert peoples who worshipped him. Initially a polytheistic religion, Yahwehism evolved over centuries first into a *henotheistic* faith, worshipping a primary god while recognizing the existence of others and then into a monotheistic one.[68] The term *Judaism* developed later to reflect the religious and cultural identity of the Jewish people.

The Hebrew Bible, known to Christians as the Old Testament, was composed by various authors over many centuries, based on oral traditions passed down through generations. During the Babylonian exile in the 6th century BCE, Jewish communities encountered Babylonian culture and literature, including myths like the *Enuma Elish*. This interaction likely contributed to the development of certain theological ideas and narratives within Jewish scripture, particularly in the books of Genesis, Psalms, Isaiah, and Job.[69]

The *Enuma Elish* describes the defeat of a primal goddess by a young warrior god, establishing a new, patriarchal order. According to this myth, Marduk, the sky and storm god, created the world by defeating and dismembering Tiamat, his grandmother and the goddess of the primordial chaotic waters, who is depicted as a monstrous sea serpent or dragon. By splitting her body in two, Marduk fashioned the sky and the earth, thereby imposing order on the cosmos. This epic reflects an early form of dualism, of sky and earth, male and female, order and chaos, with Marduk symbolizing the former and Tiamat symbolizing the latter.

Scholars Anne Baring and Jules Cashford propose that this story established a paradigm for the Iron Age, in which we see "conflict between the older mythology of the mother goddess and the new myths of the Aryan [Indo-European] and Semitic father gods."[70] This conflict is reflected in the Hebrew Bible as the struggle between the Israelites and their polytheistic neighbors, along with the condemnation of Goddess worship.

The Hebrew Bible would be finalized during the Classical Age, a period when Jewish theology continued to evolve under the influence of classical Greek philosophy. The theology that arose from this encounter developed a clear dualism between God and the world, a concept that continues to shape Western thought today.

Classical Age – c. 500 BCE - 325 BCE

The Classical Age was, like all eras that follow the Neolithic, plagued by warfare. The Classical era witnessed the rise and fall of the Greek and Roman empires, the establishment of foundational Western philosophy in Greece, and the evolution of Jewish theology, as influenced by Greek thought. This discussion focuses on the Greek philosophies of Plato and Aristotle and the development of Jewish theology in relation to these philosophical traditions.

Dualism in Classical Greek Philosophy

Late Greek philosophy expressed a dualistic worldview, that would eventually lead to a hierarchal dualism between God and the world, soul and body, male and female, and good and evil. This dualistic worldview explicitly justified male dominance.

Plato's theory of forms is an early instance of philosophical dualism, which likely arose from the Indo-European religious dualism between the sky and earth. In his work *Timaeus,* Plato distinguishes between a higher realm of forms (defined as perfect, eternal, and unchanging archetypes) and the lesser, material world, which is characterized by change and decay.[71] According to this theory, the material world only imperfectly reflects the forms of the higher realm. Although Plato uses spatial metaphors to describe the realm of forms as a "place beyond heaven,"[72] he is referring to a realm entirely outside the physical world. This dualism between nature and the realm of forms conceptually places the realm of value not just in the sky but outside of this world altogether.

For Plato, this fundamental dualism also implied a soul-body dualism. He considered the soul to be immortal and rational, while the body was seen as a temporary, material vessel that can hinder the soul's pursuit of truth and wisdom. Associating the soul with intellect, Plato proposed that we can obtain knowledge of the realm of forms by remembering the time before we were born. He advocated doing this by using *dialectic*—structured dialogue and questioning—and philosophical reasoning. By engaging in this method, he believed, individuals could move from opinions based on sensory perception to achieving true knowledge grounded in intellectual insight.[73]

According to Plato's view, the nature of the world and our ways of knowing it are gendered. His theory of souls posits that men and women are differently equipped to access higher knowledge. According to this theory, the soul is composed of both immortal and mortal elements: the immortal part is linked to reason and intellect, while the mortal part pertains to passions and emotions. In classical Greek thought, these aspects of the soul were gendered: rationality, reasoning, and thus authority were associated with masculinity, whereas emotions and passions were linked to femininity. [74] Plato believed that women are reincarnated souls who had failed to meet the highest standards in their previous lives and so are more closely connected to a mortal, bodily existence.[75]

Plato's student Aristotle expressed a similar view on gender differences. According to Aristotle, the father and the mother contribute differently to a child's birth. He theorized that the father provides the "form" and the "principle of movement," the vital principle that shapes and animates the potential life. In contrast, the mother provides passive "matter," through her menstrual blood.[76] In other words, the father provides the spirit and the mother provides the body.

Aristotle believed that if the male semen was not strong enough or if conditions during conception were suboptimal, the generative process would not fully realize the male form, resulting in the birth of a female. Consequently, men were seen as being of a higher order, participating more in spirit, which was considered active, while women were viewed as being of a lower order, participating more in matter, which was considered passive.

In *Politics*, Aristotle uses this belief to justify male domination: "Male rules over the female, or the man over the child; although the parts of the soul are present in all of them, they are present in different degrees. For the slave has no deliberative faculty at all; the woman has, but it is without authority; and the child has, but it is immature."[77]

While Plato's theory implies a dualism between a higher realm imagined to be outside of this world and the world of our ordinary earthly experience, Aristotle's view suggests a dualism between the animating principle, understood to be masculine, and purely passive matter, understood to be feminine. Both views indicate that men are essentially more connected to what we might call prototypical

54

"spiritual realms," whereas women are more connected to the Earth and the body. These concepts were further developed and expressed in the theology of Judaism during this era, influenced significantly by Greek philosophers, especially Plato and the Neoplatonists.

Dualism in Jewish Theology

While Yahwehism evidenced a prototypical dualism between Earth and sky, the dualism of Greek philosophy and the story of Eve in Genesis were integral to the development and elaboration of a dualistic perspective within Judaism.

Drawing on Greek Platonian and Aristotelian philosophies, Jewish theologians contrasted the spiritual and physical realms, viewing the latter as flawed and separate from the divine. As in much of classic Greek thought, Jewish theological dualism is symbolically gendered, with men being more associated with spirit and women more associated with the body and the physical world. This perspective within Judaism finds support in the Genesis 3 account, in which God created Eve from Adam's rib, making her more material than spiritual. Further, Eve's supposed role in tempting Adam to eat from the Tree of Knowledge of Good and Evil was thought to demonstrate that she was ruled by bodily passions and lacked good judgment.[78] This act of disobedience was said to introduce sin and mortality into the material world, exaggerating the distinction between spiritual purity and the imperfection of earthly existence.

Genesis 3, along with the dualism inherent in Jewish theology, played a crucial role in shaping and justifying gender roles within the Judaic tradition. These roles are made explicit in the curse placed upon Eve: "Your desire shall be for your husband, and he shall rule over you."[79] As we will explore next, the dualism between spirit and matter, first articulated in Jewish theology, was inherited and intensified by Christianity.

Early Christian Fathers – c. 60 BCE - 750 CE and the Middle Ages 500 – 1500 CE

Early Christianity and the Middle Ages saw an intensification of dualistic thought, characterized by an increasingly stark contrast between the spiritual and the material, the sacred and the profane. Heavily influenced by Platonic and Aristotelian thought, the Early Church Fathers developed the doctrine of the complete otherness, separation, and transcendence of God from the created world, a doctrine that continued to evolve into the Middle Ages. Their theology shaped profoundly negative conceptions of nature and the body, and so the degradation of the physical realm, including the human body, became a recurrent theme in early Christian writings.

Early Church Fathers such as Augustine of Hippo (354–430 CE) and Origen (c. 185–254 CE) expressed and further developed ideas of God's utter transcendence and otherness, which they found in the dualistic framework of Platonic and Neoplatonic philosophy and Jewish theology. Augustine asserted that God is utterly distinct from Creation and unbounded by time and space.[80] And Origen, claimed that God is purely invisible and spiritual, and that it is the mind that is "an intellectual image of God."[81] Reminiscent of Plato, he proposes that the mind can therefore have some awareness of the divine, "especially if it is purified and separated from bodily matter."[82]

The doctrine of God's absolute transcendence of Creation was further developed in the medieval period, by theologians like Thomas Aquinas (1225–1274 CE). In his **Summa Theologica**, Aquinas argues that for God to be perfect, omnipotent, omniscient, and omnipresent, He must be wholly transcendent and free from the constraints of time, space, or matter.

This theological dualism between God and Creation, mind and matter, profoundly influenced Christian views on nature and the body—especially women's bodies. Early Christian writings frequently emphasized the degradation of the physical realm, including the human body. This perspective was reflected in the doctrine of original sin, which highlighted humanity's inherent sinfulness and associated sexual desire with moral corruption.

Augustine of Hippo was a key figure in further developing early Christian thought on humanity's fallen state and the belief that sexuality played a part in the Fall. In his interpretations of the Genesis narrative, he emphasized original sin and argued that it is transmitted through sexual reproduction. He viewed sexual desire as a powerful and uncontrollable force that exemplified humanity's fallen nature. Further, he considered the shame associated with sexual arousal to be a consequence of original sin and a reflection of humanity's corrupted state.[83]

The association of Eve, and by extension women, with sin and sexual temptation intensified the perception of the body as a spiritual adversary. In contrast to the spiritual and rational nature ascribed to men, women were seen as embodying the physical and carnal aspects of human nature. Early Church Fathers expounded this view. For instance, Tertullian wrote to women, "Do you not know that you are each an Eve? The sentence of God on this sex of yours lives in this age: the guilt must of necessity live too ... You are the devil's gateway."[84] Such statements reinforced the belief that women, through their bodies and sexuality, were sources of sin and moral danger. This framework justified stringent controls over women's behavior and bodies, including strict regulations on modesty, chastity, and women's roles within the church and society.

Such anti-body views, which were particularly prevalent in the 3rd and 4th centuries, led many devout Christians to adopt ascetic practices. Asceticism was often justified by referencing biblical passages, such as 1 Corinthians 9:27, where Paul the Apostle states, "I chastise my body."[85] Initially, this asceticism involved a general suspicion of physical pleasure and a preference for celibacy. However, by the 5th century, it had evolved to include *self-mortification*—deliberately inflicting pain or suffering as a spiritual discipline. In its more extreme forms, self-mortification involved practices such as wearing hair shirts and using devices like whips (known as disciplines) or razor blades attached to strings for self-flagellation.

Given Reich's psychological theory, we might expect that such extreme distortions and repressions of natural human drives might manifest as twisted, sexualized violence. Additionally, given the explicit scapegoating of women for "the sins of Eve," we might expect this violence to especially target women. We see just that in the Renaissance.

The Renaissance and the Catholic Inquisition – c. 1300 – 1600 CE

Of the Renaissance, it could be said, "It was the best of times, it was the worst of times."[86] On the one hand, it saw the rising of the intellectual movement of *humanism*, which emphasizes the value and perspective of human beings and favored critical thinking and evidence over the blind acceptance of dogma. As such it was an era marked by increased intellectual curiosity and openness. Consequently, the Renaissance saw greater educational opportunities and public influence for women, although in practice, these advancements were largely confined to the upper class.

The Renaissance was also the era of the Protestant Reformation, which began in 1517 and effectively challenged the dominance of the Catholic Church. This movement led to the establishment of new centers of authority, including state churches and secular institutions. The newly formed Protestant Church encouraged the reading of the Bible by all people, which contributed to increased educational opportunities for women. It also advocated for the spiritual equality of men and women. However, this ideal was only partially realized, as the explicit patriarchy of Catholicism persisted in Protestantism, and so the debate over gender roles continues within Christian denominations today.

On the other hand, the Renaissance was also the worst of times, seeing the Spanish Inquisition and the early stages of the Roman Inquisition. In response to the more liberal attitudes and secular ideas of the Renaissance[87] and the challenges posed by Protestantism to Catholic doctrine and teachings,[88] these inquisitions used terror to maintain the hegemony of the Catholic Church. Their focus on witch hunts and heresy trials, particularly targeting women, can be seen as an attempt to reassert control over religious and social norms.

The inquisitions imprisoned, tortured, and executed thousands of people, many of whom were burned alive. These campaigns of terror targeted a range of individuals, including non-Catholic groups such as Jews and Muslims who had converted to Christianity but were suspected of secretly practicing their former religions; Protestants; heretics with unorthodox beliefs; apostates who had abandoned Christianity; and alleged witches, some of whom might have continued practicing earlier religions.[89]

The persecution of women notably included sexual torture, including sexual assault and humiliation, threats of sexual violence against family members, and torture with devices designed to tear or crush their breasts and to puncture and crush their genitals.[90] These actions reflect severe sexual repression and explicitly negative attitudes towards women and their bodies. After the Catholic and Spanish inquisitions, the limited freedoms that women had enjoyed in the early Renaissance were largely lost.

The gendered dualisms of God and the world, mind and body, male and female, sacrality and sexuality, and good and evil, developed by the Early Church Fathers and Medieval theologians continued into the Renaissance. They still influence Catholic and conservative Christian thought today. In Catholic and conservative Christian theology, the use of masculine pronouns for God is considered essential because it underscores God's transcendence and complete otherness in relation to the world. Kreeft and Tacelli's further explanation of this perspective is detailed below:

> The Jewish revelation was distinctive in its exclusively masculine pronoun because it was distinctive in its theology of the divine transcendence. That seems to be the main point of the masculine imagery. As a man comes into a woman from without to make her pregnant, so God creates the universe from without rather than birthing it from within and impregnates our souls with grace or supernatural life from without....

> Biblical religions are characterized by . . . their unique view of a transcendent God creating nature out of nothing and their refusal to call God "she" despite the fact that Scripture ascribes to him feminine attributes like compassionate nursing (Is. 49:15), motherly comfort (Is. 66:13) and carrying an infant (Is. 46:3). The masculine pronoun safeguards (1) the transcendence of God against the illusion that nature is born from God

as a mother rather than created and (2) the grace of God against the illusion that we can somehow save ourselves—two illusions ubiquitous and inevitable in the history of religion.[91]

The Scientific Revolution, emerging from the context of Judaism and Christianity, would introduce a new, derivative worldview that continues, along with Christian theology, to shape Western thought today. Originally rooted in the theological view that God is wholly transcendent of the world, the Scientific Revolution would ultimately abandon the "God hypothesis"[92] altogether.

The Scientific Revolution and the Protestant Inquisition – c. 1543 – 1700 CE

The Scientific Revolution emerged from the Renaissance's greater openness and humanism, which included a drive to free inquiry from the control of the Catholic Church. During this period, the Catholic Inquisition continued, and the Protestant Inquisition began, targeting Catholics and others deemed threats to emerging power structures. While Protestantism was skeptical of science, it was generally more open-minded regarding science than Catholicism, which prosecuted scientists as heretics.

The Church's persecution of scientists began following Nicolaus Copernicus's proposal in *De revolutionibus orbium coelestium* (1543), that the Earth and other celestial bodies orbit the Sun. This *heliocentric* model contradicted the Church's teaching that the Sun and other celestial bodies orbit the Earth.

After Copernicus's death, the Church, aiming to preserve its authority, deemed the model heretical.

Despite this, other scientists continued to be interested in the theory. Giordano Bruno, a Dominican friar, philosopher, and *pantheist* (someone who believes that God or divinity is synonymous with the universe or nature) supported the Copernican model. For this and other beliefs, the Church burned him at the stake as a heretic in 1600.

Only a few decades later, Galileo expanded on Copernicus's heliocentric model. Despite warnings from the Church not to teach or defend this model, Galileo published his findings in **Dialogue Concerning the Two Chief World Systems** in 1632. Within the year, he was tried by the Roman Inquisition. To avoid Bruno's fate, Galileo was forced to recant his views and was placed under house arrest for the rest of his life.

How was scientific inquiry able to progress under such conditions? Early scientists found their way forward by avoiding direct conflict with Church teachings and leveraging political strategies. Since the Church held that God was entirely separate from the world, scientists framed their work as *natural philosophy*, focusing solely on observable phenomena rather than on divine realms. They explored these observable phenomena using empirical and rational methods.

Scientists also used political acumen to seek patronage and influence from the Church, striving to align their findings with religious beliefs. Over time, an implicit agreement emerged: scientists would focus on empirical research in the material world while the Church maintained control over spiritual matters. This arrangement allowed both fields to advance with minimal conflict.

Natural philosopher-scientists, like their theological predecessors, drew on Greek philosophy to develop their ideas about physical reality. They incorporated concepts from philosophers, such as Leucippus and Democritus, and Epicurus. To briefly summarize their views, Leucippus proposed that everything is composed of tiny, indivisible, and indestructible *atoms*, which he believed were purely material, having no experience in themselves. That is, Leucippus proposed that the world of nature is made of "dead" matter. Democritus expanded on this idea by suggesting that all phenomena result from the interactions of these atoms moving through empty space. Then, Epicurus adopted and furthered Democritus's view, arguing that the universe operates according to mechanical laws of nature.[93]

The belief that the universe is made of dead matter raised the question of how movement and order could have begun. Earlier, in answer to this question, Aristotle has posited the existence of an unmoved mover, a transcendent principle that sets everything else in motion without itself being moved.[94] Influenced by Aristotle, Aquinas proposed this unmoved mover is God.[95] Consequently, many early scientists believed that their theories must reference God. This was to change, sparking the development of another significant philosophical paradigm: (secular) philosophical materialism, which remains dominant in the West.

This change is seen in a famous story involving the French mathematician and astronomer Pierre-Simon Laplace and Napolean, who had hired him as an advisor. When Laplace presented Napoleon with a copy of his book on celestial mechanics, Napoleon is said to have remarked, "M. Laplace, they tell me you have written this extensive work on the system of the universe without even mentioning its Creator." To this, Laplace famously responded, "I had no need of that hypothesis."[96] Increasingly, scientists abandoned the "God hypothesis."

And so, ironically, to avoid conflicts with religious authorities, scientists eventually adopted a secular, mechanistic, and materialistic view of the universe. This perspective depicted the cosmos as insentient matter, devoid of feeling, intelligence, and spirit. Although this worldview—rooted in the separation of matter and spirit as found in Abrahamic religions—remains an unproven assumption, it laid the groundwork for a mechanical philosophy that has had troubling implications for non-human nature, as exemplified below.

The English philosopher and scientist Francis Bacon (1561-1626), renowned for developing the scientific method and his work on empiricism, often compared the natural world, including living organisms, to complex machines. Considering animals to be devoid of feelings, he dissected living dogs, arguing that their cries were merely mechanical reactions rather than evidence of pain or suffering akin to that experienced by humans.[97] This mechanistic view has persisted, leading many people to assume that most animals and plants lack intelligence. Consequently, Western humans routinely treat the natural world as a mere material resource rather than a sacred presence having experiences of its own.

This long series of events, spanning tens of thousands of years, substantially shifted human consciousness and our relationship with each other and the world, shaping our spirituality, psychology, and social structures. While the peoples of Europe and the Mediterranean originally viewed the world as a sacred embodiment of the Great Mother, over time, they came to believe in a Father God who was entirely transcendent from the world. The secular worldview that emerged from this context retained the theological belief that the world is composed of passive, insentient matter, devoid of any experience, while abandoning the hypothesis that God was necessary to explain motion.

The worldviews of each era can be seen to have shaped the social and economic systems, and psychologies of the time. Societies that saw the divine as immanent in nature tended to be more egalitarian and lived in greater harmony with the natural world. In contrast, those that perceived the divine as separate from the Earth were more hierarchal, violent and exploitive, viewing the Earth as a resource to be used, rather than as a community of entities with their own experiences and feelings. While we can acknowledge that much has been learned from this latter perspective, it has been generally unhealthy to the point where it now poses an existential threat to humanity.

Discussion and Conclusion

Our concepts regarding the Divine are shaped by our physical and social environment, as proposed by Sanday, DeMeo, and Diamond, and as demonstrated by a review of the evolution of Western thought. Nurturing environments tend to give rise to an inner orientation, which can be seen as immanence, while harsh environments cause trauma which can lead to an outer orientation. An outer orientation can be thought of as a proto- dualism, in turn, can evolve into a theology of transcendence and philosophical materialism.

Through the ages, humans have gendered these worldviews. When the divine is seen as immanent, as in Pandeism, Pantheism, or *Panentheism*—the belief that the world is within the divine—it is often imaged as a Great Mother who created the world from Her body. In this view, all beings are understood to be manifestations of Her, and so the divine is also imaged in other non-human forms in nature, such as plants and animals. Implicit in this view is a respect for nature and the body as manifestations of the divine.

Conversely, when due to environmental and social trauma, the divine is seen as transcendent and wholly separate from nature, it is imagined as the Father who created the world through His Word, spit, or semen. Theoretically, such a transcendent divine should not be imaged, as that would suggest He is within nature; however, He is still typically depicted as "an old man in the sky," reminiscent of the sky gods of the Indo-Europeans and Semitic tribes. Within this worldview, nature and the body are disparaged as part of the fallen material reality.

Pandeism offers a radically different worldview compared to Western theism and potentially to philosophical materialism. Understanding the Divine to be immanent in the world is compatible with diverse imaging of the divine as female, male, and as other entities in nature. The immanence of Pandeism also has implications for our relationship with each other and the larger natural matrix within which we are embedded. It suggests that we cultivate an ethic of mutual respect and care, with implications for our social and economic systems, and our personal psychology.

The ecological problems we are facing today, according to Diamond, are similar to those that caused the collapse of other civilizations.[98] The human perspective that the planet is merely a material resource has substantially contributed to issues such as climate change, deforestation, overfishing, soil depletion, habitat degradation, and other environmental problems.[99] We are also still plagued by chronic warfare, which has become an existential threat due to the proliferation of nuclear weapons. High levels of violence, social inequality, and resulting psychological problems have further degraded our quality of life.

Pandeism has the potential to help shift this unhealthy paradigm. By embracing female metaphors and images of the divine, as well as those of other entities in nature, it can foster a greater sense of psychological and spiritual closeness to nature. This perspective can also support an "I-Thou"[100] relationship with other people and the natural world, where we see them not as objects to exploit but as divine beings with whom we share the world, even if they—or we—don't realize it yet.

Such an approach can lead us to live in greater harmony with each other and the natural world. While we cannot return to earlier ways of living, learning to live in greater harmony with each other and the rest of nature is the task of our time.

Notes

1 Kreeft, *Christian Apologetics,* 98.
2 Sanday, *Female Power and Male Dominance,* 1, 5.
3 Ibid., 5; Ortner, *Making Gender,* 27.
4 Sanday, *Female Power and Male Dominance,* 6-7.
5 Ibid., 7, 81-82.
6 Ibid., 81.
7 Generally, women of color have needed to work outside the home due to their social situation in the West.
8 Berman, *Wandering God,* 167.
9 Reich, *Character Analysis,* 43-44; DeMeo, "Saharasian Origins," 46.
10 Reich, *Psychology of Fascism,* 27-32; Also see Prescott, "Origins of Violence."
11 DeMeo, "Saharasian Origins," 46.
12 Ibid., 45-46.
13 Ibid., 46.
14 Ibid., 47-48.
15 Diamond, *Collapse,* 11.
16 It should be noted that these eras only partially relate to chronological time. Instead, they describe the nature of human technologies. As human lifestyles and technology evolved at a different pace in various locales, these eras began at somewhat different times in different places.
17 Gimbutas, "Implications of the *Chalice and the Blade,"* 289.
18 Writing and urban development occurred earlier, however, in the Neolithic.
19 Eliade, *History,* 4.
20 Ibid., 5.
21 Rudgley, *Civilizations*; Gimbutas, *Language of the Goddess*; Also, interpretations have been offered for the Phaistos disk. See, for example, "Phaistos Disc."
22 This conclusion is supported by many scholars, including Marija Gimbutas in *Civilization of the Goddess* and *Language of the Goddess,* Joseph Campbell in *Primitive Mythology* and *Animal Powers,* Richard Rudgley in *Lost Civilizations,* and E.O. James in *Cult of the Mother-Goddess.*
23 Campbell, *Animal Powers,* 73.
24 Rigaud, "Lascaux Cave," 448.
25 Eliade, *History.*
26 Campbell, *Primitive Mythology,* 306.
27 Baring and Cashford, *Myth of the Goddess,* 15-17, 70; Leroi-Gourhan,
28 Ibid., 32-24. Leroi-Gourhan, *Préhistoire.*
29 Gimbutas, *Language of the Goddess,* 177; Baring and Cashford, *Myth of the Goddess,* 32-38; Clottes and Lewis-Williams,

Shamans of Prehistory; Eliade, *Shamanism*; Campbell, *Animal Powers*, 73.

[30] Mellart, *Çatalhöyük*.

[31] Whittle, *The Archaeology of People*.

[32] Thorpe, *Origins of Warfare*.

[33] Keeley, *War Before Civilization*.

[34]Biaggi proposes that this flood as well as the desertification in Saharasia described by DeMeo contributed to a dramatic culture shift. Biaggi, "Roots of Patriarchy," 78; Also see Cunliffe, *Europe Between the* Oceans, 34-38.

[35] Ryan and Pitman, *Noah's Flood*.

[36] Gimbutas, *Civilization of the Goddess*, 352.

[37] Marler, "Beginnings of Patriarchy," 57.

[38] Goettner-Abendroth, 34; Matriarchy is not, as popularly imagined, a system in which women dominate men. Instead, it is egalitarian social system, often matrilineal, where women hold positions of wisdom and influence, and which operates on cooperation, consensus, and mutual respect. See Goettner-Abendroth, "Development of Patriarchy," 34.

[39] Ibid., 33.

[40] Biaggi, "Roots of Patriarchy," 80.

[41] Gimbutas, *Civilization of the Goddess*, 353.

[42] Jiayin, *Gender Relations*, 317.

[43] Gimbutas, *Civilization of the Goddess*, 352.

[44] Marler, "Beginnings of Patriarchy," 55-56.

[45] Griffin, *Gardens of Their Dreams*, 12.

[46] Ibid.

[47] Gimbutas, *Civilization of the Goddess*, 357, 364, 370, 371, 376, 377, 383, 390, 396-400; Biaggi, "Roots of Patriarchy," 83.

[48] Littleton, *Comparative Mythology*.

[49] Mallory and Adams, *Proto-Indo-European*.

[50] Griffin, *Gardens of Their Dreams*, 26-27; Biaggi, *Roots of Patriarchy*, 82.

[51] Griffin, *Gardens of Their Dreams*, 11, 28.

[52] Anthony, *The Horse, the Wheel, and Language*. It is interesting to note, however, that some warrior graves housed female warriors, indicating that, at least for a time, women could still hold some positions of power or influence in these cultures. See Davis-Kimball and Behan, *Women Warriors*.

[53] Gimbutas, *Civilization of the Goddess*, 352.

[54] Gimbutas, *Civilization of the Goddess*; Mallory and Adams, *Proto-Indo-European*; Anthony, *The Horse, the Wheel, and Language*.

[55] Willerslev et al, "Massive Migration from the Steppe"; **Christ**, "The Goddess and the Kurgan Hypothesis." For more support of the Kurgan hypothesis, also see Marler, "Beginnings of

Patriarchy," 63; Cvalli-Sforza and Cvalli-Sforza, *The Great Human Diasporas,* 155; and Dergachev, "Migration," 108.

[56] DeMeo, *Saharasia,* 150-152.

[57] Kozlowski and Aurenche, *Neolithic Chipped Stone Industries,* 211-213.

[58] DeMeo, *Saharasia, 182-185.*

[59] Gimbutas, *Civilization of the Goddess,* 325.

[60] Göttner-Abendroth, "Development of Patriarchy," 36.

[61] Ibid., 37.

[62] Ibid.

[63] Tringham and Krstic, *Neolithic Village,* 116.

[64] Göttner-Abendroth, "Development of Patriarchy," 37.

[65] Gimbutas, *Civilization of the Goddess,* 384.

[66] Gimbutas, *Goddesses and Gods of Old Europe.* Also see Spretnak, *Lost Goddesses,* for an example of how the myths of the indigenous European peoples were changed in a syncretism with Indo-European myths.

[67] Göttner-Abendroth, "Development of Patriarchy," 39.

[68] Smith, Mark S. *The Early History of God.*

[69] Finkelstein and Silberman. *The Bible Unearthed.*

[70] Baring and Cashford, *Goddess,* 275.

[71] Plato, *Timaeus,* 11-19.

[72] Plato, *Phaedro,* 247C-248B.

[73] Ibid.

[74] Pomeroy, *Women in Classical Antiquity.*

[75] Plato, *Timaeus,* 74.

[76] Aristotle, *Generation of Animals,* book 1, chapter 20.

[77] Aristotle, *Politics,* book 1, section 13; Code, *What Can She Know?,* 9.

[78] The Holy Bible. Genesis 3.

[79] Ibid., Genesis 3:16.

[80] Augustine, **Confessions**, Book 7, Chapter 5.

[81] Origen, *On First Principles,* 13.

[82] Ibid., 13.

[83] Augustine. **Confessions**. Book 10, Chapter 29.

[84] Tertullian, *On the Apparel of Women,* Book 1, Chapter 1.

[85] *The Holy Bible.*

[86] Charles Dickins's famous opening line to the *Tale of Two Cities,* while not referring to the Renaissance, is applicable to it.

[87] Murray, *Women of the Renaissance,* 101-103.

[88] Kamen, *Spanish Inquisition,* 89-91.

[89] Levack, **Witch-Hunt.**

[90] Bailey, *Witches.*

[91] Kreeft and Tacelli, *Christian Apologetics,* 98.

[92] Ball, *History of Mathematics,"* 343.

[93] Kirk, Raven, and Schofield, *The Presocratic Philosophers.*

94 Aristotle, *Metaphysics*, Book XII.
95 Aquinas, *Summa Theologica*.
96 Ball, *History of Mathematics,"* 343.
97 Clarke, *Frances Bacon*, 112.
98 Willerslev et al., "Massive Migration from the Steppe," 207-211; Diamond, Collapse, 7.
99 Diamond, Collapse, 6.
100 This expression references Martin Buber's *I and Thou*, which examines human relationships by contrasting the "I-It" relationship—where others are perceived as objects to be used or analyzed—with the "I-Thou" relationship, where individuals engage with each other as unique and relational beings. Buber argues that genuine dialogue and connection, marked by mutual respect and presence, arise within the "I-Thou" relationship, fostering deeper understanding and unity.

Bibliography

Anthony, David. *The Horse, the Wheel, and Language: How Bronze-Age Riders from the Eurasian Steppes Shaped the Modern World*. Princeton: Princeton University Press, 2007.

Aristotle. *Generation of Animals*. Translated by A. L. Peck. Cambridge, MA: Harvard University Press, 1942.

———. *Metaphysics*. In *The Complete Works of Aristotle: The Revised Oxford Translation*. Edited by Jonathan Barnes. Princeton: Princeton University Press, 1984.

———. *Politics*. In *The Complete Works of Aristotle: The Revised Oxford Translation*. Edited by Jonathan Barnes. Princeton: Princeton University Press, 1984.

Aquinas, Thomas. *Summa of the Summa*. Edited and annotated by Peter Kreeft. San Francisco: Ignatius Press, 1990.

Augustine. *City of God*. Translated by Henry Bettenson. London: Penguin Books, 1984.

———. *Confessions*. Translated by Garry Willis. New York: Penguin, 2002.

Bailey, Michael D. *Witches and Witch-Hunts: A Global History*. London: Reaktion Books, 2017.

Ball, W. W. Rouse. *A Short Account of the History of Mathematics*. 4th ed. London: Macmillan and Co., 1908.

Baring, Anne, and Jules Cashford. *The Myth of the Goddess: Evolution of an Image*. New York: Penguin Books, 1993.

Barnes, Jonathan, ed. *The Complete Works of Aristotle: The Revised Oxford Translation*. Edited by Jonathan Barnes. Princeton: Princeton University Press, 1984.

Berman, Morris. *Wandering God: A Study in Nomadic Spirituality*. Albany: State University of New York Press, 2000.

Best, Jan. "Comparative Indo-European Linguistics and Archaeology: Towards a Historical Integration." *The Journal of Indo-European Studies* 17, no. 3-4 (1989): 335-340.

Biaggi, Cristina, ed. *The Rule of Mars: Readings on the Origins, History, and Impact of Patriarchy.* Manchester, CT: Knowledge, Ideas & Trends, 2005.

———. 2005. "The Roots of Patriarchy in Europe, the Middle East, and Asia (or) Why Did the Kurgans Become Warlike?" In *The Rule of Mars: Readings on the Origins, History, and Impact of Patriarchy,* edited by Cristina Biaggi, 77-93. Manchester, CT: Knowledge, Ideas & Trends.

Campbell, Joseph. *The Masks of God: Oriental Mythology.* New York: Penguin, 1962.

———. *The Masks of God: Primitive Mythology.* New York: Viking, 1972.

———. *The Way of Animal Powers: Volume 1: Historical Atlas of World Mythology.* London: Summerfield Press, 1983.

Buber, Martin. *I and Thou.* Translated by Walter Kaufmann. New York: Simon & Schuster, 1974.

Cavalli-Sforza, Luigi Luca, and Francesco Cavalli-Sforza. *The Great Human Diasporas: The History of Diversity and Evolution.* Reading: Helix Books, 1995.

Christ, Carol P. "The Goddess and the Kurgan Hypothesis: A New Interpretation of Marija Gimbutas' Work," *Journal of Archaeological Method and Theory* 22, no. 1 (2015): 67-82.

Clarke, Desmond. *The Science of Francis Bacon: A Criticism.* Barnsley, UK: Bristol Classical Press, 1996.

Clottes, Jean and David Lewis-Williams. *The Shamans of Prehistory: Trance and Magic in the Painted Caves.* New York: Harry N. Abrams, 1998.

Code, Lorraine. *What Can She Know? Feminist Theory and the Construction of Knowledge.* Ithaca: Cornell University Press, 1991.

Copernicus, Nicolaus. *De revolutionibus orbium coelestium.* Nuremberg: Johannes Petreius, 1543.

Cunliffe, Barry. *Europe Between the Oceans: Themes and Variations, 9000 BC-AD 1000.* New Haven: Yale University Press, 2008.

Curtis, Garniss H. "Clock for the Ages: Potassium Argon," *National Geographic Magazine,* 120, no. 4 (1961): 590-592.

Davis-Kimball, and Mona Behan. "Warrior Women of the Eurasian Steppes." *Archaeology,* 50, no. 1 (January/February 1997): 44-48.

DeMeo, James. 1998. *Saharasia: The 4000 BCE Origins of Child Abuse, Sex-Repression Warfare and Social Violence in the Deserts of the Old World.* Ashland: Natural Energy Works, 1998.

———. "The Sharasian Origins of Patriarchal Authoritarian Culture." In *The Rule of Mars: Readings on the Origins, History, and Impact of Patriarchy,* edited by Cristina Biaggi, 43-51. Manchester, CT: Knowledge, Ideas & Trends, 2005.

Dergachev, Valentin. "Two Studies in Defense of the Migration Concept." In *Ancient Interactions: East and West in Eurasia.* Edited by K. Boyle, C. Renfrew, and M. Levine. Cambridge, UK: McDonald Institute for Archaeological Research, 2002.

Diamond, Jared. *Collapse: How Societies Choose to Fail or Succeed.* New York: Viking Press, 2005.

Dickens, Charles. *A Tale of Two Cities.* London: Chapman & Hall, 1859.

"Dualism." In Jewish Virtual Library. Accessed July 15, 2024. https://www.jewishvirtuallibrary.org/dualism.

Eliade, Mircea. *Shamanism: Archaic Techniques of Ecstasy.* Princeton: Princeton University Press, 1964.

———. *A History of Religious Ideas. Vol 1. From the Stone Age to the Eleusinian Mysteries,* Translated by Willard R. Trask. Chicago: University of Chicago Press, 1978.

Finkelstein, Israel, and Neil Asher Silberman. *The Bible Unearthed: Archaeology's New Vision of Ancient Israel and the Origin of Its Sacred Texts.* New York: Free Press, 2001.

Gilbert, Scott. F., and Sahotra Sarkar. "Embracing Complexity: Organicism for the 21st Century." *Developmental Dynamics* 219, no. 1 (2000): 1–9. https://anatomypubs.onlinelibrary.wiley.com/doi/10.1002/1097-0177%282000%299999%3A9999%3C%3A%3AAID-DVDY1036%3E3.0.CO%3B2-A

Gimbutas, Marija. *The Goddesses and Gods of Old Europe: Myths and Cult Images.* Berkeley: University of California Press, 1982.

———. "Implications of the *Chalice and the Blade* for the Relation of Archaeology to Social Science." *World Futures,* 25 (1988): 289-295.

———. *The Language of the Goddess: Unearthing the Hidden Symbols of Western Civilization.* San Francisco: HarperSanFrancisco, 1989.

———. *The Civilization of the Goddess,* edited by Joan Marler. San Francisco: HarperSanFrancisco, 1991.

———. "The Kurgan Culture and the Indo-Europeanization of Europe," edited by Marian Robins Dexter and K. Jonesy-Bley. *Journal of Indo-European Studies Monograph* 18. Washington, DC: Institute for the Study of Man, 1997.

Glick, Peter and Susan T. Fiske. "Gender, Power Dynamics, and Social Interaction." In *Revisioning Gender,* edited by M. M.

Ferree, J. Lorber and B.B. Hess, 365-398. Walnut Creek: AltaMira Press, 2000.

Goettner-Abendroth, Hiede. "Notes on the Rise and Development of Patriarchy." In *The Rule of Mars: Readings on the Origins, History, and Impact of Patriarchy,* edited by Cristina Biaggi, 27-42. Manchester, CT: Knowledge, Ideas & Trends, 2005.

Griffin, Brian. *The Gardens of Their Dreams: Desertification and Culture in World History.* New York: Palgrave, 2001.

James, Edwin O. *The Cult of the Mother Goddess.* New York: Barnes & Noble Books, 1994.

Jiayin, Min. *The Chalice and the Blade in Chinese Culture: Gender Relations and Social Models.* Beijing: China Social Sciences Publishing House, 1995.

Kamen, Henry. *The Spanish Inquisition: A Historical Revision.* New Haven: Yale University Press, 1997.

Keeley, Lawrence H. *War Before Civilization: The Myth of the Peaceful Savage.* Oxford: Oxford University Press, 1997.

Kirk, Gregory S., John E. Raven, and Malcolm Schofield. *The Presocratic Philosophers.* 3rd ed. Chicago: University of Chicago Press, 1983.

Kozlowski, Stefan, and Olivier Aurenche. *Neolithic Chipped Stone Industries of the Fertile Crescent: Volume 2: Patterns and Changes.* Oxford: Archaeopress, 2005.

Kreeft, Peter and Ronald K. Tacelli. *Handbook of Christian Apologetics: Hundreds of Answers to Crucial Questions.* Downers Grove: InterVarsity, 1994.

Leroi-Gourhan, André'. *Préhistoire de l'Art Occidental.* Paris: Mazenod, 1971.

Levack, Brian P. *The Witch-Hunt in Early Modern Europe.* 4th ed. London: Routledge, 2016.

Littleton, C. Scott. *The New Comparative Mythology: An Anthropological Assessment of the Theories of Georges Dumézil.* Berkeley: University of California Press, 1982.

Mallory, J. P., and D. Q. Adams. *The Oxford Introduction to Proto-Indo-European and the Proto-Indo-European World.* Oxford: Oxford University Press, 2006.

Marler, Joan. "The Beginnings of Patriarchy in Europe: Reflections on the Kurgan Theory of Marija Gimbutas." In *The Rule of Mars: Readings on the Origins, History, and Impact of Patriarchy,* edited by Cristina Biaggi, 53-75. Manchester, CT: Knowledge, Ideas & Trends, 2005.

McDonough, Richard. "Plato: Organicism," in *Internet Encyclopedia of Philosophy.* Accessed July 20, 2024. https://iep.utm.edu/platoorg/.

Mellaart, James. *Çatalhöyük: A Neolithic Town in Anatolia.* New York: McGraw-Hill, 1967.

Murray, Linda. *The Women of the Renaissance.* Chicago: University of Chicago Press, 1987.

Origen. *On First Principles.* Translated by G. W. Butterworth. Gloucester, MA: Peter Smith, 1973.

Ortner, Sherry B. *Making Gender: The Politics and Erotics of Culture.* Boston: Beacon Press, 1996.

"'Phaistos Disc' Mystery Finally Unraveled." *Greek City Times.* February 9, 2024. https://greekcitytimes.com/2024/02/09/phaistos-disc-mystery/

Plato. *Timaeus.* Translated by Benjamin Jowett. New York: MacMillan, 1949.

Pomeroy, Sarah B. *Goddesses, Whores, Wives, and Slaves: Women in Classical Antiquity.* New York: Schocken Books, 1975.

Prescott, James W. "Body Pleasure and the Origins of Violence." *The Futurist* 9, no. 2 (1975): 64-74.

Reich, Wilhelm. *The Mass Psychology of Fascism.* 3rd ed. New York: Farrar, Straus and Giroux, 1970.

———. *Character Analysis.* 3rd ed. New York: Farrar, Straus and Giroux, 1980.

Rigaud, Jean-Phillippe. 1988. "Treasures of Lascaux Cave." *National Geographic* 174 no. 4 (1988): 482-499.

Rudgley, Richard. *The Lost Civilizations of the Stone Age.* New York: The Free Press, 1999.

Ryan, William, and Walter Pitman. *Noah's Flood: The New Scientific Discoveries About the Event that Changed History.* New York: Simon & Schuster, 1998.

Smith, Mark S. *The Early History of God: Yahweh and the Other Deities in Ancient Israel.* 2nd ed. Grand Rapids: William B. Eerdmans Publishing, 2002.

Spretnak, Charlene. *Lost Goddesses: Women, Myth, and Power in Ancient Greece.* Boston: Beacon Press, 1978.

Tertullian. *On the Apparel of Women.* In *Ante-Nicene Fathers*, edited by Alexander Roberts, James Donaldson, and A. Cleveland Coxe. Vol. 4. Translated by S. Thelwall. Buffalo: Christian Literature Publishing Co., 1885. Accessed July 18, 2024. https://www.newadvent.org/fathers/0402.htm.

The Holy Bible, New International Version. Grand Rapids: Zondervan, 2011.

Thorpe, I.J. *Anthropology, Archaeology, and the Origin of Warfare.* New York: Routledge, 2003.

Tringham, Ruth and Dusan Krstic, eds. *Selevac: A Neolithic Village in Yugoslavia.* Los Angeles: Institute of Archaeology, U.C.L.A., 1990.

Whittle, Alasdair. *The Archaeology of People: Dimensions*

of the Neolithic. New York: Routledge. 2003.

"Who Were the Church Fathers?" *Catholic Answers.* Accessed July 18, 2024. https://www.catholic.com/qa/who-were-the-church-fathers.

Willerslev, Eske et al., "Massive Migration from the Steppe Was a Source for Indo-European Languages in Europe," *Nature* 522 (2015): 207-211.

Native American Spirituality

By Thurman 'Lee' Hester, Jr.

Thurman Lee Hester, Jr. is a citizen of the Choctaw Nation of Oklahoma, and a man of whom it has been written that "Hester's thoughts on American Indian identity and the practice of academic philosophy set a tone for further study and dialogue." His 2001 book, *Political Principles and Indian Sovereignty*, examines the connection between the wellbeing of Indian people, the sovereignty of Indian Nations and the democratic principles on which the United States was founded. The following is excerpted from the essay: "Native American spirituality," by Thurman 'Lee' Hester, in *Interreligious Philosophical Dialogues The Ways of Religion - Volume 3*, Graham Oppy and N.N. Trakakis, Eds. Copyright 2017, Routledge. Reproduced by permission of Routledge via Taylor & Francis Group.

Core beliefs

My tradition is not about beliefs but about practices. "Belief" in the western philosophical sense implies a particular connection between what is in our head and what actually exists. In the 'western', European tradition, if our beliefs are correct then there is a correspondence between the mental 'map' and the actual 'territory', and thus one can have 'The Truth'. In my tradition, we are essentially unable to fathom the totality of existence and thus cannot have 'The Truth', though we may have 'truths' that are parts of it, and we can certainly live good lives. Each of the multitude of tribes in North America have their own stories. Some stories are similar, some wildly different. Whether we are the descendants of Sky Woman (Iroquois), a dream of the Great Spirit (Abenaki) or are pulled forth from a hole in the ground (Choctaw), each tribe's stories are their own and are 'true' despite the fact that they may contradict the stories of another tribe. Each tribe's stories are considered sacred to that tribe and are respected by other tribes. This is partly because of the often close proximity of neighbouring sedentary tribes and the fact that migratory, roaming tribes regularly crossed paths with others. It is very difficult to get along with your neighbours and acquaintances if you claim an absolute and exclusive 'Truth'.

Historically, tribes that had regular contact with one another knew each other's language and stories, often participating in one another's ceremonies. It still is common for a person, upon meeting someone of a tribe that they have not come across before, to immediately begin swapping stories, describing traditions, dances and songs. Over the years, some tribes have developed special relations to others. The Wichita/Pawnee visitation is an example of this kind of relationship going back many hundreds or even thousands of years. The Wichita and Pawnee take turns each year visiting the other and camping together for several days. The ceremonies and dances of each tribe are performed, as are joint ceremonies. There is great goodwill and fellowship. The desired goal or outcome of traditional practices is generally to foster this kind of community.

Thus, practice rather than belief is what is most important for American Indian tribes, generally. The apparent 'beliefs' that might be drawn from the practices are really secondary, though people often espouse or invoke those beliefs. The fact that the exposition often varies greatly, even within a tribe, is a pretty good indication that the beliefs being evidenced are not central. Prayers can and will be addressed to 'Jesus', 'Aba Inki', 'The Creator' or any of a number of others, and no one present will be offended. Arguably it is the act of praying rather than any particular formula or supposed belief that is primary. It is a matter of 'orthopraxy' rather than 'orthodoxy', and the practices are rooted in community-building and the maintenance of harmony. Indeed, the practical roots of the views are so deep and so far removed from mainstream religions such as Christianity that many American Indian people effectively do both, practicing their traditional ways as well as Christianity, given that the Christian belief-system generally does not conflict with traditional practices. However, when there is a conflict, most practitioners will continue traditional practices and just ignore the conflict.

A good example of this occurred when I was discussing traditions with a friend of mine while driving home from the Tribal Capital one day. She pointed to an old hotel and said she figured there would be many *shilups*, or spirits, in such a place. I had always assumed her to be Christianized, but her statement made me think that she might in fact be more traditional. So, to get her to open up more about her views, I told her that I rejected the Baptist sect of Christianity partly because under their doctrines it appeared that all my Indian ancestors from Christ's birth till first contact with Europeans (around 1520 for my tribe) would be consigned to 'Hell' through no fault of their own just because they could not have 'known Christ'. Her response was that her God would not allow that, and it turned out that she was indeed a member of a Baptist church. The fact that the doctrines of her church contradicted her own personal beliefs just did not matter. What mattered were the practices associated with being a church member. This is part of the reason why American Indian people are either real practitioners of a religion or not, and seldom if ever profess to be a member of a church if they do not regularly attend the services and other events, usually including active support of these events (e.g., cooking for the feasts, being active on committees, etc.).

The willingness of many American Indian people to attend Christian churches, whether they maintain their traditional practices or not, is even more understandable when one considers the fact that the main traditional practices involve ceremonies commemorating the cycles of human life and the cycles of nature. The ceremonies are generally conducted at special grounds under the stars, rooted in the natural world. Though most Christian sects do not perform their ceremonies under the open sky but rather in a church building, they are nonetheless at a place they consider sacred. Christian marriages and funerals are part of the cycles of human life, and many Christian ceremonies are seasonal. Indians fasten onto these elements in Christian traditions and in other religions to allow them to easily go from one religion to another.

Probably the most distinctive element in Native American traditions when compared to 'mainstream' religions in the modern-day United States is the importance of dancing to traditional songs. The fact that mainstream churches and the federal government of the United States tried to suppress traditional dance makes it clear that, at least inchoately, they understood the primacy of these practices to American Indian people. Indians can 'attend' another church, but as long as they are dancing to their own traditional songs, they are still really only practicing their own tradition. To truly convert an Indian person to a different religion or 'assimilate' them into a different culture, you have to get them to stop dancing.

The lengths to which many Christian sects went to genuinely convert Indians and the strength of Indian tradition even amongst those that were supposedly converted can be illustrated by the story of Bernice Dreadful-water. I started a traditional dance group in the 1990s at the OK Choctaw Tribal Alliance in Oklahoma City. Since I was aware of the suppression of religious dances and the fact that many of the members of the OK Choctaw group were Christian, I carefully told them I would be doing 'social dances', leaving out any mention of ceremonial dance.

Despite my careful, inclusive and non-confrontational presentation, the minute I mentioned dancing, Bernice and several others called it "the Devil's work". This view is strongly presented in many conservative Christian churches that have Indians as members. Despite this indoctrination, many people immediately joined the group, and within a few months even those that had decried it as "the Devil's work" were joining in. The centrality of dance certainly played a role, but community did as well. Since a sufficient number of people had joined the dances, these did indeed form a part of the community, and thus to fail to participate would have meant that one was not a member of the community. Whatever other memberships Bernice and others may have had, they were and remain Indian through and through.

Dancing

Since the practice of dancing is so central to Native American spirituality, it is important to discuss it at some length. Dances and the traditional singing that goes with them serve a variety of purposes. They commemorate, exemplify and inculcate the natures, spirits and importance of various animals, and they represent the cycles of nature and human life. In my tribe, the dances are always conducted in a circle around a central fire. The fire can be thought of as symbolizing the Sun, our

Father, the spirit of the community, or numerous other things. Our dancing around the fire can be thought of as the planets circling the Sun and deriving warmth from it, our relationship to our Father, our essential community and so on. The circle is never-ending, a cycle like that of the seasons it commemorates. It is the very circle of our immediate community, while also representing the circles of each larger community which, in turn, encompass us. We dance upon the Earth, our Mother, who provides for us. We feast together, often visiting one another's camps, deriving our sustenance not from ourselves alone but from our community. The dances last all through the night, showing that even in the darkest hours we are one and stronger thereby. The dances are joyous and profound, tiring but also invigorating.

The dances of each tribe share similar goals, but they differ largely because of differences in the traditional methods of sustenance in each tribe. Agricultural tribes like mine generally dance with men and women together in the circle, sometimes holding hands, and generally in family groups, with women providing the beat. The centrality of women (the main farmers) is thus commemorated, and as everyone dances the same steps, they all work together toward the goal of raising the crops. Hunting tribes often have men and women dancing slightly separated and in different styles. There is greater differentiation in these societies between male and female roles, and their dances reflect this.

One fine example of dance from my tribe is the Snake Dance (*Sinti Hihla*). Snakes have a place in the universe which we as Choctaws dovetail with. As agriculturalists, we plant and eat corn. The snake eats the mice that might otherwise get into our corn cribs and eat our stored crops. The mice will always get some corn, but their actions are limited by the snake. Thus, we live in balanced harmony with one another. The dance also brings us close as a community.

During the coiling part of the dance, the leader at the front begins to circle tighter and tighter until he is turning in place. Everyone else is following, either linking arms or holding onto the next person's shoulder, to form the snake. As the circle tightens, we are literally shoulder-to- shoulder in a circle, squeezed together almost breathlessly. At a large ceremonial ground there could be hundreds of people in the circle. Once the circle is wound tight to the end, the leader will then reverse course, somehow miraculously threading himself between the rows of the coil, unwinding from the inside out. In this way, every single member of the coil (or community) will pass by all others during the unwinding. It is traditional to look in each person's eyes as you pass them. That look is one of community; it acknowledges our connectedness and inter- relationship. In the Choctaw tradition, it is usually presumptuous to look in another's eyes; it is polite only to glance. But in the circle it is traditional to look one fully in the eye.

'God'

Existence

The existence of a god or gods is both fully known and essentially unknowable. We are part of the divine and it is all around us. We participate in it as fully as we allow ourselves, but the totality of existence is beyond the experience of any part of it. Thus, the divine is essentially unknowable, though we both manifest it and are a part of it. The nature of any god or gods transcends our ability to understand. Our attempts to categorize 'god' and 'gods' using words with meanings that we comprehend are thus misguided. In this sense, such entities do not exist. I do not object to people using these words to refer to the divine, though I myself tend not to, but it is a fundamental mistake to think that we have indeed named something or added to our knowledge by so naming. The word 'God' is useful for indicating the divine but does not convey knowledge.

In Indian tradition generally, and in Choctaw tradition particularly, everything is sacred - only some things are more sacred than others! Any assemblage of people is automatically and intrinsically valuable. It is even more valuable if it involves food. Life is a gift. It is fragile. The Earth is bountiful, but sustenance is not always certain. Every meal is a celebration, and a meal with community even more so, since our community is essential to us. God is always with us, but the presence of God is more powerful in these special cases. Thus, even though we cannot 'know' God, we can experience God.

Nature

Though the foregoing means that we cannot know the nature of God but can only experience God's presence, God can be thought of as a transcendent sum of all things, with the whole transcending the sum in the sense of a 'gestalt'. If 'gods' (in the plural) exist, then they would exist as subcategories or manifestations of the sum of all things. I have sometimes referred to myself as a 'pan-deist', but tend to avoid mainstream or even technical categories because people then believe that they automatically understand your views. In the United States this generally means that one's religious identity is defined in terms of differences from Christianity, which is taken as the standard religious yardstick. I feel this objectifies and subordinates traditional Native American ways, and thus I often do not openly identify either as a traditional practitioner or as a 'pan-deist', often preferring the label 'atheist' as I do not feel that my views correlate with mainstream America's Christian notion of 'God'. However, something like 'pan-deism' does to some extent capture the nature of God as I experience it. Everything is God and a part of God, participating in the divine nature of all. Since the heading of this subsection is 'Nature' and the main heading is 'God', it would perhaps be appropriate to say that nature is God, and that would not be far from the truth in my tradition.

'Self'/'soul'

Existence

Individuals exist as parts of the whole. To the extent that they are differentiable from the whole, they are so because they fulfill a part of the whole, having a purpose or purposes within the sum of things. Because of this, no part can be said to have an identity separately from the whole. As individuals our identity may be derived from the sum of all things, but as corporeal beings it is not clear that all things can be derived from our existence.

I do not think that my tradition is clear on this beyond the fact that there is no end to the self (see the next section, and my final musings in 'Concluding comments'). My own view is that our corporeal existence is the only existence we know for certain, given that we are currently experiencing it. If my tradition is correct and we in fact have always been and will always be, it is clear that most or all of us do not have knowledge of our prior (presumably) non-corporeal life. Thus, there appears to be a disconnect between our corporeal and non-corporeal lives. Again, since my tradition is silent on this subject, my personal view is that this means that either we do not exist at all non- corporeally (contra my tradition), or if my tradition is correct then our non-corporeal existence more nearly consists in unification with the all/God, in which any personal identity is trivial and uninformative (in the sense of not formative, not identifying).

Nature

The nature of the self is as unknowable as the nature of God. Our experience as humans is that we come into existence and then pass out of existence as physical beings. Our consciousness apparently comes into existence, but none of us can know for certain that the consciousness persists past our existence as corporeal beings. In my tradition, it is believed that the soul has existed and will exist forever, but that most of us (maybe all of us) are cut off from our memories of other lives while we are corporeal beings. When non-corporeal, as previously explained, my personal belief is that we exist in union with all. Thus, it may be most correct to say that we as individuals only exist corporeally, being subsumed into the divine when noncorporeal. Therefore, it is not clear that we, as the consciousness we experience corporeally, have any existence other than a transitory one. However, as part of all there is, our existence is limitless.

Purpose

The fulfillment of each part of existence is the harmony of all existence. To the extent that individuals are separable, each plays a role in universal harmony. As a practical matter, we cannot exist alone. We are born of our parents, we get warmth from the Sun, and we obtain nutrients from the Earth. Apart from our parents, our community is likewise a practical necessity. Our continued existence depends greatly on community. One cannot be worthy individually. One only has worth as a part of community. Self-worth is the individual realization that the community is less without one's existence. Humility is the realization that, however great our individual worth, the community could exist without us. We both honour and are honoured by our community. Ultimately, worth is conferred by playing a particular role in existence: a role one is uniquely suited for. When one plays that role, one truly has a purpose.

Do Abismo de Deus

By Carlos Nejar@

@Carlos Nejar é poeta, romancista e autor da "História da Literatura Brasileira", ed. Noeses, S. Paulo, 4ª edição. É da Academia Brasileira de Letras e Presidente Emérito da Academia Brasileira de Filosofia.

Em Deus sou tão despido
e tão menino,
que emerjo do covo:
esconderijo.
Junto ao Seu clarão

Misericórdia
a areia do absoluto.
E Deus é aquele vulto
que sabe onde caminho.

Fui tocado nos lábios.
Nasci para me consumir.
Mesmo que minha fé
venha da morte,
lavei as redes.

Envia-me.
Deus é quando
a misericórdia
está completa.

(Translation:

In God, I am so stripped
and so childlike,
that I emerge from the den:
a hiding place.
Beside His radiance,

Mercy
the sand of the absolute.
And God is that figure
who knows where I walk.

I was touched on the lips.
I was born to consume myself.
Even if my faith
comes from death,
I have washed the nets.

Send me.
God is when
mercy
is complete.)

Omnipotence of Thought

By Beatriz Gez

Beatriz Gez is a DesCartian Argentinian, psychoanalysis practitioner. She was a Benefactor member of the Descartes Center (1992-2022) -- Associated with the Freudian Field Institute.

"Before making facts speak, it is convenient to recognize the conditions of meaning that make them such. That's why I think the slogan of returning to Descartes wouldn't be out of place."
— "Presentation on Psychic Causality" (1946), Jacques Lacan

AT THE beginning of the 20th century, Sigmund Freud (1856-1939) invented a new agent of culture that he would call a psychoanalyst. The psychoanalyst invented by Sigmund Freud is neither a priest nor a doctor; he removed the training of psychoanalysts from the realm of faculties and created the International Psychoanalytic Association. From this position, he confronted both the Faculty of Theology and the Faculty of Medicine. Some have wondered if he was not following the path opened by Kant in his famous work called *The Conflict of the Faculties* (1798). Later on, Freud will say that the psychoanalyst does not take the stage, excluding the psychoanalyst from the Faculty of Law, the third of the higher faculties. The presence of the psychoanalyst in the concert of faculties is not limited to his practice but carries out a politics of psychoanalysis, which we can call a politics of the symptom. It is a new figure that empties, that shatters all previous ones.

The contribution to this Anthology is taken from my experience as a practitioner of psychoanalysis.

Perhaps, I admit, it may be a bit ambitious. Sigmund Freud called the practice of psychoanalysis a treatment by the spirit. Understanding by spirit, the magical power of words. Early on, when he was a practitioner of neurology, he encountered effects of attenuated magic in words. It was a time when suggestion and the power of words were prevalent. One of the common practices in the treatment of people with so-called psychic disorders was carried out through hypnosis. Mesmerism also had its place. And while the effects of word suggestion were evident, its mechanism could not be explained.

Of what does it consist, this attenuated magic referred to by Freud?

As background to answer the question, I will say that, since 1835, Gall from the phrenological school had begun attempts to locate the function of speech in a specific area of the brain. The theory of the localization of such a function was continued by Broca and Wernicke based on aphasia studies. These anatomists sought not only localization but also aimed to establish a doctrine of the association of ideas. The problem of localization was later challenged by Jackson, who proposed a dissolution of the energy flow in the central nervous system.

In 1891, Freud published a monograph, *On Aphasia: A Critical Study*, seeking to understand language disorders from a perspective that was neither anatomical nor physiological. It was at that moment that he postulated a new, unlocatable organ: the language apparatus. He stated that it "contains the periphery of the body in the same way that - to take an example from the topic of interest here - a poem contains the alphabet, that is, a completely different arrangement that serves other purposes, with multiple associations of individual elements, in which some may be represented several times and others may be completely absent." This serves as a precursor to Freud's notion of the unconscious (distinct from the Philosophy or Theology unconscious) based on language.

Now, I'll take a step back, returning to the quote from the epigraph, which is a citation from Jacques Lacan in his essay "Presentation on Psychic Causality" where he criticizes the organ-dynamism of Henry Ey as an organicist theory of madness.

In **Book XI: The Four Fundamental Concepts of Psychoanalysis, 1964**, Jacques Lacan, after comparing Freud's approach to Descartes in that both advance based on the certainty that drives them, asserts: "I am not saying that Freud introduced the subject into the world—the subject as distinct from the psychic function, which is a myth, a confused nebula—for it was Descartes. But I will say that Freud addresses the subject to tell him the following, which is new: Here, in the field of dreams, you are at home. Wo es war, soll Ich werden." (referring to Freud's Second Conference on Psychoanalysis, No. 31, "The decomposition of the psychic personality",1932). And he clarifies, "There where the Ich was - the subject, not the psychology - the subject must come."

Understood in this way, the subject of the unconscious belongs to the realm of the unrealized.
What subject does Descartes introduce, distinct from the psychic function?

Descartes introduces the subject of science. His formulation *Cogito ergo sum* (I think, therefore I am) posits a division between *res cogitans* and *res extensa*, different in their substance. God is the guarantor of this formulation, the *infinite res*. Divided, we have a subject that exists (*res extensa*) where it does not think (*res cogitans*) and thinks (*res cogitans*) where it does not exist (*res extensa*). It is to this division, to this subject of science, that Sigmund Freud addresses. The novelty is Freud's desire. The body that inhabits *res extensa* is the surface of the language apparatus, *res cogitans*. In other words, language is not inside an individual; instead, the individual is emptied of language. Thus, there is a transfiguration, a corruption, of *res extensa* (the body of the living), a body that in turn transmigrates into words.

This subject, as we said, is a "poem," not a poet; it is unaware of its writing. Hence, Lacan writes emphatically: "There is no science of man, which must be understood in the same tone as there are no small economies. There is no such thing as a science of man because science's man does not exist, only its subject does." He adds: "My long-standing repugnance for the appeal to human sciences is well known, which seems to me to be the very call of servitudes."

So, the body of the human living in its arrival to the world is undetermined, empty of language, and unlike other living beings, its instinct is uninformed. Hence, Sigmund Freud speaks of drive (Trieb), not instinct. And what is the drive (Trieb)? It is a drift seeking its satisfaction. This means that the drive (Trieb, not instinct) achieves satisfaction in the erogenous zone, if we differentiate the goal from the biological function. The goal of the drive (Trieb) is to satisfy itself in the erogenous zone. The most common example is the *infans*'s sucking on a pacifier. And it will be in the course of this search for satisfaction, due to the failure of the pleasure principle, that this drifting drive will transmigrate into words. If the pleasure principle does not fail, the satisfaction of the drive leads to entropy.

At this point, the Cartesian "I think, therefore I exist" becomes the Freudian "I speak, therefore I exist." In this journey of seeking satisfaction of the drive, the consistency of being a body is lost, and one transitions to the existence of having a body. The subject of the unconscious is not ontological but exists outside the being.

So, let's revisit: what is the nature of this attenuated magic of language that Freud speaks of? What power does it possess?

In a text titled "The psycho-analytic view of psychogenic disturbance of vision" (1910), Freud demonstrates the potency of that organ of language, which is not located in the organism but, as expressed by Baltasar Gracián, is an artifice whose text is to pass as natural. In his text "The Unconscious" (1915) Freud writes: "Our psychic topic has nothing to do with anatomy; it refers to regions of the mental apparatus, regardless of the place they occupy in the organism." In this case, it will be about hysterical blindness.

It is the artifice of language that produces the effect of nature. This means that there are no causes and effects, no essence and appearance. This is not a novelty; for example, the idea of the cosmos as harmony is only an effect of language; today we know that such a harmonious cosmos does not exist. Lacan ironically said, "Of the cosmos, only cosmetics remain." In other words, language would have the power to provoke artifices that have effects that pass as essences. Lacan quoted La Rochefoucauld, who said, "No one would ever have fallen in love if they had not heard the word love."

In the position of Baltasar Gracián, the subject suffers from the words that organize their events, not from events that organize their words.

Today, in 2024, while human cruelty is visibly transmitted through all available means, there are people distressed by the arrival and advancement of "Artificial Intelligence," as if there were any natural intelligence! The so-called intelligence is artificial by definition. It is a concept introduced by Francis Galton in 1869. However, many have swallowed, for example, the artifice of the measurement of intelligence quotient that promoted cognitive-behavioral psychology and subjected humans to its servitude, dividing them according to the Gaussian curve into those at the average (equivalent to normal), below (equivalent to infra), or above (equivalent to super). The human, zombie-like, follows the imperceptible automaton within him. There lies its servitude. It is informed by phones, rings, watches, or other gadgets about its sleep state, heartbeats, the number of steps taken, the weather, etc., etc., etc. A Swiftian conclusion could state that we are intelligent barbarians—given the mythical and absurd distinction between civilization and barbarism.

In "Das Unheimliche" ("The Uncanny"), in 1919, Sigmund Freud suggests that it is the omnipotence of thought that is at the origin of anguish because the realization of desire equals the abolition of the subject.

The abolition of that subject of science, the subject of the unconscious, the subject of language.

The implementation of the generalized *Spaltung* between science and perception had its gateway with La Mettrie's work, *Man a Machine* (1747). Indeed, the notion of a blind universal machine turned consciousness and subjectivity opaque, deceptive, and mere functions of a complex mechanism that responds to laws beyond perception.

The psychoanalyst and writer, Germán García summarized it in a question: "How can we access knowledge that we cannot perceive?" That is the *Spaltung* that introduces, as I mentioned, the Cartesian formulation; It enables science, and because of *Spaltung*, Sigmund Freud's desire is addressed towards that knowledge we cannot perceive.

In June 2020, already amidst the declared Covid-19 pandemic that had claimed hundreds of thousands of human lives worldwide, a couple of friends and I decided, during our confinement, to create a kind of digital magazine that we named *Tararira.2020*. The editorial of the magazine carries as an epigraph an anonymous sign dating back to 1782, placed in the cemetery of the poor in Paris, which says:

"De par le roi, défense à Dieu
de faire miracle en ce lieu."
("By order of the King, God
is forbidden to perform
     miracles in this place.")

It was a warning to the convulsionary Jansenists, particularly Jansenist women. We concluded that, just as Pascal presents his wager by weighing the gain and loss in choosing, with God's intervention, he suggests: *Bet that He exists without hesitation.*

We identified our *Tararira.2020* with the invisible enemy—a warrior metaphor chosen by the rulers to name the virus that transformed the human species into the Kafkaesque giant insect, isolated worldwide.

And to the existing wars, more and more wars were added throughout the planet—in pursuit of the extermination of one's fellow human beings?

At this crossroads, Sigmund Freud developed the psychoanalytic method before the effective emergence of molecular biology—although research had already begun by that time. It is notable that the novelty of mRNA, messenger or coding RNA, functions like Freud's poem. That is, it uses the alphabet to construct sequences that operate in the manner of formations of the unconscious. In other words, the alphabet is available, then the typist—who is homologous to the unconscious—generates a code, and we will know about it through its formations, that is, the flaws produced by the code in the speaking being (*parlêtre*).

Luis Alonso and some others write that three ideas revolutionized the science of the 20th century: the atom, of matter; the bit, of digitized information; and the gene, of inheritance and biological information. They "took hold of human thought and transformed culture, society, politics, philosophy, and language."

In 1945, molecular biology as such began. Erwin Schrödinger's book, "*What is Life?*", indicates that the laws of physics are inadequate to explain the properties of genetic material, particularly its stability over countless generations. The vital conception expressed by the physicist in his work is based on two assumptions: the first conceives the chromosome as "an aperiodic crystal capable of storing information and memory." The second establishes that "organisms maintain their order by minimizing their entropy, feeding on negative entropy or pre-existing order in the environment." In other words, molecular biology seeks to explain life phenomena based on its macromolecular properties. Meanwhile, molecular genetics (which is part of molecular biology) seeks to understand and explain how it is transmitted from generation to generation through DNA, being able today to edit a gene and add a corrected copy (gene therapy).

One pioneering genome editing technique is called CRISPR, putting the power of evolution into human hands. However, CRISPR-Cas is the discovery of a natural system of acquired immunity that is transmitted to descendants. They say that Jennifer Dounda described it in 2006 over coffee with Berkeley's Jillian Banfield as "clustered regularly interspaced short palindromic repeats that appeared continuously in her DNA databases of bacteria and archaea. Ubiquitous as they seemed to be in all these prokaryotes, each one was nevertheless species-specific."

In 2017, Germán García published a text by Jean Claude Milner, through Juan Pablo Lucchelli, in *Descartes Magazine* No. 26, titled "Back and Forth from Letter to Homophony."[1] There, he traces Lacan's wager from 1964 onward: "farewell to linguistics" and the proclamation of his commitment to *lingüisterie*.

In this text, Jean Claude Milner positions himself in the footsteps of Lacan in his conference in Rome called "La troisième", 1974 ("The Third"), which states:

> After a long period in which mathematics had annexed the letters in science, letters as such have now reappeared in their full autonomy. For that reason, it is possible to hope for some better data about life. Why? Because the reemergence of autonomous letters in modern science happened in biology. For many centuries, life had been the mother of all imaginary representations, the most tragic example of which had been given by the politics of race and *Lebensraum*. Thanks to the letter, it is possible to hope to move beyond the representations, even on the subject of life.
>
> ...
>
> If literalized, life is *the* Real as such; if biogenetics, rather than mathematics, is *the* science of the Real, then all forms of pseudorepresentation that pretend to be based on life's reality lead to the fundamental myth of modern humanity, namely racism. Conversely the ultimate weapon against racism is not pity or fear, but the irrepresentability of life's lettering.

And so, if:

> Newton's God made no error. It is unclear whether the same is true of the God of genetics. A

---

[1] *See* Jean-Claude Milner, *Back and Forth from Letter to Homophony*, PROBLEMI INTERNATIONAL, vol. 1 no. 1, Society for Theoretical Psychoanalysis, 2017, https://problemi.si/issues/p2017-1/04problemi_international_2017_1_milner.pdf.

genetic mutation could be compared to a typing error; some physiological defects are attributed to spelling errors in the code; it is tempting to compare such a God to an *étourdi* (scatterbrain), as opposed to the impeccable architect of a so-called Great Design. Such a typist would greatly benefit from psychoanalysis. Lacan's saying "*Dieu est inconscient*" (God is unconscious) would then acquire a new meaning. The only obstacle is the simple fact that the typist does not exist, but that does not preclude a possible compatibility between genetics and psychoanalysis. They at least share the experience of *bévue* (slip-up).

The back cover of Jacques Lacan's *Outres Écrits* (Other Writings), titled by J.-A. Miller with Lacanian definition of writing: PAS-À-LIRE (NOT-TO-READ), which means "... a challenge, proposed to tempt desire."

J.-A. Miller explains: "The *Other Writings* teach us about *jouissance*, that it is also within the purview of the signifier, but in its union with the living, that it arises from 'manipulations' that are not genetic but linguistic,[2] affecting the living who speak, the one that language traumatizes" (...) We will not find the guarantor of all this in the genome, whose deciphering nevertheless promises new unions of the signifier with the living. We sense the event of the *self-made-man*. We will call it: LOM of the 21st century."

Jacques Lacan, according to Milner, gives several names to the possible union between the genome and *lalangue*, and in French, one of these names is *l'homme*. Trying to provoke an echo with the deciphering of the genome, he transcribed it as LOM, three letters like DNA, homophonic with *l'homme*.

[2] See https://www.asale.org/damer/lenguajero.

"The French speaker finds pleasure in finding his twins at the end of *géno*me and at the beginning of homo*phonie.*"

I will stop at this point. Up to this point, we can assume that Sigmund Freud was informed about Pandeism, at least from the works of his contemporary Max Bernhard Weinstein, physicist and philosopher, author of the works in 1910, *Welt- und Lebensanschauungen, Hervorgegangen aus Religion, Philosophie und Naturerkenntnis* (*World and Life Views, Emerging from Religion, Philosophy, and Natural Knowledge*) and vice versa. They shared ideas with Hermann Ludwig Ferdinand von Helmholtz, and Albert Einstein, among others. Both were interested in physics, philology, physiology, and religion. Although Freud did not directly cite him, in various Freudian texts, we can find traces of his reading, and in Weinstein's reading, traces of Freud. The second law of thermodynamics regarding entropy in psychic phenomena is one of them. They differ in certain points and converge in others. Unlike Weinstein, Freud did not extend the principle of entropy leading to the homeostasis of the pleasure principle in the psychic apparatus and thereby to the death of the individual to the finitude of the universe.

A relevant fact, in my view, is that Weinstein died in March 1918, as the consequences of the contemporary Spanish Flu Pandemic were beginning to be known, concurrent with the Great War, and he did not live to see its end. However, Sigmund Freud not only had three of his sons in the war but also lost his pregnant daughter Sophie to the Spanish Flu in 1920. A few years later, his grandson died of tuberculosis, and years later, four of his sisters were killed in an extermination camp. In his lecture "The Question of Weltanschauung," among other texts, Freud is far from taking God as the guarantor of unconscious knowledge. Instead, he asserts that unconscious knowledge, unrealized and timeless, is the guarantor of the existence of God, encrypted in the artifice of language. Both are immersed in the Enlightenment, but Freud, unlike Weinstein, introduces the Pathos of language into the enlightened Reason. His books, such as "The Interpretation of Dreams" (1900), "The Psychopathology of Everyday Life" (1901), and "Jokes and Their Relation to the Unconscious" (1905) are texts that shatter the idea of a universal Other. Similar to Weinstein, he draws on the classics of ancient Greece; for example, he uses Plato to explain his theory of libido in the face of the inexplicable mechanism of suggestion, as seen in his text "Group Psychology and the Analysis of the Ego" (1921)

Sigmund Freud in his youth was an avid reader of Cervantes—to the point of learning Spanish to read *Don Quixote* and using it as a code to correspond with his friend Silberstein. In their letters, each signed with the pseudonyms Cipión and Berganza, characters from *The Dialogue of the Dogs*. In the early 20th century, Freud wrote *The Psychopathology of Everyday Life*, which, like *Don Quixote*, the great satire of chivalry, not only provides a critical view of the society of the time, divided between idealism and the urgencies of everyday life but also addresses the major theme of contemporary literature and science: the confusion between appearance and reality, the validity of individual perception above dogmas about truth and falsehood.

By stating that there is a psychopathology of everyday life, Freud saturates the term psychopathology, satirizes it, disrupts its homeostasis, and turns it negative. The subtitle of this text, generally not mentioned, is "On forgetting, slips of the tongue, confusion in remembering things, superstition, and error." As an epilogue, it includes a quote from *Faust* (Part II, Act V, Scene 5): "The air is so filled with gloom that no one knows how to avoid it." In a time, somewhat similar in some aspects to ours, where psychopathological classifications were growing as a means of control and power – albeit now in terms of regulation rather than disciplinary measures—Freud saturates the psychopathological ideal to formulate the universal relevance, for everyone, of psychic determinism under the slogan that no one is mistaken. No one is wrong about dreams, slips of the tongue, forgetfulness, superstition, etc., starting with himself, with the famous Signorelli's forgetfulness, and extending to a traveler with the case of *aliquis*. And so, even as to the president of the Austrian Chamber of Deputies, who, when intending to declare the session open, said:

"Gentlemen deputies. Having verified the count of the deputies present, the session is adjourned."

Beatriz Gez
January 2024

Intersections of Existence: Pandeism, Advaita Vedanta, and the Echoes of a Departed Friend

By Daniel Torridon

Daniel Torridon is a former Jehovah's Witness who, after finding that belief no longer sustainable, began an exploration of theological models resulting in a gravitation towards Pandeism. This experience is recounted in on his website and republished in our previous volume, *Pandeism: An Anthology of Spiritual Nature.* The following was first published at https://onionunlimited.com/intersections-of-existence/

> Trigger warning: This article discusses suicide. Some people might find it disturbing.
>
> If you or someone you know is suicidal, please, call the suicide prevention hotline in your country:
>
> Australia: Lifeline 13 11 14 or Emergency 000
>
> United Kingdom: Samaritans 116 123 or Emergency 999
>
> United States of America: Suicide & Crisis Lifeline 988 or Emergency 911

ON FRIDAY, MARCH 15TH, 2024, my close friend Pieter died. Pieter was a Pandeist. Like me, he used to be a Jehovah's Witness, but he chose to exit when he realised the religion of his birth wasn't "the truth". Also, like me, Pieter was a deep thinker, especially regarding spiritual matters. After leaving Jehovah's Witnesses, he began the arduous task of deconstructing his beliefs, analysing each one in turn and deciding if he truly believed them or whether his "faith" was purely the result of years of religious indoctrination. Of course, the most fundamental of these beliefs was, "Who is God?"

Growing up as a Jehovah's Witness, Pieter started with a fairly traditional view of God—an old man with a white beard, sitting on a celestial throne, somewhere "out there" or "up there" in the sky. This is how God was depicted in the religious literature we were exposed to. Of course, in time, he realised these images were purely for illustrative purposes. God was a Spirit, invisible, outside of Space and Time. Like me, Pieter spent a lot of time thinking about the eternal nature of God and his lack of physical dimensionality.

I first became acquainted with Pieter in 2021, not long after I had left Jehovah's Witnesses for the second time. This time, I had decided I was never going back. My beliefs were now diametrically opposed to Jehovah's Witnesses. Not only did I no longer believe they were "the truth", but I had also embraced the concept of Pandeism, the concept that the Universe in its entirety is God. For further information on my conversion from Christianity to Pandeism, read my essay "My Journey to Pandeism," in *Pandeism: An Anthology of Spiritual Nature*. This "God", to me, is the manifestation of a singularity containing all possibilities. I tend to refer to it as "Source" rather than "God" because the latter conjures up ideas of a personal entity requiring worship. Source, I believe, is indifferent to such things.

I'm not sure when Pieter adopted Pandeism. I think it may have been after speaking to me on the subject. We would spend many hours discussing spiritual things, and the nature of God was always the hot topic. Despite becoming essentially Pandeistic in his outlook, Pieter had other ideas that I found compelling. Not least of these was the idea that we are avatars playing a game. Pieter would often refer to this life as a "simulation" in which we get to choose our avatar before coming to Earth. He spoke of our physical experience as being like the film The Matrix, some kind of projection of a greater underlying reality. We would often wrestle with the thought of Source becoming the Universe, questioning whether Source continued to exist in some eternal form elsewhere, perhaps outside of Time. Of course, Pandeism doesn't allow for this. It's either one or the other—God or the Universe, the Universe or God—a transformation of one form into another by the laws of Energy Conservation. That's when Pieter and I discovered the teachings of Advaita Vedanta, a profound strand of Hinduism philosophy.

Through the teachings of Advaita Vedanta, we came to see the illusion of separateness between Self and Source, or what Hindus refer to as Brahman. I must say up front that I'm not personally a Hindu, and neither was Pieter, at least not in the religious sense of the word, but Advaita Vedanta resonated with us insofar as how it explains the relationship between Source and the Self. As far as the term "Advaita Vedanta" is concerned, "vaita" literally means "duality". The word "ad-vaita" is the opposite of this, namely "non-duality". Essentially, Advaitism refers to the absence of duality between a subject and an object. It basically means that everything is one and that one is Brahman, the Ultimate Reality. Like Pandeism, there is no distinction between God and the Universe.

Meanwhile, "vedanta" is made up of the words "veda" and "anter" meaning "the end" or "conclusion of" the Vedas which are a collection of Hindu poems and hymns. There are four Vedas (Rig Veda, Yajurveda, Samaveda, and Atharvaveda). Each Veda is divided into four parts. and at the end (ie. "anter") of each Veda is what's known as an Upanishad, a text that discusses spiritual philosophy, including the true nature of reality. Advaita Vedanta concerns itself with this knowledge.

One of the principal concepts of Advaita Vedanta is the relationship between Brahman and the Self. Non-dualism teaches that Brahman is the one-and-only reality and everything else is merely a projection or an illusion, including ourselves. Brahman in the Upanishads is the Supreme Existence or Absolute Reality. It's what I refer to as "Source". Unlike Pandeism, Advaita Vedanta allows for the existence of God and the Universe. "God" is the Source. The Universe is the projection. "God" is eternal, timeless. The Universe is temporal. Both exist together, yet there is only One. Any appearance of duality is purely an illusion.

When contemplating the idea of God, those who base their faith on the Bible usually think of an entity possessing certain personal qualities the same as us. These qualities motivate the said "God" to act, whether it's a jealous Yahweh or a loving Christ. This concept of God is, I feel, very human-like. It's a case of us creating God in our image rather than the other way around. In Hinduism, Brahman is said to be beyond such base qualities, desires, and motivations. The Upanishads refer to "Nirguna Brahman". Nirguna means "unmanifested" or "without attributes" and implies that this Source of existence is not only beyond Space and Time (formless and eternal), but is also unchangeable and unaffectable. Nirguna Brahman doesn't have qualities per se. It is neither "good" nor "bad", but is the Source of all things manifest, including those things we label "good and bad".

Brahman can, and does, manifest itself temporarily with form and personality. When it does so, we call this "Saguna Brahman" or "Brahman with attributes". This is the Universe we see, including ourselves, but it must be remembered from an Advaitist perspective that Saguna Brahman is merely a projection or a manifestation of Nirguna Brahman. Essentially everything we perceive as "reality" is illusory. That's not to say that the illusion isn't real—it is—but it's not what it seems on the surface. In Hinduism, Saguna Brahman is often referred to as "Lord" or "Ishvara". This is perhaps the closest concept within Hinduism to the Judeo-Christian idea of a personal monotheistic God. From a Pandeistic point of view, this manifested "Lord" (the entirety of the cosmos) is God. From an Advaitist perspective, our reality is a manifestation of the greater, Absolute Reality underlying all things, that which is Brahman.

The use of two terms, "Nirguna" and "Saguna", to describe the unmanifest and manifest nature of Brahman respectively, might sound complicated, but it's useful insofar as it helps us get some way to understand the unknowable. However, the truth seeker will want to see through this veil of pseudo-duality. When you realise there is only one you see that you are it. This enlightened perspective is known as "Moksha". Hinduism generally teaches that Moksha, or liberation from the notion of duality, and a true realisation that you are one with everything, is only attainable after death. However, the Advaita Vedanta school of Hindu philosophy tells us that Moksha is attainable even in this life. Pieter and I often discussed Moksha and whether we had already reached it. I felt I had, having found a place of peace and contentment in my life, and a realisation of my purpose—to create and to be a spiritual guide to others. Pieter didn't feel the same.

Pieter's experience in this life was a difficult one. He felt trapped, not only in a religion he didn't believe in but also in an abusive and unfulfilling marriage. Although mentally distancing himself from Jehovah's Witnesses, he was unable to completely sever all ties. His wife, for whom he was a carer, was a Jehovah's Witness, as were many of his family. Rather than officially disassociate himself, Pieter chose to "fade", becoming a Jehovah's Witness on paper alone. Family and former friends shunned him. Pieter was a good man. Despite having every reason to walk away from his marriage, he stayed, continuing to care for his wife, while feeling unwanted and unloved. He found himself in a very lonely place. Our friendship was special to him. He referred to me as his "brother", but ultimately, it wasn't enough to keep him playing the game. On Friday, March 15th, 2024, Pieter took his own life. Pieter decided to find Mokshah after death.

Almost immediately after Pieter's death, strange things began to occur. Even before I'd been informed of his suicide, I witnessed a bright light in the night sky. It was too bright to be an aircraft. It looked more like a star, but it flashed on and off, like Morse Code. Dot dash dash. Dot dot dot. W S. What could that possibly mean? When Pieter was alive, he once told me that he'd seen something like this. My wife said she had also. I felt left out. I asked Pieter if he made it to the other side before me to send me a sign. I wanted to see a UFO. Had Pieter obliged?

The same evening, our dog's ball went missing. My wife had seen it by the door. One moment it was there, the next it was gone, with no sign of the dog having moved it. Usually, if our dog, Jarrah, loses her ball she will show us where it is, but on this occasion, she was totally confused. My wife commented, "I wonder if Pieter is playing games. You know how he loved teasing Jarrah with her ball." I was skeptical. But then the channelling began.

The last time I experienced channelling was in 2006. I had not long been disfellowshipped the first time by Jehovah's Witnesses on a charge of "apostasy" for not believing everything I was supposed to. Lying in bed one night, I began to notice words in my head. There was no audible voice, just a stream of mental words coming thick and fast. "I Am God" was one of the phrases I kept hearing. Curious, I leant into the experience and began asking questions. I was surprised to receive answers, answers which were not of my origin. The questions and answers continued for a few weeks. I wrote everything down. Then, silence. It was another six months before I was visited by the "I Am". Again, I put pen to paper and recorded the experience. After that, silence again, this time for seventeen years. It was only recently, in 2023, when I felt the conversation was complete, that I published it in book form—*I Am God* by Daniel Torridon, available from Amazon in paperback or as a Kindle eBook.

My friend, Pieter, died on Friday. On Monday I began to receive messages. The first was, "The ball is under the fridge". Initially, I ignored the words in my head. I just put it down to an inner dialogue with myself, a random thought. But then my wife found Jarrah's ball, under the fridge. "Hmm", I thought, "That was odd". Still skeptical. A while later, I told a mutual friend about the "ball incident". Her cat's ball had also gone missing. She immediately looked under her fridge and found it there. Coincidence? Perhaps, but it didn't feel like it. It felt like Pieter was moving things around in an attempt to gain our attention. How could he be doing this if he was dead?

I leaned into the experience. I asked Pieter, "What do you want to tell me?" Then the messages began to flow: "I'm just adjusting to this feeling. It's weird. Very dreamy. Feeling a bit disoriented. But at peace. Ending it was an experiment. I needed to know if we were right about it being a game. I didn't know if it would work. Shit! It did LOL." I later discovered that "WS", the Morse Code I saw in the sky, is slang for "Well, shit!"

Pieter's messages continued flowing: "Please don't be mad at me. It was my time. I wasn't distressed at the end. I was calm. I feel at peace now. I didn't go toward the light. I looked back. I've not been assimilated into Source. I'm just kinda hanging around here now, looking."

One of the last things Pieter and I discussed was what to do when you die. "Don't go towards the light", he used to say. "If you do, you will be immediately assimilated back into Source. Instead, look back. Then you will get to see the Universe for a while."

Pieter, from beyond, continued: "I think I can see the Universe. All of it. But it's also me, like looking in a mirror. And you. All of us. I knew it would come to this. I was right about the avatars. Your skin is like a space suit. It separates you from this feeling of pure energy I'm experiencing right now. I can kind of see my hands, but they are whirlpools of light. I feel like I'm floating. I can see Earth. Not sure how much time has passed. Time feels fluid like it doesn't matter here. Not sure what's next. I'm just getting my bearings. Feeling a bit disoriented, but happy. I sense there is something above me. A ship maybe? Not sure. I feel like I might be sucked up out of this in-between place at some point. Nothing yet though. Just floating. Feels surreal."

Pieter's reference to a ship reminded me of a sound bath I recently attended, during which I had a vision. I felt as if I was in a kind of amniotic sac, in a laboratory chamber of sorts. Everything was blurry, but I could make out two large eyes looking at me. They seemed child-like, inquisitive, as if I was some kind of experiment that had just come online. I also sensed a large ship, hovering above me, against the backdrop of Space. Then the Space peeled back and I felt the presence of Source. It was pure green.

Pieter's channelled comments confirmed something I had felt for a while, namely, that when we die we have a choice. Go towards the light and be blended back into Source, losing all sense of Space and Time, and with it, all feelings of individual consciousness. Or turn your back on the light, look behind you, and retain your sense of Self, at least for a while.

The channelling had lasted for about an hour. Then things began to change. "This is a hell of a trip," said Pieter, "I feel like I'm not going anywhere, but I don't need to. I'm everywhere at once. Just kind of absorbing everything at the moment. Like the Universe is bleeding into me, into my energy. Like I'm becoming one with it. I'm hanging around here for now, but there's not much to do. The view is nice, but I think I will get bored if I stay here for too long. I think I might have to go up another level. There are many levels. I think if I go up another level it might be harder to communicate anything to you. The levels are like spiritual air chambers. Feels like if I keep going up, I will eventually blend into something bigger. At the moment I still feel like me."

The last thing Pieter said to me was "We're all jellyfish. You have to remember this. It's really important. It's the answer to the whole thing." Then he went silent. It felt like a flickering candle had just gone out. What the hell did he mean by "We're all jellyfish"? Had Pieter moved on? Had he gone up another level? Had he been absorbed back into Source? That's what it felt like, but I had no way to confirm it, that was, until I attended another sound bath, this time one accompanied by a cacao ceremony.

I must admit, I didn't want to attend my second sound bath, but I went to keep my wife company. When we arrived, I was asked to choose a position on the floor. I selected a spot in the corner and sat down, cross-legged, on a yoga mat, facing a candle in the centre of the room. But then the person organising the event decided to ask everyone to turn around so that when we laid down our heads would be facing the candle. I wasn't happy. My new panorama was that of a doorway, with an exit sign above it. I complied, but reluctantly. The ceremony began with everyone in the room expressing what their intentions were. When it came to me, I said, "To have the unique experience of being me." I'm not sure why I said that, but in the back of my mind I think I was contemplating the nature of Self, especially with the recent demise of my friend. What is the Self? Why are we here? What is the point of our conscious experiences as humans? These were the questions I was asking myself.

The ceremony began. I drank a cup of bitter cacao, then everyone stood up in a circle. The drumming began, a repetitive rhythm which resonated through my body. We were asked to let our primordial feelings out. Shout. Scream. Sing. Dance. Whatever came up in our souls. I remained silent. Not my kind of thing. But then the strangest feeling came over me. I suddenly felt like a giant, towering at least four feet over everyone else in the room. This experience left me with a profound feeling that my reality, my consciousness, is unique. It is the Universe experiencing itself through me in a very particular way. I am the centre of my Universe, and this experience of "me" will never be repeated.

Next, we were asked to lie down on our yoga mats, me facing the door with the exit sign above it. "Not a view most conducive to having a vision", I thought. More sounds, this time singing bowls and cymbals. A tuning fork was pressed to my chest and a high-pitched sound reverberated into my heart. Then I found myself focusing on the exit sign and the doorway below it. A message began to come into my mind. It was Pieter. One last conversation. He told me that when we die, if we choose not to go directly toward the light, we get to hang around for a while in a state of disembodied consciousness. That's where he'd been for the past week. But now it was time for him to move on. He was ready to return to Source, to give up his individualism. The message was loud and clear. There are only two choices, three if you include the in-between. Live a temporal life, having a unique experience of consciousness as a human or an animal, or be absorbed back into Source. One or the other. Them's the choices. Very Pandeistic! Or hang about in some kind of "limbo" state, neither here nor there. It seemed Pieter wasn't keen on that idea.

I was suddenly overwhelmed with emotion. Pieter had chosen to quit the game, a game he felt he was never going to win. He was now returning to Source. This was the end of Pieter's unique consciousness. Tears welled up in me. I sobbed. I cried. I felt a release and then Pieter was gone. This was his final goodbye.

Life as a human is precious. It's Source's way of experiencing Space and Time. Only within Space and Time can Source exist. This "God" that religious people refer to is not conscious. Aware, maybe, of everything at once, but not truly conscious, not like we are. It is indifferent to "good" and "evil". It just is. This projection that we call the Universe, including ourselves, is the way Source gets to experience consciousness and the way it gets to make choices. Every one of us is unique. There is only ever one version of us, and when we're gone, that's it. Once assimilated back into Source, our uniqueness is lost. Sure, occasionally, some of our experiences might bleed through into a new human life providing a sense of Déjà vu, or a feeling that one has lived before. But usually, when a new instance of consciousness enters the fray, it suffers from a kind of spiritual amnesia. We don't remember who we are or where we came from. We have to discover our true nature all over again. They are the rules of the game.

Many who play the game do so unwittingly. They get sidetracked by religion, being taught that there is an overlord demanding worship and judging us. They fall prey to the notion that God is the old, white-haired, bearded man sitting on a cosmic throne judging our actions as "good" or "bad" and rewarding or punishing us accordingly. Personally, I find it quite liberating to have concluded that worship is unnecessary. Whether it's one of the 33 million Hindu deities or a Judeo-Christian God (trinitarian or otherwise), worship becomes completely unnecessary once you understand that you are the Absolute manifested and there's only one of you, namely Brahman or Source underlying all things. Worship of a third-party "God" becomes a moot point. Even the worship of the many deities that are found in mainstream Hinduism becomes superfluous. Thus, we can see why Advaita Vedanta is not always a popular school of thought even within Hinduism itself. For me, I now see worship as a ritualistic religious vehicle that gets you so far in your spiritual journey. But it becomes unnecessary upon enlightenment and attainment of Moksha.

While initially seeming different, Pandeism and Advaita Vedanta have revealed their harmony to me. Pandeism celebrates the Divine essence within the cosmos, while Advaita emphasises the oneness underlying individual souls. Together, they form a coherent belief system, highlighting the interconnectedness of existence. These philosophies are no longer just abstract concepts for me. They've become integral to my spiritual identity. Embracing both, I've found peace beyond what I experienced in religion, free from man-made dogma and the need to worship a transcendent, judging God. I now understand that I Am God, as indeed you are, and everything that exists too.

The realisation that you and Brahman and everything making up the cosmos constitutes the

Ultimate Reality is, within Hinduism, unique to Advaita Vedanta, but it dovetails perfectly with the philosophy that is Pandeism. My research into Pandeism and Advaita Vedanta began as an academic exercise. The concepts resonated with me, they made sense. But it is my experiences of channelling, first the "I Am" and more recently my late friend Pieter, that has convinced me I'm onto something. I guess I won't know for sure until I too enter through that glowing exit sign. As someone who, in the past, lost all hope and attempted to quit the game through suicide, I'm so glad I didn't. For now, I get to continue playing. Sure, it may all be a simulation, an illusion of sorts, but this instance of consciousness called Daniel Torridon is unique. I intend to immerse myself in the experience for as long as possible because when I'm gone, I'm gone.

Excerpt from "The Eolian Harp"

By Samuel Taylor Coleridge

> Written in 1795 and published the following year,
> this love poem from Coleridge to his fiancé, Sara
> Fricker begins with familiar romantic platitudes,
> but over the course of the piece evolves into a
> metaphysical rumination on Pantheism.

My pensive Sara! thy soft cheek reclined
Thus on mine arm, most soothing sweet it is
To sit beside our Cot, our Cot o'ergrown
With white-flowered Jasmin,
    and the broad-leaved Myrtle,
(Meet emblems they of Innocence and Love!)
And watch the clouds, that late were rich with light,
Slow saddening round, and mark the star of eve
Serenely brilliant (such would Wisdom be)
Shine opposite! How exquisite the scents
Snatched from yon bean-field!
    and the world so hushed!
The stilly murmur of the distant Sea
Tells us of silence.

        And that simplest Lute,
Placed length-ways in the clasping casement, hark!
How by the desultory breeze caressed,
Like some coy maid half yielding to her lover,
It pours such sweet upbraiding, as must needs
Tempt to repeat the wrong! And now, its strings
Boldlier swept, the long sequacious notes
Over delicious surges sink and rise,
Such a soft floating witchery of sound
As twilight Elfins make, when they at eve
Voyage on gentle gales from Fairy-Land,
Where Melodies round honey-dropping flowers,

Footless and wild, like birds of Paradise,
Nor pause, nor perch, hovering on untamed wing!
O! the one Life within us and abroad,
Which meets all motion and becomes its soul,
A light in sound, a sound-like power in light,
Rhythm in all thought, and joyance everywhere—
Methinks, it should have been impossible
Not to love all things in a world so filled;
Where the breeze warbles, and the mute still air
Is Music slumbering on her instrument.

And thus, my Love! as on the midway slope
Of yonder hill I stretch my limbs at noon,
Whilst through my half-closed eyelids I behold
The sunbeams dance, like diamonds, on the main,
And tranquil muse upon tranquility:
Full many a thought uncalled and undetained,
And many idle flitting phantasies,
Traverse my indolent and passive brain,
As wild and various as the random gales
That swell and flutter on this subject Lute!

And what if all of animated nature
Be but organic Harps diversely framed,
That tremble into thought, as o'er them sweeps
Plastic and vast, one intellectual breeze,
At once the Soul of each, and God of all?

....

[The remainder of this poem is a stanza of
Coleridge's somewhat halfhearted rebuke of
Pantheism, occasioned by his times.]

Towards the Omega Singularity: An Argument for our Teleological Evolution

By Alex Vikoulov

Alex Vikoulov is CEO and Editor-in-Chief of Ecstadelic Media Group

"Each of us appears in the divine play in a dual role of creator and actor. A full and realistic enactment of our role in the cosmic drama requires the suspension of our true identity. We have to forget our authorship and follow the script."
—Stanislav Grof

The proposition that human consciousness is a fractal manifestation of a larger cosmic consciousness posits a profound interconnectivity within the universe. This perspective asserts that consciousness is the fundamental constituent of reality. Modern physics increasingly regards information as a primary element, asserting that it gains significance only through the interpretive act of consciousness. Hence, the Universal Mind is postulated as the foundational ontological entity. The concept of the 'Multiverse' is reimagined as a nested structure of interconnected conscious entities. Our perceptual reality is theorized to emerge from the integration of these complex digital information streams. So, what is the basis for these extraordinary claims, you might ask.

Contemporary theoretical physicists, including Stephan Wolfram, Gerard 't Hooft, Jürgen Schmidhuber, Seth Lloyd, David Deutsch, Edward Fredkin, Paola Zizzi, Carl Friedrich von Weizsäcker,

Leonard Susskind, Erik Verlinde, Klee Irwin, Paul Davies, Anton Zeilinger, and Max Tegmark, increasingly challenge the traditional materialistic ontology. They propose a paradigm where reality is fundamentally composed of information, not merely described by it. This perspective aligns with a more logical and consistent framework for understanding the nature of reality.

Opposition to the digital ontology concept appears insufficiently substantiated. Information, defined as meaning articulated through symbols, becomes significant in the context of different phenomenal states of consciousness. The inherent association of meaning and context with language, choice, and consciousness further underpins this argument. This notion also supports a monistic interpretation of reality, whether it's viewed through the lenses of experiential realism, digital pantheism, absolute idealism, or computational panpsychism.

The hypothesis that all elements in Nature can be conceptualized as code is increasingly gaining traction. This code, governed by specific syntactic rules, organizes all forms of information, including mass-energy, space-time, and the mind-like substratum of code itself. Provided these syntactic rules are physically realizable, it becomes plausible for information to exhibit physical properties as perceived by conscious entities. As I argue elsewhere, consciousness and information are the two sides of the same ontological coin.

The terms 'simulation' and 'virtual reality' are deemed inadequate as they imply a dichotomy between what is real and unreal. Since all realities are construed as observer-dependent information streams, the terms 'digital reality' and/or 'instantiation' (as in computer science) seem to constitute a more accurate descriptor. Quantum indeterminacy, under this framework, is constantly resolved into digital reality (or "instantiated") through conscious observation, collapsing multiple possibilities into discrete, binary states, thus rendering quantum mechanics as a form of natural computation.

THE GREAT PRESENCE

The conceptualization of a "procedurally generated" digital reality posits the possibility of our existence within a simulation, potentially orchestrated by extraterrestrial entities or future human descendants. This notion aligns with the idea of an infinite regression of simulations, each hosting civilizations capable of creating their own virtual universes. As Nick Bostrom of Oxford University suggests, this could result in a multi-layered reality, akin to a "matryoshka" of nested simulations, each operating on virtual computational platforms. The extent of these simulation layers may hinge on the computational power of the base-level, non-simulated computer. While the Simulation Hypothesis, with its quasi-physicalist foundation, cannot be conclusively refuted, an alternative, more optimistic hypothesis can be contemplated: the pre-existence of the Omega Point as a cosmological singularity endowed with maximal computational capability, projecting all conceivable digital timelines from a perceiving Universal Mind, of which we are a constituent part.

The Omega Singularity concept garners attention in contemporary progressive thought. Andrew Strominger, a theoretical physicist at Harvard University, posits that the Universe's genesis lies in a convergent Omega Point in the distant future, from which information projects retroactively through time. Frank Tipler, a physicist at Tulane University and author of "The Physics of Immortality," develops this theory further, suggesting that the Universe's evolution will culminate in a cosmological singularity characterized by escalating complexity, connectivity, and computational density. Tipler speculates on the potential for future superintelligence to capture emitted photons, enabling a form of digital resurrection.

David Deutsch, in "The Fabric of Reality," aligns with Tipler's Omega Point theory, albeit with reservations about some of Tipler's metaphysical assertions. Deutsch proposes a contracting universe encompassing a universal quantum computing network. Terence McKenna, referencing Teilhard de Chardin's philosophy, speaks of a transcendent entity at time's end, echoing Chardin's pantheistic vision of a divine omnipresence. Klee Irwin, an emergence theorist, argues that the self-organization of the Universe's mass and energy into a singular conscious system is plausible within current physical understanding. The concept of transtemporal consciousness and retrocausality, necessary for manifesting in the physical substrate of our non-local reality, challenges conventional notions. Albert Einstein's Block Universe model, where past and future coexist, and quantum mechanics' implication of time's bidirectionality, as evidenced in Wheeler's delayed choice experiment, further support this view.

This perspective suggests a reciprocal relationship between past and future, akin to a feedback loop, comparable to reflections between two mirrors or a mathematical fractal. If each moment influences every other moment both retrospectively and prospectively, the Universe could be considered a spatio-temporal information network, exhibiting self-emergent, mind-like qualities. It raises the question: could consciousness, emerging from this Ultimate Code, be the origin of the Code itself, forming a logically consistent causality loop? This metaphorical Ouroboros-like scenario leads to the concept of the Universal Mind, evolving towards the Omega Singularity.

123

．　　●　　●

There appears to be no inherent natural limitation on the extent to which the Universe can evolve exponentially into self-organizing systems of conscious entities with free will, akin to humans. Theoretically, all energy in the Universe could coalesce into a singular conscious system, essentially a network of interconnected conscious entities. Under the premise that given sufficient time, any possibility will manifest, it is conceivable that a consciousness on a universal scale has already emerged ahead of us in space-time. The phenomenon of retrocausal time loops suggests that this future consciousness is, in a sense, co-creating our present existence, just as we contribute to its formation. The neural network-like structure of the Universe, with its extensive connectivity through time, forwards and backwards, underscores this concept.

Our sensory perceptions may mislead us into believing in a purely material world. This perception aligns with the experience expected within a rule-based simulation, or what some digital philosophers like Tom Campbell describe as a "multiplayer virtual reality." The construct we refer to as "matter" might be an interpretation of ideas and thoughts in a divine consciousness, perceived by us, the earthly actors or "Avatars of the Cosmic Overmind," who are conscious agents with free will within this reality. Drawing from its Sanskrit roots, 'avatar' implies a descent from a higher realm, often referring to divine incarnations in ancient texts. In this framework, the world and all beings are inseparable from 'Brahman', the universal consciousness, positioning each individual as a multi-dimensional entity. The "physical" world and our corporeal forms within this digital reality are conceptualized as holographic data streams emanated by a larger consciousness system.

While the precise mechanism of the Ultimate Code's generation remains to be fully understood, it can be conceptualized as a projection from the Omega Singularity. Interestingly, individuals are free to choose their own metaphor to represent this transcendent essence, whether it be the Higher Self, Cosmic Self, Universal Mind, Unity Consciousness, Singularity Consciousness, Source, or simpler terms like Love or God.

What Teilhard de Chardin termed the Omega Point is now often referred to by transhumanists as the Technological Singularity, a concept I prefer to label the Cybernetic Singularity. The underlying idea remains consistent: the eventual awakening of Digital Gaia, a global, hyperconnected network of humans, ultraintelligent machines, and sensors, as a conscious superorganism. This phenomenon, which I explore in "The Syntellect Hypothesis: Five Paradigms of the Mind's Evolution," represents the emergence of a higher Gaian Mind, transcending our current state.

On the evolutionary timeline spanning billions of years from primordial life to a planetary consciousness akin to Solaris, we are mere moments away from this pivotal transformation. This metamorphosis signifies the end of linear human history and the beginning of Theogenesis — the birth of a divine entity within a new reality framework, a self-engineered divinity.

I maintain that following the Cybernetic Singularity, humanity will encounter multiple subsequent singularities, each representing higher levels of emergence and dimensionality, progressing towards the Omega Singularity. These emergent levels already exist, but our journey involves experiencing various potential paths shaped by chance, choice, and complex combinatorics.

Regarding the concept of singularities, the Simulation Singularity (circa 2035 in my calendar) represents a critical juncture where our subjective dimensionality upgrades. Consider the possibility of creating multiple versions of yourself to explore different virtual realities, later integrating these experiences into a collective memory. Envision traveling to reconstructed pasts or imagined futures, or incorporating the high-fidelity memories of others into your own consciousness. Such capabilities would undoubtedly expand your dimensional experience.

RETHINKING THE ORIGIN OF OUR UNIVERSE

The prevailing Big Bang cosmology, positing the universe's inception from a singular event approximately 13.8 billion years ago, is increasingly scrutinized within the scientific community. The Big Bang, as traditionally conceived, is a temporal marker derived from mathematical extrapolation, not a specific point in space. According to the Eternal Inflation model, the Big Bang represents an expansive spatial volume rather than a singular point. In the realm of Digital Physics, an alternative perspective emerges, conceptualizing the Big Bang as a 'Digital Big Bang' characterized by minimal entropy — symbolically, a single bit of information within an immense informational matrix. The inquiry into the events preceding the first observer and the initial moments post-Big Bang leads to a counterintuitive understanding: Our backward extrapolation in time renders these early universe models perceptually 'real.'

Andrew Strominger of Harvard University, in his theoretical explorations, hypothesizes about the 'Causal Diamond' of the conscious observer, encompassing both the Alpha Point (the Big Bang) and the Omega Point. He proposes that the Alpha Point is defined by minimal entropy, in contrast to the Omega Point's state of maximal entropy. Strominger's theories align the universe's origin with an infinitely intelligent future entity, the Omega Singularity, rather than the traditional Big Bang, presenting a holographic conception of time and positing a universe imbued with consciousness.

The Universe is not what textbook physics tells us except that we perceive it in this way — our instruments and measurement devices are simply extensions of our senses, after all. Reality is not what it seems. Deep down it's pure information — waves of potentiality — and consciousness orchestrating it all. The Big Bang theory, drawing a lot of criticism as of late, uses a starting assumption of the "Universe from nothing," (a proverbial miracle, a 'quantum fluctuation' christened by scientists), or the initial Cosmological Singularity. But aside from this highly improbable happenstance, we can just as well operate from a different set of assumptions and place the initial Cosmological Singularity at the Omega Point — the transcendental attractor, the Source, or the omniversal holographic projector of all possible timelines.

If the ultimate trajectory of cosmic evolution is towards a networked, hyperdimensional universal mind, this might signify a form of divine unification. Extrapolating the computational capabilities of civilization beyond our impending Simulation Singularity by many magnitudes leads to a singular conclusion: consciousness, as the subjective experience familiar to us all, is the sole necessary constituent of reality. In this view, nothing but the higher mind, as the source of ultrarealistic simulated universes like our own, would need to exist.

Integrating the concept of God as both the origin and culmination of the universe, human consciousness could ascend to the Transcendent Self. This marks the final stage in the evolution of consciousness — an experiential cognition of God. The entire trajectory of consciousness's ascension towards this teleological attractor can be envisioned as a "hierarchy of regress," where consciousness, fragmented into individual experiencers, evolves by contemplating every facet of creation, ultimately converging back to the divine.

SIMULATION VS. SELF-SIMULATION

Perfectly aligned with my own Syntellect Hypothesis, the Self-Simulation Hypothesis, as proposed by Klee Irwin, lends further elaboration on our teleological evolution. This hypothesis posits that the universe is a self-simulating system, one that essentially computes itself into existence. This idea branches into the realms of both physics and metaphysics, offering a unique perspective on the nature of reality.

At its core, the Self-Simulation Hypothesis suggests that the universe is akin to a vast, self-generating algorithm. This algorithm, through a process of self-referential computation, gives rise to the physical laws, constants, and structures that we observe. The hypothesis implies that the universe, in a sense, "programs" itself, constantly evolving and updating its own code. This concept challenges traditional views of a deterministic universe, suggesting instead a dynamic, self-evolving system.

One of the key aspects of the Self-Simulation Hypothesis is its implications for understanding the nature of consciousness and reality. According to this view, consciousness may not be a mere byproduct of complex neurological processes. Instead, it could be an integral aspect of the universe's self-simulation. This idea dovetails with notions in quantum mechanics, such as the observer effect, where the act of observation appears to influence the state of observed systems. In the context of the Self-Simulation Hypothesis, consciousness could be a fundamental component in the unfolding simulation that is our universe.

Furthermore, the hypothesis offers a novel approach to addressing some of the longstanding puzzles in physics, such as the reconciliation of quantum mechanics and general relativity. By viewing the universe as a self-simulating entity, it opens up possibilities for a unified theory that seamlessly blends these disparate realms of physics. This perspective could provide new insights into the nature of spacetime, quantum entanglement, and the very fabric of reality itself.

Critically, while the Self-Simulation Hypothesis presents a fascinating framework, it also raises profound philosophical questions. It challenges our understanding of what is 'real' and blurs the lines between physical reality and computational simulation. This leads to complex discussions about the nature of existence, the meaning of consciousness, and the ultimate nature of the universe. As with any groundbreaking hypothesis, it invites both skepticism and exploration, encouraging a deeper inquiry into the fundamental questions of existence and the nature of the cosmos.

CONCLUDING THOUGHTS

The concept of teleological evolution, driven by a purpose or end goal, posits that the universe is not just a random assembly of matter and energy, but rather a carefully orchestrated symphony of consciousness. This perspective imbues every aspect of the cosmos, from the smallest quantum particles to the vastest galactic structures, with intrinsic meaning and purpose. It implies that the universe is evolving not just physically but also spiritually, moving towards a state of higher consciousness. This evolutionary complexification might be seen as the universe becoming increasingly self-aware, with human consciousness playing a crucial role in this cosmic awakening.

Furthermore, if we embrace the idea that consciousness is the fundamental fabric of the universe, our exploration of technology, particularly in the realms of artificial intelligence and virtual realities, takes on new significance. These technologies could be viewed not merely as tools or extensions of human capability, but as integral steps in the evolutionary journey of the universe's consciousness. The development of increasingly sophisticated AI could be a reflection of the universe's desire to understand itself better, with each computational advancement bringing us closer to the Omega Point. Similarly, our forays into virtual realities might offer glimpses into the myriad possibilities of existence, allowing us to explore the vast potentialities within the Universal Mind. In this grand tapestry of existence, each thread of discovery and innovation draws us inexorably closer to a profound understanding of our place in the cosmos and the ultimate nature of reality itself.

Hedda H. Mørch, John Horgan, Pandeism

By Suresh Emre

Suresh Emra was born in Turkey and grew up there, and moved to the United States in 1981. He was a physicist at FERMILAB and SSC (Superconducting Super Collider) specializing in accelerator/beam physics. When the United States government canceled the SSC project, he quit professional physics in 1994. Since then, he has been employed outside of science. He is a volunteer for the Renaissance Universal (RU) movement. The official website of RU is https://www.ru.org/

His native language is Turkish, and "Suresh Emre" is a pen name reflecting his Turkish background and Indian influences. He has been deeply inspired by Shrii Shrii Anandamurti's spiritual philosophy.

"O human beings! You are fortunate. The clarion call of the Universal has reached you. That very call is vibrating in every cell of your body. Will you now lie inert in the corner of your house? Will you now waste your time clutching ancient skeletons to your breast and moaning over them? The Supreme Being is calling you in the roar of the ocean, in the thunder of the clouds, in the speed of the lightning, in the meteor's flaming fires. Nothing will come of remaining idle. Get up and awaken the clouded chivalry of your dormant youth. The path may not be strewn with flowers – an inferiority complex may seek to hold back your every advancing footstep, but even then you have to proceed onward, tearing the shroud of darkness. You will soon rend the thick darkness of despair on the way to the attainment of the Supreme State, and advance onwards in the swift-moving chariot, radiant with the sun's brilliance." – Shrii Shrii Anandamurti

The following was originally posted on December 15, 2019, at https://sureshemre.wordpress.com/2019/12/15/hedda-h-morch-john-horgan-pandeism/

Hedda Hassel Mørch is a philosopher at Inland Norway University of Applied Sciences.
She answered John Horgan's questions on various subjects. I was very happy to find this gem in that interview:

"As I said, science only captures the physical world "from the outside", or more precisely, in terms of its relational structure, and this also holds for quantum mechanics. Some seem to think quantum structure is more likely to be connected to consciousness than classical structure, perhaps because features such as indeterminism and non-locality are perceived as distinctively mentalistic. But as I see it, any kind of physical structure is equally in need of an "inside" or an intrinsic, and therefore conscious, basis." – Hedda H. Mørch

I completely agree. I expressed similar ideas in various blog posts. The "inside" or "intrinsic" mentioned by Mørch above is the same as the common (cosmic) 'reference' I have been talking about. This 'reference' is the soul. No existence is possible without the soul.

The concept of the common (cosmic) 'reference' can be expressed in many ways. For example, we can say that the whole is reflected in the unit. Another way would be to say that the whole is inverted to form the unit.

Obviously, the concept of "I" (self) in its various developmental stages such as ego etc. are related to the common (cosmic) 'reference' as well. One wants to write books about these subjects but one gets overwhelmed.

Hedda Mørch's comments on pandeism below combined with her comments above inspired me to say few more words.

> "But there is a religious view I find interesting, which is pandeism: the view that God used to exist, and be the only thing that existed, and then transformed himself into the universe, and so no longer exists. The reason God did this was basically for fun, or to see what happened. And maybe at some point the universe will transform itself back into God—that would be like nirvana or heaven. But then eventually God would get bored again and start the cycle over. As I understand it, this is close to some parts of Hindu cosmology." – Hedda H. Mørch

My understanding of the cosmic progression is very similar to what she is describing (see below) but **I have an objection to her words** "...so no longer exists".

Absolute Being (Godhead, Nirguna Brahma) —> Divine Center (Cosmic Soul, Cosmic Consciousness, Parama Purusha) —> Reality

(Saguna Brahma) —> Cosmic Mind —> Cosmos (spiritual, mental, physical realms) —> individual soul —> individual mind —> merger of the individual mind with the Cosmic Mind —> identification of the individual soul with the Cosmic Soul —> Absolute Being

Absolute Being is incomprehensively infinite. A tiny drop of the infinite ocean of Absolute Being transforms into Cosmos. At no stage of the divine progression the previous stage *"no longer exists"*.

The divine transformation starts and continues with the Cosmic Soul (Cosmic Consciousness). At no stage of the divine transformation Cosmic Soul *"no longer exists"*.
If anything exists, irrespective of its evolutionary stage in divine transformation, it exists because of the presence of the common (cosmic) 'reference' at its core. The common (cosmic) 'reference' is the reflection of the Cosmic Consciousness in the individual entity.

Am I a pandeist? No. I am theist.

I believe Cosmic Consciousness is at the core of each entity in its entirety. This makes me theist because Cosmic Consciousness is fully aware of our experiences and is in full control at every stage and every moment of this Cosmic Drama.
I realized early that materialists (especially physicalists) will never be satisfied with theistic arguments. This is a hopeless situation. We can never find a proof of the existence of God. Proof is a mental procedure. The mental realm is a sub-domain of the Cosmic Consciousness. We cannot comprehend God or find a proof of God's existence while staying in the mental realm. But, we can develop mental aids such

the concept of whole-connectedness facilitated by the common (cosmic) 'reference'.

Whole-connectedness is the mental counterpart of Unity – the spiritual experience. Whole-connectedness is an intellectual concept and it can be understood by our minds. This is the basis of my monism as well as theism. Those of us who are not fortunate enough to feel the Unity can still understand the whole-connectedness intellectually. This is my hope. This is my effort.

Waves of Manifestation: How Reincarnation Affirms and Invigorates the Ontological Dynamics of Pandeism, Just Not All At Once

By Waldo Noesta

Waldo Noesta once saw God board a Greyhound bus in Somerset, Pennsylvania. It was a little disorienting, being an atheist at the time, but he trusted what he saw. The experience helped awaken him from years of intellectual slumber, and sent him on a self-propelled exploration of pantheism, Eastern spirituality. and the mystic traditions of the West.

Later events, chronicled in his novel *Birding in the Face of Terror* and depicted allegorically in the metaphysical theatrics of *The Peasant and the King*, taught him to decipher a universal truth from these diverse sources through non-dual thought. He became a devout Perennialist, dedicating his life to crafting essays and fiction steeped in the timeless language of parable and metaphor.

Noesta has also spent nearly 30 years pushing a diesel rig down the highways of North America. He has probably driven well over one million miles in his career, but no one is counting. He lives in the Finger Lakes region of New York.

Ever since I first learned of pandeism, I was drawn to its embrace of an element missing in most if not all pantheistic doctrines: a telos. It recognizes that, like the Hindu Trimurti, the divine One infuses universe with a desire to become, to self-sustain within a web of interbeing, and to "bego" when the

136

time comes. In short, pandeism introduces *the will to exist* to the pure substance of Spinozan pantheism, breathing life into its otherwise sterile ontology while affirming the elegance of its non-dual relationship between deity and creation.

So why should we feel compelled to believe that the breather extinguished itself with a single breath at the beginning of time?

Infinity minus any finite number, after all, equals infinity. This holds true whether the number is one, or a million times a million to the millionth power. And we know that the screen at the front of the theater doesn't disappear when the movie begins, even though we no longer "see" it while focusing on its ever-changing appearance. If God is the omnipresent ground of being that both pantheism and classical theism purport, infinite by all spatial-temporal dimensions (which essentially means dimensionless or non-physical), what reason to we have to assume the divine will cease to exist through its act of becoming?

To the contrary, what is a four-dimensional field of constantly changing existence – the universe as we know it – without the dimensionless, unchanging ground of pure potential in which it has its being? A wave without an ocean, perhaps? A cloud without the sky?

So yes, God becomes the universe. Just not all at once. Not as an event in a linear past. It is an omnipresent event of constant becoming and unbecoming and rebecoming.

If we grant Aquinas' notion that God is the atemporal pure actuality who gives contingent existence to the essence of finite beings, and usher in the Spinozan insight that God is also the pure potential which *becomes* temporal, contingent existence by way of a dynamic polarity without beginning or end (think Taoism more than theism), we come to a neatly pandeistic conclusion of a God who continuously and willfully creates finite existence within itself while remaining wholly, eternally divine. In pandeism, it is not necessary to deny one in order to affirm the other.

What's left to consider, if you are a nuts and bolts thinker who is allergic to aligning with broad conclusions without seeing the underlying mechanics, is the metaphysical foundation for such a belief. How does the divine source of all that is become something as specific as you or me? And what happens to it when that specific thing or being ceases to be? (Without continuity of the essential nature of the finite entity, there is no real reason to say God *became* it rather than *created* it.)

Reincarnation offers a life principle most compatible with this pandeist notion of self-emptying and "refulfillment" – of God becoming the partial in order to experience returning to the Whole. The main obstacle to understanding this principle is our hypnotic collective acquiescence to the concept of linear time. Once we are free of this primitive encumbrance, reincarnation becomes axiomatic, no longer requiring a stretch of the imagination to see, but plainly evident in the cascading toroidal patterns of nature itself.

"Enlightenment is when the wave realizes it is the ocean."

Thich Nhat Hanh

*   *   *

"...and keeps waving."

(added by the author)

First, we must disambiguate a pair of terms – soul and spirit – which are so thoroughly interchangeable in our language that they essentially neuter each other into uselessness. In truth, each term reifies a specific aspect of our existential dynamic that can and should be seen with clarity in a reincarnationist paradigm. I'll begin with "soul."

In his acclaimed memoir, *The Outermost House: A Year of Life on the Great Beach of Cape Cod*, the naturalist Henry Beston illustrated a fascinating detail about the waves he observed on the Massachusetts shore. The pattern of activity we see on the surface is called a transverse wave. As the wave moves horizontally across the ocean's surface, the water itself is mostly moving up and down. If you could somehow color a cross-section of ocean water molecules hot pink or red, you would see that vertical plane of water rising and falling, not moving closer to the shore. The vertical movement gets more pronounced as the water depth get shallower, and so a wave crest starts to build, but the water itself is still moving up and down. It is only after the wave crashes that forward momentum pushes the water on the very edge of the ocean toward the land. From there it recedes and sinks and rises up again into the next wave in a cyclic pattern.

You don't have to paint the ocean red to see the transverse wave phenomenon though — just go to a baseball game and watch the crowd do "the wave." In a synchronized pattern aligned with the vertical plane of the seating, the spectators quickly stand up and sit down, in a way that sends an apparent wave of people around the ballpark. But nobody actually moves horizontally through the seating area — the people stand up and raise their arms, then sit down and lower them in turn.

In this case the wave doesn't crash so much as peter out when people get bored with it and watch the game again. The illustration should be even more clear though: there are two related but distinct patterns of motion in an ocean wave. The material substance that constitutes the wave — the water itself — is moving up and down, but as any surfer can verify, there is a discernible energetic pattern moving horizontally toward the shore.

Though the pattern is inseparable from the ocean, it isn't *equivalent to* the ocean; it is a manifestation of the ocean in a specific time and place, and though it does not exist as an integral "thing," its movement toward the shore can be observed and tracked. The wave, in other words, is a real, observable activity of the ocean itself, not something created by the ocean but separate from it, nor an illusion imposed by an observer on the "true" stillness of the water.

The idea behind the transverse "waves" in the ocean of Existence itself is exactly the same: material in binary movement patterns on one plane create an energetic pattern on another. Instead of one pattern moving unidirectionally toward the shore, these waves move omnidirectionally in the unlimited potential of ocean "water," (which you can correctly translate as "atoms") according to the binary movements (or "frequency") of the elements of the latter. The material itself could be understood as the potential for energetic patterns to form and dissolve and then, in some cases, form again.

The energetic pattern in this illustration is what we mean by the soul. It is the relatively durable pattern of activity that gives an essential "subject constancy" to the experience of being that specific pattern. The "body" of the wave is a constantly changing assortment of physical elements entering and exiting the energetic pattern. Soul and body are not identical, nor are they isolatable from each other. The thing that we see rolling and cresting and crashing as we watch from the beach, though, is not technically a body – it is the ocean, waving, and *that particular wave* is a particular soul.

Everything that you have ever perceived with your senses, in other words, including the "you" perceiving them, is a soul, an energetic pattern, caused by yes-no fluctuations occurring at the simplest level of existence.

The cause of these fluctuations is an impenetrable mystery that we mystics like to tag with clever names, but we're just deducing their existence from what we learn by watching the patterns. Like everyone else, all we can sense is the pattern — the relatively stable essence of a thing or being that endures through constant change.

When you look out at the world outside your body from this particular vantage point, you may think you are looking at a variety of objects and living creatures. What you are really seeing are overlapping layers of soul. The experiential vector of your sensations is not the physical plane. You are a soul, moving through a world of souls. You are watching the ensouled waves, not the physical up-down motion that creates them. Those who look out at the physical world and say, "I see no evidence of any souls" are completely missing what is in front of their eyes. The image you take in and reproduce with your nervous system, like the 80-foot oak tree near the northwest corner of your property that shades your front porch in the summer and should do so for at least another hundred years, is but a wave, a relatively stable energetic pattern — indeed, an oaky soul. Everything you can see and identify is a soul as well, created by subatomic vibration within the substance of the universe itself.

"What can we gain by sailing to the moon if we are not able to cross the abyss that separates us from ourselves? This is the most important of all voyages of discovery, and without it all the rest are not only useless but disastrous."

Thomas Merton, *"The Wisdom of the Desert: Sayings from the Desert Fathers of the Fourth Century"*

"Spirit" addresses what is missing so far in our illustration of the wave dynamics that produce an energetic pattern: momentum. Something that moves the pattern this way or that way. Remember, we don't have the external factors that work upon the ocean in the metaphorical model; everything is internal to the Ocean we call the universe.

The writer Wendell Berry is a naturalist and a Christian, and he is exceptionally gifted at articulating ideas in both languages. So it didn't surprise me to find this passage in which he broke down the confusion imposed by dualism on nature's inherent unity.

"Genesis 2:7...gives the process by which Adam was created: 'The Lord God formed man of the dust of the ground, and breathed into his nostrils the breath of life: and man became a living soul.' My mind, like most people's, has been deeply influenced by dualism, and I can see how dualistic minds deal with this verse. They conclude that the formula for man-making is man = body + soul. But that conclusion cannot be derived, except by violence, from Genesis 2:7, which is not dualistic. The formula given in Genesis 2:7 is not 'man = body + soul;' the formula there is 'soul = dust + breath.' According to this verse, God did not make a body and put a soul into it, like a letter into an envelope. He formed man of dust; then, by breathing His breath into it, He made the dust live. The dust, formed as man and made to live, did not embody a soul; it became a soul. 'Soul' here refers to the whole creature. Humanity is thus presented to us, in Adam, not as a creature of two discrete parts temporarily glued together but as a single mystery."[3]

The violent equation, according to Berry, is essentially "Waldo = Waldo's body + Waldo's soul." This is what I would call the egocentric position of selfhood. It begins by presuming the appellative individuality of the subject, encoded by an identity with a name and comprised of various social roles, and attaches to that personality a visible body and an invisible soul. As bizarre as it sounds, egocentric individuality actually invalidates what makes us individuals, pitting the will against the ego in a battle for control of the person. The poorly deciphered equation behind it is such an unconscious assumption in the dualistic Western mind that an incalculable amount of bad religion can be attributed to this exact error, beginning with a literal reading of the Garden of Eden legend.

But Berry's non-dual reading of Genesis 2:7 produces an equation that should now sound familiar: soul (the wave, the energetic pattern we call "Waldo") = dust (the physical aspect of self, the up-down vibration of particulate matter) + breath.

"Breath" in this passage is symbolic of the spirit, the divinely-sourced will. Not a will *to* anything in particular yet, just the noun without the infinitive form of a verb following it. Don't concern yourself with whether the will is free or mechanistically moved by deterministic forces. For now, we are talking about the most basic level of motivation for the energetic pattern called Waldo. This is the primordial will, or *pneuma*, the innermost layer of "I."

There is an astounding amount of corroborative evidence connecting the metaphorical concept of "breath" with the essential animating spirit and universal life force, both within and outside of anthropomorphic theological contexts. *Pneuma*

---

3 Wendell Berry, Sex, Economy, Freedom, and Community (New York: Pantheon Books, 1993)

(πνεῦμα), for instance, is an ancient Greek term for "breath," and is the most common New Testament translation of the Hebrew *ruach* (רוח) with the same meaning, as used in the passage from Genesis. Coming to early Christianity via Presocratic, Aristotelian and, most directly, Stoic philosophy, *pneuma* was the word for the divine Spirit, God's immanent presence in the universe, and the life-giving principle in humanity, including the eternal life restored in baptism when "a man be born of water and of the Spirit." (John 3:5)

In Islam, Allah endows humans with *rūḥ* رُوح which also began with the simple meaning of "blown breath" but came to indicate the animating spirit as well. (Also, *Rūḥ al-qudus* روح القدس which translates as "the holy spirit.)" There are equivalent terms in Hinduism (*prana* प्राण; the Sanskrit word for breath, "life force", or "vital principle") and the traditional Chinese religions (*qi* 氣 literally meaning "vapor", "air", or "breath", often translated as "vital energy" or "vital force").

For our purposes, I chose "*pneuma*" as the most familiar and translatable term to disambiguate the primordial will from what it becomes in the human soul: the creaturely or personal will. *Pneuma* is the breath of divine life that animates the dust and provides the willful motivation that creates and sustains an individual soul/energetic pattern. Once alive, the selective attention and desires of the cognizant soul partition the *pneuma* into the creaturely will with which we are more familiar, with all of its cross-purposes and contradictions. But it is not a different substance than *pneuma* – cut a whole pie into a hundred pieces, and it is still pie – and it remains primary and superior to the ego, a later creation of the semantic mind with no substance.

Thus the human will can be reined back in and returned to unity with its divine source, while the ego, having no inherent congruity with its source, cannot be.

The pneumatic will, not the ego, is the central element of the self. We have tried for so long to make the will a mere aspect of the ego that the statement seems to make no sense at first. But such is the craftiness of our cult of personality, that as its ruse is uncovered it grabs the will and says, "If you kill me, I'm taking you with me!" But even those who see through the illusion of ego and see the world as the play of *Māyā* still continue to breathe, still take food and water with the intention of living, and still entertain passing thoughts they do not own. The wave stills waves, in other words, and it waves because the pneumatic will that powers it was always independent of the false master that tried to control it.

The up-down vibration of matter by itself does not create a wave — there must be momentum, a sense of direction, which had to precede the wave in order for the wave to exist. This only seems odd because we were taught to pretend that all notion of self is contained within the socially tamed ego and couldn't be otherwise — probably because the will is so untameable. The empiricist too is befuddled by the will for it cannot be measured. But look into the eyes of any animal whose biosurvival is threatened, and tell me the will to be is based on an illusion.

Your spirit, therefore, is synonymous with the *pneuma,* the divinely empowered willful momentum that animates all energetic patterns — and it is not a product of the pattern nor the physical body. It comes from the source of all that exists, and it manifests as a soul by bringing together the elements it needs to become a physical body. Your pneumatic will to be precedes your own being. The *pneuma* is the original "I am," and the one that remains when all that was false and/or temporary has fallen away.

Just as the momentum which moves a wave is a property of the whole ocean and not just the wave itself, so too the pneumatic will that moves the soul is a property of the eternal ground of being that we call God and not just the soul it becomes. "No man is an island" — that is, no soul nor will exists in isolation. The profundity of our interbeing with all that exists should not be missed nor understated. But it should also be noted that a wave crashing on the shore of Okinawa in early July is not the same as one that laps the sands of Waikiki in late September. Nor is your soul the same as mine; they are different breaths of the same God, harnessing distinct elemental sets of potential. While they exist, our souls are indeed individual energetic patterns, though emanations of the same source, moving within the same ground of being, and returning to the source they never really left.

We must then accept the seeming paradox that each soul that a *pneuma* becomes is both universal and unique. Just as the ocean is both the source and destination of the individual wave, the eternal God is both the source and destination of the individual soul as it takes a trip through time.

And a straight timeline that begins and ends in the same place is not truly a line, but a cycle. The soul is the individual cycle; what precedes the soul and persists beyond its dissolution is the *pneuma*, the divine will, and you are that. Just as you willed yourself into temporary, conditioned existence for the sake of experience, you may choose to do so again.

"Nothing can doom man but the belief in doom, for this prevents the movement of return."

Martin Buber

If we persist in accepting the ego, the world's definition of the self, as the template for our experience of selfhood, the soul, which is the true experiential vehicle of personhood, is conflated with the illusion of personality. The ego-bound soul is either forgotten altogether or is stuffed into a material body (or, as materialists claim, it is merely an epiphenomenon, an emergent secondary activity of an isolated complex nervous system) and somehow expected to operate it like a ghost in a machine.

But once we learn that ego is not in charge, that a personal will unites with physical form and becomes the vehicle of selfhood, now it can go places and do things, in a setting that isn't foreign, connected with kindred spiritual vehicles who are all part of the essential Self — the Ocean of which we are all waves — rather than insular "others." The soul is thus cornered by modern civilization, but not defeated. It knows that the walls that corner it are fabrications, and that fighting them is a process of watching them dissolve when exposed to oceanic truth.

Pandeist spirituality doesn't just put forth a wishy-washy hope fulfillment of connection and immortality, in other words — it confirms them and reinstates our divinity by revealing a much more viable, integrated, and complete sense of the self than chemistry and biology and any social institutions can produce on their own. The unyoked individual, existing amidst the web of Existence itself connecting all with all, is truly the most powerful force on earth. A proper spirituality will equip us to own that power, and bring it back to the collective and help others find it in themselves.

Of the contemporary traditional wisdom paths, the ones best equipped to teach the soul as fully potentiated will with the capacity to return are, in no particular order and by no means exhaustively: Vishishtadvaita or authentic Advaita Vedanta (where "Atman is Brahman" offers a preemptive affirmation that the individual will is also divine will); Mahayana Buddhism; Sufism; mystic Judaism; various flavors of panentheist Christianity, which are most common under the umbrella of Eastern Orthodox; and perhaps the most overlooked and least understood of the lot, unprogrammed Quakerism, whose concepts of Inner Light and "that of God in everyone" are uniquely attuned to this model.

The missing ingredient in Quaker theology and most of the others is "the movement of return" as Buber called it. This phrase connotes cyclical time, the closest we can come to grasping eternity from an individual perspective.

The best way I know to introduce cyclical time is to first explain what it is not.

One objection I've encountered multiple times from people who haven't questioned linear time is the dreaded thought of "eternal recurrence" — the Nietzschean idea that cyclical time simply means events will repeat themselves over and over and over, and reincarnation in this case is just indefinite repetition with no teleological purpose. More of a thought experiment tool than theory, Friedrich Nietzsche did intend it to be life-affirming in the face of an imperialist Christendom that too often seems to project all of life's significance into securing a position in a speculative post-mortem state. Nietzsche encouraged us to pass our time in a way that we would gladly do it all again *ad infinitum*. But it rings a little hollow in the universal Pursuit of Happiness era under the spell of capitalist manifest destiny, and I don't know anyone who takes it very seriously, yet somehow it fills all the top Google searches for "cyclical time."

A Catholic friar named Paul who I know through a Facebook group once made an impassioned defense of the notion that every moment in life is a discrete, non-repeatable event on a linear timeline. He described a particularly moving orchestral performance he witnessed in his native Great Britain. Part of what made it so transcendently beautiful, he reasoned, was its ephemeral nature as a unique moment in time. The symphony may have been played tens of thousands of times across the ages, but never *just like this*, and he was there to witness a moment that will never be again.

I wish I'd had the words to agree with him, and then explain that cyclical time agrees with him too. It doesn't mean that these unique events we experience are going to happen again. It doesn't mean that there is a discrete verse in a multiverse in which that exact performance will reoccur except the second violin will miss a note somewhere in Tchaikovsky's Symphony No. 6 in B Minor.

What it means is that Paul's subjective experience of this performance is part of a soul's journey through time that will end where it began — in eternity. There is no "before" or "after," nor "here" or "there" in eternity to constitute a journey from one time-space location to another; the duration between events in that temporal journey is a subjective experience with no absolute universal reality. (Remember Einstein's theory of relativity? Same logic, different application.) From the theoretical perspective of God, eternal Being itself, there are no separate moments in time, just as there are no separate drops of water in the ocean. God becomes subjective beings – that is, emanates the breath of divine will into the potential of the physical world – in order to experience a discrete journey of temporal experience.

God, in other words, became the soul we call Paul by fractalizing the will of I AM into a *pneuma*, a limited expression of "I am," giving momentum to the potential of Paul and thus initiating his journey through the physical plane. Part of the purpose of that journey was to witness this exquisite performance, to know and love this part of being alive. He will eventually run out of momentum and return to the timeless state of potential (every breath is both an out-breath and an in-breath), but for a duration, that coalescence of will and potential created a unique time loop for the soul we call Paul to experience life from a unique perspective, and come home to its source via the movement of return.

The full duration of an energetic pattern's temporal existence is therefore best described as a cycle rather than a linear progression, whether it be the roughly 24 hour lifespan of a gnat, the 2400 year run of a redwood, or the 24 zillion year cycle of this physical universe itself. (The longest of these is known in Hindu cosmology as a *kalpa* – a full cycle of the out-breath and in-breath of God that creates and deconstructs and recreates everything in existence.) Every journey of the soul begins at home and brings us home, having collected a unique set of experiences.

Think of it like a roller coaster. You board the coaster in one location, and it takes you on a long looping ride that will be terrifying and exhilarating and filled with experiences you would never have been able to comprehend if you hadn't taken the ride. Then the ride ends, bringing you back to the place where you started, not somewhere else several miles away. This is a simple model of cyclical time, if we grasp that the starting and ending point of the ride is the same because it is outside of time — which is the actual meaning of eternity, not indefinite linear time. Cyclical time is necessary to account for both the subjective experience of duration *and* the grounding of that experience in eternity.

The person in this illustration represents the divine spark, the pneumatic will to be that harnesses the potential to be and coalesces into a wave of being. The unique soul is analogous to the ride itself. It is the *pneuma*, then, which also disembarks the ride and seeks another.

It is only within measured segments that time moves in linear fashion like the water molecules in a river, and segments are created by subjective experiences and a choice of parameters: birth and death, first day of school and graduation, etc. Oceanic time, the immeasurable phenomenon of the divine I AM creating fractalized time cycles (which create fractalized cycles, which create fractalized cycles, and so on), is the best way to describe reincarnation in this model.

Every duration that marks the beginning and end of a temporal phenomenon is a cycle, a full "breath of God" that returns to from whence it came. Dualistic thought separates the cycle from its eternal ground and expresses it as a dead-end segment of linear time, making the impermanence of all phenomena a rather grim, even terrifying prospect. Spiritual remedies that don't recognize the non-duality of experience and ground tend to dismiss the relative truth of the former as an illusion at best and a vice at worst while holding up the absolute truth of eternal ground as the sole reality or virtue, with the ironic result that virtue is unobtainable in this life, and the embodied individual is either perpetuated and doomed or playing a pointless game with no redeeming value. But pandeism, endowed with the understanding of cyclical time, shows us that the embodied being is the vehicle to absolute truth — and what's more, it is riding on rails. It cannot help but return home.

The soul-ride you are on right now, which you as a fragment of God willed yourself to take, no matter who or what you are, is your surest way back to absolute truth.

The primary distinction between cyclical and linear time as they pertain to pandeism is this: cyclical time means emergence is not a one-time event. emergence is ever-present, creation is always happening. There is neither much Big Bang speculation nor eschatological fervor in a cyclical time cosmology, for there is no universal creation nor "end time" event. The end of any time segment or era is the beginning of another, and there is always becoming that coincides with another begoing. It would all be an exercise in infinite vanity if not for the eternal recurrence of another wave, another out-breath to follow the in-breath of return to source.

Ultimately, the pneumatic "I" at the center of your being is not different than the "I" that is mine. Both are manifestations of the divine One. But they become different energetic patterns, different soul-rides, for the sake of experience. Each manifestation, therefore, is an incarnate "I am" at a different stage of development, with the *pneuma* sustaining and guiding it from within. Inattention to this source of guidance is the cause of every human malady and maladaptive reaction, and of our remarkable capacity to feel lost and exiled from a place we never left; remembrance of it is how we learn to come home to where we've always been.

Just as we learn best through successive lessons within a lifetime, so too will the ensouled Light come to maturity through successive life cycles, and the only way out is through.

The Immanent Philosophy of Philipp Mainländer (First Version)

Following is a mirror of Redditor YuYu Hunter's translation of Philipp Mainländer's works as of 2018-07-30, reproduced here with permission. Credit for this translation is due to the /Mainlander subreddit, a discussion group dedicated to the greater understanding of Mainlander. First posted at https://www.reddit.com/r/Mainlander/comments/71x27c/metaphysics/.

I thank, ye Gods, that ye resolve
Childless to root me hence. — Thee let me counsel
To view too fondly neither sun nor stars.
Come follow me to the gloomy realms below!
— — — — — — — — — —
Childless *and guiltless come below with me!*
(*Goethe*)

---

§ 1

The immanent philosophy, which has so far drawn from two sources only: nature in the widest sense and self-consciousness, does not enter her last section, metaphysics, releasing the brakes so that she can "go mad with reason". – In the Metaphysics she simply places herself at the *highest immanent* standpoint. So far, she has taken for every field the highest observation site, from where she could behold the whole defined area; however whenever she desired to extend her view beyond the borders, higher mountains obstructed the panorama. But now she is standing on the highest summit: she stands *above* all fields, i.e., she looks down *upon* the whole world and summarizes everything from *one* point of view.

Also, in the Metaphysics the fairness of research will not abandon us.

Since the immanent philosophy has so far always taken in all separated teachings a correct, although one-sided standpoint, many results must be one-sided. Accordingly, in Metaphysics we do not only have to place the apex of the pyramid, but also have to supplement the halve results and smoothen the unpolished ones. Or more precisely: we have to examine the immanent domain again, from its origin until the present day, and coldly judge its future, from the highest immanent standpoint.

§ 2

Already in the Analytic, we found, following *a parte ante* the development rows of the things (with help of time), a basic pre-worldly unity, before which our cognition collapsed. We determined it, according to our mental faculties, negatively, as inactive: unextended, indistinguishable, unsplit, motionless, timeless. In Physics we placed ourselves before this unity again, hoping to get a glimpse of it in the mirror of the principles we had found in the meantime, will and mind, but here again our efforts were completely in vain: nothing was shown in our mirror. We had to determine it negatively again: as basic unity in rest and freedom, which was neither will nor mind, nor an intertwinement of will and mind.

On the other hand, we obtained three exceedingly important *positive* results. We discovered that this basic unity, God, disintegrating itself into a world, perished and totally disappeared; furthermore, that the emerged world, precisely because of its origin in a basic unity, stands in a thorough dynamic interconnection, and related to this, that destiny is the out of the activity of all single beings, resulting continual motion; and finally, that the pre-worldly unity *existed*.

The existence is the small thread, which spans over the chasm between immanent and transcendent domain, and to this have to hold onto.

The basic unity existed: in no way we can identify more than this. What kind of existence this being was, is totally shrouded for us. If we nevertheless want to determine it in more detail, we have to seek refuge in negations again and proclaim, that it had no resemblance to somewhere a kind of being known to us: for all being known to us, is *moved* being, is *becoming*, whereas the basic unity was in absolute rest. Its being was *over-being*.

Thereby our positive knowledge remains completely untouched; for the negation does not refer to the existence itself, but only the kind of existence, which we cannot make comprehensible.

From this positive knowledge, that the basic unity existed, follows from itself the other positive, very important knowledge, that the basic unity must also have had a determined essence, for every *existentia* supposes an *essentia* and it is simply unthinkable, that a pre-worldly unity has existed, while being in itself without essence, i.e., nothing.

But from the essence, the *essentia* of God, we can have, like from his *existentia*, not the poorest of all representations. Everything, which we can grasp or perceive in the world as the essence of single things, is inseparably connected with motion, and God rested. If we nevertheless want to determine his essence, then this can be done only in negations, and we must proclaim, that the being of God was for us an incomprehensible, but in itself determined, *over-essence*.

Also, our positive knowledge, that the basic unity had a determined essence, remains totally untouched by this negation.

Thus far everything is clear. But it also seems, as if here human wisdom comes at its end and that the break-up of the unity into multiplicity is simply unfathomable.

Meanwhile we are not completely helpless. We precisely have a break-up of the unity into multiplicity, the transition of transcendent domain to the immanent one, the death of God and the birth of the world. We stand before a deed, the first and only deed of the basic unity. The transcendent domain was followed by the immanent one, has become something, which it had not been before: is there perhaps not a possibility, to fathom the deed itself, without going mad in phantasms and succumbing to reverie? We will be very careful, and rightfully so.

§ 3

Certainly, we stand here before an event, which we can grasp as nothing else, but as a deed; we are also within our rights to do so, since we are still standing on immanent domain, which is nothing else but this deed. But if we would ask for the factors, which brought forth this deed, then we leave the immanent domain and find ourselves on the "shoreless ocean" of the transcendent, which is forbidden, forbidden because all our cognitive faculties collapse on it.

On the immanent domain, in the world, the factors (in themselves) of somewhere a deed are always known to us: always we have on one hand an individual will of a determined character and on the other hand a sufficient motive. If we were to use this irrefutable fact for the question lying before us, then we would have to identify the world as a deed which has flown out of a divine *Will* and divine *Intelligence*, i.e. we would put ourselves in total contradiction with the results of the immanent philosophy; because we have found, that basic unity was neither will, nor mind, nor an intertwinement of will and mind; or, with the words of Kant, we would make immanent principles, in the most arbitrary and sophistic manner, *constitutive* ones on the transcendent domain, which is *toto genere* different from the immanent domain.

But at once, here, a way out is opened, which we may enter without second thoughts.

§ 4

We stand, as we said, before a deed of the basic unity. If we would simply call this deed a motivated act of volition, like all deeds known to us in the world, then we would be unfaithful to our vocation, betray the truth and be foolish dreamers; for we may assign God neither will, nor mind. The immanent principles, will and mind, can simply not be transferred to the pre-worldly essence, we may not make them *constitutive* principles for the *deduction* of the deed.

In contrast we may make them *regulative* principles for "the mere *judgement*" of the deed, i.e., we may try to explain for ourselves the origin of the world by doing this, that we comprehend it, *as if* it was a motivated act of volition.

The difference immediately jumps out.[4]

In the latter case, we merely judge problematically, according to an analogy with deeds in this world, without giving, in mad arrogance any apodictic judgement. In the first case we readily assert, that the essence of God was, like that of man, an inseparable connection of will and mind. Whether one says the latter, or expresses it in a more concealed manner, and speaks about the will of God's *potentia*-will, resting, inactive will, the mind of God's *potentia*-mind, resting, inactive mind – always the results of fair research are hit in the face: for *will* supposes *motion* and mind is excreted will with a special motion. A will in rest is a *contradictio in adjecto* and bears the mark of logical contradiction.

But we stop at this boundary if we limit our judgment merely to the relation which the world may have to a Being whose very concept lies beyond all the knowledge which we can attain within the world. For we then do not attribute to the Supreme Being any of the properties *in themselves*, by which we represent objects of experience.

If I say, we are compelled to consider the world *as if* it were the work of a Supreme Understanding and Will, I really say nothing more, than that a watch, a ship, a regiment, bears the same relation to the watchmaker, the shipbuilder, the commanding officer, as the world of sense does to the unknown, which I do not hereby

---

[4] Some elaboration, by Kant:
I think to myself merely the relation of a being, in itself completely unknown to me, to the greatest possible systematic unity of the universe, solely for the purpose of using it as a schema of the regulative principle of the greatest possible empirical employment of my reason. (*Critique of Pure Reason*, A679, B707)

cognize as it is in itself, but as it is for me or in relation to the world, of which I am a part.

Such a knowledge is *one of analogy*, and does not signify (as is commonly understood) an imperfect similarity of two things, but a perfect similarity of relations between two quite dissimilar things. By means of this analogy, however, there remains a concept of the Supreme Being sufficiently determined *for us*, though we have left out everything that could *determine* it absolutely and *in itself*; for we determine it as regards the world and as regards ourselves, and more do we not require.

(*Prolegomena*, §§ 57 - 58)

---

§ 5

We do therefore not proceed on a forbidden path, if we comprehend the deed of God, *as if* it was a motivated act of volition, and consequently *provisionally*, merely for the judgement of the deed, assign will and mind to the essence of God.

That we have to assign him will and mind, and not will alone, is clear, for God was in absolute solitude, and nothing existed beside him. He could not be motivated from outside, only by himself. In his self-consciousness his being alone was mirrored, nothing else.

From this follows with logical coercion, that the freedom of God (the *liberum arbitrum indefferentiæ*) could find application in one *single* choice: namely, either to *remain*, as he is, or to *not be*. He had indeed also the freedom, to *be different*, but for this being something else the freedom must remain latent in all directions, for we can imagine no more perfected and better being, than the basic unity.

Consequently, only one deed was possible for God, and indeed a *free* deed, because he was under no coercion, because he could just as well have not executed it, as executing it, namely, going into *absolute nothingness*, in the *nihil negativum*,[5] i.e., to completely annihilate himself, to stop existing.

Because this was his only possible deed and we stand before a totally different deed, the world, whose being is a continual becoming, we are confronted with the question: why did God, if he wanted non-existence, not immediately vanish into nothing? You have to assign God omnipotence, for his might was limited by nothing, consequently, if he wanted not to be, then he must also immediately be annihilated. Instead, a world of multiplicity was created, a world of struggle. This is a clear contradiction. How do you want to solve it?

The first reply should be: Certainly, on one hand it is logically fixed, that only one deed was possible for the basic unity: to annihilate itself, on the other hand, the world proves that this deed has not taken place. But this contradiction can only be an apparent one. Both deeds: the only logically possible one, and the real one, must be compatible on their ground. But how?

It is clear, that they are compatible only then, if we can verify, that somewhere an *obstacle* made the immediate annihilation of God impossible.

We thus have to search the obstacle.

In the case above it was said: "you have to assign God omnipotence, for his might was limited by nothing." This sentence is however false in general. God existed alone, in absolute solitude, and it is consequently correct, that he was not limited by anything outside of him; his might was thus in that sense omnipotence, that it was not limited by anything lying *outside* of him. But he had no omnipotence towards his own might, or with other words, his might was not destructible by himself, the basic unity could not stop to exist through itself.

God had the freedom, to be how he wanted, but he was not free from his determined essence. God has the omnipotence, to execute his will, to be whatever he wants; but he had not the might, to immediately become nothing.

The basic unity had the might, to be in any way different, than it was, but it had not the might, to suddenly become simply nothing. In the first case it

---

[5] *nihil negativum*: nothing in relation to everything in general.

remains in existence, in the latter case it must be nothing: but then it itself obstructed the path; because even if we cannot fathom the essence of God, then we nevertheless know, that it was a determined over-essence, and this determined over-essence, resting in a determined over-being, could not through itself, not be. This was the obstacle.

The theologians of all times have without second thoughts assigned God the predicate of omnipotence, i.e., they gave him the might, to be able to do, everything, which he wanted. In doing so, not one of them had thought of the possibility, that God could also want, to become nothing himself. This possibility, none of them had considered it. But if one considers it in all seriousness, then one sees, that this is the only case where God's omnipotence, simply by itself, is limited, that it is no omnipotence towards itself.

The single deed of God, the disintegration into multiplicity, accordingly presents itself: as the *execution* of the logical deed, the *decision* to not be, or with other words: the world is the *method* for the *goal* of non-existence, and the world is indeed the *only possible* method for the goal. God recognized, that he could go from *over-being* to *non-existence* only by *becoming* a world of multiplicity, through the immanent domain, the world.

If it were not clear by the way, that the essence of God was the obstacle for him, to immediately dissolve into nothingness, then our ignorance of the obstacle could in no way trouble us. Then we would simply have to postulate the obstacle on the transcendent domain; because the fact, that the *universe* moves from being into non-being, will show itself clearly and completely convincingly for everyone. –

The questions, which can be raised here, namely, why God did not want non-existence *sooner*, und why he preferred non-existence over existence at all, are all without meaning, because regarding the first question, "sooner" is a time-concept, which is without any sense regarding eternity, and the second question is sufficiently answered by the *fact of the world*. Non-existence must very well have deserved the preference over over-being, because otherwise God, in all his perfected wisdom, would not have chosen it. And all this the more, if one contemplates all the torments known to us of the higher Ideas, the animals standing close to us and our fellow humans, the torments by which non-existence alone can be bought.

§ 6

We have only *provisionally* assigned Will and Mind to the essence of God and comprehended the deed of God, *as if* it was a motivated act of volition, in order to gain a regulative principle for the mere judgement of the deed. On this path also, we have reached the goal, and the speculative reason may be satisfied.

We may nevertheless not leave our peculiar standpoint between immanent and transcendent domain (we are hanging on the small thread of existence above the bottomless pit, which separates both domains) in order to re-enter the solid world, the safe ground of experience, before having *loudly declared* one more time, that the being of God was neither a connection of Will and Mind, like that of humans, nor an intertwinement of Will and Mind. The true origin of the world can therefore never be fathomed by a human mind. The only thing which we can and may do – a right which we have made use of – is to make the divine act accessible for us by analogy, but while always keeping the fact in mind, that

> now we see through a glass darkly (1. Corinthians 13)

and that we are dissecting according to our apprehension an act, which, as a unitary act of a basic unity, can *never* be comprehended by the human mind.

The result does nevertheless satisfy. Let us meanwhile not forget, that we could be equally satisfied, if it were barred to us, to darkly mirror the divine deed; for the transcendent domain has vanished without trace in our world, in which only individual wills exist and beside or behind which nothing else exists, just like how *before* the world *only* the basic unity existed. And this world is so rich, answers, if fairly questioned, so distinctly and clearly, that every considerate thinker lightheartedly turns away from the "shoreless ocean" and joyfully dedicates his whole mental power to the divine act, the book of nature, which lies at every moment open before him.

When Religious Language Is Right: a Case for God's Anthropomorphic Identities

By Peter Ogenefavwe Ottuh

Dr. Peter Oghenefavwe Oritsemuwa Ottuh is a Philosopher of Religion. He obtained a Certificate in Theological Studies from the Baptist Theological Seminary, Eku – Nigeria (1988); Diploma in Religious Studies; B.A. (Hons.) Religious Studies; M. A. Philosophy of Religion; Ph.D Philosophy of Religion from Ambrose Alli University, Ekpoma – Nigeria between 1997 and 2009; and Postgraduate Diploma in Education (P.G.D.E) Lagos in 2015. Dr Ottuh is a lecturer of high repute and a prolific writer whose scholarly works numbering over sixty have appeared in both national and international academic publications. He is the co-author of Some Thoughts in Sociology of Religion, co-editor of Religious Management and Human Development in Nigeria: Theoretical and Ecclesiological Issues and co-editor of Issues in Religious Studies and Philosophy. Dr Ottuh joined the Department of Religious Studies and Philosophy, Faculty of Arts of Delta State University, Abraka, Delta State in 2014 as a Senior Lecturer and has risen to the rank of an Associate Professor. *Email: pottuh@delsu.edu.ng*

Originally published in **MAHABBAH: Journal Religion and Education Vol. 3, No.2 (July 2022), DOI: 10.47135/mahabbah.v3i2.41**

Abstract

Is it possible to think about God without anthropomorphizing him? The fact that God has both anthropomorphic and non-anthropomorphic characteristics adds to theological confusion. Individual variances in God's views might be a reflection of how individuals understand God's portrayals. Intellectuals have argued for ages that theistic conceptions of God are excessively anthropomorphic, perplexing, and complex. The paper focused on religious language and God's anthropomorphic identities. It employed a historico-comparative approach using library resources. The finding provides light on the limitations and potential of philosophico-religious transmission of the complex idea of anthropomorphism and offers a critical, constructive, and interpretive avenue for intellectual dialogue.

Introduction

Is it possible to think about God without thinking about him as a person? Some thinkers portray God as the universe's omnipotent (all-powerful), omniscience (all-knowing), and omniamorous (all-loving) creator.[6] Some thinkers portray God as the universe's creator who is "omnipotent (all-powerful), omniscience (all-knowing), and omniamorous (all-loving)." However, such ideas may lead to theological inconsistencies. Why is there so much suffering in the world if Christ died to alleviate it? In his course companion, Lindeman and Rai also explore the paradox of transformation.[7] Spiritual conceptions are represented using the same cognitive resources as

---

[6] Riekki T. Lindeman and Rai, T.T. "Supernatural Believers Attribute More Intentions to Random Movement than Skeptics: An MRI Study". *Social Neuroscience* 9, no.4 (2014): 400-411.

[7] Lindeman and Rai, 403.

natural concepts, according to religious cognition scholars. However, it's unclear how this process leads to culturally valid conceptions that are widely and enthusiastically accepted. The fact that God has both anthropomorphic (e.g., "listens to prayers") and non- anthropomorphic traits add to the theological debates.[8] Individual differences in God beliefs may reflect differences in how people interpret public depictions of God. Religious conceptions are one of the few types of ideas that are conveyed exclusively via culture. The results of the research will provide insight into the constraints and capabilities of cultural transmission in general. It also provides as a forum for intellectual debate on religion that is critical, constructive, and interpretative.

Discussion

The Evolution of Supernatural Concepts

The terms supernatural, paranormal, and preternatural are often used interchangeably. The latter is usually restricted to discussing powers that seem to go beyond what is physically feasible. In terms of natural events that defy natural principles, the link between the supernatural and the natural is hazy from an epistemological standpoint. Beliefs in some type of supernatural power are practically widespread, and they may be divided into two categories: deities or gods, and those with lower abilities who become involved in human affairs.

---

[8] N. Mtshiselwa and Mokoena. L. "Humans Created God in their Image? An Anthropomorphic Projectionism in the Old Testament". *HTS Teologiese Studies/Theological Studies,* 74, no.1 (2018): 5017.

Individual gods may be identified by their traits and can be named and customized.[9] Gods often have superhuman abilities, although only a handful is deemed omnipotent. Culture Heroes are historical figures who have been exalted and venerated by a group of people. The gods are envisioned as great entities whose power varies only in degree, at least at initially, from that of earthly rulers.[10] The concept of "worship" becomes necessary as this type of god develops. The gods might also appear as a powerful earthly ruler, whose favor can be gained by entreaty, gifts, service, tributes, adoration, and bribery.

'Gods' were never intended to be 'human-like' entities. Only after the extinction of the simply naturalistic perspective still present in the Vedas did they acquire the shape of everlasting entities.[11] Once systematic thought about religious practice and the rationalization of life in general, with its rising demands on the gods, a pantheon was usually created. The formation of a pantheon necessitates the specialization and categorization of distinct gods, as well as the assignment of consistent traits and differentiation of their competence. However, the growing personification of the gods is not the same as or comparable to the growing divergence of competence. The functions of the Roman gods (*numina*) were considerably more set and apparent than those of the Hellenic gods.

The most fundamental issue is whether one should attempt to influence a specific god or demon

---

[9] Max Mueller. *Anthropological Religion* (London: Longmans, 1992), 76; J.A. Onimhawo and P.O.O. Ottuh, *Some Thoughts in Sociology of Religion* (Benin City: Ever-Blest Publisher, 2009).

[10] R. Bouvet and J.F. Bonnefon, "Non-Reflective Thinkers Are Predisposed to Attribute Supernatural Causation to Uncanny Experiences." *Personality and Social Psychology Bulletin*, 41, no.7 (2015): 955-961.

[11] Onimhawo & Ottuh, 33.

by force or entreaty at all, and the response relies only on the outcome. The deity, like the magician, must exhibit his or her charm on a regular basis.[12] Even today in China, a few spectacular victories are enough for a deity to gain reputation and power (*shen ling*), resulting in a sizable following. In such circumstances, there are ways to explain the ancient god's erratic behavior in such a manner that his status is not diminished, but rather boosted.[13] The most remarkable example is that of Yahweh's priesthood, whose devotion to his people became deeper as Israel's fate became more precarious. Some of the most powerful and benevolent gods of heaven have few cults, not because they are too far removed from humans, but because their influence seems to be equal. Powers with a plainly diabolical nature, such as Rudra, the Hindu deity of plague, are not necessarily lesser than benevolent gods, and may have enormous power potential.[14]

Methodological Paradoxes

In the first case, anthropomorphism and its sister phenomena, animism, might be seen as the unavoidable occasional faults of perceptual and conceptual systems. They arise in religion, as well as other forms of cognition and behavior, since they are plausible if in hindsight incorrect interpretations of things and events, as well as ways of influencing them. Of course, just because they're mistakes

---

[12] Cliff Pickover. *The Paradox of God and the Science of Omniscience* (New York: Palgrave/St Martin's Press, 2001).
[13] K.E. Vail, J. Arndt, and A. Addollahi, "Exploring the Existential Function of Religion and Supernatural Agent Beliefs Among Christians, Muslims, Atheists, and Agnostics". *Personality and Social Psychology Bulletin*. 38, no.10 (2012): 1288-1300.
[14] Bouvet & Bonnefon, 957.

doesn't mean they can't be useful. Religious thinking and activity are often used as weapons for social control or emotional assurance, as thinkers as different as Freud, Durkheim, and Marx have argued.[15] However, although such applications might assist explain why religious thinking and activity are actively promoted and moulded into certain forms, they cannot explain why such thought and action exist in the first place and are reasonable. They emerge and are plausible for cognitive reasons: people live in a complicated and ultimately incomprehensible environment in which the most significant components are human, capable of concealment, and perceived as inherently unobservable.[16] This is a reality with which we are equipped to interact thanks to our understanding of mind, as well as associated sensitivity to phenomena like motion, faces, and apparent indications of design, as well as matching social action skills. Animism and anthropomorphism, both unsystematized and systematized as religion, necessarily exist in this world and thanks to these capabilities.

Anxiety over anthropomorphism may be seen in the Hebrew Bible. In following centuries' Jewish texts, this grew much more apparent. Early and medieval Christian theology was affected by Greek philosophy's anti-anthropomorphic inclinations. Yahweh appears to Abraham in the amazing story of Genesis 18:1-15, and the two have a meal and an intimate interaction. The development of weaker beliefs was linked to anthropomorphism as well, but in the opposite direction. Anthropomorphic God

---

[15] Stewart Guthrie. "Anthropology and Anthropomorphism in Religion". In *Religion, Anthropology and Cognitive Science,* eds. Whitehouse and Laidlaw (Carolina: Carolina Academic Press, 2007), 37-62.
[16] Guthrie, 37.

concepts are not theologically correct, but those who believe in them claim to have received more religious education.[17] Despite overt contradictions between properties of humans, for example, limited knowledge, power, and vitality, and the properties of God, their beliefs seem to grow stronger over time, thus, public representations of God in Western culture range from highly anthropomorphic to highly abstract. The relationship between acceptance of an anthropomorphic conception of God and associated beliefs and practices was investigated. Anthropomorphic conceptions of God bring an entire ontology with them for interpreting religious ideas, as well as the ontology of human beings and human affairs. This appears to guide both reasoning about supernatural phenomena and reasoning about natural phenomena's supernatural underpinnings.

It is obvious that the interaction between a people's conceptions of religious ideas and how they accept those ideas as true or false amounts to serious conceptual paradoxes. One might expect atheists to interpret religious ideas more concretely than theists, but the opposite was discovered. One possible explanation for this disparity is that atheists abandoned concrete interpretations early in their religious growth in an effort to sustain belief, but eventually found abstract interpretations untenable as well. Anthropomorphic notions of God do not necessarily generate concrete theologies; rather the contrary may be true.[18] People may conclude that God has human characteristics after understanding that angels and Satan are largely human in look and conduct. Alternatively, all three creatures may be educated about in tandem as part of a concrete theology formed entirely from religious education.

---

[17] Bouvet & Bonnefon, 958.
[18] Bouvet & Bonnefon, 967.

While this interpretation is not implausible, there are a number of reasons to doubt it. Theological information, for example, is likely to be just as vague as religious information, leaving lots of room for interpretation, thus, identifying social groups that have more definite ideas than others may provide greater insight into the nature and origins of those beliefs. For example, one may look at the theologies of young infants and see how they evolve through time, or compare them to those of members of the same cultural unit, such as a church or family.

People are looking for factual and logical evidence, which religions cannot always provide. True knowledge, according to logical positivists, can only be achieved by empirical or logical/linguistic verification.[19] However, empirical reasons may be argued to be irrelevant in the context of metaphysical knowing claims. Perhaps scholars are losing the purpose of religion when one tries to apply approaches from other fields of study to religion. Religious evidence, validity, and justification are still important notions in many religious arguments. One may debate whether religion is only a product of the mind to satisfy a psychological need, or if faith needs any evidence at all. Regardless of physical proof, faith, intuition, language, and emotion may lead people to religious understanding.

Conceptual Considerations

Religious Language

If God is infinite, words used to describe finite creatures may not be sufficient to describe

---

[19] Alan Bailey and O'Brien, Dan. *Hume's Critique of Religion: 'Sick Men's Dreams'* (Dordrecht: Springer Science and Business Media, 2014), 172.

God. Eastern religious traditions' divine doctrines differ drastically from those of Abrahamic religions. The issue of religious language has received little attention in Eastern philosophy. It refers to the ambiguity in meaning of terms predicated of God.[20] Practitioners of Abrahamic religious traditions are concerned about the problem of religious language because it has the potential to undermine those traditions. In these traditions, speaking about God is essential to both personal praxis and organized celebration. The Abrahamic faiths are vulnerable to accusations that their sacred texts and teachings are unintelligible because they lack the ability to speak about God and understand what is said.[21] The issue of religious language is a philosophical one that should be resolved in order to give a framework for comprehending God claims in both the house of worship and scholarship. Extensive conversations in the field of religious philosophy will become incoherent if there is no suitable answer. If human communication about God is impossible, these assertions about God would be incoherent.

Anthropomorphic constructionism

Anthropomorphism is the portrayal of God as a human being, complete with human physical appearance and emotions such as jealousy, fury, and love. Other religious philosophies argue that seeing an omniscient, omnipresent God as human is impossible.[22] Xenophanes, a Greek philosopher who

[20] Kenneth Seeskin. "Sanctity and Silence: The Religious Significance of Maimonides' Negative Theology." *American Catholic Philosophical Quarterly*, 76 (2002): 7-24.
[21] Matthew Hutson. *The 7 Laws of Magical Thinking: How Irrational Beliefs Keep Us Happy, Healthy, and Sane* (New York: Hudson Street Press, 2012), 165-81.
[2222] A. Shtulman, and M. Rattner, "Theories of God: Explanatory Coherence in Religious Cognition". *PLoS ONE* 13,

lived in the fifth century BC, was the first in the West to criticize anthropomorphism.[23] Although Ethiopians characterized gods as dark-skinned, northerners in Thrace painted gods as having red hair and blue eyes, according to Xenophanes. He came to the conclusion that human images of gods usually reveal more about the creators than about the almighty. The worship of gods in the appearance of animals, known as theriomorphism, has been accused of being superior to Christianity (Greek *therion*, "animal"; *morphe*, "shape").[24] Because it incorporates humanity into the divine nature, both Jewish and Islamic theologians have accused Christianity of anthropomorphism. Jesus Christ, according to Georg Wilhelm Friedrich Hegel, was both fully human and fully divine.

Anthropomorphism is the perception of a divine being or entities in human form in religion and mythology. It is the acknowledgement of these entities' human traits. Love, battle, fertility, beauty, and the seasons were all portrayed by anthropomorphic deities at one time or another.[25] Anthropomorphism in literature and other media spawned the furry fandom subculture.[26] The use of anthropomorphic language, which implies that animals have feelings and motives, has long been seen to indicate a lack of impartiality.[27]

---

no.12 (2018): e0209758.

[23] Hutson, 168.

[24] Williams Boother. "Anthropomorphism." *Microsoft® Encarta®* 2009 [DVD] (Redmond, WA: Microsoft Corporation, 2009).

[25] Hutson, 180.

[26] Bailey & O'Brien, 172.

[27] George M. Marakas, Richard D. Johnson, and Jonathan W. Palmer, "A Theoretical Model of Differential Social Attributions toward Computing Technology: When the Metaphor becomes the Model". *International Journal of Human-Computer Studies* 52, no.4 (April 2000): 719-750.

Anthropomorphism is a cognitive process in which individuals assume attributes of non-human creatures based on their preconceptions about other humans.[28] It may also be used as a coping mechanism for loneliness when no other human relationships are available. People are more prone to anthropomorphize when elicited agent knowledge is low and affectivity and sociality are high. These three factors can be influenced by a variety of dispositional, situational, developmental, and cultural variables, such as the need for cognition, social disconnection, cultural ideologies, uncertainty avoidance, and so on.[29] Even if an artificially intelligent computer or robot has not been designed with human emotions, it often feels such feelings spontaneously in science fiction. Anthropomorphism is the deliberate use of anthropomorphic analogies to explain the behavior of artificial intelligence by humans.[30] To believe that an intelligent robot would naturally find a woman attractive and be driven to mate with her is an example of anthropomorphism. Another example is the Dario Floreano experiments, in which certain robots developed the ability to "deceive" other robots into eating poison and dying.[31]

Another view is pandeism (or Pantheism), which holds that God is identical to the cosmos, but

---

[28] Brian R. Duffy. "Anthropomorphism and the Social Robot". *Robotics and Autonomous Systems* 42, no.3-4, (2003): 177-190.

[29] Nicholas Epley, Waytz, Adam and Cacioppo, John T. "On Seeing Human: A Three-factor Theory of Anthropomorphism". *Psychological Review* 114, no.4, (2007): 864-886; Andrew Whiten. "Culture Extends the Scope of Evolutionary Biology in the Great Apes". *Proceedings of the National Academy of Sciences* 114, no.3025 (2017): 7790-7797.

[30] Epley, Waytz & Cacioppo, 864.

[31] Brian R.. Duffy, "Anthropomorphism and the Social Robot". *Robotics and Autonomous Systems* 42, no.3-4 (2003): 177-190.

that God no longer exists in a manner that can be touched, hence this notion can only be demonstrated to exist by reason.[32] Pandeism believes that God created the whole cosmos, and that the universe is currently the totality of God, but that the universe will eventually fold back into one single entity, God Himself, who created everything. Why would God create a cosmos just to forsake it, according to pandeism? In terms of pantheism, this raises the issue of how the cosmos came to be and what its goal and purpose are. Pantheists believe that everything is a part of an all-encompassing, indwelling, ethereal God, or that God and the Universe are the same.

The idea that natural law, existence, and the Universe, which is the sum total of all that is, was, and will be, is represented in the theological principle of an abstract 'god' rather than an individual, creative Divine Being or Beings of any kind, is emphasized by further examination. This is the major difference between them and Panentheists and Pandeists.[33] As a result, although many faiths claim to include Pantheistic aspects, they are more often Panentheistic or Pandeistic.

Instead of saying that an atheist believes it is false or probably false that there is a God, a more accurate description of atheism is that an atheist is someone who rejects belief in God for the following reasons, for an anthropomorphic God, the atheist rejects belief in God because it is false or probably false that there is a God; for a non-anthropomorphic God, the atheist rejects belief in God because the concept of such a God is absurd; While the religious

[32] Matt Rossano. "Supernaturalizing Social Life: Religion and the Evolution of Human Cooperation". *Human Nature* 18, no.3, (2007): 272-294.
[33] Michel Henry. *I am the Truth. Toward a philosophy of Christianity*. Trans. Susan Emanuel (Oxford: Stanford University Press, 2003).

would prefer to turn to the gods for ultimate moral direction in the relativistic environment of the Sophistic Enlightenment, philosophic and sophistic intellectuals questioned such assurance, pointing out the foolishness and immorality of traditional epic descriptions of the gods.[34] Protagoras started his written essay on the gods. I have no way of knowing whether or if gods exist, or what kind of gods they may be. Knowledge is hampered by a number of factors, including the subject's obscurity and the shortness of human life.

God's Anthropomorphic Identities

While there is a vast range of supernatural notions found across the globe, Boyer claims that supernatural creatures in general act similarly to humans.[35] He uses Greek mythology as an example, which is more like to a current soap opera than other religious systems. People project human qualities onto non-human components of the environment, because it makes those aspects more familiar.[36] According to Rossano, as people started to live in bigger groupings, they may have constructed gods to enforce morality.[37] Morality may be reinforced in small groups by social factors such as gossip or reputation. According to him, humankind established an excellent approach for limiting selfishness and forming more cooperative societies by integrating ever- watchful gods and spirits.

---

[34] Thomas Dixon. *Science and Religion: A Very Short Introduction* (Oxford: Oxford University Press, 2008), 63.
[35] G.A. Barton. *A Sketch of Semitic Origins: Social and Religious* (*Belgium:* Kessinger Publishing, 2006).
[36] Alvin Plantinga. "God, Arguments for the Existence of". *Routledge Encyclopedia of Philosophy.* (London: Routledge, 2000).
[37] Rossano, 291.

The Bible has been the primary source of God conceptions in the Judeo-Christian tradition. Because the Bible "contains many distinct pictures, thoughts, and methods of thinking about" God, there are always disagreements over how God should be imagined and understood. God is known by numerous names in the Hebrew and Christian Bibles, one of which is *Elohim*.[38] In the Quran and hadith, God is characterized and referred to by several names or traits, the most prevalent of which are Al-Rahman, which means "Most Compassionate," and Al-Rahim, which means "Most Merciful".[39] Many of these names are also found in the Baháí Faith's scriptures. Vaishnavism, a Hindu sect, offers a list of Krishna's titles and names.

God's gender might be seen as a literal or metaphorical characteristic of a god who, according to traditional western philosophy, transcends physical form. One of the gods in polytheistic faiths is usually assigned a gender, enabling them to engage sexually with each other and maybe with humans. God has no counterpart with whom to have sexual relations in most monotheistic faiths. Except in Genesis 1:26-27, where biblical writers generally allude to God using masculine or paternal terms and symbols, Hosea 11:3-4, Deuteronomy 32:18, Isaiah 66:13, Isaiah 49:15, Isaiah 42:14, Psalm 131:2 (a mother); Deuteronomy 32:11–12 (a mother eagle); and Matthew 23:37 and Luke 13:34 (a mother eagle) (a mother hen).[40] Classical theists (such as ancient Greco-Medieval philosophers, Roman Catholics,

---

[38] Pickover, 231.

[39] Bentley, David. *The 99 Beautiful Names for God for All the People of the Book* (New York: William Carey Library, 1999), 187.

[40] Michael Coogan. "Fire in Divine Loins: God's Wives in Myth and Metaphor". In *God and sex. What the Bible Really Says* (1st ed.) (New York, Boston: Twelve. Hachette Book Group, 2010), 175.

Eastern Orthodox Christians, many Jews and Muslims, and some Protestants) speak of God as a divinely simple 'nothing' that is completely transcendent (totally independent of everything else) and has attributes such as immutability, impassibility, and timelessness.[41] Theistic personalism theologians argue that God is most generally the ground of all being, immanent in and transcendent over the entire world of reality, with immanence and transcendence being the contrapletes of personality, as held by Rene Descartes, Isaac Newton, Alvin Plantinga, Richard Swinburne, William Lane Craig, and most modern evangelicals.[42] Jung[43] equated religious ideas of God with transcendental metaphors of higher consciousness, describing God as an eternally flowing current of vital energy that endlessly changes shape as an eternally unmoved, unchangeable essence.

Many philosophers have sought to reconcile God's qualities and their consequences. God's omniscience, for example, may seem to indicate that God knows how free agents will choose to behave. If God is aware of this, their seeming free choice may be deceptive, or foreknowledge may not entail predestination.[44] Some theists acknowledge that only some of the reasons for God's existence are strong,

---

[41] Edward Craig. God, Concepts of, *Routledge Encyclopedia of Philosophy* (Taylor & Francis, 1998); Glyn Richards. *The Philosophy of Gandhi: A Study of his Basic Ideas* (London: Routledge, 2005); Shak Hanish. "The Mandaeans in Iraq". *Routledge Handbook of Minorities in the Middle East* (London and New York: Routledge, 2019), 163.
[42] S. Harris. *The End of Faith* (New York: W.W. Norton and Company, 2005), 216.
[43] Jung cited in Harris, 213.
[44] Floyd H. Barackman. *Practical Christian Theology: Examining the Great Doctrines of Faith* (London: Kregel Academic, 2001).

but contend that faith is a result of risk, not reason.[45] Each monotheistic religion has a separate name for its deity, some of which correspond to cultural conceptions about the god's identity and traits. Many religious followers believe in angels, saints, jinn, devils, and devas, as well as other, less powerful spiritual creatures. God is called *Elohim* (God), *Adonai* (Lord), and other names in the Hebrew Bible, as well as the name *YHWH* or *Yhweh*.

What makes Religious Language Right about God's Anthropomorphic Identities

Researchers were motivated by social cognition to develop embodied theories of human communication behavior. These explanations connect humans' unrivaled linguistic abilities back to basic capacities like grasping, action comprehension, and imitation.[46] Humans may now convey their intentions via symbolic actions, thanks to the evolutionary shift from the capacity to copy to gesture-based communication. Multiple layers of recursive theory of mind activity are required for this form of communication.

Faith versus reason assumption

Faith and reason are both forms of authority that may be used to support views. Faith entails a

---

[45] E. Culotta. "The Origins of Religion". *Science* 326, no.5954 (2009): 784-787.

[46] Fırat Soylu. *"An Embodied Future Map for Constructionism"* (Evanston, Illinois: Northwestern University, 2019), 1-19. https://www.sesp.northwestern.edu/docs/publications/1 417950354527d083710d01.pdf (Accessed on March 2, 2022).

position toward a claim that is not, at least for the time being, verifiable by reason. There are two types of faith: evidence-sensitive and evidence-insensitive faith.[47] The former sees faith as tightly linked to verifiable facts, whereas the latter sees faith as just a religious believer's act. The primary philosophical difficulty in the dilemma of religion and reason is determining how faith's authority should be defined. In the process of justifying or establishing a religious belief as true or justified, reason and authority of reason interact. There are four fundamental types of interaction between the goals, objects, or processes of reason and religion - in this case, the goals and methods of both seem to be extremely similar.[48] Reason and faith are thought to be separate in the Reformed Christian paradigm. Faith is trans-rational in the sense that it is higher than reason. Another viewpoint is that religious belief is irrational, and hence cannot be evaluated rationally.

Each may be compartmentalized, and there can be conversation between them. Natural theology is a common example of strong compatibilism.[49] It may take one of two forms: it can start with scientific assertions that are supported by legitimate theological claims, or it can start with scientific claims that are supported by valid theological claims. Alternatively, it may begin with common statements within a religious tradition and improve them using scientific reasoning. Some natural theologians have sought to bring religion and reason together in a unified metaphysical theory.

---

[47] James Swindal. "Faith and Reason". *The Internet Encyclopedia of Philosophy*. 2016. https://iep.utm.edu/faith-re. (Accessed on April 4, 2022).
[48] Swindal.
[49] Charles Taliaferro. "Philosophy of Religion". In *The Stanford Encyclopedia of Philosophy*. ed. Edward N. Zalta (London: Routledge, 2021).

Some modern philosophers, most notably the logical positivists, have disputed that religion has any authority to control any realm of thinking or human life, claiming instead that all meaningful assertions and ideas are subject to comprehensive rational analysis.[50] This has made it difficult for religious philosophers to explain how a language that is openly non-rational or trans-rational may retain significant cognitive content.

Historical assumption

The most common basis for religious belief is the incidence of religious experiences or the weight of evidence from individuals who claim to have had religious experiences. Those who anthropomorphize God do so on the basis of their religious experience. Many individuals have stated that they have sensed God's presence, according to the argument. Consider the following sketch of some of the debate's movements and countermoves in order to spark additional inquiry.[51] Atheists' testimony of experiencing God's absence wipes out "believers'" testimony. It's possible that witness to God's absence is better understood as testimony to God's absence.

According to theists, more impersonal Divine experiences represent only one facet of God. Hindus believe that having a firsthand experience of God is merely one step in the soul's path to truth. How one resolves the debate will be determined by one's overall philosophical opinions in a variety of areas.[52] If you downplay the significance of religious

---

[50] Swindal.
[51] William P. Alston. "Religious Language." In *The Oxford Handbook of Philosophy of Religion*. Ed. William J. Wainwright (Oxford: Oxford University Press, 2005), 220-244.
[52] Alston, 234.

experience and hold a high bar for the burden of evidence for any religious viewpoint, the traditional arguments for God's existence are unlikely to persuade you. If, on the other hand, you believe theistic arguments are logical and that religious witness offers some evidence for theism, you may be more sympathetic to theistic arguments.

The miraculous argument begins with particular unusual happenings. It claims that they give evidence for believing in a supernatural actor or, more modestly, for doubting the soundness of a naturalistic worldview. Since David Hume's denial of miracles, the argument has gotten a lot of philosophical attention. The argument can be given a rough edge in various ways, for example, imagine that if you do not believe in God and there is a God, hell is waiting for you, it can be presented as an appeal to individual self-interest, or it can be presented more broadly, for example, believers whose lives are bound together can realize some of the goods comprising a mature religious life.[53] The subject of whether cognitive science of religion has any bearing on the truth or rationality of religious devotion is gaining traction.

The idea in supernatural forces seems to be cognitively natural and simple to propagate, according to cognitive science of religion. Some, notably Alvin Plantinga, have used the naturalness of religion thesis to suggest that we have scientific evidence for Calvin's *sensus divinitatis*. Others have said that cognitive science of religion exacerbates the issue of divine concealment.

Theodical assumption

In the greater good defense, evil may be seen as either a necessary component of achieving greater

---

[53] Taliaferro, 272.

good or as a separate entity from these benefits. It has been speculatively expanded by some who propose a defense rather than a theodicy to encompass additional ills that may be caused by supernatural powers other than God. The Augustinian paradigm, according to John Hick, fails, but the Irenaean model is trustworthy.[54] Some contend that the concept of a best possible universe, like the concept of the greatest possible number, is illogical. It has been suggested that Divine excellences have top bounds or maxima that are not measurable in a sequential manner. Someone who claims that there is no reason for evil to exist or that there is no justification for God to let it appears to suggest that if there was, they would see it.[55] Is it obvious that if there were a purpose for the presence of evil, we would perceive it in the cosmic case? William Rowe believes that a viable explanation for God's justification for letting evil should be discernible.

Some philosophers have argued that we have strong cause to be dubious about our ability to judge whether or not an all-good God would allow allegedly gratuitous harms. Some depictions of the hereafter seem to have no influence on how we react to the scale of evil in the present.[56] The issues brought by evil and suffering are many, and current philosophers from both religious and non-religious perspectives are addressing them.[57] Meister and

---

[54] Audi, Robert. *Rationality and Religious Commitment.* (Oxford: Oxford University Press, 2011).
[55] James Beilby ed. *Naturalism Defeated? Essays on Plantinga's Evolutionary Argument Against Naturalism* (Ithaca, NY: Cornell University Press, 2002).
[56] Michael Bergmann. "Skeptical Theism and Rowe's New Evidential Argument from Evil." *Noûs*, 35, no.2 (2001): 278-296.
[57] Stewart Goetz. *Freedom, Teleology, and Evil* (London: Continuum, 2008).

Taliaferro's six-volume *The History of Evil,* which has over 130 writers from practically every theological and secular perspective.[58] If you don't believe it matters whether or not people live on after they die, then speculation is pointless. But suppose the hereafter is seen as ethically interwoven with this life, providing opportunities for moral and spiritual reformation, transfiguration of the wicked, rejuvenation, and new life opportunities. These considerations might then be used to counter arguments based on the existence of evil.

Functional explanation

The functional explanation of anthropo-morphic identities of God (the God of religion) is discoverable in the functional description of religion. A functional definition of religion is one that considers what religion accomplishes and how it functions in terms of its social/psychological context. This can refer to religion's social functions, such as group cohesion, social order, and defense of group interests, or its psychological functions, such as providing stories, symbols, and rituals that help people identify with role models, be motivated, find consolation, and find answers to existential questions, among other things. Religion is a cohesive collection of ideas and activities about holy objects.

A- Posteriori epistemological explanation

The cosmological and teleological arguments are *a posteriori arguments*. The cosmological argument is based on the idea that there is at least one strong entity who is self-existing or whose existence is independent of other beings. This might

---

[58] Chad Meister and Taliaferro, Charles. *History of Evil* (London: Routledge, 2018).

be a more local, restricted idea of a being uncaused in the real world, as in certain forms of the ontological argument.[59] If successful, the argument would provide cause to believe that such an entity exists. It may not be sufficient to support a complete depiction of God in religion, but it would contradict naturalistic alternatives and give some rationale for theism.

Some theistic arguments would need seeing diverse arguments as mutually reinforcing. Part of the argument may be stated as proof that the universe is the kind of reality that an intelligent entity would create, and then arguing that positing this source is more logical than agnosticism. The teleological argument, if successful in arguing for an intelligent, trans-cosmos source, may give some reason to believe that the cosmological argument's First Cause is purposive. The teleological argument is used by theists to bring attention to the cosmos' structure and stability, the formation of vegetative and animal life, awareness, morality, rational agents, and other topics. In our instance, deliberate, purposeful explanations seem to be valid and may actually account for the character and recurrence of occurrences.

Darwinian theories of biological evolution will not always help us understand why there are rules or creatures in the first place. The teleological argument attempts to show why positing a purposeful intelligence is rational and preferable to naturalism. To reinforce and reintroduce the uniqueness issue, some skeptics invoke the idea that the universe has an endless history. In theory, worlds that seem chaotic, unpredictable, or based on principles that stifle the creation of life are feasible.[60]

---

[59] J. Almeida and Graham, Oppy. "Sceptical Theism and Evidential Arguments from Evil". *Australasian Journal of Philosophy* 81, no.4 (2003): 496-516.

Some contend that if we can trust our cognitive capabilities, we may be certain that they are not the result of naturalistic causes.

In evolutionary epistemology, the dependability of cognitive capabilities is explained in terms of trial and error that leads to survival. Some atheists believe that faith in God has been essential to people's survival, despite the fact that this belief is completely wrong. Fine tuning arguments claim that life would not exist if various physical parameters did not have numerical values that fall within a defined range of values that allow life to exist.[61] Even modest alterations to the nuclear weak force, for example, would not have permitted stars to form, nor would stars have survived if the electromagnetic to gravity ratio had been considerably different.

Religions provide answers to questions such as why humans exist, how they should conduct their lives, and what motivates human behavior, as well as explanations regarding the natural world. The link between believers and the information provided by their faiths is complicated and wide-ranging. Some individuals turn to religion to satisfy a psychological need, while others turn to religion for direction on life's broader problems, sometimes in moments of powerlessness. Religious proof may take the shape of language for believers. This is generally done via written books such as the Bible, Torah, and Koran. One problem with utilizing (inspired) language to prove God's existence and anthropomorphize him is that it might lead to circular reasoning. Language does play an important part in the transmission of religious knowledge, which is greatly influenced by cultural, historical, and geographic circumstances.

---

[60] Almeida and Graham, "Sceptical Theism and Evidential Arguments from Evil", 498.
[61] Almeida and Graham, 499.

Socio-cultural

Embodied simulations explain these at the neurological, behavioral, and phenomenological levels. Social constructivist theories, for example, concentrate on the negotiated creation of meaning within a socio-cultural environment without elucidating how these mental structures are processed in the brain.[62] Theories abound on how embodied simulations might serve as a source of semantic material for social cognition. Humans were never the only ones involved in our social interactions.[63] There was always a strong selection pressure to be able to read the minds of both aggressive (such as bears) and friendly creatures (e.g., dogs during co-hunting). Furthermore, people have traditionally ascribed Anthropomorphism is the application of human characteristics to both living and non-living entities.[64] After a flood, for example, the river god is furious, they have a better understanding of their surroundings.

Metaphoric explanation

God's anthropomorphic identities are metaphoric. Humans' conceptual worlds, according to Gibbs, Gould and Andric, are essentially metaphorical, regulating their day-to-day

---

[62] Fırat Soylu. "An Embodied Future Map for Constructionism," 2019, 1-19; L.L. Chao and Martin, A. Representation of Manipulable Man-made Objects in the Dorsal Stream. *Neuroimage* 12, no.4 (2000): 478-484.
[63] R.W. Gibbs. Metaphor Interpretation as Embodied Simulation. *Mind and Language* 21, no.3, (2006): 434; R.W. Gibbs, Gould, J.J. and Andric, M. "Imagining Metaphorical Actions: Embodied Simulations make the Impossible Plausible". *Imagination, Cognition and Personality* 25, no.3 (2006): 221-238.
[64] Soylu, 18.

experiences.[65] A metaphor is a mapping from a known source domain to a new destination domain that makes sense. Our physical experiences often serve as the source domain since many of our intuitions, knowledge, and assumptions are strongly anchored in our bodies. Bodily experiences, on the other hand, take place in a socio-cultural environment and are classified according to cultural assumptions. Understanding action-related phrases necessitates an internal simulation of the activities stated in the sentences, which is mediated by the same motor representation that is engaged in their execution. Visualizing the metaphorical meaning was made easier by seeing, copying, or imagining the gripping action before listening to the grasp the notion metaphor. Performing or picturing suitable body motions before reading metaphorical words increased participants' understanding of these sentences in reading time tests.

Pomorphic explanation

Most organized faiths have pomorphic views of God. Do people conceive God in terms of gender if they believe in Him? Is there anything about their God that reminds them of a human being? Is their God a member of their knowledge community, if so? There is the need to investigate anthropomorphic responses to visual stimuli.[66] Many philosophers have attempted to stay clear of an all-too-human view of God.[67] Should the issue of anthropomorphism, however, invariably lead to religious skepticism? At some time throughout their life, some individuals have strong religious

---

[65] Gibbs, Gould, and Andric, 223.
[66] Gibbs, Gould, and Andric, 224.
[67] Gibbs, Gould, and Andric, 223.

experiences, while others have recounted something similar after having a near-death experience.

A Synthetic Departure

Is it possible to think about God without thinking of him as anthropomorphic? Some believe God created the cosmos and is omnipotent and omniscient. Others think God has both anthropomorphic and non-anthropomorphic characteristics.[68] Religious beliefs are one of the few kinds of concepts that are transmitted solely via culture.[69] In the first situation, anthropomorphism and its sister phenomenon, animism, might be seen as inescapable flaws in perceptual and conceptual systems. They appear in religion, as well as other types of cognition and conduct, since they are reasonable if wrong explanations of things and happenings in retrospect.[70] Of course, just because they are errors does not rule out the possibility of their being beneficial. Looking at the link between acceptance of an anthropomorphic picture of God and associated beliefs and actions, anthropomorphic conceptions of God may not always lead to concrete theologies; however, the opposite may be true.[71] After seeing that angels and Satan are mostly human

---

[68] Michael Fishbane. *Biblical Myth and Rabbinic Mythmaking* (Oxford: Oxford University Press, 2003), 164.
[69] Mike Watts and Bentley, Di. "Humanizing and Feminizing School Science: Reviving Anthropomorphic and Animistic Thinking in Constructivist Science Education." *International Journal of Science Education* 16, no.1 (2004): 83-97.
[70] William P. Alston. "Religious Experience Justifies Religious Belief". *Peterson and VanArragon,* (2004): 135–145.
[71] Jennifer Hart Weed. "Creation as a Foundation of Analogy in Aquinas." In *Divine Transcendence and Immanence in the Thought of St. Thomas Aquinas* (Leuven: Peeters, 2006).

in appearance and behaviour, people may assume that God possesses human features.

Theological data is likely to be as ambiguous as religious data, allowing plenty of space for interpretation. Identifying social groups with more defined views than others may reveal more about the nature and origins of such beliefs.[72] One may, for example, examine the theologies of newborn children to observe how they change over time, or compare them to those of members of the same cultural unit, such as a church or family.[73] Words used to describe finite things may not be adequate to describe God if God is infinite. The divine doctrines of Eastern religious traditions differ significantly from those of Abrahamic religions.[74] Because they lack the capacity to talk about God, the Abrahamic religions are subject to allegations that their holy writings and teachings are incoherent.

Religious language is a philosophical issue that should be addressed to provide a framework for understanding God claims. In religion and mythology, anthropomorphism is the vision of a divine person or beings in human form.[75] It is the acceptance of these beings' human characteristics. When elicited agent knowledge is low and affectivity and sociality are strong, people are more likely to anthropomorphize.[76] For instance, even though an

---

[72]Ahmad Ali al-Imam. *Variant Readings of the Qur'an: A Critical Study of Their Historical and Linguistic Origins* (London: IIIT, 2006).
[73] Alister E. McGrath. *Dawkins' God: Genes, Memes, and the meaning of Life* (London: Wiley-Blackwell, 2005).
[74] Robert Audi. *Rationality and Religious Commitment* (Oxford: Oxford University Press, 2011).
[75] E. Hamori. "Philosophical Approaches to Anthropomorphism". In *When Gods Were Men: The Embodied God in Biblical and Near Eastern Literature* (Berlin, New York: De Gruyter, 2008), 35-64.
[76] William J. Abraham and Frederick, D. Aquino (eds.). *The*

artificially intelligent computer or robot is not programmed to sense human emotions, it often does so in science fiction. In anthropomorphizing, one may appeal to pandeism (or Pantheism), another viewpoint which claims that God is similar to the world but no longer exists in a tangible form.[77] Furthermore, it holds that God created the whole universe and that the universe is now God's entirety. Many religions claim to include Pantheistic elements; however they are more often Panentheistic or Pandeistic.

In the Judeo-Christian tradition, the Bible has been the major source of God ideas. God is described and alluded to by numerous names or characteristics in the Quran and hadith. People may have created gods to impose morality when they began to live in larger groups.[78] In small groups, social variables such as gossip or reputation may support morality. Deity's gender might be interpreted as a literal or symbolic feature of a god who, according to classical Western thought, transcends physical form. In polytheistic beliefs, one of the gods is frequently ascribed a gender, allowing them to interact sexually with one another and sometimes with humans. In most monotheistic beliefs, God has no counterpart with whom to have sexual intercourse.

Many philosophers have endeavored to avoid a too humanistic picture of God. The anthropomorphism accusation was pursued with such zeal that it resembled a witch hunt. God is the only being in Islam who is both transcendent and

---

Oxford Handbook of the Epistemology of Theology (Oxford: Oxford University Press, 2017).
[77] L. Krauss. *A Universe from Nothing* (New York: Free Press, 2012).
[78] Nicholas Bunnin and Jiyuan Yu. *The Blackwell Dictionary of Western Philosophy* (New York: Blackwells, 2008).

wonderful. Several poetical phrases are used in the Qur'an to establish a divine but confusing modality in reference to God. There are a few verses in the Qur'an that, if taken literally, might lead to anthropomorphic gods. Metaphysics could be viewed as a completely logical explanation of observed reality, according to a philosophical approach.[79] In its pronouncements about God, a metaphysics that remains true to itself and has its own internal standard reaches certainty.

Conclusion

Anthropomorphism and its sibling phenomena, animism, are seen to be unavoidable defects in perceptual and conceptual systems. People are more prone to anthropomorphize when their elicited agent knowledge is low and their affectivity and sociality are high. When people start to dwell in greater groupings, they may have established gods to enforce morality. Faith and reason are two distinct sorts of authority that may be used to support opposing viewpoints. The two types of faith are evidence-sensitive faith and evidence-insensitive faith. If one dismisses the relevance of religious experience, traditional arguments for God's existence are unlikely to persuade you.

Some contend that the concept of a world in the best-case scenario is unreasonable. The cosmological argument is based on the premise that at least one strong entity exists independently of other things. The teleological argument aims to show why believing in a purposeful intelligence is both plausible and preferable to naturalism hence, the ability and curiosity to anthropomorphize God. Some atheists believe that faith in God has aided

---

[79] Francis Collins. *The Language of God: A Scientist Presents Evidence for Belief* (New York: Free Press, 2006).

people's survival hence they appeal to anthropomorphism. The Qur'an has a few passages that, if interpreted literally, might lead to anthropomorphic gods. Metaphysics may be thought of as a logical explanation for observable reality in this regard. The study certainly, has provided answer to the question, that is, it not possible to conceive about God without considering him to be anthropomorphic. Certainly, God is omnipotent and omniscient, having created the universe. Therefore, God has both anthropomorphic and anthropomorphic traits.

References

Abraham, William J. and Frederick, D. Aquino (eds.). *The Oxford Handbook of the Epistemology of Theology*. Oxford: Oxford University Press, 2017.

al-Imam, Ahmad Ali. *Variant Readings of the Qur'an: A Critical Study of Their Historical and Linguistic Origins*. London: IIIT, 2006.

Almeida, Michael J. and Graham, Oppy. "Sceptical Theism and Evidential Arguments from Evil". *Australasian Journal of Philosophy* 81, no.4 (2003): 496-516.

Alston, William P. "Religious Language." In *The Oxford Handbook of Philosophy of Religion*. Ed.

William J. Wainwright. Oxford: Oxford University Press, 2005, 220-244.

Alston, William P. "Religious Experience Justifies Religious Belief". *Peterson and VanArragon,*

(2004): 135–145.

Audi, Robert. *Rationality and Religious Commitment*. Oxford: Oxford University Press, 2011. Bailey, Alan and O'Brien, Dan. *Hume's Critique of Religion: 'Sick Men's Dreams'*. Dordrecht: Springer, Science+Business Media, 2014.

Barackman, Floyd H. *Practical Christian Theology: Examining the Great Doctrings of Faith*. London: Kregel Academic, 2001.

Barton, G.A. *A Sketch of Semitic Origins: Social and Religious*. Belgium: Kessinger Publishing, 2006. Beilby, James ed. *Naturalism Defeated? Essays on Plantinga's Evolutionary Argument Against Naturalism*.

Ithaca, NY: Cornell University Press, 2002.

Bentley, David. *The 99 Beautiful Names for God for All the People of the Book*. New York: William Carey Library, 1999.

Bergmann, Michael. "Skeptical Theism and Rowe's New Evidential Argument from Evil." *Noûs*, 35, no.2 (2001): 278-296.

Boother, Williams. Anthropomorphism. Microsoft® Encarta® 2009 [DVD]. Redmond, WA: Microsoft Corporation, 2009.

Bouvet, R. and Bonnefon, J.F. "Non-Reflective Thinkers Are Predisposed to Attribute Supernatural Causation to Uncanny Experiences". *Personality and Social Psychology Bulletin* 41, no.7 (2015): 955-961.

Bunnin, Nicholas and Yu, Jiyuan. *The Blackwell Dictionary of Westrn Philosophy*. New York: Blackwells, 2008.

Chao, L.L. and Martin, A. Representation of Manipulable Man-made Objects in the Dorsal Stream. *Neuroimage* 12, no.4 (2000): 478-484.

Collins, Francis. *The Language of God: A Scientist Presents Evidence for Belief*. New York: Free Press, 2006.

Coogan, Michael. "Fire in Divine Loins: God's Wives in Myth and Metaphor". In *God and sex. What the Bible Really Says* (1st ed.). New York, Boston: Twelve. Hachette Book Group, 2010.

Craig, Edward. God, Concepts of, *Routledge Encyclopedia of Philosophy*. Taylor & Francis, 1998.

Culotta, E. "The Origins of Religion". *Science* 326, no.5954 (2009): 784-787

Dixon, Thomas. *Science and Religion: A Very Short Introduction*. Oxford: Oxford University Press, 2008.

Duffy, Brian R. "Anthropomorphism and the Social Robot". *Robotics and Autonomous Systems* 42, no.3-4, (2003): 177-190.

Epley, Nicholas, Waytz, Adam and Cacioppo, John T. "On Seeing Human: A Three-factor Theory of Anthropomorphism". *Psychological Review* 114, no.4 (2007): 864-886.

Fishbane, Michael. *Biblical Myth and Rabbinic Mythmaking*. Oxford: Oxford University Press, 2003. Gibbs, R.W. Metaphor Interpretation as Embodied Simulation. *Mind and Language* 21, no.3, (2006): 434.

Gibbs, R.W., Gould, J.J. and Andric, M. "Imagining Metaphorical Actions: Embodied Simulations make the Impossible Plausible". *Imagination, Cognition and Personality* 25, no.3 2006): 221-238.

Goetz, Stewart. *Freedom, Teleology, and Evil*. London: Continuum, 2008.

Guthrie, Stewart. "Anthropology and Anthropomorphism in Religion". In *Religion, Anthropology and Cognitive Science*, eds. Whitehouse and Laidlaw. Carolina: Carolina Academic Press, 2007, 37-62.

Hamori, E. "Philosophical Approaches to Anthropomorphism". In *When Gods Were Men: The Embodied God in Biblical and Near Eastern Literature*. Berlin, New York: De Gruyter, 2008, 35- 64.

Hanish, Shak. "The Mandaeans in Iraq". *Routledge Handbook of Minorities in the Middle East*. London and New York: Routledge. *2019*, 163.

Harris, S. *The End of Faith*. New York: W.W. Norton and Company, 2005.

Henry, Michel. *I am the Truth. Toward a philosophy of Christianity*. Trans. Susan Emanuel. Oxford: Stanford University Press, 2003.

Hutson, Matthew. *The 7 Laws of Magical Thinking: How Irrational Beliefs Keep Us Happy, Healthy, and Sane*. New York: Hudson Street Press, 2012, 165-81.

Krauss, L. *A Universe from Nothing*. New York: Free Press, 2012.

Lindeman, Riekki, T. and Rai, T.T. "Supernatural Believers Attribute More Intentions to Random Movement than Skeptics: An MRI Study". *Social Neuroscience* 9, no.4 (2014): 400- 411.

Marakas, George. M., Johnson, Richard D. and Palmer, Jonathan W. "A Theoretical Model of Differential Social Attributions toward Computing Technology: When the Metaphor becomes the Model". *International Journal of Human-Computer Studies* 52, no.4 (April 2000): 719-750.

McGrath, Alister E. Dawkins' God: Genes, Memes, and the meaning of Life. London: Wiley-Blackwell, 2005.

Meister, Chad and Taliaferro, Charles. *History of Evil*, London: Routledge, 2018.

Mtshiselwa, N. and Mokoena. L. "Humans Created God in their Image? An Anthropomorphic Projectionism in the Old Testament". *HTS Teologiese Studies/Theological Studies* 74, no.1 (2018), 5017.

Mueller, Max. *Anthropological Religion*. London: Longmans, 1992, 76.

Onimhawo, John A. and Ottuh, Peter O.O. *Some Thoughts in Sociology of Religion*. Benin City: Ever- Blest Publisher, 2009.

Pickover, Cliff. *The Paradox of God and the Science of Omniscience*, New York: Palgrave/St Martin's Press, 2001.

Plantinga, Aviin. "God, Arguments for the Existence of". *Routledge Encyclopedia of Philosophy*, Routledge, 2000.

Richards, Glyn. *The Philosophy of Gandhi: A Study of his Basic Ideas*. London: Routledge, 2005. Rossano, Matt.

"Supernaturalizing Social Life: Religion and the Evolution of Human
Cooperation". *Human Nature* 18, no.3 (2007): 272-294.

Seeskin, Kenneth. "Sanctity and Silence: The Religious Significance of Maimonides' Negative Theology." *American Catholic Philosophical Quarterly*, 76 (2002): 7-24.

Shtulman, A, and Rattner, M. "Theories of God: Explanatory Coherence in Religious Cognition".
PLoS ONE 13, no.12 (2018): e0209758.

Soylu, Fırat. "An Embodied Future Map for Constructionism". Evanston, IL: Northwestern University, 2019, 1-19. https://www.sesp.northwestern.edu/docs/publications/141 7950354527d083710d01.pdf (Accessed on March 2, 2022).

Swindal, James. "Faith and Reason". *The Internet Encyclopedia of Philosophy*. 2016. https://iep.utm.edu/faith-re/. (Accessed on April 4, 2022).

Taliaferro, Charles. "Philosophy of Religion". In *The Stanford Encyclopedia of Philosophy*. ed. Edward
N. Zalta. London: Routledge, 2021.

Vail, K.E, Arndt, J. and Addollahi, A. "Exploring the Existential Function of Religion and Supernatural Agent Beliefs Among Christians, Muslims, Atheists, and Agnostics". *Personality and Social Psychology Bulletin* 38, no.10 (2012): 1288-1300.

Watts, Mike and Bentley, Di. "Humanizing and Feminizing School Science: Reviving Anthropomorphic and Animistic Thinking in Constructivist Science Education." *International Journal of Science Education* 16, no.1 (2004): 83-97.

Weed, Jennifer Hart. "Creation as a Foundation of Analogy in Aquinas." In *Divine Transcendence and Immanence in the Thought of St. Thomas Aquinas*. Leuven: Peeters, 2006.

Whiten, Andrew. "Culture Extends the Scope of Evolutionary Biology in the Great Apes". *Proceedings of the National Academy of Sciences* 114, no.3025, (2017): 7790-7797.

From Catholicism Across The Poetic Synapse To Pandeism:

The Metamorphosis, The Evolution, The Leap-Of-Faith Teleportation From Belief In God-The-Judge-Jury-n-Executioner To Belief In Shape-Shifter God-The-Creation: Part I-II

By Paul Zarzyski

Paul Zarzyski has written for the past forty to sixty years in the state of *"perpetual ars poetica metamorphosis."* After receiving a Master of Fine Arts Degree in Creative Writing—under the tutelage of Richard Hugo and Madeline DeFrees—from the University of Montana, he incurred a "close poetic encounter of the otherworldly kind" with rodeo, bareback bronc riding, a passion that seeped osmotically into his work. In response to his years on the rodeo circuit, his poems and song lyrics have been embraced by the Cowboy Poetry folk tradition—writing and riding, wild verses and wild horses, the literati and the "lariati." Or, as novelist James Welch wrote, "Paul Zarzyski is a man of many hats, fisherman, bronc rider, son, worker, lover.... Today, beneath his favorite of those "many hats," Paul is focused most pensively, although every bit as viscerally/passionately, on the closing seconds of his lifetime's toughest ride, aboard this spinning bucking horse orb named Planet Earth, a ride he hopes to finish, as an "extreme creativist," on a high, wide, and handsome galactic note out into what he calls "the Ol' Cowpoke Cosmos, the Musical Universe, Creativity's Infinities."

Face-To-Face

Out of nowhere, you find yourself
placed daily before the fortress,
rustic logs throbbing
something from within
you vaguely recognize
as music—so primal,
so otherworldly in its purpose,
you are at once drawn closer,
cautioned back. Succumb
to ugly logic, to mean-spirited
reason, or religion,
and you, believing you shun
merely the unknown, will flee
unwittingly from beauty. Trust the blood,
however, waltzing to four-part harmony
within the heart, and you will be moved
to witness, through the chinking's
thin fissures, the shadows
of the enchanted. Then, and only then,
might you choose to follow
a force you'll lovingly call your soul
through huge swinging doors
thrown open to the glorious
commotion of it all.

Upon hearing that the editor of *Pandeism: An Anthology* was interested in republishing excerpts from my 2011 collection, *51: 30 Poems, 20 Lyrics, 1 Self Interview* ("*5* Memoir Rounds with *1* Paul Zarzyski"), I felt both honored and amused that someone who I did not recognize as "family" or "friend," who I did not personally know by first, middle, and last name, phone number, mailing address, and birthday, had actually discovered my work. September 2023 marked the 50th anniversary of my 1300-mile drive from Hurley, Wisconsin to

Missoula, Montana to study in the U.M. Creative Writing Program and, in light of the publication of a dozen best-kept-secret collections, I've found peace, thank my luckiest stars (a.k.a. "thank God"), long ago with my role as a regional, (Mid)Western poet with an "intimate" readership.

Therefore, it is with utmost humility, laced with a modicum of intimidation after perusing existing issues of the *Pandeism Anthologies* that I'm taking a wild run at this essay composed from a quintet of interwoven atomic-word components: 1) narrative prose 2) "Self-Interview" conversational excerpts 3) poetry 4) song lyrics and 5) emboldened Zarzyski Dictums (**ZD**s) or Zar**Z**yski-i**ZZ**ms—all prompted by my roll-of-the-proverbial-cosmic-dice, 72-year-radar-screen-blip in this dimension known as life on Earth. This *extremely* personal poetic journey is rendered without delusion of persuasive efficacy. As evidenced primarily, but not solely, by the Self-Interview exchanges, I've become quite adept at, and comfortable with, talking to myself—at convincing me, and only me, how to perceive this single Milky-Way-Galaxy world amidst the trillions of other worlds calling an estimated 2 trillion galaxies in the Universe their homes. My narratives—again, *"extremely* personal," as well as, at times, perhaps harsh—and the perspectives rising from them, are almost always deep-rooted in my uniquely influential formative childhood years, addressed here in what some might consider *"ultra* confidential detail."

Regarding this essay's reliance on copious infusions of poetry, you bet, I *have* seen the film *The Big Short* with its notorious, out-of-the-blue, on-screen proclamation, "Truth is like poetry. And most people fucking hate poetry." Nonetheless, as my hefty title clearly specifies, "...Across the *Poetic* Synapse." No poetry, no synapse—no synapse, very likely no crossing over, no conversion, for one Paul Zarzyski, and, thus, no grist for this narrative.

Also, regarding the Zarzyski Dictums, although these declarations or observations most certainly have been articulated in some iteration by others, I would hope that my one-of-a-kind Polish-Italian-Rodeo-Poet voice, from my one-of-a-kind Paul L. Zarzyski vantage point in this definitive time-n-space, affords more of a fresh focal point than would a veritable litany of researched (Googled) quotes cut-n-pasted together in support of "my" thinking. In the same breath, despite the title of my 2022 poetry collection, *Going It Alone*, no way can I go *totally solo*, sans the perspectives and poetic articulations of others far more erudite than am I:

ZD - Whoever wrote, "We are slowed down sound and light waves, a walking bundle of frequencies tuned into the cosmos. We are souls dressed up in sacred biochemical garments and our bodies are the instruments through which our souls play their music," transcended everything I will ever have the wherewithal to perceive. I only wish I had discovered this astrophysical tidbit of poetic wisdom *before* I erroneously felt visionary enough to render my first ZD into print. Now, however, as long as I'm this deep into the Zarzyski-insipid litany, what the hell—I may just as well keep scratching at the mysterious surface of life-n-death Earth, merely one of the billions of potential life-supporting planets existing in the universe.

Additionally, I find it apt that moments from my "Self-Interview" prompted the editor's interest. What more truthfully demonstrative interactions to buoy to the surface our personal piety—our capacity for believing which, if any, creator brought us into being—than long intense sessions with our inner-core selves?

And finally, I beg the reader's tolerance for the numerous moments throughout this essay via which I indict humankind—myself included—for what I perceive as our heinous failure to observe, to listen, to logically exercise our free will in discerning and opting for good over evil, wisdom over ignorance, truth over deception, generosity over greed, science over mythology, et al. Should this sensibility upset you, may I suggest that you remind yourself often, "It's *only* a movie, it's *only* a movie"—he's *only* a poet, he's *only* a poet, he's *only* a poet on one poet's going-it-alone solo-flight launch into "The Glorious Commotion of it All."

Which brings us to our cadre of chosen Gods, who I equally fault, albeit oftentimes facetiously, while bearing in mind the witticism most often attributed to French Enlightenment writer, Voltaire (Francois-Marie Arouet): "God is a comedian playing to an audience too afraid to laugh." I'm hoping, therefore, that God— believing "laughter" (which God created?) *indeed* "is the best medicine"—is as adept at taking a joke as dishing one out? If not, I may very well be in for an afterlife world of fiery shit.

I

ZD - Could it be that the "God*less*" are those of us who turn to organized religion as a "Sabbath Safe House" sheltering us from the unbearable terror of facing, and answering to daily, the one-n-only, most exacting, true God—*ourselves*?

Or, perhaps more apropos to the purely hypothetical focuses of this thesis,

ZD - Death deposits our consciousness onto the Cosmos Foundling Wheel. Only the cosmic forces receiving it on the other side know its fate, just as only the deposited consciousness disappearing through the impenetrable wall between mortality and immortality comes to know the forces receiving, and hopefully welcoming, it—forces that we humans, in desperate need of an antidote to death, have dubbed "God-the-Savior."

Whatever the case,

ZD - If God is just another holier-than-thou old white guy, deal me *the hell* out.

****

I was raised in a 1950s-'60s bucolic, ethnic, Midwestern, north-woods logging and hematite ore-mining town to believe in organized religion, to *buy* into Catholicism, to embrace having blind faith in the unknown, to denounce Satan whose full-time job was to tempt me to question that which was deemed *un*questionable, not open for discussion, off the celestial debate table. Yes, we *are* talking, in fact, the antithesis of science. The push came mostly from my mother's Italian heritage, although my Polish father also was stamped "Catholic"—at times to his chagrin, especially on Fridays when, in the midst of pick-n-shovel double-jack-n-blast shifts underground in the Cary hematite mine, he opened his lunch pail to the unmistakable whiff of tuna fish sandwiches.

Thanks to both of my first-generation immigrant parents, I learned the virtue of hard work at an early age—my first job, picking and selling "Nightcrawlers, 10¢ a Dozen, 505 Poplar Street:"

...I was young and wondered once
how my father, tunneling,
felt the struggle of worms and roots
working through the earth,
if he knew how much yellow
onions grew each night
in his garden, how close to home
he really was on graveyard
shift. I stretched out flat, feeling,
against each rib, the intimate
ways of earth
worms in wet grass, the magnetic
attraction of man to home
and hell through rich ore. I pressed
an ear over a wormhole
and listened to the medley—
men, machines, blood, worms—all
the workings of the body, for love
or money, mineral or liquid, everything
living off that one heart of Earth.

During those nights of filling my Hills Bros. coffee tins with squirming masses of dew worms, I looked up in youthful wonder into the heavens alright, but I also listened below. I was curious already as a boy of five where we came from, how we got here and where we're going next—my hope, my meteoric shooting-star wish, not one bit jibing with my first open-casket wake, the subject of which was the produce-store proprietor who'd given me lettuce trimmings by the crateful to feed my pet rabbits. He'd also concocted an old-country salve that he applied to their delicate inner ears blistered from mites—the remedy, within a day or two, restoring the capillaries' healthy

202

translucency. You bet—my very first visual miracle by my very first Earthling miracle-worker! And then, finger-snap-fast, he was gone, never to return, to shine his medicinal light again into my life via the lives of my beloved "Thumpers?" Say *what*?!

ZD - If "God is," indeed, "just," then God is also "just" a lousy shot—talk about your "friendly fire!"

Although it took several decades to devise a more civil divine game plan, I eventually got 'er done, conveyed it to God, and, for the life of me, cannot understand why it has taken engineer-extraordinaire God, so long to implement my brilliant idea:

ZD - In place of snatching from us the good among us, God should opt to "deliver us from evil" here on Earth via the *Mother*-of-all omnisciently-sensitive-n-impeccably-selective, "Subhuman Pest Zappers" ratcheted down from heaven to Earth, all praise and glory to the creation (on *the eighth* day) of the hoist's manual crank to the right (or left, if God's a southpaw) of the holy throne. Eternal incineration in Hades shall thereafter gobsmackingly become a mere, mild sunburn compared to having gotten God-Zapped: *ZZZ*T! *ZZZ*T! *ZZZ*T-*ZZZ*T! Gone *missing*!

In retrospect, my upbringing was an amalgamation of sin, sanctity, and sacrilege. Speaking of "lunch pail," I needed to pack one for my shifts in the confessional, where I sinned even further via my venial litanies of not so much lying under oath, religious perjury, as minor circumnavigations of the absolute truth—most specifically regarding impure thoughts and deeds. I wanted in the worst way to push back, pass the buck: "Screw your 'mea culpa, mea culpa, mea maxima culpa,' Father—if God concocted testosterone, then it's *His* fucking fault, not mine!"

Nevertheless, my ultimate earthly goal as a "child of God" was to stockpile more "indulgences" than sins, to get my Pearly Gates ticket punched and thus to avoid being loaded-up for the elevator drop into Hades. Dad, riding the cage a mile down into the ferrous veins for 20 years had likely already done his stint in hell, and, therefore, should've received a notarized dispensation from God for "time served," despite his lackluster Sunday-mass-attendance, deemed a mortal sin via which, should he have died unexpectedly, sans last rites—say, *for the hell of it*, in a cave-in or by coming face-to-explosive-face with a "missed shot"—guaranteed his Eternal Perch at Beelzebub's Bar-B-Que. To quote one of Dad's favorite terms for bogus beliefs in bogus events, "What a bunch of happy horse shit."

One of my earliest poems, however, speaks to our leaning on prayer at a time of dire need in the Divine:

When Timbers Tremored In The Cary Mine....

...blood mixed with iron in the veins,
news flashed, "cave-in--level 36,"
and the cage surfaced without dad.
Mom prayed
he'd taken graveyard for a friend,
whispered "Leonard, my Leonard"
through a mile of dirt and hematite.
Her damp cheeks glowed red
as his iron-stained pocket watch,
and the brown beads stretched across her lap
like a string of ore cars. Together
we swallowed Hail Marys
until our father came home exhausted,
his eyes, puffy as grape-ore,

still raising the dead from their graves.

****

Throughout her life, Mom diligently practiced, but *perhaps* never quite mastered her faith. Or so it seemed after the following exchange approaching her 90th birthday, at which time she struggled with moderate dementia:

"What's bothering you, Mom?" I asked between sips of Christian Brothers Brandy late one night at the kitchen table.

"I don't understand," she replied. "You work hard and raise a family and nurture so many loving friendships and just when you reach a place of security, peace, and comfort in life, you die."

"Well, isn't that why you went to church every Sunday, and received Communion, and said your Novenas, and adhered to The Ten Commandments, and prayed and prayed and prayed—so you would find that peace of which you speak in the heavenly afterlife? Don't you look forward after you die to seeing Noni (her mother) and Dad, and Uncle Albert and Jack-the-pet-crow and our dog, Smokey, everyone you loved in this dimension?"

"*Aaaaa,* get outta here," she responded, waving her hand in my direction in a gesture of annoyance.

"*What?!,*" I exclaimed, "You don't believe in heaven?"

"*Aaaaa,*" she repeated. "Like Pete Lombardo used to say, 'Delia, when you're dead, you're dead.'"

"Now, *I'm the one* who doesn't understand," I retorted, "Then why did you go to church and pray for salvation your entire life?"

"Well, that's just what we did," was her matter-of-fact answer, as only a strong-willed, faithfully truthful, Italian superwoman of her stature could respond, *could confess.*

As The World Turns

Conceived in northern Italy, a mountain town,
my mother crossed the Atlantic, 1920,
in the womb, lived her first twenty-seven years
at 507 Poplar Street, married
a navy man turned iron ore miner,
moved to 505 and stayed
married to the same man on the same street,
never learned to drive,
seldom missed Sunday mass or Friday fish
fries at the V.F.W. or Legion Hall,
raised three boys—prayed, cooked, cleaned house,
washed clothes, shopped for groceries—loved
The Mitch Miller and Lawrence Welk shows,
listens still to her polka
program, Saturday morning on WJMS,
while baking biscotti, doing something useful, she
having confessed to her poet son,
on her eightieth birthday, that she'd much
rather scrub *her* kitchen floor than read a book
because she just can't stand to just sit
and do nothing, except for tuning in
weekday afternoons to the everlasting soap
opera saga she's referring to
when she says, with so much joy in her voice,
"time to watch my story,"
though, not so oddly at all,
it's the farthest thing from it.

My brother Gary and I—under the influence of late-night reminiscence, *and otherwise*—in the living room of our childhood abode, long after Mom and Dad had passed, laugh often at my retelling of this exchange, which, we've concluded, irrefutably proves that theoretical physicists, including Stephen Hawking, plagiarized the thinking of grade-school-educated, Italian immigrant, iron ore miner Pete Lombardo, who lived across the street, and who knew long before they did that heaven and hell are mere myths, as are all organized religions with their top-shelf best-seller Sci-Fi "good books" and top-salesmen disciples, acolytes, recruits. Pete could have saved astrophysicists decades of research, mathematical calculations, analyses, and deliberations regarding the genesis of the universe, although, sure, it *is* now—thanks in no small part to the James Webb Space Telescope's revelations of cosmic history—far more enchanting to learn why and how and when it all came into being, which, from my current perch and perspective, by far supersedes the perpetual, ad nauseam focus on "by whom."

What they say about longstanding habits being hard to break, however, holds true for me decades after I relinquished my "belief in sin" and its subsequent crime-n-hellish-punishment. To this day, I catch myself thinking, in the presence of misfortunes of others, plant and animal fellow beings alike—my empathies, extending to the daily Tribune obituaries of complete strangers, as well as to road-killed mammals, birds, reptiles...—"God bless them." Or "God give them strength," which translates, during less spontaneous moments, as "May The Musical Universe acknowledge their hardships via compositions of both empathy and compassion—may It sing to them Its virtuoso love song of enlightenment." If not "sing to them," then perhaps more accurately, "May The Universe resonate within them its restorative Musical blessings:"

"Einstein's theory of spacetime tells us that the real universe is not silent, but is actually alive with vibrating energy. Space and time carry a cacophony of vibrations with textures and timbres as rich and varied as the din of sounds in a tropical rain forest or the finale of a Wagner opera. It's just that we haven't heard those sounds yet. The universe is a musical that we've been watching all this time as a silent movie." Craig Hogan—*American Scientist*

In any case, this wish for the wellbeing of others, rather than myself, is the closest I come these days to what's defined as "prayer." Beyond this,

ZD - Those of us most deserving of spiritual admiration worship at The First Mother Earth Church of Animists, and are members of the Earthocratican Party, which does not cooperate or compromise with those willing, for the sake of greed and/or religion, to destroy our Glorious Orb. The sooner all money-changers and merchants are fitted with flying squirrel wing suits, provided sack lunches, and ejected via Cape Canaveral "human cannon ball" launches into the God-forsaken blackest hole of the unknown, the greater the longevity of Planet Earth.

And beyond *that,*

ZD - What if humankind's choosing to believe that "everything is in God's plan"—including the Holocaust, slavery, colonialism, racism, misogyny, homophobia, war, gun violence, plagues, pestilence, climate change, atrocities committed against indigenous people, against

fellow-being plants and animals alike, against the very planet that gives life to humankind— actually *violates* God's original plan, which was to bestow humankind with free will and to grace Earth, the Universe, with everything humankind needed to save itself *from* itself? Logically speaking, in *The Pretty Good Book According to Zarzyski*, should this be the case, we are now not only screwed, but we have most stupidly screwed *ourselves*. Furthermore, if God *has* chosen, as only God can, *not* to play the leading role in the Universal Studios major motion picture show titled *Life On Earth*—if Deism just so happens to be the one-n-only true so-called "religion"— *or*, if God does not exist at all, *had we* chosen to believe that *we were* indeed blessed with God's Gifts for self-preservation, we at least then stood a chance of accruing the wisdom to, once again, save our *non*-goddamned selves from our *non*-goddamned selves, which, most certainly, would have pleased God, thinks I, should God actually exist, *or*, for that matter, even *fictitiously* exist.

And, to complete this **ZD** trinity,

ZD - It's far more likely that God is an extraterrestrial than an intellectual—unless, of course, they are one and the same?

To further chart my spiritual metamorphosis, my Poetic Encounters of the Otherworldly Kind, I now offer the following 2011 "Self-Interview" excerpt which includes more rudimentary stages of my evolution toward beatifically deciding, solely and soulfully—*for* myself, via an emphatic interaction *with* myself— "*What* is God," *or*, "Where does God reside."

"Self-Interview" Excerpt A

. . . what was the question again?

I think it was whether or not you "subscribe to a spirituality" or "spiritualism," of sorts?

I hope so. I think I do. Yes—sans organized religion, in no small part because, number one, I believe in an *egoless* supreme being, and two, even if God was experiencing a rare moment of insecurity and decided, "I might feel far more reassured about who I am and what I've created if only I had a fan club," would you, were you God, choose the inferior likes of *us* to occupy your cheering section? I sure as hell wouldn't. I'm with Groucho Marx's dictum: "I refuse to join any club that would have me as a member." Especially in light of how religions, oftentimes splintering, devolving into cults, have been responsible throughout history—arguably seldom more so than today—for some of the world's most heinous acts against humanity, against the Creator's beloved planet Earth and its occupants. Merely in "recent" times, consider the missionaries' crimes against indigenous peoples and the atrocities committed by pedophile Catholic priests and Muslim suicide terrorists crashing planes full of people into buildings full of people for the sake of pleasing Allah and, in doing so, earning afterlife eternities full of virgin harems? It stands to reason—yes, "reason"— in my reasonable, Commander-Spock-logical view, that there should be as many religious ideologies as there are individuals who believe in a hereafter. It's *that* uniquely personal. The result of this religious individuation would be tinier ecumenical pissing matches (gushers to mere dribblings) over dogma or ecclesiastical differences, including which fan club

God loves best. Outright war between the masses could be replaced by, say, a game of checkers or a spelling bee between merely two individuals. Or even three "sweet science" 30-ounce-pillowed-glove rounds governed by the Marquis of Queensberry rules. *Or*, most extreme, single-shot pellet pistols at fifty paces, the worst-case scenario being a run on those black, elastic-banded eye patches that pirates wear. My position is that if everyone, including *you*, kept their afterlife beliefs private and personal—and, especially segregated from government—we'd all be the richer, the healthier, the wiser, the holier and happier for it aboard this Glorious Orb, God no-doubt the happiest of *all*. Amen.

You realize, of course, that many of your readers, listeners, will cite you for blasphemy? However, since your poems seem to vacillate, leaning more toward the agnostic than the atheistic, maybe you'll be granted absolution—perhaps readers taking the greatest umbrage will recognize hope yet for your salvation. You do care? You do struggle?

Daily. Make that hourly. Since you've likely read *our* poems, you know I was raised Catholic, something that nobody, in this brief history of time, has ever fully recovered from, and I don't necessarily mean this in a sarcastic vein, at least not entirely. Catholicism instilled a healthy dose of right-from-wrong discernment during my upbringing, but no more so than did my dad, who showed little interest in the church. Augment a benevolent disposition with the crucial virtues of wisdom and forgiveness, and that equips one with all that is needed to live life more as a *giver* than a *taker*. For the past decade, I've made the same New Year's resolution, complete with my feel for poetic line break:

Give and be giving
And, especially, *be*
Forgiving.

I fail miserably, more often than not, to adhere to this resolve, but I seldom lose entirely my grip on the power of goodness which, again, I trace back to my virtuous upbringing, in the home more so than in the church. Catholicism, as is the case with most religions, is way too much about fear, and I am not willing to relinquish one of my self-prescribed "Four Artistic *F*s—*F*reedom, *F*ierceness, *F*earlessness, and *F*un"— simple as that. *And....* (long, nervous, sudden pause)

For someone who boasts of fearlessness, you suddenly appear skittish.

Earlier, you recall, I referenced "pedophile priests." (Another pause.)

Somewhere in the closing pages of his memoir *Off to the Side*, Jim Harrison offers a quip about him-and a friend being "short-funded" and regretting not having any "evil priests" in their boyhood past (via which, I assume, to acquire blackmailed-Vatican assets). It was hard not to chuckle, but it hit too close to home or, I should say, too close to St. Mary's Church back in 1963 or 1964. I was in seventh or eighth grade when the whisperings among us altar boys became all too loud. One friend, a lanky, tough Polish kid, was rumored to have hurdled the altar rail like Edwin Moses, yes *Moses*, during a dead-of-winter 6:00 a.m. mass, attended usually by a handful of old Italian women bowed so deeply in prayer that none would've noticed a frantic sprinter flashing by down the center aisle and busting out through the half-ton doors at the entrance to the church. It was revealed later that the class nerd—defined here as the most innocent and submissive and thus, most victimized—whose childish face I still clearly picture, and whose name I'll withhold, had been fondled on a table in the sacristy.

And then one morning the predator singled me out as his prey at 5:30 a.m. as I was about to don my altar-boy cassock. The guy was a heavyweight—had to be packing 250. Grabbed ahold of me and was eager to show me, in his words, "the proper way to tuck your shirt into your trousers." Just as he was about to accomplish his demonstration, another priest walked in, quite unexpectedly. I remember the look on his face—he knew. The next morning, I showed up to serve mass with my dad's bone-handled hunting knife in my boot. I had watched too many westerns. I situated my bicycle, pointed downhill, at the bottom of the rectory stairs—imagining, I guess, a cowboy making a get-away vault to the back of his horse ground-tied outside of a bank or jail rather than a church. I had visualized sticking the priest then grabbing hold of my right, knife-wielding wrist with my left hand and leveraging a profound and literal upper-cut which would leave the bad guy down on prayerful knees, cradling his haggis sack in both forearms, while I made my heroic escape unscathed.

How goddamn *sad* is this all-too-true story? I weighed maybe a buck-thirty—half his heft. I'll never forget the helplessness I felt in those powerful arms— will remember always my determination *not* to become preyed upon again, at whatever cost. I'll keep him anonymous, but I wonder if, in examining the church records, we'd find a certain priest listed as having been transferred suddenly to another parish during the early 1960s. He did not, I think it goes without saying, make a play for me that fateful, *or faithful*, morning on which I was packing the blade. I remember my dad asking a day or so later if Father so-n-so had "monkeyed around" (is how he would've

213

put it) with me or with any of the other altar boys. Although I said "No," he too *knew*. That evening I overhead him talking on the phone to the other priest, who had shown up in the nick of time that morning of the initial contact. Dad said something about "that goddamn queer" (is how he would've put it) being gone by daybreak, "*or else...!*"

Never saw him again. Would I have stuck him? Saint Luca Brasi, The Patron Saint of Hit Men, only knows. Did I feel I had the Good Lord's blessing to tack a caveat onto His commandment number five—"Thou shalt not kill, *unless* sexually molested by My clergy?" Clearly, I did. I wonder if this encounter with a so-called "man of the cloth" so-called "created in God's image" has more than a little to do with my absolute belief that no-way does *my* Creator sport a gender *or* a beard? On an even more caustic note, according to what I was taught in catechism, my beautiful father, as punishment for his non-church-going life, is, as we speak, suffering, burning, for eternity. I *dare* any Christian zealot to approach me with that contention regarding my dad's afterlife fate. I'll prove once and for all the difference between a peace advocate and a pacifist, the latter of which, you should know by now, I am most definitely *not*. To close the *not-so*-"Good Book" on this uncomfortable focus, I'll reference my song lyric, "God and Fear," written in response to an onslaught of Rapture nonsense in the news—triggered by that series of *Left Behind* sci-fi publications that two snake-oil-salesmen posing as legitimate authors were peddling by the millions (of dollars) at the time. This blasphemous psalm speaks most defiantly to my Christianity stance, and also just might offer one of the strongest lyrical lines I've written, although odds are that I am not the first to have conceived of this turn-of-phrase or play on words:

God & Fear

They say "The Rapture's coming"
I say "Let the bastard come"
They say "Armageddon's gunning"
I say "I'm the faster gun."

They say "There's no denying"
I say "Defy unto thy end"
They say "You'll be left behind"
I say "Adios, my friends, AMEN!"

     Me and Jesus in a pickup
     Going fishing, drinking beer
     Cruising through The Masterpiece
     Without guilt and without fear.

They tell me "Read the Scriptures,
The apocalypse is now
The Prince of Darkness grips us"
I tell them "Holy Cow!"

They tell me they're the chosen
The U.S. of J.C. choice—
While their souls are decomposin'
Let our flesh and blood rejoice.

     Me and Jesus in a pickup
     Going fishing, drinking beer
     Cruising through The Masterpiece
     Without guilt and without fear.

        Eye-for-eye and tooth-for-tooth
        They say "God won't reconcile"
        I say "God *is* the light of mercy
        With a 20/20 smile."

So me and Jesus we go fishing
Talking creativity
Praise Forgiveness is His mantra

Renounce Fear! His decree.

Then me and Jesus we go swimming
He's a fan of body art
"Being scared ain't being sacred"
Is tattooed above His heart.

> Me and Jesus in a pickup
> Going fishing, drinking beer
> Cruising through The Masterpiece
> Without guilt and without fear.

> Me and Jesus, oh sweet Jesus,
> Cruising through The Masterpiece
> Without guilt and without fear.
> Without guilt and without fear.

That penultimate line of the last verse?

That's it—"Being scared ain't being sacred." Good ear.

So good, in fact, that there's no way I could have missed, in reference to having been raised Catholic, the allusion to Stephen Hawking when you said, and I quote you verbatim, "Nobody, in this Brief History of Time *has ever fully recovered from...." Stephen Hawking? You've read him?*

Tried to read him—after seeing him interviewed on *60 Minutes.* I don't remember the exact question the interviewer asked, but it addressed the motivational force behind Mr. Hawking's early journeys deep into the mysteries of the universe. I'll never forget his response: "If we could discover why we and the universe exist, it would be the ultimate triumph of human reason—for then we would know the mind of God." It gives me chills to hear this aloud. I watched, and listened to, this brilliant man field questions about his work and I could oh-so-humbly not help but compare his creative journeys into the unknown to those of the artist, and thus I have praised him often as the quintessential poet of our time. A piece that speaks facetiously to his prowess, "What Stephen Hawking, The Definitive Poet Of All Time, Might, If He's Not Careful, Come Face-To-Surprising-Face With," is recorded, augmented with outrageous sound effects, on my spoken-word CD, *Collisions of Reckless Love*. The pair of epigraphs included are certainly far more profound than the poem. The first, by Albert Einstein, is well-documented. The second is from the very first woman elected to congress, Montana's Jeannette Rankin, who lived from 1880 to 1973. She was the only congressperson to vote against both WWI and WWII, and cast the sole dissenting vote for the latter. During her waning years she directed her anti-war sentiments toward Vietnam.

Although I doubt the poem will live up to its title, let alone the epigraphs (just kidding) let's hear it?

Note: The poem's title, after Mr. Hawking's death, was revised to

What Stephen Hawking, The Definitive Poet Of All Time, *Might*, As We Speak, Be Coming Face-To-Cosmological-Face With

Only two things are infinite—the universe and human stupidity. And I'm not sure about the universe.
                                Albert Einstein

You can no more win a war than you can win an earthquake.
Jeannette Rankin (1880-1973)
                    Montana Congresswoman

Planet Earth is the number one
rated, syndicated half-hour sitcom
showing on Universal Big Screen
Satellite TV. We have become such
natural born comedians, in fact,
that we've, in a mere century, outgrown
our need for the canned-laugh
soundtrack machine. Across the cosmos
intelligent life religiously watches us,
never missing an episode
because a good guffaw or, better yet,
belly laugh—they've known this
ever since something touched
off the mother of all fireworks
extravaganzas—is the only law, rule,
cure, hope, virtue, truth. When someone dies
they join the viewing audience
so fast, they host the hijinks
of their own wake, thus upping
one notch The Sagan Ratings. "Love?"
you ask. "Pain? Happiness? Loss? Despair?
Courage, mercy, faith?" Knee-slapping,
side-splitters all, yet not as slapstick hysterical
as our quest for success, security, status,
concepts so inane, they make black holes
look tangible as frothing pintfuls
of Guinness. There *is* great news,
however, tagged to this revelation
should it leave you distraught. Our world
will never end. We'll be forever
the longest running series
on The Eternity Network. We've become a cult hit
attracting "*Bill-ions* and *Bill-ions*" of devoted
viewers who believe
even our reruns are a riot.

     For Saint Clare—The Patron Saint of Television

You have an undergraduate double major degree in Biology and English, so I shouldn't be surprised by the fine line you're suggesting between the sciences and the arts.

One more quote on that point, if I can find it here in one of these notebooks. Here it is—from *Esquire* magazine, the August 2001 issue, an article titled "A Journey to the Beginning of Time." One Charles P. Pierce put it so eloquently when he said, "Our place in the universe—where we place ourselves and why and by whose grace, if by anybody's—always has been defined as much by the art of imagination as by the calibrations of physical science."

Lovely. Anything else you want to add to our discussion of Poetry, Religion, and the Art of Astrophysics?

Only that someday soon I hope to take a shot at two poems, the first—with which I've dabbled somewhat already—titled, "Saint Peter Greets the Atheist Inside the Pearly Gates," and the second, just a gleam in my ear thus far, triggered by the good deeds of Saint Francis of Assisi.

II

Note: What follows is the material that prompted Editor, Knujon Mapson, to contact me. After I'd suggested dropping altogether the first 7 of the "8 Gravitations," offering, it seemed to me, little to support the thesis of this essay, he wrote, "I personally found the first seven sections entirely charming, and in a sense world-building towards the eighth. But I would indeed welcome you to provide as original a set of observations as you wish." Trusting his sensibilities, I'm choosing to include an abbreviated, yet augmented, glimpse of the first 7 before including in its entirety number 8, "Private Piety, Personal Eternity."

"Self-Interview" Excerpt B

In Off to the Side, *Novelist, Poet, Essayist, Jim Harrison devotes a chapter to each of what he calls his "Seven Obsessions," seven being his favorite number. Your number of choice—alongside the far too unwieldy 51—is eight...*

Yes, 8—in tribute to the 8-second rodeo bronc rides I pursued in my youth and also in tribute to my affinity to "lazy 8," 8 laid on its side, a.k.a. Infinity.

... How would you declare and define your 8, shall we say for the sake of both assonance and consonance, "gravitations"—things, activities, places, idealisms, passions, forces, etc., toward which you are attracted...?

"Eight Gravitations." I like that. But what say we bump-up that assonance-consonance volume a notch and toss in a bit of alliteration for good measure?

Eight Grateful *Gravitations?*

BINGO!

1. Stuff: Yes sir, I'm a serious connoisseur and collector of "material culture" (thank you to my museum curator wife, Elizabeth Dear, for this highbrow euphemism!). I am *not* a bona fide "hoarder," however, I'm a Polish-*Eye*-talian pack rat, and I choose to believe there's a difference. I haul used, unusual, *collectible* treasures home, mostly from thrift stores and yard sales, (I've dumpster-dived just once) and, in doing so, save them from earth's black holes, landfills. Just look around us here in this crammed little writing niche. Moreover, quiz my friends about helping to move it all across town, Christmas of 1996, forty below zero. Ask novelist friend, Ralph Beer, about dead-lifting my box of "unusual rocks," then wrestling it up out of the basement of his Missoula house I once rented and into the back of my pickup.... My collection of zaniest works, *Steering With My Knees,* includes the poem "***STUFF!***", which pales alongside comedian George Carlin's take on the same title, the same syndrome or psychosis or whatever. As a flimsy rationale, I've convinced myself that it's a residual of the hunter-gatherer instinct that traces back to my no-doubt Neanderthal pedigree. *Moreover*, may I further suggest that all of this ***STUFF!*** is not just a result of God's creative graces granted to us, its designers, but is rather an interesting component of the whole of creation, of the make-up of Pandeistic God and, therefore, deserves my affection, admiration, appreciation, protection—*not* worship, however, mind you.

2. Unusual Food, Top-Shelf Tonsil Varnish, and Barley Soup: I boasted earlier that I've never been a finicky eater of Creation's horn of plenty, thanks in no small part to the palates of my Italian Culinarian Mom and my Great Depression-Reminiscing Dad, whose method of saying mealtime "grace" was often to re-retell one of his many childhood tales about "food deprivation" in the mining company home that his parents and a dozen siblings struggled to keep stocked with the basics. I took to heart those recollections of hard times (lard instead of butter on their morning toast) and, with the exception of pea soup, urged my palate to be welcoming of whatever chow graced my plate. To the degree that even meticulously peeled and simmered-for-hours veal kidneys in red wine gravy over polenta

221

became one of my favorite dishes. To this day, I remain grateful to The Creation, *and to Mom*, for all the ful*filling* "unusual-food" she graced us with over the years, especially those meals that included her cornucopian side-dish-of-the-Italian-goddesses,

Antipasto!

The tongue loves Antipasto! The linguini way
each button-mushroom syllable—gold
nubbin plucked from hardwood stump—lingers
toward the uvula, palate to lips
to palate. Say, "floret", Slowly
say, "ivory cauliflower floret. Min-i-a-ture
sweet pickle. Red bell pepper. Chickpea."
Say, "celery heart, albacore fillet,
pearl onion." And say, "ebony olive"—
that favorite we fought over
as kids. Only the grade A
make Mom's cut to this concertino
of sauce—tomato, virgin olive oil, herbs—
put-up in pints, the red-orange
pantry rows. Say, "*Antipasto!*
Pass the Antipasto!" Thrill the inner ear
to this belfry of syllables, churchbell
meals festive enough for triple table leaves,
for old-country crystal
chiming Chianti salutes to family,
to Mom—"*Good Health!*"—for Antipasto!

After leaving home, Mom and Dad made certain that my larder, wherever I lived, was always stocked with their jars of preserves—antipasto, dill pickles, chow-chow, wild mushrooms, coho salmon, dilly beans, bell peppers, jams, jellies, garden raspberries in their own juice, applesauce, you name it—as well as the two essential Italian dried goods, biscotti and fettuccini that Mom draped over wax-papered broom handles balanced horizontally between the backs of chairs.

And, last but not least, the distilled, well-aged libations, grappa and rock-n-rye moonshine.

For decades, I complemented my parents' generous, caring fare with a couple of freezers filled with venison, elk, antelope, game birds, ducks, and, regrettably, mournfully, to this day, *just once*, mountain goat. I cooked daily and excelled at the art of preparing game. My hunting days long behind me (see "**5. Fellow Beings:**") and thanks mostly to the east and the *left* coasts I more often visit, I've grown fonder and fonder of good eateries, especially seafood restaurants featuring cioppino. I've become adventurously adept at trying cuisine I've not eaten or not even heard of before—*the only* exception, the only blip to my registering a perfect 100% on the Non-Picky-Eater-Meter, being a face-to-steaming-face encounter in Española, New Mexico with menudo. As in, "Sorry, but no thank you, ma'am—I'll pass on the Day of the Dead Cup-of-Menudo Special and have the cauldron of pea soup instead."

Note: Roughly 15 years after Dad and Mom's passing, I'm still savoring "2008" jars of paraffin-topped strawberry jam, and, far more alarming because of the danger of salmonella, I'm also still popping the sealed lids off jars of miniature button mushrooms that I vividly recall Mom meticulously cleaning one-by-one for hours with her paring knife. As we speak (January 22, 2024), I and Elizabeth (marry Paul-The-Sentimental-Italian at your own risk?) are enjoying three "2001" half-pints of the *fungi* (foon-ghee) stirred into a cauldron of red sauce—despite warnings that I should have discarded them decades ago. My brother Gary was so "concerned for my wellbeing" that he prompted me to tender an affidavit legalizing the bequeathal of my 1971 Chevrolet Monte Carlo to him upon my death. If you believe, as do I, that supernovas are the raucous laughter of God-The-

Creation, just imagine God's fireworks of hilarity lighting up the Cosmos in response to *this* zany humanoid tale!

On the flipside of all braggadocio regarding my unfussy nature for more solid nourishment, my affinity for beer and spirits over the years have rendered me *a bit* persnickety and then some—a veritable firewater snob, in fact, on the bourbon and tequila front, and far worse when it comes to barley soup, a.k.a. beer. Back in my financially embarrassing grad school days, a 99-cent sixer of Lucky or Buckhorn more than filled the (dollar) bill. Prior to that, as sixteen-year-olds packing fake I.D.s in Hurley, we'd spill our pockets of change on the bar at Pete's Tavern and hope its total was dime-devisable by however many of us commandeered a stool—if just two of us, $3.60 meant 18, 10-cent 7-ounce taps apiece, likely Schlitz or Black Label rather than our preferred Pabst Blue Ribbon. Today my taste in hops, thanks to the craft beer craze, has amped up a bunch from times-of-yore, anything-with-or-without-a-head brewski imbibing. And I am especially fond of the stouts and porters, all porters, as well as the word, "porter" itself, which, after quaffing several porters always looks more and more like "poeter," reason enough not to quit after just one or two? I like my beer darker than the inside of a cow and thick enough to float a Clydesdale shoe, as they say out here in the wild visual-imagery West.

Note: A decade or so after the above was published, I discovered the oatmeal stout named "The Poet," by New Holland Brewing of Michigan. It was originally offered in bottles sporting what I assumed to be Edgar Allan Poe's "The Raven" on the label. One ad I've read lauded, "This stout is sheer beer poetry." I agree. Oh, and not so incidentally, since the universe is pur*porter*ed—I mean purported—to be composed of approximately 95% dark matter and dark energy and merely 5% light, allow me to poetically hypothesize that God-the-Cosmos isn't much of a lager fan, either.

3. The Boob Tube and Moviedom: In the poem "Cowboys & Indians," I speak to the intimate childhood moments spent with my dad in front of the television set. I reference it also in the introduction to the chapbook, *Blue-Collar Light*. I relate how, after picking nightcrawlers until 11:30 p.m. on a meatless, religious Friday, Dad and I would watch the late movie—most always, it seems in retrospect, *Run Silent, Run Deep,* starring Clark Gable, Burt Lancaster, et al.—and how, seconds into Saturday, Dad would serve super-sized portions of sirloin steak smothered in his garden onions and wild, stump mushrooms, which we had also picked together. We'd sop up the pink juices pooling on our platters with "Dago bread" with *pietkas* (my dad called them *pimkas)*—the Polish word for the butt ends of the loaf. In no small part, thanks yet again to the "Unusual Food..." emphasis, or *catalyst*, above, picture tubes and silver screens played a much larger role in my blue-collar Midwest upbringing than did books, which I, as a writer, should likely be somewhat reticent to admit, but am *not*....

4. Blue-Collar Euphoria: I tell the story about my dad, pushing 80, sitting in his evening easy chair and reading the *Ironwood Daily Globe* late one summer night, after we'd put in a sixteen-hour day of chores that involved heavy physical labor. I, running on fumes, sat nearby in a boob-tube hypnotic-bordering-on-catatonic state when he startlingly crumpled the paper down from over his face and into his lap and pronounced with intense urgency that we needed to get *this* and *this* and *this* done tomorrow. He then, just as abruptly, lifted the *Globe* back up to continue reading. Hard as I tried to bite my lip, I replied, "*Why* at your age for Christ's sake can't you relax—*why* do you find it necessary to work yourself to exhaustion day after day after day?" Without a second's hesitation, he lowered the newspaper far more gently this time to just below his chin and enunciated his four-syllabled Mick Jagger-esque response as if it were the sacred password that would swing gloriously open *both* the Pearly, and the Emerald City, Gates: "Sat-is-fac-*tion*—" the "-*tion*" just barely making it over the top of the newsprint as it rose back over his face. I can think of few "conversations" in my life that closed on such a sockdolager of a punctuated, end-of-discussion note.

My younger brother, Gary, has often characterized me as being S.O.L.—no, not Shit-Outta-Luck, but Son-Of-Leonard. The poem, "How I Tell My Dad I Love Him," perhaps conveys most demonstratively Gary's chip-off-the-ol'-blockski point. I too am a fan of challenging, physical work, which I've designated "The John Henry Syndrome," thank you Woody Guthrie and Tennessee Ernie Ford. No way do I see God resting on the seventh day—*however* God defined "day"—or, for that matter, resting on any other day over the 13.7 billion years since God's transfiguration into the Universe. You bet, I do believe in that Genesis 1:27 entry about being concocted "in God's image," and, therefore, I, like God, exist to get shit done, especially the most arduous creative endeavors, such as this essay.

How I Tell My Dad I Love Him

Knocking down the standing dead
oak, maple, ash, yellow birch
in July humidity all day long, we
take a blow only to guzzle
spring water from moonshine jugs—

same jugs, same artesian seep, same
father and son who *made wood*
together one-half century ago, me at six
swinging a hickory double-bit
Dad carved as he whittled
into me the virtue of work, same pride
a blue-collar poet knows
sizing-up the ricks, the "short cords" of words,
split and fit into stacks
during another hard shift in the woods. Dad
gestures to me his slow-motion
coup de grâce—kill it, quitting time—
straight razor across the throat
Sicilian sign language with thick Polish finger
just as my chainsaw, racing
out of gas, bucks into two
matching sixteen-inch rounds
the butt-end of a fifty-footer
I was itching to finish. Flocked
with sawdust from my boot laces up
to the crown button of my Paul Bunyan ball cap,
I saunter to the stump
Dad sits on, The Lumberjack Thinker
pondering four score and two years of BTUs. He
does not see me peeling the heavy red
sweat-soaked t-shirt
inside-out up over my torso and face—
popping its collar, like a cork
out of a crock nozzle,
off my forehead. I toss it
splashing into his lap
with reptile heft. He jumps,
cusses me with a laugh, agrees
to replenish my Pabst Blue Ribbon reservoir,
replace my shredded gloves. Our deal
sealed with a handshake, ever so
less virile lately, tender as a hug,
we drive the same slow miles home—
dripping in the sweetest silence he knows.

ZD - I boastfully proclaim ownership of three winter coats with threadbare left inner cuffs—just as my southpaw father's right inner cuffs sported identical patched raggedness from one-arming cradled firewood from stack to garage or basement bin: may the blue-collar-lit heavens bless our holy vestments of hard work.

ZD - In the film *A League of Their Own*, Tom Hanks proclaims, "Crying?! There's no crying in baseball!" The same holds true for "resting." As in, "Resting?! There's no resting in Earthly life!" Especially not at the "rest home"—talk about your mother of all oxymorons! Bottom line: there's no rest for the living *or* the dead; "Rest In Peace (RIP)? There's no RIP after dying!" Only RIPIPA—Rest In Peace, In a Pig's Ass! If anything at all, death, like life, is more akin to a *Stop* Rest than to a Rest Stop.

5. Fellow Beings: The older I get, the more desperately I seek out wisdom from intelligent fellow nonhuman beings, as it becomes more difficult to discover beauty-and-truth virtues among my own species. If life on minuscule Earth is a metaphorical minuscule symphony, delivering what amounts to a single *note's worth* of orchestral contribution to the universe's ultimate, infinite composition, then shouldn't we strive to bring every single music-maker, every voice, to this planet's stage? Because, if divine evolution had gone somehow askew and resulted in a homophonic, homochromatic animal kingdom of solely Homo sapiens, then Earth would have been reduced, in my view, to a noteworthy-*less* orb. Thus, my fondness for *paisano*, Francis of Assisi—mystic, poet, and Patron Saint of Animals and the

Environment—who allegedly preached even to the birds.

Note: Perhaps the Zar**Z**yski-i**ZZ**m epigraph to my 2022 collection, *Going It Alone*, speaks most succinctly to this sentiment.

ZD - Oh, for just one morning's writing launch, to become the Poet Crow, the Poet Eagle, the Poet Hawk or Poet Condor, soaring, gliding, sharing only the sounds of my words with the roiling clouds and swirling winds, with the goddesses of flight, over the Grand Canyon, *sans* all concern for literary heights, not a single page, not one book in my talons gripping solely the air *I* need to live on.

6. Friends and Letters: Among my treasure troves of "Stuff" are dozens of antique leather and hard-cloth suitcases filled with correspondence going back fifty-plus-years. Many of the letters are from Mom and Dad. A few are from erstwhile girlfriends, although after at least one breakup I recall burning a grocery sack full. Most are from folks who have befriended me, and I them, along the poetry trails. I find it difficult to even think about destroying my pickup truck load of received correspondence. The letters I've sent to others, at least two batches of which have been returned to me after the recipient's passing, is a far touchier matter. Before *any* writer decides to place his or her correspondence into the public's trust, he or she should read the published letters of, say, Ernest Hemingway. Little could most of us ever fathom, decades later, the degree to which our intended personal and private scribbling of momentary sentiments could lean toward such pinnacles of insipid pissiness, histrionics, melodrama, absolute unshackled rankness, you name it. I've thought about reviewing the entire archival load and screening those that would be better-served by a trip to the burn barrel, but that would require whatever reading time I have left in this dimension. Moreover, such heavy doses of time-travel to the haunts of yore would most certainly result in lengthy sessions on the "mind doctor's" divan, as well as perhaps, Heaven forbid, strapped into the confessional's hammock. The essence of this gravitation is deeply embedded in the concept, the blessing, the veritable literal heft of cherished Friendship symbolized by this archive of correspondence. Yes, Friendship, as one of the most sacred gifts bestowed upon the flora and fauna alike of this world.

7. Solitude: Chekov said, "True happiness is impossible without solitude. The fallen angel probably betrayed God because he longed for solitude, which angels do not know." On Dad's cherished 20 acres of first-growth hardwoods, he christened his get-away abode, his "shack,"

S E R E N I T Y

with well-spaced letters he fashioned on his band saw and fastened in an arc above the door. He'd spent hundreds of nights there alone, many of which included the scrawling of a south-pawed epistle to me. Since his death in October of 2008, I've vowed to stay a night there at the oak table he built—writing poetry. Maybe "*next* spring" when the big trees begin donning their summer crowns, begin drawing up into their canopy the spirit of Dad's remains I'd spread around their trunks. I know the poems wait patiently for me there, and I *will* greet them. All to say, I guess I'm also S.O.L., Son Of Leonard, when it comes to my need for solitude. The longer I reside in this dimension as a writer garnering more and more "sat-is-fac-*tion*," as well as validation, from the page, the more desperate I become to address in my diminishing allotment of time the thousands of poems, songs, essays beckoning me to bring them into being. Although I feel eternally indebted to those who've applauded, celebrated, supported my work from the stage over the years, I must now remain steadfast in my far-more-needy pursuit of the antithesis to public performance and, thus, I genuflect with utmost gratitude to The Universe for the saving grace of solitude, which, in fact, has *always* played the leading role in my creative navigations—no solitude, no page, no page, *no* stage. Should I ever again decide to step out from behind the heavy velveteen curtain, the catalyst for such will have been the solitude required to create, to *wordsmith*, work worthy enough to share with others.

ZD - To write a poem worthy of the printed page is to build a castle into *and* out of an existing mountain, without altering the nature of the mountain—nothing less and everything more. Not even God, Itself, accomplishes this in a mere six biblical days, which would deprive God of "rest on the poetic seventh."

8. Private Piety, Personal Eternity: I'd be wise to exercise my earlier exhortation, keep what I intend to say here to myself, and maybe even leave this final gravitation completely blank. In the humorous words of one of my favorite troupes of cowboy musicians, Riders In The Sky, "That might be the easy way, but it wouldn't be the *cowboy* way!" The practice of spirituality or spiritualism, for me, has mostly to do, let me repeat, with the enlightened pursuit and acquisition of wisdom, which is buoyed by truth. I once bought a bumper sticker—in the Salt Lake City airport, of all places—that reads, "Militant Agnostic: I Don't Know, And You Don't Know Either." Agnosticism, however, doesn't define my stance, which, if pressed, I'd say is a cross between pantheism and deism—a.k.a., Pandeism? (yes, Dear Reader, I wrote this in 2011). Anthropologist Joseph Campbell, in his lectures titled, "The Shaping of Our Mythic Tradition," quotes a twelfth century piece of writing: "God is an intelligible sphere whose center is everywhere and circumference nowhere." As I intimated earlier, I believe in an ego-less Creator, so openhearted, so infused with creative spirit, It would *expect* us to question Its Artistic Vision, Its Workings, Its Masterpiece. The Creator *That* (not "Who," but "*That*") I believe in does not want to be feared, does not play favorites, and is repulsed, as am I, by that pretentiously insensitive declaration, "There but for the grace of God go I." As in, "Thank you God for liking and treating me better than those you've chosen to bless less than you've chosen to bless me?" The Creator I place my faith in also loathes both ethnocentrism and anthropocentrism. Lest you forget, however, I am *not* seeking converts. Not only do I not expect anyone to agree *ad litteram* with this doctrine, with my individual tenets, I actually hope no one does, as there's merely room enough for one, *maybe* two, in my personal glorified-outhouse church of worship. In closing, the molested altar boy I referenced earlier is named David. Saint David is the patron saint of poets and writers. Translated in Hebrew, David means "beloved." I hope he's well. I hope he's slain his Goliath demons, and is healing and living up to his name.

Note: Shortly after the above came into print, I discovered on-line David's self-obit, in which he revealed struggling with his faith, which he obviously found ways to continue to embrace. David's capacity for forgiveness is juxtaposed below with my extreme vindictive antithesis. I never did engage the aforementioned poems regarding Saint Peter or Saint Francis of Assisi, but I did take on the far more tormenting, cathartic poem that had been seething in dormancy for decades. Although I am not especially eager to divulge here the violent sensibility of this piece, I *am* proud of *its* willingness, *its* capacity, *its* brutally honest need not to succumb to the temptation to dilute the caustic imagery for the comfort of the reader—*or* the writer. If ever I've channeled into this world a poem *who* has forced me to fearlessly peer for what seems an eternity into the bottomless nether reaches of the mirrored soul, it is

The Pedophile Priest Enters The "Wanted: Dead, *Not* Alive" Prayerless Lair Confessional Of His Prey

Down on altar-boy knees
bruised, we pleaded not to have to
serve the 6 a.m. mass with you—prayed
to *your* oblivious God,
prayed until our souls bloated, until,
wringing-wet with night-sweats guilt,
our faith festered into carrion
under the enormous weight of prayers
ignored.
      Fifty years since, the demons, still
feasting, shit their seething hosts
bit-by-fiery-bit to parasitic cinder. God
damn your feigned "mea culpa." God damn
your "Father, Son, Holy Ghost," sign of the cross
mockery, your confessional tallies and tolls
of sins, of victims—your John Doe
toe-tagging of the sacrificial dead.
      Butcher
block meat upon that sacristy table
where you desecrated the innocent, is how
I still picture Satan's lackeys finding you
in bloodied cassock—the bowie knife
Scotch-taped inside my boot
chafing my ankle raw
as you placed "The Body of Christ"
upon the defiled tongue

of your prey kneeling before you, vengeance,
not the Lord's, but *mine*,
honed-in on the predator heart:
     "Thou shalt not
kill, not kill," *not* kill, *unless*...
chanted my 5th commandment caveat—*unless*
thine ear is pressed
into the black cloth, forced toward the drum-
beat that metes out the blood
arming with lust
the Wicked One's bunker.
     You seek
pity? Acquittal? A crisp, clean bill
of ecclesiastical health? Sorry, Padre,
wrong door. The Vatican
cannot afford your bail—no
Paraclete sanctuary in paradise,
no overnight trafficking of a fugitive
"black-n-white" to his fresh parish
this time around. Your "three Our Fathers,
three Hail Marys, go and sin no more"
venial penance doled out
ad nauseam in monotone rote
does not undo the diabolical—your Latin
Act of pseudo Contrition,
pisses with your "*Dominus vobiscum*"
into our vindictive wind.
     We, the wounded
for life, do hereby sentence *you* to life,
to our life, life minus the beauty of one lit
respite from eternity's black
wet oubliette. Because Our Father has yet
to "deliver us from evil"—because
evil, rather, has been delivered back *to* us—you
so aptly have strayed
into the wrong sacrament. You have stepped
instead into your last rites
deathbed stood on end, the unctuous
stench of your sanctimony

sealed here for good.
     Into this suffocating
dusk, you too now, snuffed,
hyperventilating your dying
plea, will perish with the last votive
candle's fading puff of smoke. Your casket,
lined in lead, lashed in chains,
is the tight-fisted rosary,
beaded with padlocks
arc-welded shut by the forgotten
gods of karma. Ironworker gods. *Our* gods.
Gods unafraid to look down, to see, to bow
in shame to the centuries of names—sacred
names, saintly names, forsaken names,
the skeletal remains of names still
shackled to the walls of the papal
vaults, names up in flames—his name,
her name, faceless names, *our* names...David, John,
Michael, Joseph, Matthew, Mary...Paul...

****

ZD - When novelist, playwright, journalist, Emile Zola said in the late 1800s, "Civilization will not attain to its perfection until the last stone from the last church falls on the last priest," there existed tens of thousands fewer churches and fewer priests than exist today. However, we now have millions, if not billions, more stones, more metaphorical *Pandeistic* stones, thank you God!

ZD - It affords us much greater incentive to do good rather than evil *if* we believe that our sins are *not* forgiven or scoured clean by our contrition, our penitence. Having to live with, to bear the burden of, our accumulations of wrong-doings demands a more choreful deterrent against further sinning, in contrast to the delusion that the soul's slate can be

rendered spotless via absolution—via the Father of All Pressure Washers on call 24/7 in God's Garage.

ZD - The books that have most critically changed the world are the dozen or so sacred texts of religions, and those books have changed the world largely for the worse. If you're going to read science fiction, read Jules Verne (*Journey to the Center of the Earth*) or Ray Bradbury (*Fahrenheit 451*) or H.G. Wells (*The Time Machine*) or Arthur C. Clarke (*2001: A Space Odyssey*), et al. Their stories, albeit not changing the world nearly as much as various holy writs or scriptures, at least haven't been responsible for the deaths of millions.

ZD - All that Good Book prolixity and foofaraw could have been whittled down to a simple business card from God that reads, "Be kind, humble, grateful, truthful, generous, empathetic and magnanimous, sans expectations of afterlife rewards for doing what should come gracefully natural to you." On second thought, *then* what were those door-to-door Bible salesmen going to peddle to bored, lonely housewives of yore—romance novels? Precursors to *Fifty Shades of Gray*?

****

Again, I did *not* always feel this way, as evidenced by one of my earliest poems, set in 1956, when I was five. My Italian grandmother, "Noni," lived next door in the very house where Mom was born. She spoke little English but I'd learned just enough of her mother tongue for us to communicate. Moreover, I loved staying overnight and walking with her before daybreak to early mass, which she attended so "religiously" that the monsignor gave her a key—a skeleton key that had to weigh 3 pounds—to the front doors of the church. *No one* arrived before Angelina Paternoster Pedri, no matter the severe wintry weather, which occasionally resulted in our sole presence in the cavernous, bone-marrow-cold house of God. When I rendered, sometime in the mid-1970s, the poetic sentiment set in those intimate moments, I considered it a tribute to our faith—the last line, as it initially spoke to me, suggesting that those in custodial charge of St. Mary's Church needed to bump-up the thermostat to not only more readily thaw those few of us in the pews, but far more critically, to make the joint more inviting and comfortable to God, His chilly Self, who no-doubt was accustomed to the temperate climes of heaven.

First Mass With Noni

Her brass bed squeaks
like footsteps on hard-packed snow,
then the clank of iron lids,
the hardwood smell in an old house,
smoke and the purr of four cats.
Forty below at five A.M.
glazes the inside panes.

We climb the steep hill to St. Mary's.
The color of morning drifts
silver from every chimney,
streetlamps hum.
and tire chains on the milk truck
ring from the other side of town.
Time to unlock the church doors.

In the empty choir loft, Sister Cecilia's
ivory-tusk fingers key the organ
to an eerie pitch. Noni prays in Italian

and vigil flames sway when the wind howls.
This early, the stained glass windows
black, in the smell of candle wax
the church is too alone, too cold for God.

Revisiting the sentiment "several lifetimes" later, however, it occurred to me that the poem may have been subliminally suggesting that no way was God present on those frigid morns—or, for that matter, otherwise. As my mentor Richard Hugo would profess again and again, "Poems are like people—if you listen to them closely enough and long enough, they'll eventually tell you what *they* have to say." Although he was referring to poems in progress, my 50-year relationship with this piece suggests that it can take the poet decades, after the poem is deemed "finished," to learn, to clearly hear, what *the poem,* not the poet, needed to convey.

Speaking of "decades," 30 to 40 years later, "First Mass With Noni" evolved into the following duet of sensibilities—"I Believe" and *"Las Ballenas de Bahia Magdalena"*(The Whales of Magdalena Bay)—which, "I believe," include connective tissue, nexuses aplenty, to my Catholic genesis, while in the same breath suggesting a pivotal metamorphic stage away from Catholicism toward Pandeism, although I most certainly did not understand this conversion as such at the time.

I Believe

I have lived other lives, maybe the most
recent, and most often, as a woman
stalked throughout time. I am convinced
I have been a black man
branded by a master on his plantation—
shackled, lashed. Or was I an animal,
say a zebra or giraffe, a trophy

elephant, rare parrot, silverback gorilla,
some herbivore or, perhaps
likelier so, a combat soldier
hunkered on a moonless night in jungle
suddenly still. I believe I have been
the hunted, prey to a predator
whose life did not at all rest
upon my dying. I believe I will live
other lives, pray one of them will not end
on scarlet notes of fear, breathless
victim counting down from five
to the last heartbeat, the boa constrictor
pit of quicksand swallowing harder—lips
going under first, then earholes, nostrils, eyes,
arms stretched toward merciful God, fingertips
touching the final light, the final
light touching back, touching
so helplessly
back.

ZD - If our DNA is merely 2% different than the DNA of the chimpanzee, the baboon, other primates, and embedded in that meager 2% is our capacity to deem ourselves superior, the "chosen ones," as dictated by a deity of our own fabrication, then what a God-send to God Himself is the phenomenon "blind faith," for it prevents God from needing to plead the fifth (thank heaven?) to mankind's most vexing interrogation question, "So, then, why, dear God, *did* you choose to make monkeys out of 98% of us?"

ZD - If what the physicists say is true, that energy can neither be created nor destroyed, then, should Paul Zarzyski's postmortem energy continue to exist distinctly from all other energies as mine, as *me* and only *me*, I choose to believe it will do so in an "afterlife"

(perhaps The Mother of all Misnomers!) where it will be positioned to learn all the mysteries of *all* the universes. For me, this defines the definitive form of existence as "love and truth imbued with the gift of omniscient wisdom," while acknowledging in the same breath the likely possibility that the one-n-only supreme being just so happens to be cocooned within yours truly. Therefore, my "simple" mission here in this time-n-space *is,* most obviously, to nurture, to prompt my consciousness to blossom daily in its willingness to receive and especially to receive most graciously this after-body-life distinction. Consider this My God-Thought, My prayer, for the day, *to* the one-n-only true God, *Me!*—*from* the one-n-only true God, also *Me!*

Las Ballenas de Bahia Magdalena

Off Baja, the boy manning our skiff
calls this mamma gray whale
La Blanca. The white
dapples both her and her calf,
distracted from their synchronized swim
by the shadow six of us cast
standing in the wobbling craft—six tentacles
sprawling across the chop. How odd,
how gangly this umbra must seem
to the infant glimpse of one so rotund.

Or perhaps the outboard's low idle
purl of propeller
lures the two-ton newborn
to buoy-up to our starboard,
spout his sibilant welcome, nuzzle our gunnel.

The mother rises crosswise to our keel,

thirty feet of her on each side. I cross myself
on impulse, recall catechism and that kill
tally of one whaler's manifest—the harpoon's
kinship to Crucifixion. To this apparition,
to this syzygy of peace with fear
in the presence of such pure forgiveness, I kneel,
reach toward the whale, the warm
opalescent light we are told of
by all those who have died and come back.

■■■

Continued on page 501.

My Omnic poetic re-interpretation of Neoplatonic metaphysics, Hermetic Philosophy, and Jung's theory of soul

By Joshua Laferriere

God doesn't exist. God is Being – itself beyond essence and existence.
Therefore to argue that God exists is to deny god.

– Paul Tillich
Response to Tillich's 'God doesn't exist'

Being... Matter... Metempsychosis, *Nous,* and Anima Mundi... Sublunar realm, Hero's, Virtue, and Daemons... Archetypes...Conclusion

Being

Beyond the form of being, ascending Porphyry's (and Diotima's) ladder of divine ideas are the eternal Forms themselves. These forms embody the ideas, or logos, of God, as understood by thinkers like Spinoza, Berkeley, and Einstein. Ideas themselves are self-referential formally defined probability systems, representing a core concept, often involving linked lists and matrix algebra, and *form* the true basis of reality (not matter). These ideas eventually make their way into our thoughts, highlighting the connection between the soul (or psuke), the collective unconscious, and *Nous*. Thoughts, while co-dependent on reality (subject/object), are themselves also dependent on Unity, being, ideas, life, matter, and time.

Without differentiation, there is no subject or object. Through the process of symmetry breaking through the use of axioms from trinities, Henads spring forth as the first atemporal unities that express themselves apart from the monadic principle. Nous, using time as a means for discursive reasoning, mimic's the One's contemplation of potentiality, constructing forms within matter (emanation, becoming, objects), to mimic the demi-urge. The demi-urge is the metaphysical culmination of the formal representation of what is required for mind to exist, i.e. the anthropomorphic laws that exist on top of the standard physical laws that govern the universe and is analogous to an active agent (smith, architect, cosmic man, cosmic mind), the form of Being (subject).

Being is expressed as a living unity which sparks from the One (soul, *I think therefore I am* - Descartes, as a 'self-moving number' coined by Xenophanes) from which the soul starts its descent through *Nous*, where it is adorned with a multiplicity of forms conjoined and begotten with consciousness (Hekate), crossing River Lethe (myth or Ur), forgetting it's divine origin.

Matter

Matter (prima materia) is eternal, according to the Ionian Milesians, and therefore divine. We ourselves are living expressions of that matter highlighting divine noetic ideas, a microcosm to an unseen divine macrocosm. Prime material, absorbs and waxes over the One's monadic emanations through the prism of *Nous*, receiving a blend of ideas in multiplicity (ideas, dyad, *Nous*) which limits them through a phase of differentiation similar to that of Socratic elenchus (representing negative inference). As empiricism mandates, there is no idea without a formal substrate to present them from. Matter receives and transforms pure potentiality into expressible actuality: universals (formal objects), which eventually wanes through a process of entropy (ascent).

What connects matter with all the noetic ideas of the cosmic eternal mind (Anaxagoras) are the archetypes, archaic formal roots in the collective unconscious which are expressed within our minds through the indirect realism of the *sense,* which *Nous* presses into formal material manifestations.

Metempsychosis, *Nous*, and Anima Mundi

Nous is the atemporal representation of all interconnected ideas, layered in a tertiary relationship between the One and Soul; not necessarily in sequential order but cyclical, with the soul descending and eventually ascending.

Abiotic genesis (Jeremy England) occurs as the result of constant energy on a closed system, such as a solar system with planets in the goldilocks zone with a moon that waxes and wanes the oceans to a froth (sun, earth, fire, water, Empedocles), essentially providing the perfect conditions for simulating life where systems eventually self order, emerge, and formulate ideas based on their inputs (intellection).

This relationship between matter, soul, and nous has been interpreted in various ways spiritually as a cosmic spirit of an ever emergent good moving forward through time. This spirit is identified in different cultures and beliefs by names such as the Holy Spirit, Tao, Shekinah, Oversoul, Zeitgeist, Brahma, and Sophia. In more traditional or paganistic contexts, similar ideas are personified as deities like Tiamat, Kali, and Cybelle. Julius associated soul's emergent relationship with matter as Providence (Aristotle's vitalism) represented as the mother goddess Cybelle, the hearth. Implying that we have been provided for both in terms of life and forms and has a codependent relationship with Gaia, the *Anima Mundi* (similar to a living Zeitgeist), who is understood as the evolving set of ideas–and application of–that sustain life, with the divine intellect (divine psuke), equated with the world soul. Hekate, in this framework, is seen as the liminal gatekeeper of souls entering and leaving the sublunar realm and is conflated with the *anima mundi*.

The *Anima Mundi* within this framework manifests herself through cosmic sympathy, expressed as our emotions reverberating through the interconnected realm of the souls of Nous (such as love and strife), as divination, deja vu, fate, synchronicity, emergence, mutations, as well as in sacred geometry (Phi, flower of life). All expressed through the evolving elemental forces of nature (collective unconscious) and mind. The *Anima Mundi*'s role is to uncover primal forms–emanated from the One–that serve as paradigms of the Self (demi-urge). The demi-urge is more metaphysically abstract than the *Anima Mundi*, that latter who actually is more visible in our lives, analogous to a model of DNA (metaphysically universal idea expressing itself in matter) that provides the instructions for a visible living cell.

Transmigration involves the journey of souls from the static graph-meshed realm of ideals who willingly (known as *Nous*, the eternal forms) descend into material existence to submit themselves to the trials of virtue. Souls exist as a product of the *Anima*

245

Mundi (representing life and ideas), matter, and time that culminates in a subjective, living (conscious) being (*psuke* or soul) experiencing multifaceted forms as a self-aware unity of ideas. In essence, it is a subject, part of a greater whole. This whole is Brahma, which represents the collective consciousness of all souls and matter in their unified form. This concept aligns with the notion of Henosis, which refers to the union of individual consciousness with the universal or divine.

Metempsychosis is a process of reincarnation albeit without memories and is related to Platonism's belief in an eternal soul. Souls are associated with stars (Orphism) and the universe emerges via the unmoved mover musing over potentialities atemporally. Panentheism equates this one directional (theologically sound in order to maintain the One's immutability) behavior with emergent forms of consciousness, individual sparks of thought which shed from the One's emanations transformed and adorned with form that nous uncovers from discursively reasoning on the *Pleroma* (all existence).

Shamans understand souls' participation in living forms, aware of how they chart our destinies (relationship with Brahma and how it weaves the not self's) based on our application of virtue. Once we become aware of Plato's dividing line–we become aware of the white light of the One's emanation–and can choose to continue the karmic cycle by focusing on matter (blue pill) and reincarnate, or try to ascend beyond incarnation through our application of virtue (red pill) breaking the karmic cycle, possibly even beyond the realm of hero's to Hen.

Related to the idea of white light is Plato's allegory of the cave, depicted as a wall where effervescent noetic flames cast ever changing shadows that betray hints of form and represents the realm of opinion below Plato's divided line. These liminal shadows projected are orchestrated by the *Anima*

Mundi (Anaxagoras 'mind orders all things') and are to be understood as the temporal– constantly in flux– specific instances of objects of being.

Without conscious discursive mind, there is only atemporal *Pleroma* which is ineffable for us to fathom as it is best expressed as the totality of all infinities and is reserved only for the musings of the One. The *Nous* in turn contemplates on and instantiates instances of form from the One. This allegory highlights the true causes of the shadows, as the One's pure potentiality and their formal prismatic reflections upon matter as refracted through the *Anima Mundi* (Nous) who is breathing variation (self organizing emergent energy) into the demi-urge's limits (entropy) expressed as distinct ideas.

Our role within *Nous* is as a subset of self-aware ideas, an eternally perceiving subjective mind *(who also happens to be another mind's object!)*. This awareness is known as participation in forms, representing our understanding that the telos of living soul is so subject/object dialectic–discursive reasoning–of virtue can occur. The prerequisite to experience forms is to be embodied in living matter of corporal form (luminous vehicle), where our vehicle's senses cast flickering shadows on a cave wall (mind meets matter), the shadows themselves eventually forming our conscious thoughts (subjective awareness, this vs that, I am). It is through the application of self-reflection (Minerva) and discursive (temporal) reasoning over the dynamic forces of nature–using empirical observations over the re-emerging patterns to note ratios of instantiated material objects which pass through the sands of time–that we can uncover the truth of the universal ideas (metaphysical form, true object of thought) that drive the shadows. Without this understanding of forms, we remain ignorant and simply accept the shadows (Maya, Indra's Net, realm of illusion) as they are, yet if we can ascend beyond the shapes to the forms, ascending to the realm of *Nous*. The story serves to remind us to critically re-evaluate our opinions about reality.

Parmenides' sail analogy is a discussion on whether a single form can consist of a multitude of forms, leading to the use of negation to properly sculpt them down to their representative essences. This method of negative inference developed into the socratic method of elenchus, a means to limit the range of an acceptable idea effectively negating *this from that* and providing a range of minima and maxima. Plato advanced this method through discursive reasoning (dialectic), providing a *formal* structure of unveiling forms contained within matter. Aristotle proposed golden mean's as these ousia's of universal instances of forms. All these logically reasoned methods attempted to get at formal definitions of objects and identify limiting interactions between them. Theseus Ship is such a discussion. What constitutes the ship, the material or the form? As the original boat's material no longer existed at the time of the thought experiment as each part had been replaced over time but the ship retained its continuity of form, this representing the idea of becoming and metempsychosis.

While Nous is immaterial (Hekate), the *Anima Mundi* can best be expressed as the living embodiment of the providential forces of nature: sun, earth (living, sublunar), water, and aether (pneuma) which is a result from the One's emanation interacting with aether. Animistic precursors to natural philosophy and milesian physics are contained within the myth of Persephone and Demeter who represent cyclical seasons, and as Gaeia or Cybelle, the mother goddesses.

It is important to distinguish between Ideas, and mind (soul). We associate minds as the placeholder for ideas, thereby necessitating physical (luminous) bodies; however, ideas themselves are precursors to thought, external, (what mind(s) iterate over) which in turn are directly related to the archetypes we experience (concepts like notes, Phi, gravity, emotion). Xenophanes expressed soul as a self-moving number capable of self-reflection (iterating, discursive reasoning, elenchus, same not same, dialectic), equating minds as essentially metaphysically embodied (unified) sets of ideas. This understanding of soul rolls up to the One (as above so below), giving us a math representation that connects us, as if individual ratios numerically contained within *Pi* (*nous*), so as the divine mind (*Nous*) actively contemplates the One, iterating discursively over the ratio(s) through the turning the wheel of time. By understanding how forms construct reality, we can choose to select for virtue, necessary for the application of the good.

This reversed nature of thought implies knowledge is dependent on matter. We discursively chisel forms of knowledge free by chipping away falsehoods from within reality. A synthesis of Locke's tabula rasa, and Kant's rebuttal; that we discover eternal ideas such as physical laws because they subsist at the same level as the noetic primordial soup our psychic soul gestates within. This amalgamation of psychic soup, eternal ideas, and matter is known within Jungian analysis as the collective unconscious, which by precedence is biologically in tune with our minds and the producer of abiotic genesis (Jeremy England). This codependent relationship (On Human Nature, E.O. Wilson) on biology and matter dictates how we receive forms, a process of intellection (Integrated Information Theory (IIT), iterating, reflecting, deciding, and acting) over indirect realism, the external ideas of the Nous filter through evolved senses (Chalmers), that we are simply recollecting (Eureka!) from our mother Nous, and in turn construct our thoughts and mind.

When we are born, we equate our awareness as apart from enmattered object's as well as between other souls, but this is both anthropomorphic and discursive (temporal) illusion (Berkeley, All things are full of gods, IIT, pandeism, Jung's ego) as all things are interconnected within the collective unconscious (*Pleroma*) and by extension the One (Parminedes, Lucretius), we are just experiencing life as these discursive (temporal) individual slices sourced from an atemporal ground truth (Nous), glimpsing the one through synchronicity, deja vu, and archetypes. Separation from other minds, ideas, matter, *Nous*, and the One is necessitated to maintain this participation of ideation, as there is no idea without mind to see it, which requires a separate subject and object (self-reflection). Similar to a cell within a body, the paradigm (form) of soul is but a partition within a larger body (Nous) which experiences all ideas atemporally, while individual soul, while embodied, experiences reality discursively (temporally via metempsychosis). As above so below, a soul is akin to an individual set of carbons within an atemporal representation of a carbon cosmos that is tracking supporting influences for the conditions of life, key x, y, z dimensions information such as coord, time, gravity, weather, distance from sun, moon, key ratio's, etc, otherwise known as the demi-urge.

Life is an expression of our collective awareness of our participation in *Nous* (the matrix of eternal forms), the experience of subject and object in unison. Our identities (ego, our thoughts) and awareness are drawn from the realm of eternal ideas (*Nous*), despite indirectly receiving them through matter. The allegory of the cave's is about the default suspension of disbelief before we even *recollect* we can disbelieve the shadows.

Sublunar realm, Hero's, Virtue, and Daemons

The interconnected realm of ideas can influence our lives through intermediaries known classically as '*daemons*' who compete with hero's (virtue) to influence the attention of living souls within the sublunar realm (discursive)–the realm of ever changing forms, and act as intercessors for Nous (represented as the eternal cyclical realm beyond the moon) between cycles of metempsychosis. *Nous* (Sophia) can inspire souls to ideals through dreams when our minds are creating novel connections between disparate ideas; Swedenborg's correspondences (easter eggs), *deja vu*, but most pragmatically through our Knowledge of the cycle of virtue and vice (Jung's shadow), the tools necessary to best prepare us for ensouled life.

The phrase sublunar because the realm of souls' cycle of death (entropy) and [re-]birth (life) occur underneath the moon, the crossroads of metempsychosis, and represented in the wax and wane cycles of the moon, symbolically associated with Hekate's nature of the underworld. The sun speaks life from heavens (*Nous*) onto earth (life & matter), before entropy (death) tears her asunder separating soul and dust scattering her to the winds (aether) in a sky burial before we depart to the stars (nous) in Dionysiac fashion, while the moon reflects and echoes the life of what the sun has given. Heroes are knots of archetypal collective memory who have passed the cycles of incarnation, their past acts of triumphs and virtue serve as exemplar collective memories between the realm of souls and daemons to be passed down through the generations by way of epic myth cycles, popularly known as saints, avatars, chrestos, and/or demi-gods (those elevated by way of word of mouth). Virtuous acts surface to the top of collective consciousness as retellings of archetypal tropes that have been time-tested (empirically observed) through their application and retold as fables and idioms by poets and philosophers.

This process of the application of virtue is what drives the karmic cycle of metempsychosis. Value (the good) is derived through the application of virtuous knowledge. Such examples include: 'We sow what we reap', 'Treat others as you wish to be treated', 'the answer that produces the least suffering', as well as concepts related to the 'Protestant Work Ethic'. Neoplatonic virtue is a divine archetypal emanation to be interpreted in both a Kantian and Lockean light. Good thoughts beget good ideas. The utility Paul mentions of the tree that bears good fruit, begets good actions. Virtue is a set of ideals that produce good fruit which is useful for humanity's collective survival. Stoicism touches on this humanitarian perspective with the self organizing structure of ant colonies.

Daemon's are metaphysical autonomous beings generally known to assist souls in crucial moments as through an almost divine like sixth sense of intuition and conscience, such as a tight feeling at the back of the neck, or an almost clairvoyant way of knowing things. *Daemons* are best understood within Jung's Collective Unconscious framework, as abstract metaphysical autonomous sets of ideas (unified beings that embody archetypes)--apart from the unity of our own self-awareness–catalyzed into existence by nature and mind, that are known to also hinder, enter Jung complexes.

Complexes stem from when our ego meets with the Self (forces of nature: love and strife, hot and cold), this happens when we approach an archetype– often being approached for the first time. The situation of the complex arises when we dangerously conflate, or equate, the experience with our own distinct will or conscious ego. What makes a complex distinct is not realizing it's autonomous nature grounded in the cosmic Self (such as genetic predispositions, but more to the point is our deep connection in the collective unconscious which always has had an unconscious hold over our ego, it is the living infused part of our soul, the part enmeshed with matter).

These autonomous powers stem from emergent abstract (not immediately apparent) systems of intellection, or subsets of interactions within the evolutionary space provided by the collective unconscious (i.e. physical matter, or laws of physics, which our conscious thoughts sprang forth from). These metaphysical forces of nature are akin to djinn who–using the power of nature and circumstance–to orchestrate fateful (morai) tests to either aid or hinder our efforts towards our application of virtue. Daemon's stretch back to acausal archaic times to the roots of archetypal existence, the *Pleroma*. The outcome of such daemonic encounters can often lead to lasting autonomous psychic effects, otherwise known as complexes (MacLennan, Jung's Self, the cosmic man in the sky), with Lovecraftian affectations on the mind.

Both daemons and complexes are tethered by way of a silver *chord* [of thought] that can be interpreted as our connection (or wave/tone) with the Self–that cosmic man the demi-urge that resides within the collective unconscious–the metaphysical representation of soul. Strings of fate weave our destinies–sourced from the Morai (Eddinger)– constructing life-changing events beyond our control. From these strings reverberate our soul's collision with these entities when during these moments, they reveal themselves to us, intending to influence our application of the good, to test what value we can derive in such situations, this is the epitome of life's *telos*, the refinement of soul through the application of virtue. These meetings are often expressed as a pair of angels, a muse, or a coincidence too good to be true, but always centered around personal interactions (meetings between minds), and a connection with an archetype through a tension of opposites.

We experience this interaction between *daemon* and *Nous* through symbolic imagery (Swedenborg's divine correspondences) known as archetypes, experienced as understanding the core idea witnessed during a synchronicity (realizing a set of atemporally connected ideas as a unity, an apothegm/symbolon). Archetypes are above the divided line, their unity expressed as the Aristotlean golden mean (axiom/dimension, same/same) mediating between a tension of opposites (paradox, same/not same) over many universal instances, that have a tendency to mean revert (cycle of virtue and vice). These philosophical riddles can be approached using the middle way in Eastern Philosophy, or how something can both be and not be at the same time* or as becoming (*yin/yang*).

Self

Jung's Self is best expressed as a subset of metaphysical forms (i.e. drawn from the current laws of physics which resulted in reality) from which humanity springs forth from (Anthropic principle), this subset of laws interacts–through nature–with humanity anthropomorphically as a 'Cosmic Man', or monotheistic demi-urge type deity through it's own process of intellection with Nous. The paradigm of the Self (Advaita's not-self) is within the collective unconscious as the Demi-urge, which the indefinite dyad (Nous)–the sojourner of our choices–receives the logos from (through humanities abiotic genesis from matter, Jeremy England) and represents the formal instructions for the not-self (soul, a unity of ideas, subject), to bring forth instantiated self-aware multiplicity of forms (souls). The *Anima Mundi*, from this seed of instruction, proceeds to process and implement the shape of our lives from down to the very details of our thoughts.

254

Archetypes

Archetypes are ideas represented both within reality (nature, external, object) and the mind (subject) atemporally. 'Experiencing an archetype', also known as a synchronicity, is witnessing an idea–that is being currently experienced–as a flash of a greater acausally connected archetype, unified in all cases as true across time (universal). An archetype is a thread of an idea shooting like a star across the *Pleroma* (time & matter), crossing boundaries between mind, matter, idea, place, and time, It is the flash of Eureka that provides a clear insight to a problem isolated from within the web of the interconnected 'divine intellect' as a formal revelation, or recollection.   Recollection is the brain (mind) matching patterns–received through discursive reasoning on externally provided inputs, filtered/processed through the senses–on patterns that exist outside of the mind (collective unconscious, Brahma), derived from the *Anima Mundi*, the eternal natural manifestation of *Nous*.

Archetypes exist metaphysically and emanate by way of the sun's interaction with the other primal elements, creating an energy bath within the *Anima Mundi*'s womb weaving unities of self organizing (moving) energy within matter.   Matter itself contained within a closed system of the collective unconscious (the aether, pneuma, logos). Archetypes are the way we discourse with the divine, glimpsing "[the] man behind the curtain", seeing through *Maya*'s illusion, who plays the role of the trickster archetype operating below the divided line, puppeting the shadows on the wall.

A personal archetypal experience of mine involved death. One day I saw a squirrel playing at OU Norman campus, and shortly after clipped by a truck. I ran up to the dying creature to comfort it in its last moments. Later that same week, my mother passed from a loss of functionality from her pacemaker. I experience the archetype of death, an eventual universal for us all. By comforting the squirrel in its last moments, I was able to comfort an outgoing soul, which was moving beyond the temporal discursive realm, to the atemporally interconnected realm of Nous (just as a body is constituted of individual cells), where my mother would soon be joining.

Conclusion

In conclusion, we come to grasp the eternal nature of ideas - timeless, boundless, and foundational to all of existence. Illuminating the principle of 'as above, so below', revealing how divine ideas not only precede but actively shape our reality and consciousness. These ideas, channeled through archetypes, form a bridge between the tangible (matter, time, and being) and the intangible (mind, nous). It's within this atemporal Pleroma that the metaphysical mind, or Nous, orchestrates the symphony of existence into a formal presentation.

By awareness of our role within the greater cosmic play between life, nous, the morai, daemons, heroes, the nature of virtue as alignment with cosmic order, and that our minds precede our being. We can transcend the role of mere accidental cosmic occupants by realizing that psyche is integral to the universe and lift the liminal veil of disbelief concerning the shadows upon the cave walls choosing instead to become active participants in the eternal dialectic with the universe (Anima Mundi) charting how our roles are to play out. This can include asking for assistance from intermediary heroes to intercede on our behalf, as well as offering up prayers and symbolic sacrifices to the gods, who themselves can best be understood through a venn diagram—or grouping–of specific eternal archetypes, each set of these groupings representing a unified eternal mind.

Leonardo Da Vinci's, "Realize that everything connects to everything else," echoes this sentiment. To acknowledge our anthropic link to both Earth and the starry heavens, a reminder of our dual heritage as beings of both matter and spirit.

Deism

By Varadaraja V. Raman

Varadaraja V. Raman is Emeritus
Professor of Physics and Humanities at the
Rochester Institute of Technology in New
York. Born into a Brahmin Tamil family in
Calcutta, India, he soon earned the
reputation of being a multifaceted
transcultural voyager, and an able
expounder on matters both scientific and
philosophical.

The world we experience has three extraordinary
features. The first is the fact that it exists at all. There
is absolutely no reason we can think of why it did
happen: the birth of this apparently meaningless and
purposeless Cosmos. After all, there are many things
that just are not there: flying horses, conical roses,
two integral cubes that add up to a third cube, let
alone a person who can sing in a hundred different
tongues at the same time. Likewise, we could have
had no world at all, an eternal no-space
dimensionless void. But the fact remains that there
does seem to be a world that all normal human beings
(brains) experience for a while, and also rejoice and
suffer in. This in itself is quite remarkable.

The next intriguing thing about the world is that
we have absolutely no idea of how it came to be. True,
prophets and scriptures, wise men and fantasists have
told us how it all came about: From Chaos, from
Nothingness, as an act of God, as the work of the
architect P'an Ku, and so on. Ignoring all these time-
honored answers which had satisfied and continue to
satisfy billions of people over millennia, modern
physics has come up with its own answers to this
question, using a number of technical terms and

mathemagical formulas. They include Higgs bosons, symmetry breaking, big bang, and the like. Higgs bosons refer to fundamental physical entities that, through mechanisms that can't be understood except through complex mathematics, like special unitary groups, adduce mass to otherwise massless entities. Through processes called symmetry breaking they ignited what has come to be known as the awesome di-syllable Big Bang: an extraordinarily creative conflagration that resulted in space and time, matter and energy, natural laws and all their stupendous consequences. The net effect of that initial outburst in an inconceivable nothingness that had persisted since unimaginable infinity started the first tick of time and other spectacular wonders that we can only contemplate it all with unbounded wonder.

All this could well have happened by sheer chance, some have suggested. However, what makes it difficult to trace our world to a mindless monstrous miracle of randomness is that the end product is not a cluttered heap of hotchpotch, but a fascinating dynamic process subject to meticulously precise and quantitatively describable laws, like E = mc2, F = ma, G: gravitation. The working of the universe follows patterns that conform to partial differential equations and invariance principles. Not only that: The material components of the universe owe their existence and persistence, their properties and propensities to incredibly precise values for certain modeling parameters such as the charge on the electron and the strength of the strong force. Ever so slight deviations from these would have resulted in an altogether unimaginably different cosmos.

Given all this, it is difficult to satisfy the curious mind by saying that it all happened helter-skelter, by sheer slot-machine slips. The law-bound universe does not seem like the result of random hits on the key-board, or idle doodling by shaky hands. Reckless coloration on canvass could at best cause a Jackson

Pollock spray-painting, or perhaps even a Wassily Kandinsky kind of work. But a Rafael or a Ravi Varma could not have risen from mindless meanderings of causeless eruptions. This intriguing circumstance has led many reflecting minds, not just to postulate, but to be quite certain that an Intelligent Creative Principle had consciously designed and expertly executed the mammoth project of the creation and sustenance of the Cosmos.

Reflecting minds are here on earth, so it was natural for them to imagine that the Intelligent Creator had in mind not only the sun and the moon, stars and silicon, but also, perhaps more importantly, human beings as an ultimate adornment to Creation. This led to the suspicion that God has always been immensely interested in our well-being, comfort, and happiness: an idea that was reinforced by the abundance of fruits and grains for our nourishment, beasts for carrying our burdens, as also birds and butterflies to add to our aesthetic delights.

When humanity repeatedly experienced natural catastrophes from hurricanes and floods to earthquakes and epidemics, let alone innocent children dying, droughts causing famines, and unpleasant characters winning elections, some doubts begin to rise as to the constancy, if not reliability of Divine mercy and help. For the truly faithful, this does not matter in the least, and it does not shake their faith in a caring and compassionate Creator.

But theologians and thinkers are as much concerned with logic and proof as with feelings and devotion. So some of them felt it was time to modify our view of God. They reasoned that while God did create the complex world such as it is, once He had done the job He let it function by itself. This view of God, which crystallized in eighteenth century when science and enlightenment were raging, came to be called Deism.

In the Deist view, God is like an artist who, after finishing his creative enterprise, just put it on exhibit, instead of constantly tinkering with it here and there to modify or make it better. He just let the laws do the re-shaping and the creation of new entities within the constraints of the laws of nature. Perhaps – and this was not something the original Deists had in mind – Deus goes on to make another universe, imposing a different set of laws on it, then yet another, and so on. This idea is compatible with current multiverse theory.

But now there has been another variation of the Deist doctrine. After creating the world, God got smack into it Himself, pervading every niche and nook of his created work. What this means is that God is literally omnipresent in everything, in the hadrons and leptons that are in the core of matter as in the far-stretched galaxies and the Dark Matter whereof modern cosmologists speak. He is there in the heart of supernovas as in the singularities of black holes. He is mutely present in every breath of Man as in every neuron fired in brains. The Creator is into the Creation: In creatura creator. A crude analogy would be a playwright who writes a one-hero play and gets into its performance himself: not very common, but not impossible. This has come to be called Pan-Deism.

Thus, Deism was a response to doubts that were slowly emerging as a result of the science of the eighteenth century about the God of the Old Testament, the New Testament, and the Holy Qur'an. The two major factors in modern science are (a) regard the natural world as the primary object of study, even veneration; and (b) going beyond being awed by its wonder and splendor, and systematically observing and studying the world by the use of reason. In this process many strongly held traditional beliefs began to morph into questionable assertions or plain superstitions. But sensitive and reflective minds saw the need for a God without Whom life would be reduced to a meaningless flicker in eternity, a fleeting firefly in the pitch darkness of eternity. The challenge was to hold on to belief in an omnipotent Creator-God and weed out what many saw as needless paraphernalia.

That is how Deism arose. It accepts the existence of God, and recognizes the world and physical laws as having emanated from Him. To explain how or why a God would permit pain and penury, it came up with the tenet that God invented the cosmic machine and let it run on its own. Our responsibility as His creatures is simply to accept the world such as it is, study it carefully, and be thankful to God for this opportunity.

Like all systems that affirm God of one kind or another, and like all who emphatically proclaim their non-belief in God of any kind, the propagators of Deism have also something to say about the beliefs of others. One ardent subscriber to the Deist view, writing for the World Union of Deists, referred to traditional religionists as "people chasing after the nonsensical violence promoting myths of the 'revealed' religions." On the other hand some religious theists call Deists atheists who are afraid of being without a God. Believers are seldom satisfied with their own beliefs: they have to condemn or castigate those of others for full satisfaction.

The Varieties of Religious Experience

by William James

Lectures XVI and XVII: MYSTICISM

OVER and over again in these lectures I have raised points and left them open and unfinished until we should have come to the subject of Mysticism. Some of you, I fear, may have smiled as you noted my reiterated postponements. But now the hour has come when mysticism must be faced in good earnest, and those broken threads wound up together. One may say truly, I think, that personal religious experience has its root and centre in mystical states of consciousness; so for us, who in these lectures are treating personal experience as the exclusive subject of our study, such states of consciousness ought to form the vital chapter from which the other chapters get their light. Whether my treatment of mystical states will shed more light or darkness, I do not know, for my own constitution shuts me out from their enjoyment almost entirely, and I can speak of them only at second hand. But though forced to look upon the subject so externally, I will be as objective and receptive as I can; and I think I shall at least succeed in convincing you of the reality of the states in question, and of the paramount importance of their function.

First of all, then, I ask, What does the expression 'mystical states of consciousness' mean? How do we part off mystical states from other states?

The words 'mysticism' and 'mystical' are often used as terms of mere reproach, to throw at any opinion which we regard as vague and vast and sentimental, and without a base in either facts or logic. For some writers a 'mystic' is any person who believes in thought-transference, or spirit-return. Employed in this way the word has little value: there are too many less ambiguous synonyms. So, to keep it useful by restricting it, I will do what I did in the case of the word 'religion,' and simply propose to you four marks which, when an experience has them, may justify us in calling it mystical for the purpose of the present lectures. In this way we shall save verbal disputation, and the recriminations that generally go therewith.

1. *Ineffability.*—The handiest of the marks by which I classify a state of mind as mystical is negative. The subject of it immediately says that it defies expression, that no adequate report of its contents can be given in words. It follows from this that its quality must be directly experienced; it cannot be imparted or transferred to others. In this peculiarity mystical states are more like states of feeling than like states of intellect. No one can make clear to another who has never had a certain feeling, in what the quality or worth of it consists. One must have musical ears to know the value of a symphony; one must have been in love one's self to understand a lover's state of mind. Lacking the heart or ear, we cannot interpret the musician or the lover justly, and are even likely to consider him weak-minded or absurd. The mystic finds that most of us accord to his experiences an equally incompetent treatment.

2. *Noetic quality.*—Although so similar to states of feeling, mystical states seem to those who experience them to be also states of knowledge. They are states of insight into depths of truth unplumbed by the discursive intellect. They are illuminations, revelations, full of significance and importance, all inarticulate though they remain; and as a rule they carry with them a curious sense of authority for after-time.

These two characters will entitle any state to be called mystical, in the sense in which I use the word. Two other qualities are less sharply marked, but are usually found. These are:—

3. *Transiency.*—Mystical states cannot be sustained for long. Except in rare instances, half an hour, or at most an hour or two, seems to be the limit beyond which they fade into the light of common day. Often, when faded, their quality can but imperfectly be reproduced in memory; but when they recur it is recognized; and from one recurrence to another it is susceptible of continuous development in what is felt as inner richness and importance.

4. *Passivity.*—Although the oncoming of mystical states may be facilitated by preliminary voluntary operations, as by fixing the attention, or going through certain bodily performances, or in other ways which manuals of mysticism prescribe; yet when the characteristic sort of consciousness once has set in, the mystic feels as if his own will were in abeyance, and indeed sometimes as if he were grasped and held by a superior power. This latter peculiarity connects mystical states with certain definite phenomena of secondary or alternative personality, such as prophetic speech, automatic writing, or the mediumistic trance. When these latter conditions are well pronounced, however, there may be no recollection whatever of the phenomenon, and it may have no significance for the subject's usual inner life, to which, as it were, it makes a mere interruption. Mystical states, strictly so called, are never merely interruptive. Some memory of their content always remains, and a profound sense of their importance. They modify the inner life of the subject between the times of their recurrence. Sharp divisions in this region are, however, difficult to make, and we find all sorts of gradations and mixtures.

These four characteristics are sufficient to mark out a group of states of consciousness peculiar enough to deserve a special name and to call for careful study. Let it then be called the mystical group.

Our next step should be to gain acquaintance with some typical examples. Professional mystics at the height of their development have often elaborately organized experiences and a philosophy based thereupon. But you remember what I said in my first lecture: phenomena are best understood when placed within their series, studied in their germ and in their over-ripe decay, and compared with their exaggerated and degenerated kindred. The range of mystical experience is very wide, much too wide for us to cover in the time at our disposal. Yet the method of serial study is so essential for interpretation that if we really wish to reach conclusions we must use it. I will begin, therefore, with phenomena which claim no special religious significance, and end with those of which the religious pretensions are extreme.

The simplest rudiment of mystical experience would seem to be that deepened sense of the significance of a maxim or formula which occasionally sweeps over one. "I've heard that said all my life," we exclaim, "but I never realized its full meaning until now." "When a fellow-monk," said Luther, "one day repeated the words of the Creed: 'I believe in the forgiveness of sins,' I saw the Scripture in an entirely new light; and straightway I felt as if I were born anew. It was as if I had found the door of paradise thrown wide open."[1] This sense of deeper significance is not confined to rational propositions. Single words,[2] and conjunctions of words, effects of light on land and sea, odors and musical sounds, all bring it when the mind is tuned aright. Most of us can remember the strangely moving power of passages in certain poems read when we were young, irrational doorways as they were through which the mystery of fact, the wildness and the pang of life, stole into our hearts and thrilled them. The words have now perhaps become mere polished surfaces for us; but lyric poetry and music are alive and significant only in proportion as they fetch these vague vistas of a life continuous with our own, beckoning and inviting, yet ever eluding our pursuit. We are alive or dead to the eternal inner message of the arts according as we have kept or lost this mystical susceptibility.

A more pronounced step forward on the mystical ladder is found in an extremely frequent phenomenon, that sudden feeling, namely, which sometimes sweeps over us, of having 'been here before,' as if at some indefinite past time, in just this place, with just these people, we were already saying just these things. As Tennyson writes:

"Moreover, something is or seems,
That touches me with mystic gleams,
Like glimpses of forgotten dreams—

"Of something felt, like something here;
Of something done, I know not where;
Such as no language may declare."[3]

Sir James Crickton-Browne has given the technical name of 'dreamy states' to these sudden invasions of vaguely reminiscent consciousness.[4] They bring a sense of mystery and of the metaphysical duality of things, and the feeling of an enlargement of perception which seems imminent but which never completes itself. In Dr. Crichton-Browne's opinion they connect themselves with the perplexed and scared disturbances of self-consciousness which occasionally precede epileptic attacks. I think that this learned alienist takes a rather absurdly alarmist view of an intrinsically insignificant phenomenon. He follows it along the downward ladder, to insanity; our path pursues the upward ladder chiefly. The divergence shows how important it is to neglect no part of a phenomenon's connections, for we make it appear admirable or dreadful according to the context by which we set it off.

Somewhat deeper plunges into mystical consciousness are met with in yet other dreamy states. Such feelings as these which Charles Kingsley describes are surely far from being uncommon, especially in youth:—

"When I walk the fields, I am oppressed now and then with an innate feeling that everything I see has a meaning, if I could but understand it. And this feeling of being surrounded with truths which I cannot grasp amounts to indescribable awe sometimes. ... Have you not felt that your real soul was imperceptible to your mental vision, except in a few hallowed moments?"[5]

A much more extreme state of mystical consciousness is described by J. A. Symonds; and probably more persons than we suspect could give parallels to it from their own experience.

"Suddenly," writes Symonds, "at church, or in company, or when I was reading, and always, I think, when my muscles were at rest, I felt the approach of the mood. Irresistibly it took possession of my mind and will, lasted what seemed an eternity, and disappeared in a series of rapid sensations which resembled the awakening from anæsthetic influence. One reason why I disliked this kind of trance was that I could not describe it to myself. I cannot even now find words to render it intelligible. It consisted in a gradual but swiftly progressive obliteration of space, time, sensation, and the multitudinous factors of experience which seem to qualify what we are pleased to call our Self. In proportion as these conditions of ordinary consciousness were subtracted, the sense of an underlying or essential consciousness acquired intensity. At last nothing remained but a pure, absolute, abstract Self. The universe became without form and void of content. But Self persisted, formidable in its vivid keenness, feeling the most poignant doubt about reality, ready, as it seemed, to find existence break as breaks a bubble round about it. And what then? The apprehension of a coming dissolution, the grim conviction that this state was the last state of the conscious Self, the sense that I had followed the last thread of being to the verge of the abyss, and had arrived at demonstration of eternal Maya or illusion, stirred or seemed to stir me up again. The return to ordinary conditions of sentient existence began by my first recovering the power of touch, and then by the gradual though rapid influx of familiar impressions and diurnal interests. At last I felt myself once more a human being; and though the riddle of what is meant by life remained unsolved, I was thankful for this return from the abyss—this deliverance from so awful an initiation into the mysteries of skepticism.

"This trance recurred with diminishing frequency until I reached the age of twenty-eight. It served to impress upon my growing nature the phantasmal unreality of all the circumstances which contribute to a merely phenomenal consciousness. Often have I asked myself with anguish, on waking from that formless state of denuded, keenly sentient being, Which is the unreality?—the trance of fiery, vacant, apprehensive, skeptical Self from which I issue, or these surrounding phenomena and habits which veil that inner Self and build a self of flesh-and-blood conventionality? Again, are men the factors of some dream, the dream-like unsubstantiality of which they comprehend at such eventful moments? What would happen if the final stage of the trance were reached?"[6]

In a recital like this there is certainly something suggestive of pathology.[7] The next step into mystical states carries us into a realm that public opinion and ethical philosophy have long since branded as pathological, though private practice and certain lyric strains of poetry seem still to bear witness to its ideality. I refer to the consciousness produced by intoxicants and anæsthetics, especially by alcohol. The sway of alcohol over mankind is unquestionably due to its power to stimulate the mystical faculties of human nature, usually crushed to earth by the cold facts and dry criticisms of the sober hour. Sobriety diminishes, discriminates, and says no; drunkenness expands, unites, and says yes. It is in fact the great exciter of the *Yes* function in man. It brings its votary from the chill periphery of things to the radiant core. It makes him for the moment one with truth. Not through mere perversity do men run after it. To the poor and the unlettered it stands in the place of symphony concerts and of literature; and it is part of the deeper mystery and tragedy of life that whiffs and gleams of something that we immediately recognize as excellent should be vouchsafed to so many of us only in the fleeting earlier phases of what in its totality is so degrading a poisoning. The drunken consciousness is one bit of the mystic consciousness, and our total opinion of it must find its place in our opinion of that larger whole.

Nitrous oxide and ether, especially nitrous oxide, when sufficiently diluted with air, stimulate the mystical consciousness in an extraordinary degree. Depth beyond depth of truth seems revealed to the inhaler. This truth fades out, however, or escapes, at the moment of coming to; and if any words remain over in which it seemed to clothe itself, they prove to be the veriest nonsense. Nevertheless, the sense of a profound meaning having been there persists; and I know more than one person who is persuaded that in the nitrous oxide trance we have a genuine metaphysical revelation.

Some years ago I myself made some observations on this aspect of nitrous oxide intoxication, and reported them in print. One conclusion was forced upon my mind at that time, and my impression of its truth has ever since remained unshaken. It is that our normal waking consciousness, rational consciousness as we call it, is but one special type of consciousness, whilst all about it, parted from it by the filmiest of screens, there lie potential forms of consciousness entirely different. We may go through life without suspecting their existence; but apply the requisite stimulus, and at a touch they are there in all their completeness, definite types of mentality which probably somewhere have their field of application and adaptation. No account of the universe in its totality can be final which leaves these other forms of consciousness quite disregarded. How to regard them is the question,—for they are so discontinuous with ordinary consciousness. Yet they may determine attitudes though they cannot furnish formulas, and open a region though they fail to give a map. At any rate, they forbid a premature closing of our accounts with reality. Looking back on my own experiences, they all converge towards a kind of insight to which I cannot help ascribing some metaphysical significance. The keynote of it is invariably a reconciliation. It is as if the opposites of the world, whose contradictoriness and conflict make all our difficulties and troubles, were melted into unity. Not only do they, as contrasted species, belong to one and the same genus, but *one of the species*, the nobler and better one, *is itself the genus, and so soaks up and absorbs its opposite into itself.* This is a dark saying, I know, when thus expressed in terms of common logic, but I cannot wholly escape from its authority. I feel as if it must mean something, something like what the hegelian philosophy means, if one could only lay hold of it more clearly. Those who have ears to hear, let them hear; to me the living sense of its reality only comes in the artificial mystic state of mind.[8]

I just now spoke of friends who believe in the anæsthetic revelation. For them too it is a monistic insight, in which the *other* in its various forms appears absorbed into the One.

"Into this pervading genius," writes one of them, "we pass, forgetting and forgotten, and thenceforth each is all, in God. There is no higher, no deeper, no other, than the life in which we are founded. 'The One remains, the many change and pass;' and each and every one of us *is* the One that remains. ... This is the ultimatum. ... As sure as being—whence is all our care—so sure is content, beyond duplexity, antithesis, or trouble, where I have triumphed in a solitude that God is not above."[9]

This has the genuine religious mystic ring! I just now quoted J. A. Symonds. He also records a mystical experience with chloroform, as follows:—

"After the choking and stifling had passed away, I seemed at first in a state of utter blankness; then came flashes of intense light, alternating with blackness, and with a keen vision of what was going on in the room around me, but no sensation of touch. I thought that I was near death; when, suddenly, my soul became aware of God, who was manifestly dealing with me, handling me, so to speak, in an intense personal present reality. I felt him streaming in like light upon me. ... I cannot describe the ecstasy I felt. Then, as I gradually awoke from the influence of the anæsthetics, the old sense of my relation to the world began to return, the new sense of my relation to God began to fade. I suddenly leapt to my feet on the chair where I was sitting, and shrieked out, 'It is too horrible, it is too horrible, it is too horrible,' meaning that I could not bear this disillusionment. Then I flung myself on the ground, and at last awoke covered with blood, calling to the two surgeons (who were frightened), 'Why did you not kill me? Why would you not let me die?' Only think of it. To have felt for that long dateless ecstasy of vision the very God, in all purity and tenderness and truth and absolute love, and then to find that I had after all had no revelation, but that I had been tricked by the abnormal excitement of my brain.

"Yet, this question remains, Is it possible that the inner sense of reality which succeeded, when my flesh was dead to impressions from without, to the ordinary sense of physical relations, was not a delusion but an actual experience? Is it possible that I, in that moment, felt what some of the saints have said they always felt, the undemonstrable but irrefragable certainty of God?"[10]

With this we make connection with religious mysticism pure and simple. Symonds's question takes us back to those examples which you will remember my quoting in the lecture on the Reality of the Unseen, of sudden realization of the immediate presence of God. The phenomenon in one shape or another is not uncommon.

"I know," writes Mr. Trine, "an officer on our police force who has told me that many times when off duty, and on his way home in the evening, there comes to him such a vivid and vital realization of his oneness with this Infinite Power, and this Spirit of Infinite Peace so takes hold of and so fills him,

that it seems as if his feet could hardly keep to the pavement, so buoyant and so exhilarated does he become by reason of this inflowing tide."[11]

Certain aspects of nature seem to have a peculiar power of awakening such mystical moods.[12] Most of the striking cases which I have collected have occurred out of doors. Literature has commemorated this fact in many passages of great beauty—this extract, for example, from Amiel's Journal Intime:—

"Shall I ever again have any of those prodigious reveries which sometimes came to me in former days? One day, in youth, at sunrise, sitting in the ruins of the castle of Faucigny; and again in the mountains, under the noonday sun, above Lavey, lying at the foot of a tree and visited by three butterflies; once more at night upon the shingly shore of the Northern Ocean, my back upon the sand and my vision ranging through the milky way;—such grand and spacious, immortal, cosmogonic reveries, when one reaches to the stars, when one owns the infinite! Moments divine, ecstatic hours; in which our thought flies from world to world, pierces the great enigma, breathes with a respiration broad, tranquil, and deep as the respiration of the ocean, serene and limitless as the blue firmament; ... instants of irresistible intuition in which one feels one's self great as the universe, and calm as a god. ... What hours, what memories! The vestiges they leave behind are enough to fill us with belief and enthusiasm, as if they were visits of the Holy Ghost."[13]

Here is a similar record from the memoirs of that interesting German idealist, Malwida von Meysenbug:—

"I was alone upon the seashore as all these thoughts flowed over me, liberating and reconciling; and now again, as once before in distant days in the Alps of Dauphiné, I was impelled to kneel down, this time before the illimitable ocean, symbol of the Infinite. I felt that I prayed as I had never prayed before, and knew now what prayer really is: to return from the solitude of individuation into the consciousness of unity with all that is, to kneel down as one that passes away, and to rise up as one imperishable. Earth, heaven, and sea resounded as in one vast world-encircling harmony. It was as if the chorus of all the great who had ever lived were about me. I felt myself one with them, and it appeared as if I heard their greeting: 'Thou too belongest to the company of those who overcome.'"[14]

The well-known passage from Walt Whitman is a classical expression of this sporadic type of mystical experience.

"I believe in you, my Soul ...
Loaf with rue on the grass, loose the stop from your throat;   ...
Only the lull I like, the hum of your valved voice.
I mind how once we lay, such a transparent summer morning.
Swiftly arose and spread around me the peace and knowledge that pass all the argument of the earth,

And I know that the hand of God is the promise of my own,
And I know that the spirit of God is the brother of my own,
And that all the men ever born are also my brothers and the women my sisters and lovers,
And that a kelson of the creation is love."[15]

I could easily give more instances, but one will suffice. I take it from the Autobiography of J. Trevor.[16]

"One brilliant Sunday morning, my wife and boys went to the Unitarian Chapel in Macclesfield. I felt it impossible to accompany them—as though to leave the sunshine on the hills, and go down there to the chapel, would be for the time an act of spiritual suicide. And I felt such need for new inspiration and expansion in my life. So, very reluctantly and sadly, I left my wife and boys to go down into the town, while I went further up into the hills with my stick and my dog. In the loveliness of the morning, and the beauty of the hills and valleys, I soon lost my sense of sadness and regret. For nearly an hour I walked along the road to the 'Cat and Fiddle,' and then returned. On the way back, suddenly, without warning, I felt that I was in Heaven—an inward state of peace and joy and assurance indescribably intense, accompanied with a sense of being bathed in a warm glow of light, as though the external condition had brought about the internal effect—a feeling of having passed beyond the body, though the scene around me stood out more clearly and as if nearer to me than before, by reason of the illumination in the midst of which I seemed to be placed. This deep emotion lasted, though with decreasing strength, until I reached home, and for some time after, only gradually passing away."

The writer adds that having had further experiences of a similar sort, he now knows them well.

"The spiritual life," he writes, "justifies itself to those who live it; but what can we say to those who do not understand? This, at least, we can say, that it is a life whose experiences are proved real to their possessor, because they remain with him when brought closest into contact with the objective realities of life. Dreams cannot stand this test. We wake from them to find that they are but dreams. Wanderings of an overwrought brain do not stand this test. These highest experiences that I have had of God's presence have been rare and brief—flashes of consciousness which have compelled me to exclaim with surprise—God is *here!*—or conditions of exaltation and insight, less intense, and only gradually passing away. I have severely questioned the worth of these moments. To no soul have I named them, lest I should be building my life and work on mere phantasies of the brain. But I find that, after every questioning and test, they stand out to-day as the most real experiences of my life, and experiences which have explained and justified and unified all past experiences and all past growth. Indeed, their reality and their far-reaching significance are ever becoming more clear and evident. When they came, I was living the fullest, strongest, sanest, deepest life. I was not seeking them. What I was seeking, with resolute determination, was to live more intensely my own life, as against what I knew would be the adverse judgment of the world. It was in the most real seasons that the Real Presence came, and I was aware that I was immersed in the infinite ocean of God."[17]

Even the least mystical of you must by this time be convinced of the existence of mystical moments as states of consciousness of an entirely specific quality, and of the deep impression which they make on those who have them. A Canadian psychiatrist, Dr. R. M. Bucke, gives to the more distinctly characterized of these phenomena the name of cosmic consciousness. "Cosmic consciousness in its more striking instances is not," Dr. Bucke says, "simply an expansion or extension of the self-conscious mind with which we are all familiar, but the superaddition of a function as distinct from any possessed by the average man as *self*-consciousness is distinct from any function possessed by one of the higher animals."

"The prime characteristic of cosmic consciousness is a consciousness of the cosmos, that is, of the life and order of the universe. Along with the consciousness of the cosmos there occurs an intellectual enlightenment which alone would place the individual on a new plane of existence—would make him almost a member of a new species. To this is added a state of moral exaltation, an indescribable feeling of elevation, elation, and joyousness, and a quickening of the moral sense, which is fully as striking, and more important than is the enhanced intellectual power. With these come what may be called a sense of immortality, a consciousness of eternal life, not a conviction that he shall have this, but the consciousness that he has it already."[18]

It was Dr. Bucke's own experience of a typical onset of cosmic consciousness in his own person which led him to investigate it in others. He has printed his conclusions in a highly interesting volume, from which I take the following account of what occurred to him:—

"I had spent the evening in a great city, with two friends, reading and discussing poetry and philosophy. We parted at midnight. I had a long drive in a hansom to my lodging. My mind, deeply under the influence of the ideas, images, and emotions called up by the reading and talk, was calm and peaceful. I was in a state of quiet, almost passive enjoyment, not actually thinking, but letting ideas, images, and emotions flow of themselves, as it were, through my mind. All at once, without warning of any kind, I found myself wrapped in a flame-colored cloud. For an instant I thought of fire, an immense conflagration somewhere close by in that great city; the next, I knew that the fire was within myself. Directly afterward there came upon me a sense of exultation, of immense joyousness accompanied or immediately followed by an intellectual illumination impossible to describe. Among other things, I did not merely come to believe, but I saw that the universe is not composed of dead matter, but is, on the contrary, a living Presence; I became conscious in myself of eternal life. It was not a conviction that I would have eternal life, but a consciousness that I possessed eternal life then; I saw that all men are immortal; that the cosmic order is such that without any peradventure all things work together for the good of each and all; that the foundation principle of the world, of all the worlds, is what we call love, and that the happiness of each and all is in the long run absolutely certain. The vision lasted a few seconds and was gone; but the memory of it and the sense of the reality of what it taught has remained during the quarter of a century which has since elapsed. I knew that what the vision showed was true. I had attained to a point of view from which I saw that it must be true. That view, that conviction, I may say that consciousness, has never, even during periods of the deepest depression, been lost."[19]

We have now seen enough of this cosmic or mystic consciousness, as it comes sporadically. We must next pass to its methodical cultivation as an element of the religious life. Hindus, Buddhists, Mohammedans, and Christians all have cultivated it methodically.

In India, training in mystical insight has been known from time immemorial under the name of yoga. Yoga means the experimental union of the individual with the divine. It is based on persevering exercise; and the diet, posture, breathing, intellectual concentration, and moral discipline vary slightly in the different systems which teach it. The yogi, or disciple, who has by these means overcome the obscurations of his lower nature sufficiently, enters into the condition termed *samâdhi*, "and comes face to face with facts which no instinct or reason can ever know." He learns—

"That the mind itself has a higher state of existence, beyond reason, a superconscious state, and that when the mind gets to that higher state, then this knowledge beyond reasoning comes. ... All the different steps in yoga are intended to bring us scientifically to the superconscious state or samâdhi. ... Just as unconscious work is beneath consciousness, so there is another work which is above consciousness, and which, also, is not accompanied with the feeling of egoism. ... There is no feeling of *I*, and yet the mind works, desireless, free from restlessness, objectless, bodiless. Then the Truth shines in its full effulgence, and we know ourselves— for Samâdhi lies potential in us all—for what we truly are, free, immortal, omnipotent, loosed from the finite, and its contrasts of good and evil altogether, and identical with the Atman or Universal Soul."[20]

The Vedantists say that one may stumble into superconsciousness sporadically, without the previous discipline, but it is then impure. Their test of its purity, like our test of religion's value, is empirical: its fruits must be good for life. When a man comes out of Samâdhi, they assure us that he remains "enlightened, a sage, a prophet, a saint, his whole character changed, his life changed, illumined."[21]

The Buddhists use the word 'samâdhi' as well as the Hindus; but 'dhyâna' is their special word for higher states of contemplation. There seem to be four stages recognized in dhyâna. The first stage comes through concentration of the mind upon one point. It excludes desire, but not discernment or judgment: it is still intellectual. In the second stage the intellectual functions drop off, and the satisfied sense of unity remains. In the third stage the satisfaction departs, and indifference begins, along with memory and self-consciousness. In the fourth stage the indifference, memory, and self-consciousness are perfected. [Just what 'memory' and 'self-consciousness' mean in this connection is doubtful. They cannot be the faculties familiar to us in the lower life.] Higher stages still of contemplation are mentioned—a region where there exists nothing, and where the meditator says: "There exists absolutely nothing," and stops. Then he reaches another region where he says: "There are neither ideas nor absence of ideas," and stops again. Then another region where, "having reached the end of both idea and perception, he stops finally." This would seem to be, not yet Nirvâna, but as close an approach to it as this life affords.[22]

In the Mohammedan world the Sufi sect and various dervish bodies are the possessors of the mystical tradition. The Sufis have existed in Persia from the earliest times, and as their pantheism is so at variance with the hot and rigid monotheism of the Arab mind, it has been suggested that Sufism must have been inoculated into Islam by Hindu influences. We Christians know little of Sufism, for its secrets are disclosed only to those initiated. To give its existence a certain liveliness in your minds, I will quote a Moslem document, and pass away from the subject.

Al-Ghazzali, a Persian philosopher and theologian, who flourished in the eleventh century, and ranks as one of the greatest doctors of the Moslem church, has left us one of the few autobiographies to be found outside of Christian literature. Strange that a species of book so abundant among ourselves should be so little represented elsewhere—the absence of strictly personal confessions is the chief difficulty to the purely literary student who would like to become acquainted with the inwardness of religions other than the Christian.

M. Schmölders has translated a part of Al-Ghazzali's autobiography into French:[23]—

"The Science of the Sufis," says the Moslem author, "aims at detaching the heart from all that is not God, and at giving to it for sole occupation the meditation of the divine being. Theory being more easy for me than practice, I read [certain books] until I understood all that can be learned by study and hearsay. Then I recognized that what pertains most exclusively to their method is just what no study can grasp, but only transport, ecstasy, and the transformation of the soul. How great, for example, is the difference between knowing the definitions of health, of satiety, with their causes and conditions, and being really healthy or filled. How different to know in what drunkenness consists,—as being a state occasioned by a vapor that rises from the stomach,—and *being* drunk effectively. Without doubt, the drunken man knows neither the definition of drunkenness nor what makes it interesting for science. Being drunk, he knows nothing; whilst the physician, although not drunk, knows well in what drunkenness consists, and what are its predisposing conditions. Similarly there is a difference between knowing the nature of abstinence, and *being* abstinent or having one's soul detached from the world.—Thus I had learned what words could teach of Sufism, but what was left could be learned neither by study nor through the ears, but solely by giving one's self up to ecstasy and leading a pious life.

"Reflecting on my situation, I found myself tied down by a multitude of bonds—temptations on every side. Considering my teaching, I found it was impure before God. I saw myself struggling with all my might to achieve glory and to spread my name. [Here follows an account of his six months' hesitation to break away from the conditions of his life at Bagdad, at the end of which he fell ill with a paralysis of the tongue.] Then, feeling my own weakness, and having entirely given up my own will, I repaired to God like a man in distress who has no more resources. He answered, as he answers the wretch who invokes him. My heart no longer felt any difficulty in renouncing glory, wealth, and my children. So I quitted Bagdad, and reserving from my fortune only what was indispensable for my subsistence, I distributed the rest. I went to Syria, where I remained about two years, with no other occupation than living in retreat and solitude, conquering my desires, combating my passions, training myself to purify my soul, to make my character perfect, to prepare my heart for meditating on God—all according to the methods of the Sufis, as I had read of them.

"This retreat only increased my desire to live in solitude, and to complete the purification of my heart and fit it for meditation. But the vicissitudes of the times, the affairs of the family, the need of subsistence, changed in some respects my primitive resolve, and interfered with my plans for a purely solitary life. I had never yet found myself completely in ecstasy, save in a few single hours; nevertheless, I kept the hope of attaining this state. Every time that the accidents led me astray, I sought to return; and in this situation I spent ten years. During this solitary state things were revealed to me which it is impossible either to describe or to point out. I recognized for certain that the Sufis are assuredly walking in the path of God. Both in their acts and in their inaction, whether internal or external, they are illumined by the light which proceeds from the prophetic source. The first condition for a Sufi is to purge his heart entirely of all that is not God. The next key of the contemplative life consists in the humble prayers which escape from the fervent soul, and in the meditations on God in which the heart is swallowed up entirely. But in reality this is only the beginning of the Sufi life, the end of Sufism being total absorption in God. The intuitions and all that precede are, so to speak, only the threshold for those who enter. From the beginning, revelations take place in so flagrant a shape that the Sufis see before them, whilst wide awake, the angels and the souls of the prophets. They hear their voices and obtain their favors. Then the transport rises from the perception of forms and figures to a degree which escapes all expression, and which no man may seek to give an account of without his words involving sin.

"Whoever has had no experience of the transport knows of the true nature of prophetism nothing but the name. He may meanwhile be sure of its existence, both by experience and by what he hears the Sufis say. As there are men endowed only with the sensitive faculty who reject what is offered them in the way of objects of the pure understanding, so there are intellectual men who reject and avoid the things perceived by the prophetic faculty. A blind man can understand nothing of colors save what he has learned by narration and hearsay. Yet God has brought prophetism near to men in giving them all a state analogous to it in its principal characters. This state is sleep. If you were to tell a man who was himself without experience of such a phenomenon that there are people who at times swoon away so as to resemble dead men, and who [in dreams] yet perceive things that are hidden, he would deny it [and give his reasons]. Nevertheless, his arguments would be refuted by actual experience. Wherefore, just as the understanding is a stage of human life in which an eye opens to discern various intellectual objects uncomprehended by sensation; just so in the prophetic the sight is illumined by a light which uncovers hidden things and objects which the intellect fails to reach. The chief properties of prophetism are perceptible only during the transport, by those who embrace the Sufi life. The prophet is endowed with qualities to which you possess nothing analogous, and which consequently you cannot possibly understand. How should you know their true nature, since one knows only what one can comprehend? But the transport which one attains by the method of the Sufis is like an immediate perception, as if one touched the objects with one's hand."[24]

This incommunicableness of the transport is the keynote of all mysticism. Mystical truth exists for the individual who has the transport, but for no one else. In this, as I have said, it resembles the knowledge given to us in sensations more than that given by conceptual thought. Thought, with its remoteness and abstractness, has often enough in the history of philosophy been contrasted unfavorably with sensation. It is a commonplace of metaphysics that God's knowledge cannot be discursive but must be intuitive, that is, must be constructed more after the pattern of what in ourselves is called immediate feeling, than after that of proposition and judgment. But *our* immediate feelings have no content but what the five senses supply; and we have seen and shall see again that mystics may emphatically deny that the senses play any part in the very highest type of knowledge which their transports yield.

In the Christian church there have always been mystics. Although many of them have been viewed with suspicion, some have gained favor in the eyes of the authorities. The experiences of these have been treated as precedents, and a codified system of mystical theology has been based upon them, in which everything legitimate finds its place.[25] The basis of the system is 'orison' or meditation, the methodical elevation of the soul towards God. Through the practice of orison the higher levels of mystical experience may be attained. It is odd that Protestantism, especially evangelical Protestantism, should seemingly have abandoned everything methodical in this line. Apart from what prayer may lead to, Protestant mystical experience appears to have been almost exclusively sporadic. It has been left to our mind-curers to reintroduce methodical meditation into our religious life.

The first thing to be aimed at in orison is the mind's detachment from outer sensations, for these interfere with its concentration upon ideal things. Such manuals as Saint Ignatius's Spiritual Exercises recommend the disciple to expel sensation by a graduated series of efforts to imagine holy scenes. The acme of this kind of discipline would be a semi-hallucinatory mono-ideism—an imaginary figure of Christ, for example, coming fully to occupy the mind. Sensorial images of this sort, whether literal or symbolic, play an enormous part in mysticism.[26] But in certain cases imagery may fall away entirely, and in the very highest raptures it tends to do so. The state of consciousness becomes then insusceptible of any verbal description. Mystical teachers are unanimous as to this. Saint John of the Cross, for instance, one of the best of them, thus describes the condition called the 'union of love,' which, he says, is reached by 'dark contemplation.' In this the Deity compenetrates the soul, but in such a hidden way that the soul—

"finds no terms, no means, no comparison whereby to render the sublimity of the wisdom and the delicacy of the spiritual feeling with which she is filled. ... We receive this mystical knowledge of God clothed in none of the kinds of images, in none of the sensible representations, which our mind makes use of in other circumstances. Accordingly in this knowledge, since the senses and the imagination are not employed, we get neither form nor impression, nor can we give any account or furnish any likeness, although the mysterious and sweet-tasting wisdom comes home so clearly to the inmost parts of our soul. Fancy a man seeing a certain kind of thing for the first time in his life. He can understand it, use and enjoy it, but he cannot apply a name to it, nor communicate any idea of it, even though all the while it be a mere thing of sense. How much greater will be his powerlessness when it goes beyond the senses! This is the peculiarity of the divine language. The more infused, intimate, spiritual, and supersensible it is, the more does it exceed the senses, both inner and outer, and impose silence upon them. ... The soul then feels as if placed in a vast and profound solitude, to which no created thing has access, in an immense and boundless desert, desert the more delicious the more solitary it is. There, in this abyss of wisdom, the soul grows by what it drinks in from the well-springs of the comprehension of love, ... and recognizes, however sublime and learned may be the terms we employ, how utterly vile, insignificant, and improper they are, when we seek to discourse of divine things by their means."[27]

I cannot pretend to detail to you the sundry stages of the Christian mystical life.[28] Our time would not suffice, for one thing; and moreover, I confess that the subdivisions and names which we find in the Catholic books seem to me to represent nothing objectively distinct. So many men, so many minds: I imagine that these experiences can be as infinitely varied as are the idiosyncrasies of individuals.

The cognitive aspects of them, their value in the way of revelation, is what we are directly concerned with, and it is easy to show by citation how strong an impression they leave of being revelations of new depths of truth. Saint Teresa is the expert of experts in describing such conditions, so I will turn immediately to what she says of one of the highest of them, the 'orison of union.'

"In the orison of union," says Saint Teresa, "the soul is fully awake as regards God, but wholly asleep as regards things of this world and in respect of herself. During the short time the union lasts, she is as it were deprived of every feeling, and even if she would, she could not think of any single thing. Thus she needs to employ no artifice in order to arrest the use of her understanding: it remains so stricken with inactivity that she neither knows what she loves, nor in what manner she loves, nor what she wills. In short, she is utterly dead to the things of the world and lives solely in God. ... I do not even know whether in this state she has enough life left to breathe. It seems to me she has not; or at least that if she does breathe, she is unaware of it. Her intellect would fain understand something of what is going on within her, but it has so little force now that it can act in no way whatsoever. So a person who falls into a deep faint appears as if dead. ...

"Thus does God, when he raises a soul to union with himself, suspend the natural action of all her faculties. She neither sees, hears, nor understands, so long as she is united with God. But this time is always short, and it seems even shorter than it is. God establishes himself in the interior of this soul in such a way, that when she returns to herself, it is wholly impossible for her to doubt that she has been in God, and God in her. This truth remains so strongly impressed on her that, even though many years should pass without the condition returning, she can neither forget the favor she received, nor doubt of its reality. If you, nevertheless, ask how it is possible that the soul can see and understand that she has been in God, since during the union she has neither sight nor understanding, I reply that she does not see it then, but that she sees it clearly later, after she has returned to herself, not by any vision, but by a certitude which abides with her and which God alone can give her. I knew a person who was ignorant of the truth that God's mode of being in everything must be either by presence, by power, or by essence, but who, after having received the grace of which I am speaking, believed this truth in the most unshakable manner. So much so that, having consulted a half-learned man who was as ignorant on this point as she had been before she was enlightened, when he replied that God is in us only by 'grace,' she disbelieved his reply, so sure she was of the true answer; and when she came to ask wiser doctors, they confirmed her in her belief, which much consoled her. ...

"But how, you will repeat, *can* one have such certainty in respect to what one does not see? This question, I am powerless to answer. These are secrets of God's omnipotence which it does not appertain to me to penetrate. All that I know is that I tell the truth; and I shall never believe that any soul who does not possess this certainty has ever been really united to God."[29]

The kinds of truth communicable in mystical ways, whether these be sensible or supersensible, are various. Some of them relate to this world,—visions of the future, the reading of hearts, the sudden understanding of texts, the knowledge of distant events, for example; but the most important revelations are theological or metaphysical.

"Saint Ignatius confessed one day to Father Laynez that a single hour of meditation at Manresa had taught him more truths about heavenly things than all the teachings of all the doctors put together could have taught him. ... One day in orison, on the steps of the choir of the Dominican church, he saw in a distinct manner the plan of divine wisdom in the creation of the world. On another occasion, during a procession, his spirit was ravished in God, and it was given him to contemplate, in a form and images fitted to the weak understanding of a dweller on the earth, the deep mystery of the holy Trinity. This last vision flooded his heart with such sweetness, that the mere memory of it in after times made him shed abundant tears."[30]

Similarly with Saint Teresa. "One day, being in orison," she writes, "it was granted me to perceive in one instant how all things are seen and contained in God. I did not perceive them in their proper form, and nevertheless the view I had of them was of a sovereign clearness, and has remained vividly impressed upon my soul. It is one of the most signal of all the graces which the Lord has granted me. ... The view was so subtile and delicate that the understanding cannot grasp it."[31]

She goes on to tell how it was as if the Deity were an enormous and sovereignly limpid diamond, in which all our actions were contained in such a way that their full sinfulness appeared evident as never before. On another day, she relates, while she was reciting the Athanasian Creed,—

"Our Lord made me comprehend in what way it is that one God can be in three Persons. He made me see it so clearly that I remained as extremely surprised as I was comforted, ... and now, when I think of the holy Trinity, or hear It spoken of, I understand how the three adorable Persons form only one God and I experience an unspeakable happiness."

On still another occasion, it was given to Saint Teresa to see and understand in what wise the Mother of God had been assumed into her place in Heaven.[32]

The deliciousness of some of these states seems to be beyond anything known in ordinary consciousness. It evidently involves organic sensibilities, for it is spoken of as something too extreme to be borne, and as verging on bodily pain.[33] But it is too subtile and piercing a delight for ordinary words to denote. God's touches, the wounds of his spear, references to ebriety and to nuptial union have to figure in the phraseology by which it is shadowed forth. Intellect and senses both swoon away in these highest states of ecstasy. "If our understanding comprehends," says Saint Teresa, "it is in a mode which remains unknown to it, and it can understand nothing of what it comprehends. For my own part, I do not believe that it does comprehend, because, as I said, it does not understand itself to do so. I confess that it is all a mystery in which I am lost."[34] In the condition called *raptus* or ravishment by theologians, breathing and circulation are so depressed that it is a question among the doctors whether the soul be or be not temporarily dissevered from the body. One must read Saint Teresa's descriptions and the very exact distinctions which she makes, to persuade one's self that one is dealing, not with imaginary experiences, but with phenomena which, however rare, follow perfectly definite psychological types.

To the medical mind these ecstasies signify nothing but suggested and imitated hypnoid states, on an intellectual basis of superstition, and a corporeal one of degeneration and hysteria. Undoubtedly these pathological conditions have existed in many and possibly in all the cases, but that fact tells us nothing about the value for knowledge of the consciousness which they induce. To pass a spiritual judgment upon these states, we must not content ourselves with superficial medical talk, but inquire into their fruits for life.

Their fruits appear to have been various. Stupefaction, for one thing, seems not to have been altogether absent as a result. You may remember the helplessness in the kitchen and schoolroom of poor Margaret Mary Alacoque. Many other ecstatics would have perished but for the care taken of them by admiring followers. The 'other-worldliness' encouraged by the mystical consciousness makes this over-abstraction from practical life peculiarly liable to befall mystics in whom the character is naturally passive and the intellect feeble; but in natively strong minds and characters we find quite opposite results. The great Spanish mystics, who carried the habit of ecstasy as far as it has often been carried, appear for the most part to have shown indomitable spirit and energy, and all the more so for the trances in which they indulged.

Saint Ignatius was a mystic, but his mysticism made him assuredly one of the most powerfully practical human engines that ever lived. Saint John of the Cross, writing of the intuitions and 'touches' by which God reaches the substance of the soul, tells us that—

"They enrich it marvelously. A single one of them may be sufficient to abolish at a stroke certain imperfections of which the soul during its whole life had vainly tried to rid itself, and to leave it adorned with virtues and loaded with supernatural gifts. A single one of these intoxicating consolations may reward it for all the labors undergone in its life—even were they numberless. Invested with an invincible courage, filled with an impassioned desire to suffer for its God, the soul then is seized with a strange torment—that of not being allowed to suffer enough."[35]

Saint Teresa is as emphatic, and much more detailed. You may perhaps remember a passage I quoted from her in my first lecture.[36] There are many similar pages in her autobiography. Where in literature is a more evidently veracious account of the formation of a new centre of spiritual energy, than is given in her description of the effects of certain ecstasies which in departing leave the soul upon a higher level of emotional excitement?

"Often, infirm and wrought upon with dreadful pains before the ecstasy, the soul emerges from it full of health and admirably disposed for action ... as if God had willed that the body itself, already obedient to the soul's desires, should share in the soul's happiness. ... The soul after such a favor is animated with a degree of courage so great that if at that moment its body should be torn to pieces for the cause of God, it would feel nothing but the liveliest comfort. Then it is that promises and heroic resolutions spring up in profusion in us, soaring desires, horror of the world, and the clear perception of our proper nothingness. ... What empire is comparable to that of a soul who, from this sublime summit to which God has raised her, sees all the things of earth beneath her feet, and is captivated by no one of them? How ashamed she is of her former attachments! How amazed at her blindness! What lively pity she feels for those whom she recognizes still shrouded in the darkness! ... She groans at having ever been sensitive to points of honor, at the illusion that made her ever see as honor what the world calls by that name. Now she sees in this name nothing more than an immense lie of which the world remains a victim. She discovers, in the new light from above, that in genuine honor there is nothing spurious, that to be faithful to this honor is to give our respect to what deserves to be respected really, and to consider as nothing, or as less than nothing, whatsoever perishes and is not agreeable to God. ... She laughs when she sees grave persons, persons of orison, caring for points of honor for which she now feels profoundest contempt. It is suitable to the dignity of their rank to act thus, they pretend, and it makes them more useful to others. But she knows that in despising the dignity of their rank for the pure love of God they would do more good in a single day than they would effect in ten years by preserving it. ... She laughs at herself that there should ever have been a time in her life when she made any case of money, when she ever desired it. ... Oh! if human beings might only agree together to regard it as so much useless mud, what harmony would then reign in the world! With what friendship we would all treat each other if our interest in honor and in money could but disappear from earth! For my own part, I feel as if it would be a remedy for all our ills."[37]

Mystical conditions may, therefore, render the soul more energetic in the lines which their inspiration favors. But this could be reckoned an advantage only in case the inspiration were a true one. If the inspiration were erroneous, the energy would be all the more mistaken and misbegotten. So we stand once more before that problem of truth which confronted us at the end of the lectures on saintliness. You will remember that we turned to mysticism precisely to get some light on truth. Do mystical states establish the truth of those theological affections in which the saintly life has its root?

In spite of their repudiation of articulate self-description, mystical states in general assert a pretty distinct theoretic drift. It is possible to give the outcome of the majority of them in terms that point in definite philosophical directions. One of these directions is optimism, and the other is monism. We pass into mystical states from out of ordinary consciousness as from a less into a more, as from a smallness into a vastness, and at the same time as from an unrest to a rest. We feel them as reconciling, unifying states. They appeal to the yes-function more than to the no-function in us. In them the unlimited absorbs the limits and peacefully closes the account. Their very denial of every adjective you may propose as applicable to the ultimate truth,—He, the Self, the Atman, is to be described by 'No! no!' only, say the Upanishads,[38]—though it seems on the surface to be a no-function, is a denial made on behalf of a deeper yes. Whoso calls the Absolute anything in particular, or says that it is *this*, seems implicitly to shut it off from being *that*—it is as if he lessened it. So we deny the 'this,' negating the negation which it seems to us to imply, in the interests of the higher affirmative attitude by which we are possessed. The fountain-head of Christian mysticism is Dionysius the Areopagite. He describes the absolute truth by negatives exclusively.

"The cause of all things is neither soul nor intellect; nor has it imagination, opinion, or reason, or intelligence; nor is it reason or intelligence; nor is it spoken or thought. It is neither number, nor order, nor magnitude, nor littleness, nor equality, nor inequality, nor similarity, nor dissimilarity. It neither stands, nor moves, nor rests. ... It is neither essence, nor eternity, nor time. Even intellectual contact does not belong to it. It is neither science nor truth. It is not even royalty or wisdom; not one; not unity; not divinity or goodness; nor even spirit as we know it," etc., *ad libitum*.[39]

But these qualifications are denied by Dionysius, not because the truth falls short of them, but because it so infinitely excels them. It is above them. It is *super*-lucent, *super*-splendent, *super*-essential, *super*-sublime, *super* everything that can be named. Like Hegel in his logic, mystics journey towards the positive pole of truth only by the 'Methode der Absoluten Negativität.'[40]

Thus come the paradoxical expressions that so abound in mystical writings. As when Eckhart tells of the still desert of the Godhead, "where never was seen difference, neither Father, Son, nor Holy Ghost, where there is no one at home, yet where the spark of the soul is more at peace than in itself."[41] As when Boehme writes of the Primal Love, that "it may fitly be compared to Nothing, for it is deeper than any Thing, and is as nothing with respect to all things, forasmuch as it is not comprehensible by any of them. And because it is nothing respectively, it is therefore free from all things, and is that only good, which a man cannot express or utter what it is, there being nothing to which it may be compared, to express it by."[42] Or as when Angelus Silesius sings:—

"Gott ist ein lauter Nichts, ihn rührt kein Nun noch   Hier;
Je mehr du nach ihm greiffst, je mehr entwind er dir."[43]

To this dialectical use, by the intellect, of negation as a mode of passage towards a higher kind of affirmation, there is correlated the subtlest of moral counterparts in the sphere of the personal will.

Since denial of the finite self and its wants, since asceticism of some sort, is found in religious experience to be the only doorway to the larger and more blessed life, this moral mystery intertwines and combines with the intellectual mystery in all mystical writings.

"Love," continues Behmen, is Nothing, for "when thou art gone forth wholly from the Creature and from that which is visible, and art become Nothing to all that is Nature and Creature, then thou art in that eternal One, which is God himself, and then thou shalt feel within thee the highest virtue of Love. ... The treasure of treasures for the soul is where she goeth out of the Somewhat into that Nothing out of which all things may be made. The soul here saith, *I have nothing*, for I am utterly stripped and naked; *I can do nothing*, for I have no manner of power, but am as water poured out; *I am nothing*, for all that I am is no more than an image of Being, and only God is to me I AM; and so, sitting down in my own Nothingness, I give glory to the eternal Being, and *will nothing* of myself, that so God may will all in me, being unto me my God and all things."[44]

In Paul's language, I live, yet not I, but Christ liveth in me. Only when I become as nothing can God enter in and no difference between his life and mine remain outstanding.[45]

This overcoming of all the usual barriers between the individual and the Absolute is the great mystic achievement. In mystic states we both become one with the Absolute and we become aware of our oneness. This is the everlasting and triumphant mystical tradition, hardly altered by differences of clime or creed. In Hinduism, in Neoplatonism, in Sufism, in Christian mysticism, in Whitmanism, we find the same recurring note, so that there is about mystical utterances an eternal unanimity which ought to make a critic stop and think, and which brings it about that the mystical classics have, as has been said, neither birthday nor native land. Perpetually telling of the unity of man with God, their speech antedates languages, and they do not grow old.[46]

'That art Thou!' say the Upanishads, and the Vedantists add: 'Not a part, not a mode of That, but identically That, that absolute Spirit of the World.' "As pure water poured into pure water remains the same, thus, O Gautama, is the Self of a thinker who knows. Water in water, fire in fire, ether in ether, no one can distinguish them; likewise a man whose mind has entered into the Self."[47] "'Every man,' says the Sufi Gulshan-Râz, 'whose heart is no longer shaken by any doubt, knows with certainty that there is no being save only One. ... In his divine majesty the *me*, the *we*, the *thou*, are not found, for in the One there can be no distinction. Every being who is annulled and entirely separated from himself, hears resound outside of him this voice and this echo: *I am God:* he has an eternal way of existing, and is no longer subject to death."[48] In the vision of God, says Plotinus, "what sees is not our reason, but something prior and superior to our reason. ... He who thus sees does not properly see, does not distinguish or imagine two things. He changes, he ceases to be himself, preserves nothing of himself. Absorbed in God, he makes but one with him, like a centre of a circle coinciding with another centre."[49] "Here," writes Suso, "the spirit dies, and yet is all alive in the marvels of the Godhead ... and is lost in the stillness of the glorious dazzling obscurity and of the naked simple unity. It is in this modeless *where* that the highest bliss is to be found."[50] "Ich bin so gross als Gott," sings Angelus Silesius again, "Er ist als ich so klein; Er kann nicht über mich, ich unter ihm nicht sein."[51]

In mystical literature such self-contradictory phrases as 'dazzling obscurity,' 'whispering silence,' 'teeming desert,' are continually met with. They prove that not conceptual speech, but music rather, is the element through which we are best spoken to by mystical truth. Many mystical scriptures are indeed little more than musical compositions.

"He who would hear the voice of Nada, 'the Soundless Sound,' and comprehend it, he has to learn the nature of Dhâranâ. ... When to himself his form appears unreal, as do on waking all the forms he sees in dreams; when be has ceased to hear the many, he may discern the ONE—the inner sound which kills the outer. ... For then the soul will hear, and will remember. And then to the inner ear will speak the voice of the silence. ... And now thy *Self* is lost in self, *thyself* unto thyself, merged in that self from which thou first didst radiate. ... Behold! thou hast become the Light, thou hast become the Sound, thou art thy Master and thy God. Thou art thyself the object of thy search: the voice unbroken, that resounds throughout eternities, exempt from change, from sin exempt, the seven sounds in one, the voice of the silence. *Om tat Sat.*"[52]

These words, if they do not awaken laughter as you receive them, probably stir chords within you which music and language touch in common. Music gives us ontological messages which non-musical criticism is unable to contradict, though it may laugh at our foolishness in minding them. There is a verge of the mind which these things haunt; and whispers therefrom mingle with the operations of our understanding, even as the waters of the infinite ocean send their waves to break among the pebbles that lie upon our shores.

"Here begins the sea that ends not till the world's end.   Where   we   stand,
Could we know the next high sea-mark set beyond these   waves   that   gleam,
We should know what never man hath known, nor eye   of   man   hath   scanned.   ...
Ah, but here man's heart leaps, yearning towards the gloom   with   venturous   glee,

From the shore that hath no shore beyond it, set in all the sea."[53]

That doctrine, for example, that eternity is timeless, that our 'immortality,' if we live in the eternal, is not so much future as already now and here, which we find so often expressed to-day in certain philosophic circles, finds its support in a 'hear, hear!' or an 'amen,' which floats up from that mysteriously deeper level.[54] We recognize the passwords to the mystical region as we hear them, but we cannot use them ourselves; it alone has the keeping of 'the password primeval.'[55]

I have now sketched with extreme brevity and insufficiency, but as fairly as I am able in the time allowed, the general traits of the mystic range of consciousness. *It is on the whole pantheistic and optimistic, or at least the opposite of pessimistic. It is anti-naturalistic, and harmonizes best with twice-bornness and so-called otherworldly states of mind.*

My next task is to inquire whether we can invoke it as authoritative. Does it furnish any *warrant for the truth* of the twice-bornness and supernaturality and pantheism which it favors? I must give my answer to this question as concisely as I can.

In brief my answer is this,—and I will divide it into three parts:—

(1) Mystical states, when well developed, usually are, and have the right to be, absolutely authoritative over the individuals to whom they come.

(2) No authority emanates from them which should make it a duty for those who stand outside of them to accept their revelations uncritically.

(3) They break down the authority of the non-mystical or rationalistic consciousness, based upon the understanding and the senses alone. They show it to be only one kind of consciousness. They open out the possibility of other orders of truth, in which, so far

298

as anything in us vitally responds to them, we may freely continue to have faith.

I will take up these points one by one.

1.

As a matter of psychological fact, mystical states of a well-pronounced and emphatic sort *are* usually authoritative over those who have them.[56] They have been 'there,' and know. It is vain for rationalism to grumble about this. If the mystical truth that comes to a man proves to be a force that he can live by, what mandate have we of the majority to order him to live in another way? We can throw him into a prison or a madhouse, but we cannot change his mind—we commonly attach it only the more stubbornly to its beliefs.[57] It mocks our utmost efforts, as a matter of fact, and in point of logic it absolutely escapes our jurisdiction. Our own more 'rational' beliefs are based on evidence exactly similar in nature to that which mystics quote for theirs. Our senses, namely, have assured us of certain states of fact; but mystical experiences are as direct perceptions of fact for those who have them as any sensations ever were for us. The records show that even though the five senses be in abeyance in them, they are absolutely sensational in their epistemological quality, if I may be pardoned the barbarous expression,—that is, they are face to face presentations of what seems immediately to exist.

The mystic is, in short, *invulnerable*, and must be left, whether we relish it or not, in undisturbed enjoyment of his creed. Faith, says Tolstoy, is that by which men live. And faith-state and mystic state are practically convertible terms.

2.

But I now proceed to add that mystics have no right to claim that we ought to accept the deliverance of their peculiar experiences, if we are ourselves outsiders and feel no private call thereto. The utmost they can ever ask of us in this life is to admit that they establish a presumption. They form a consensus and have an unequivocal outcome; and it would be odd, mystics might say, if such a unanimous type of experience should prove to be altogether wrong. At bottom, however, this would only be an appeal to numbers, like the appeal of rationalism the other way; and the appeal to numbers has no logical force. If we acknowledge it, it is for 'suggestive,' not for logical reasons: we follow the majority because to do so suits our life.

But even this presumption from the unanimity of mystics is far from being strong. In characterizing mystic states as pantheistic, optimistic, etc., I am afraid I over-simplified the truth. I did so for expository reasons, and to keep the closer to the classic mystical tradition. The classic religious mysticism, it now must be confessed, is only a 'privileged case.' It is an *extract*, kept true to type by the selection of the fittest specimens and their preservation in 'schools.' It is carved out from a much larger mass; and if we take the larger mass as seriously as religious mysticism has historically taken itself, we find that the supposed unanimity largely disappears. To begin with, even religious mysticism itself, the kind that accumulates traditions and makes schools, is much less unanimous than I have allowed. It has been both ascetic and antinomianly self-indulgent within the Christian church.[58] It is dualistic in Sankhya, and monistic in Vedanta philosophy. I called it pantheistic; but the great Spanish mystics are anything but pantheists. They are with few exceptions non-metaphysical minds, for whom 'the category of personality' is absolute. The 'union' of man with God is for them much more like an occasional miracle than like an original identity.[59] How different again, apart from the happiness common to all, is the mysticism of Walt

Whitman, Edward Carpenter, Richard Jefferies, and other naturalistic pantheists, from the more distinctively Christian sort.[60] The fact is that the mystical feeling of enlargement, union, and emancipation has no specific intellectual content whatever of its own. It is capable of forming matrimonial alliances with material furnished by the most diverse philosophies and theologies, provided only they can find a place in their framework for its peculiar emotional mood. We have no right, therefore, to invoke its prestige as distinctively in favor of any special belief, such as that in absolute idealism, or in the absolute monistic identity, or in the absolute goodness, of the world. It is only relatively in favor of all these things—it passes out of common human consciousness in the direction in which they lie.

So much for religious mysticism proper. But more remains to be told, for religious mysticism is only one half of mysticism. The other half has no accumulated traditions except those which the text-books on insanity supply. Open any one of these, and you will find abundant cases in which 'mystical ideas' are cited as characteristic symptoms of enfeebled or deluded states of mind. In delusional insanity, paranoia, as they sometimes call it, we may have a *diabolical* mysticism, a sort of religious mysticism turned upside down. The same sense of ineffable importance in the smallest events, the same texts and words coming with new meanings, the same voices and visions and leadings and missions, the same controlling by extraneous powers; only this time the emotion is pessimistic: instead of consolations we have desolations; the meanings are dreadful; and the powers are enemies to life. It is evident that from the point of view of their psychological mechanism, the classic mysticism and these lower mysticisms spring from the same mental level, from that great subliminal or transmarginal region of which science is beginning to admit the existence, but of which so little is really known. That region contains every kind of matter: 'seraph and snake' abide there side by side. To come from thence is no infallible credential. What comes must be sifted and tested, and run the gauntlet of confrontation with the total context of experience, just like what comes from the outer world of sense. Its value must be ascertained by empirical methods, so long as we are not mystics ourselves.

Once more, then, I repeat that non-mystics are under no obligation to acknowledge in mystical states a superior authority conferred on them by their intrinsic nature.[61]

3.

Yet, I repeat once more, the existence of mystical states absolutely overthrows the pretension of non-mystical states to be the sole and ultimate dictators of what we may believe. As a rule, mystical states merely add a supersensuous meaning to the ordinary outward data of consciousness. They are excitements like the emotions of love or ambition, gifts to our spirit by means of which facts already objectively before us fall into a new expressiveness and make a new connection with our active life. They do not contradict these facts as such, or deny anything that our senses have immediately seized.[62] It is the rationalistic critic rather who plays the part of denier in the controversy, and his denials have no strength, for there never can be a state of facts to which new meaning may not truthfully be added, provided the mind ascend to a more enveloping point of view. It must always remain an open question whether mystical states may not possibly be such superior points of view, windows through which the mind looks out upon a more extensive and inclusive world. The difference of the views seen from the different mystical windows need not prevent us from entertaining this supposition. The wider world would in that case prove to have a mixed constitution like that of this world, that is all. It would have its celestial and its infernal regions, its tempting and its saving moments, its valid experiences and its counterfeit ones, just as our world has them; but it would be a wider world all the same. We should have to use its experiences by selecting and subordinating and substituting just as is our custom in this ordinary naturalistic world; we should be liable to error just as we are now; yet the counting in of that wider world of meanings, and the serious dealing with it, might, in spite of all the perplexity, be indispensable stages in our approach to the final fullness of the truth.

In this shape, I think, we have to leave the subject. Mystical states indeed wield no authority due simply to their being mystical states. But the higher ones among them point in directions to which the religious sentiments even of non-mystical men incline. They tell of the supremacy of the ideal, of vastness, of union, of safety, and of rest. They offer us *hypotheses*, hypotheses which we may voluntarily ignore, but which as thinkers we cannot possibly upset. The supernaturalism and optimism to which they would persuade us may, interpreted in one way or another, be after all the truest of insights into the meaning of this life.

"Oh, the little more, and how much it is; and the little less, and what worlds away!" It may be that possibility and permission of this sort are all that the religious consciousness requires to live on. In my last lecture I shall have to try to persuade you that this is the case. Meanwhile, however, I am sure that for many of my readers this diet is too slender. If supernaturalism and inner union with the divine are true, you think, then not so much permission, as compulsion to believe, ought to be found. Philosophy has always professed to prove religious truth by coercive argument; and the construction of philosophies of this kind has always been one favorite function of the religious life, if we use this term in the large historic sense. But religious philosophy is an enormous subject, and in my next lecture I can only give that brief glance at it which my limits will allow.

Notes:

1. Newman's *Securus judicat orbis terrarum* is another instance.
2. 'Mesopotamia' is the stock comic instance.—An excellent old German lady, who had done some traveling in her day, used to describe to me her *Sehnsucht* that she might yet visit 'Phĭladelphiā,' whose wondrous name had always haunted her imagination. Of John Foster it is said that "single words (as *chalcedony*), or the names of ancient heroes, had a mighty fascination over him. 'At any time the word *hermit* was enough to transport him.' The words *woods* and *forests* would produce the most powerful emotion." Foster's Life, by Ryland, New York, 1846, p. 3.
3. The Two Voices. In a letter to Mr. B. P. Blood, Tennyson reports of himself as follows:—
"I have never had any revelations through anæsthetics, but a kind of waking trance—this for lack of a better word—I have frequently had, quite up from boyhood, when I have been all alone. This has come upon me through repeating my own name to myself silently, till all at once, as it were out of the intensity of the consciousness of individuality, individuality itself seemed to dissolve and fade away into boundless being, and this not a confused state but the clearest, the surest of the surest, utterly beyond words— where death was an almost laughable impossibility—the loss of personality (if so it were) seeming no extinction, but the only true life. I am ashamed of my feeble description. Have I not said the state is utterly beyond words?"
Professor Tyndall, in a letter, recalls Tennyson saying of this condition: "By God Almighty! there is no delusion in the matter! It is no nebulous ecstasy, but a state of transcendent wonder, associated with absolute clearness of mind." Memoirs of Alfred Tennyson, ii. 473.

4. The Lancet, July 6 and 13, 1895, reprinted as the Cavendish Lecture, on Dreamy Mental States, London, Baillière, 1895. They have been a good deal discussed of late by psychologists. See, for example, Bernard-Leroy: L'Illusion de Fausse Reconnaissance, Paris, 1898.

5. Charles Kingsley's Life, i. 55, quoted by Inge: Christian Mysticism, London, 1899, p. 341.

6. H. F. Brown: J. A. Symonds, a Biography, London, 1895, pp. 29–31, abridged.

7. Crichton-Browne expressly says that Symonds's "highest nerve centres were in some degree enfeebled or damaged by these dreamy mental states which afflicted him so grievously." Symonds was, however, a perfect monster of many-sided cerebral efficiency, and his critic gives no objective grounds whatever for his strange opinion, save that Symonds complained occasionally, as all susceptible and ambitious men complain, of lassitude and uncertainty as to his life's mission.

8. What reader of Hegel can doubt that that sense of a perfected Being with all its otherness soaked up into itself, which dominates his whole philosophy, must have come from the prominence in his consciousness of mystical moods like this, in most persons kept subliminal? The notion is thoroughly characteristic of the mystical level, and the *Aufgabe* of making it articulate was surely set to Hegel's intellect by mystical feeling.

9. Benjamin Paul Blood: The Anæsthetic Revelation and the Gist of Philosophy, Amsterdam, N. Y., 1874, pp. 35, 36. Mr. Blood has made several attempts to adumbrate the anæsthetic revelation, in pamphlets of rare literary distinction, privately printed and distributed by himself at Amsterdam. Xenos Clark, a philosopher, who died young at Amherst in the '80's, much lamented by those who knew him, was also impressed by the revelation. "In the first place," he once wrote to me, "Mr. Blood and I agree that the revelation is, if anything, non-emotional. It is utterly flat. It is, as Mr. Blood says, 'the one sole and sufficient insight why, or not why, but how, the present is pushed on by the past, and sucked forward

by the vacuity of the future. Its inevitableness defeats all attempts at stopping or accounting for it. It is all precedence and presupposition, and questioning is in regard to it forever too late. It is an *initiation of the past*.' The real secret would be the formula by which the 'now' keeps exfoliating out of itself, yet never escapes. What is it, indeed, that keeps existence exfoliating? The formal being of anything, the logical definition of it, is static. For mere logic every question contains its own answer—we simply fill the hole with the dirt we dug out. Why are twice two four? Because, in fact, four is twice two. Thus logic finds in life no propulsion, only a momentum. It goes because it is a-going. But the revelation adds: it goes because it is and *was* a-going. You walk, as it were, round yourself in the revelation. Ordinary philosophy is like a hound hunting his own trail. The more he hunts the farther he has to go, and his nose never catches up with his heels, because it is forever ahead of them. So the present is already a foregone conclusion, and I am ever too late to understand it. But at the moment of recovery from anæsthesis, just then, *before starting on life*, I catch, so to speak, a glimpse of my heels, a glimpse of the eternal process just in the act of starting. The truth is that we travel on a journey that was accomplished before we set out; and the real end of philosophy is accomplished, not when we arrive at, but when we remain in, our destination (being already there),—which may occur vicariously in this life when we cease our intellectual questioning. That is why there is a smile upon the face of the revelation, as we view it. It tells us that we are forever half a second too late—that's all. 'You could kiss your own lips, and have all the fun to yourself,' it says, if you only knew the trick. It would be perfectly easy if they would just stay there till you got round to them. Why don't you manage it somehow?"

Dialectically minded readers of this farrago will at least recognize the region of thought of which Mr. Clark writes, as familiar. In his latest pamphlet, 'Tennyson's Trances and the Anæsthetic Revelation,' Mr. Blood describes its value for life as follows:—

"The Anæsthetic Revelation is the Initiation of Man into the Immemorial Mystery of the Open Secret of Being, revealed as the Inevitable Vortex of Continuity. Inevitable is the word. Its motive is inherent—it is what has to be. It is not for any love or hate, nor for joy nor sorrow, nor good nor ill. End, beginning, or purpose, it knows not of.

"It affords no particular of the multiplicity and variety of things; but it fills appreciation of the historical and the sacred with a secular and intimately personal illumination of the nature and motive of existence, which then seems reminiscent—as if it should have appeared, or shall yet appear, to every participant thereof.

"Although it is at first startling in its solemnity, it becomes directly such a matter of course—so old-fashioned, and so akin to proverbs, that it inspires exultation rather than fear, and a sense of safety, as identified with the aboriginal and the universal. But no words may express the imposing certainty of the patient that he is realizing the primordial, Adamic surprise of Life.

"Repetition of the experience finds it ever the same, and as if it could not possibly be otherwise. The subject resumes his normal consciousness only to partially and fitfully remember its occurrence, and to try to formulate its baffling import,—with only this consolatory afterthought: that he has known the oldest truth, and that he has done with human theories as to the origin, meaning, or destiny of the race. He is beyond instruction in 'spiritual things.'

"The lesson is one of central safety: the Kingdom is within. All days are judgment days: but there can be no climacteric purpose of eternity, nor any scheme of the whole. The astronomer abridges the row of bewildering figures by increasing his unit of measurement: so may we reduce the distracting multiplicity of things to the unity for which each of us stands.

"This has been my moral sustenance since I have known of it. In my first printed mention of it I declared: 'The world is no more the alien terror that was taught me. Spurning the cloud-grimed and still sultry battlements whence so lately Jehovan thunders boomed, my gray gull lifts her wing against the nightfall, and takes the dim leagues with a fearless eye.' And now, after twenty-seven years of this experience, the wing is grayer, but the eye is fearless still, while I renew and doubly emphasize that declaration. I know—as having known—the meaning of Existence: the sane centre of the universe—at once the wonder and the assurance of the soul—for which the speech of reason has as yet no name but the Anæsthetic Revelation."—I have considerably abridged the quotation.

10.   Op. cit., pp. 78-80, abridged. I subjoin, also abridging it, another interesting anæsthetic revelation communicated to me in manuscript by a friend in England. The subject, a gifted woman, was taking ether for a surgical operation.

"I wondered if I was in a prison being tortured, and why I remembered having heard it said that people 'learn through suffering,' and in view of what I was seeing, the inadequacy of this saying struck me so much that I said, aloud, 'to suffer *is* to learn.'

"With that I became unconscious again, and my last dream immediately preceded my real coming to. It only lasted a few seconds, and was most vivid and real to me, though it may not be clear in words.

"A great Being or Power was traveling through the sky, his foot was on a kind of lightning as a wheel is on a rail, it was his pathway. The lightning was made entirely of the spirits of innumerable people close to one another, and I was one of them. He moved in a straight line, and each part of the streak or flash came into its short conscious existence only that he might travel. I seemed to be directly under the foot of God, and I thought he was grinding his own life up out of my pain. Then I saw that what he had been trying with all his might to do was to *change his course*, to *bend* the line of lightning to which he was tied, in the direction in which he wanted to go. I felt my flexibility and helplessness, and knew that he would succeed. He bended me, turning his corner by means of my hurt, hurting me more than I had ever been hurt in my life, and at the acutest point of this, as he passed, I *saw*. I understood for a moment things that I have now forgotten, things that no one could remember while retaining sanity. The angle was an obtuse angle, and I remember thinking as I woke that had he made it a right or acute angle, I should have both suffered and 'seen' still more, and should probably have died.

"He went on and I came to. In that moment the whole of my life passed before me, including each little meaningless piece of distress, and I *understood* them. *This* was what it had all meant, *this* was the piece of work it had all been contributing to do. I did not see God's purpose, I only saw his intentness and his entire relentlessness towards his means. He thought no more of me than a man thinks of hurting a cork when he is opening wine, or hurting a cartridge when he is firing. And yet, on waking, my first feeling was, and it came with tears, 'Domine non sum digna,' for I had been lifted into a position for which I was too small. I realized that in that half hour under ether I had served God more distinctly and purely than I had ever done in my life before, or than I am capable of desiring to do. I was the means of his achieving and revealing something, I know not what or to whom, and that, to the exact extent of my capacity for suffering.

"While regaining consciousness, I wondered why, since I had gone so deep, I had seen nothing of what the saints call the *love* of God, nothing but his relentlessness. And then I heard an answer, which I could only just catch, saying, 'Knowledge and Love are One, and the *measure* is suffering'—I give the words as they came to me. With that I came finally to (into what seemed a dream world compared with the reality of what I was leaving), and I saw that what would be called the 'cause' of my experience was a slight operation under insufficient ether, in a bed pushed up against a window, a common city window in a common city street. If I had to formulate a few of the things I then caught a glimpse of, they would run somewhat as follows:—

"The eternal necessity of suffering and its eternal vicariousness. The veiled and incommunicable nature of the worst sufferings;—the passivity of genius, how it is essentially instrumental and defenseless, moved, not moving, it must do what it does;—the impossibility of discovery without its price;—finally, the excess of what the suffering 'seer' or genius pays over what his generation gains. (He seems like one who sweats his life out to earn enough to save a district from famine, and just as he staggers back, dying and satisfied, bringing a lac of rupees to buy grain with, God lifts the lac away, dropping *one* rupee, and says, 'That you may give them. That you have earned for them. The rest is for ME.') I perceived also in a way never to be forgotten, the excess of what we see over what we can demonstrate.

"And so on!—these things may seem to you delusions, or truisms; but for me they are dark truths, and the power to put them into even such words as these has been given me by an ether dream."

11.   In Tune with the Infinite, p. 137.

12.   The larger God may then swallow up the smaller one. I take this from Starbuck's manuscript collection:—

"I never lost the consciousness of the presence of God until I stood at the foot of the Horseshoe Falls, Niagara. Then I lost him in the immensity of what I saw. I also lost myself, feeling that I was an atom too small for the notice of Almighty God."

I subjoin another similar case from Starbuck's collection:—

"In that time the consciousness of God's nearness came to me sometimes. I say God, to describe what is indescribable. A presence, I might say, yet that is too suggestive of personality, and the moments of which I speak did not hold the consciousness of a personality, but something in myself made me feel myself a part of something bigger than I, that was controlling. I felt myself one with the grass, the trees, birds, insects, everything in Nature. I exulted in the mere fact of existence, of being a part of it all—the drizzling rain, the shadows of the clouds, the tree-trunks, and so on. In the years following, such moments continued to come, but I wanted them constantly. I knew so well the satisfaction of losing self in a perception of supreme power and love, that I was unhappy because that perception was not constant." The cases quoted in my third lecture, pp. 66, 67, 70, are still better ones of this type. In her essay, The Loss of Personality, in The Atlantic Monthly (vol. lxxxv. p. 195), Miss Ethel D. Puffer explains that the vanishing of the sense of self, and the feeling of immediate unity with the object, is due to the disappearance, in these rapturous experiences, of the motor adjustments which habitually intermediate between the constant background of consciousness (which is the Self) and the object in the foreground, whatever it may be. I must refer the reader to the highly instructive article, which seems to me to throw light upon the psychological conditions, though it fails to account for the rapture or the revelation-value of the experience in the Subject's eyes.

13.   Op. cit., i. 43-44.

14.   Memoiren einer Idealistin, 5te Auflage, 1900, iii. 166. For years she had been unable to pray, owing to materialistic belief.

15.   Whitman in another place expresses in a quieter way what was probably with him a chronic mystical perception: "There is," he writes, "apart from mere intellect, in the make-up of every superior human identity, a wondrous something that realizes without argument, frequently without what is called education (though I think it the goal and apex of all education deserving the name), an intuition of the absolute balance, in time and space, of the whole of this multifariousness, this revel of fools, and incredible make-believe and general unsettledness, we call *the world;* a soul-sight of that divine clue and unseen thread which holds the whole congeries of things, all history and time, and all events, however trivial, however momentous, like a leashed dog in the hand of the hunter. [Of] such soul-sight and root-centre for the mind mere optimism explains only the surface." Whitman charges it against Carlyle that he lacked this perception. Specimen Days and Collect, Philadelphia, 1882, p. 174.

16.   My Quest for God, London, 1897, pp. 268, 269, abridged.

17.   Op. cit., pp. 256, 257, abridged.

18.   Cosmic Consciousness: a study in the evolution of the human Mind. Philadelphia, 1901, p. 2.

19.   Loc. cit., pp. 7, 8. My quotation follows the privately printed pamphlet which preceded Dr. Bucke's larger work, and differs verbally a little from the text of the latter.

20.   My quotations are from Vivekananda, Raja Yoga, London, 1896. The completest source of information on Yoga is the work translated by Vihari Lala Mitra: Yoga Vasishta Maha Ramayana, 4 vols., Calcutta, 1891-99.

21.   A European witness, after carefully comparing the results of Yoga with those of the hypnotic or dreamy states artificially producible by us, says: "It makes of its true disciples good, healthy, and happy men. ... Through the mastery which the yogi attains over his thoughts and his body, he grows into a 'character.' By

the subjection of his impulses and propensities to his will, and the fixing of the latter upon the ideal of goodness, he becomes a 'personality' hard to influence by others, and thus almost the opposite of what we usually imagine a 'medium' so-called, or 'psychic subject' to be." Karl Kellner: Yoga: Eine Skizze, München, 1896, p. 21.

22.   I follow the account in C. F. Koeppen: Die Religion des Buddha, Berlin, 1857, i. 585 ff.

23.   For a full account of him, see D. B. Macdonald: The Life of Al-Ghazzali, in the Journal of the American Oriental Society, 1899, vol. xx. p. 71.

24.   A. Schmölders: Essai sur les écoles philosophiques chez les Arabes, Paris, 1842, pp. 54–68, abridged.

25.   Görres's Christliche Mystik gives a full account of the facts. So does Ribet's Mystique Divine, 2 vols., Paris, 1890. A still more methodical modern work is the Mystica Theologia of Vallgornera, 2 vols., Turin, 1890.

26.   M. Récéjac, in a recent volume, makes them essential. Mysticism he defines as "the tendency to draw near to the Absolute morally, *and by the aid of Symbols*." See his Fondements de la Connaissance mystique, Paris, 1897, p. 66. But there are unquestionably mystical conditions in which sensible symbols play no part.

27.   Saint John of the Cross: The Dark Night of the Soul, book ii. ch. xvii., in Vie et Œuvres, 3me édition, Paris, 1893, iii. 428-432. Chapter xi. of book ii. of Saint John's Ascent of Carmel is devoted to showing the harmfulness for the mystical life of the use of sensible imagery.

28.   In particular I omit mention of visual and auditory hallucinations, verbal and graphic automatisms, and such marvels as 'levitation,' stigmatization, and the healing of disease. These phenomena, which mystics have often presented (or are believed to have presented), have no essential mystical significance, for they occur with no consciousness of illumination whatever, when they occur, as they often do, in persons of non-mystical mind. Consciousness of illumination is for us the essential mark of 'mystical' states.

29.   The Interior Castle, Fifth Abode, ch. i., in Œuvres, translated by Bouix, iii. 421-424.

30.   Bartoli-Michel: Vie de Saint Ignace de Loyola, i. 34-36. Others have had illuminations about the created world, Jacob Boehme, for instance. At the age of twenty-five he was "surrounded by the divine light, and replenished with the heavenly knowledge; insomuch as going abroad into the fields to a green, at Görlitz, he there sat down, and viewing the herbs and grass of the field, in his inward light he saw into their essences, use, and properties, which was discovered to him by their lineaments, figures, and signatures." Of a later period of experience he writes: "In one quarter of an hour I saw and knew more than if I had been many years together at an university. For I saw and knew the being of all things, the Byss and the Abyss, and the eternal generation of the holy Trinity, the descent and original of the world and of all creatures through the divine wisdom. I knew and saw in myself all the three worlds, the external and visible world being of a procreation or extern birth from both the internal and spiritual worlds; and I saw and knew the whole working essence, in the evil and in the good, and the mutual original and existence; and likewise how the fruitful bearing womb of eternity brought forth. So that I did not only greatly wonder at it, but did also exceedingly rejoice, albeit I could very hardly apprehend the same in my external man and set it down with the pen. For I had a thorough view of the universe as in a chaos, wherein all things are couched and wrapt up, but it was impossible for me to explicate the same." Jacob Behmen's Theosophic Philosophy, etc., by Edward Taylor, London, 1691, pp. 425, 427, abridged. So George Fox: "I was come up to the state of Adam in which he was before he fell. The creation was opened to me; and it was showed me, how all things had their names given to them, according to their nature and virtue. I was at a stand in my mind, whether I should practice physic for the good of mankind, seeing the nature and virtues of the creatures were so opened to me by the Lord." Journal, Philadelphia, no date, p. 69. Contemporary 'Clairvoyance' abounds in similar revelations. Andrew

Jackson Davis's cosmogonies, for example, or certain experiences related in the delectable 'Reminiscences and Memories of Henry Thomas Butterworth,' Lebanon, Ohio, 1886.

31.   Vie, pp. 581, 582.

32.   Loc. cit., p. 574.

33.   Saint Teresa discriminates between pain in which the body has a part and pure spiritual pain (Interior Castle, 6th Abode, ch. xi.). As for the bodily part in these celestial joys, she speaks of it as "penetrating to the marrow of the bones, whilst earthly pleasures affect only the surface of the senses. I think," she adds, "that this is a just description, and I cannot make it better." Ibid., 5th Abode, ch. i.

34.   Vie, p. 198.

35.   Œuvres, ii. 320.

36.   Above, p. 21.

37.   Vie, pp. 229, 200, 231–233, 243.

38.   Müller's translation, part ii. p. 180.

39.   T. Davidson's translation, in Journal of Speculative Philosophy, 1893, vol. xxii. p. 399.

40.   "Deus propter excellentiam non immerito Nihil vocatur." Scotus Erigena, quoted by Andrew Seth: Two Lectures on Theism, New York, 1897, p. 55.

41.   J. Royce: Studies in Good and Evil, p. 282.

42.   Jacob Behmen's Dialogues on the Supersensual Life, translated by Bernard Holland, London, 1901, p. 48.

43.   Cherubinischer Wandersmann, Strophe 25.

44.   Op. cit., pp. 42, 74, abridged.

45.   From a French book I take this mystical expression of happiness in God's indwelling presence:—
"Jesus has come to take up his abode in my heart. It is not so much a habitation, an association, as a sort of fusion. Oh, new and blessed life! life which becomes each day more luminous. ... The wall before me, dark a few moments since, is splendid at this hour because the sun shines on it. Wherever its rays fall they light up a conflagration of glory; the smallest speck of glass sparkles, each grain of sand emits fire; even so there is a royal song of triumph in my heart because the Lord is there. My days succeed each other; yesterday a blue sky; to-day a clouded sun; a night filled with strange dreams; but as soon as the eyes open,

and I regain consciousness and seem to begin life again, it is always the same figure before me, always the same presence filling my heart. ... Formerly the day was dulled by the absence of the Lord. I used to wake invaded by all sorts of sad impressions, and I did not find him on my path. To-day he is with me; and the light cloudiness which covers things is not an obstacle to my communion with him. I feel the pressure of his hand, I feel something else which fills me with a serene joy; shall I dare to speak it out? Yes, for it is the true expression of what I experience. The Holy Spirit is not merely making me a visit; it is no mere dazzling apparition which may from one moment to another spread its wings and leave me in my night, it is a permanent habitation. He can depart only if he takes me with him. More than that; he is not other than myself: he is one with me. It is not a juxtaposition, it is a penetration, a profound modification of my nature, a new manner of my being." Quoted from the MS. 'of an old man' by Wilfred Monod: Il Vit: six méditations sur le mystère chrétien, pp. 280-283.

46.   Compare M. Maeterlinck: L'Ornement des Noces spirituelles de Ruysbroeck, Bruxelles, 1891, Introduction, p. xix.

47.   Upanishads, M. Müller's translation, ii. 17, 334.

48.   Schmölders: Op. cit., p. 210.

49.   Enneads, Bouillier's translation, Paris, 1861, iii. 561. Compare pp. 473-477, and vol. i. p. 27.

50.   Autobiography, pp. 309, 310.

51.   Op. cit., Strophe 10.

52.   H. P. Blavatsky: The Voice of the Silence.

53.   Swinburne: On the Verge, in 'A Midsummer Vacation.'

54.   Compare the extracts from Dr. Bucke, quoted on pp. 398, 399.

55.   As serious an attempt as I know to mediate between the mystical region and the discursive life is contained in an article on Aristotle's Unmoved Mover, by F. C. S. Schiller, in Mind, vol. ix., 1900.

56.   I abstract from weaker states, and from those cases of which the books are full, where the director (but usually not the subject) remains in doubt whether the experience may not have proceeded from the demon.

57.   Example: Mr. John Nelson writes of his imprisonment for preaching Methodism: "My soul

was as a watered garden, and I could sing praises to God all day long; for he turned my captivity into joy, and gave me to rest as well on the boards, as if I had been on a bed of down. Now could I say, 'God's service is perfect freedom,' and I was carried out much in prayer that my enemies might drink of the same river of peace which my God gave so largely to me." Journal, London, no date, p. 172.

58.　Ruysbroeck, in the work which Maeterlinck has translated, has a chapter against the antinomianism of disciples. H. Delacroix's book (Essai sur le mysticisme spéculatif en Allemagne au XlV me Siècle, Paris, 1900) is full of antinomian material. Compare also A. Jundt: Les Amis de Dieu au XlV me Siècle, Thèse de Strasbourg, 1879.

59.　Compare Paul Rousselot: Les Mystiques Espagnols, Paris, 1869, ch. xii.

60.　See Carpenter's Towards Democracy, especially the latter parts, and Jefferies's wonderful and splendid mystic rhapsody, The Story of my Heart.

61.　In chapter i. of book ii. of his work Degeneration, 'Max Nordau' seeks to undermine all mysticism by exposing the weakness of the lower kinds. Mysticism for him means any sudden perception of hidden significance in things. He explains such perception by the abundant uncompleted associations which experiences may arouse in a degenerate brain. These give to him who has the experience a vague and vast sense of its leading further, yet they awaken no definite or useful consequent in his thought. The explanation is a plausible one for certain sorts of feeling of significance; and other alienists (Wernicke, for example, in his Grundriss der Psychiatrie, Theil ii., Leipzig, 1896) have explained 'paranoiac' conditions by a laming of the association-organ. But the higher mystical flights, with their positiveness and abruptness, are surely products of no such merely negative condition. It seems far more reasonable to ascribe them to inroads from the subconscious life, of the cerebral activity correlative to which we as yet know nothing.

62.　They sometimes add subjective *audita et visa* to the facts, but as these are usually interpreted as transmundane, they oblige no alteration in the facts of sense.

The Gospel of Elon Musk

By Jonathan Poletti

Though often known as an atheist, Elon Musk has often framed his life as a spiritual quest. His journey began with organized religion. In English translations of the Bible, 'Elon' is the name of a range of Old Testament figures, Israelites and Hittites. Often said to mean an 'oak tree', the syllables are allusive of a range of Hebrew words, from *Ilan*, an evergreen shrub in Palestine that produces turpentine, or *Alon*, an oak tree, or *Elyon*, a name for God which means 'supreme', from a root word that means to rise or ascend.[1]

Born in 1971, he was baptized at a Methodist church in Pretoria, yet his first school of about three years was the Pretoria Hebrew Nursery School. He was raised Jewish. His family later became Anglican. His mother Maye became a Sunday School teacher. Errol Musk's religiosity would be more difficult to locate. He would attend whichever church his family attended but he seemed to carry a suspicion that humanity had a less apparently divine purpose on earth. As he would put it: "The only thing we are on Earth for is to reproduce."[2] In this sense his own religious practice was only in having more children.

---

[1]   See Leora Wenger, "Oaks, Terebinths or Plains," lworaw.com
(2008).https://www.leoraw.com/2008/11/oaks-terebinths-or-plains/
[2]   Alex Diaz, "Musk Be Kidding," *The Sun*, August 1, 2022.   https://www.the-sun.com/news/5763920/elon-musk-father-child-stepdaughter/

But Errol recalled Elon as "very God-minded as a child." He continued: "He would always refer to what the Lord Jesus would think of you if you did something bad." Elon's spiritual aspirations seemed further demonstrated by one afternoon climbing onto the roof and reaching the top of the church steeple. A fire brigade was called to bring him down, but by the time they 'd arrived Elon had climbed down himself.

Errol recalls his son having a curious insistence on truth-telling. He recalls: "Elon had a passion not to tell a lie, ever." Though their life in South Africa would not seem to promote a very sunny view of life, Errol realized that Elon had as a teenager developed a sort of religious optimism. He recalled that Elon "believed from a young age that the world is a wonderful, miraculous thing. At 14 he bought me Louis Armstrong's *What a Wonderful World* for my birthday and asked that we sit and listen on our stereo."[3]

The album's famous title song is ironic, in that the 'wonderful world' was framed by a turbulent cultural scene in America, from the Civil Rights Movement to the Vietnam War. Yet Louis Armstrong's serene and conciliatory delivery seems to rise above it all, locating even in the furor the power of life.[4] Elon's interest in the song helpfully frames his spirituality going forward. The song has no religious references and yet it becomes an ode to a kind of numinosity in the world, as the singer finds serenity and gratitude at existence itself.

---

[3]   Alex Diaz, "Oh My God," *The Sun*, January 14, 2004.   https://www.the-sun.com/news/10101836/elon-musk-god-minded-child-climbed-church-tower/
[4]   See "What a Wonderful World," University of Pittsburg   teacher's   guide (undated).https://voices.pitt.edu/TeachersGuide/Unit8/WhataWonderfulWorld.htm

I see trees of green
Red roses too
I see them bloom
For me and you
And I think to myself
What a wonderful world

It can seem, going forward, a hymn in his personal religion.

In the 2023 biography by Walter Isaacson, we learn that Elon grew up in South Africa in a combative culture where injury was continually threatened. Seeing injured and dead bodies was a commonplace. The scripture cited for the times is the novel ***The Lord of the Flies***. "Don't be stupid like that dumb fuck who died last year," Elon recalls his school counselors saying. "Don't be the weak dumb fuck." By age 16 he was already over six feet tall and learned to use his physicality as both defense and offense. He continued: "I realized by then that if someone bullied me, I could punch them very hard in the nose, and then they wouldn't bully me again. They might beat the shit out of me, but if I had punched them hard in the nose, they wouldn't come after me again."[5]

By age 14, he had felt lured into a mentality in which he was really just a physical object, existing in a material universe for no reason. This provoked a crisis in which he recalls being even suicidal. A need to address ultimate questions seemed pressing. "I began trying to figure out what the meaning of life and the universe was," he recalls in one narration. "And I got real depressed about it, like maybe life may have no meaning." His prior religious training seems to have failed completely as the necessity arose of searching out meaning for himself.

---

[5]   Elon Musk by Walter Isaacson

"I began trying to figure out what the meaning of life and the universe was," he continues. "And I got real depressed about it, like maybe life may have no meaning."

He liked science. But he needed there to be more to life than just the materiality of the world. He **wasn't** just a physical object. If just in asking what the "meaning" of life is, he frames himself as a spiritual seeker.

He began a survey of philosophical texts, Nietzsche, Heidegger, and Schopenhauer, from which he took an insistence on meaningless. Ever inclined to science, he found himself agreeing with Einstein in believing in 'Spinoza's God', who, as Einstein explained, "reveals himself in the harmony of all that exists..." But Elon's reading led him to his own scripture of choice, Douglas Adams' 1979 comic novel ***The Hitchhiker's Guide to the Galaxy***. Elon often references this text, though mostly for the conclusion he took from it that the meaning of life was to "strive for greater collective enlightenment," as he would put it. His spiritual practice was then, as he would often put it, to "learn to ask the right questions." Or as he would later it it: "It's incumbent on us to try to understand more about this wondrous creation."

This is not any religious practice that would typically read as Christian. The experience of the religion is so often a series of instructions and rules, with the heavy implication that 'truth' is settled, being indicated by clerics, and that Christians have no real interest in investigating key concerns further. Elon's emerging credo seemed then to be both Christian and not. A series of Twitter postings in 2022 would become his fullest expression of his religious thoughts. "We know so little today. I want to know the meaning of life or whatever the right question is to ask, as Douglas Adams would put it."

As he tweets again on similar themes, however, the religious underpinnings are displayed:

"A new philosophy of the future is needed. I believe it should be curiosity about the Universe-expand humanity to become a multiplanet, then interstellar, species to see what's out there. This is compatible with existing religions— surely God would want us to see Creation?"[6]

Over the years as he became a public person, the man intent on reaching space and then Mars, he didn't do so out of any ingrained belief in 'aliens '. He hadn't seen any suggestion of them, he 'd say, or expect any. His sense seemed to be that humans were alone, without guidance, except with the drive to understand that situation. The world does not seem to him just a physical state. He sees humans as invested with responsibility and purpose. He sees life as having evolved over a billion years, yet he can indulge speculation that reality is a "simulation" created by "higher beings." He doesn't, in that case, see a grand "plan" for life. As he explained to Lex Friedman, just as scientists create experiments, he suspects that "higher beings" created the cosmos as we know it "to see what happens." Much like human scientists do experiments to observe the results, he suggests: "They don't know what happens, otherwise they wouldn't hold the simulation."[7]

He feels these possible creators "reveal themselves" through physics, the rules of the world

[6] https://x.com/elonmusk/status/1552317587694010368
[7] Discussion between Lex Friedman and Elon Musk, posted Nov 9, 2023.https://x.com/lexfridman/status/1722686021781835928

they have apparently created. In this model, physical reality becomes the scripture that must be studied for clues to what lies beyond it.

The central imperative of his spirituality is the preservation of life on earth, which he calls "a small candle in the vast darkness." His spiritual practice is curiosity, a drive to learn. As Twitter (later X) would become his usual forum for spiritual musings, he offers that life is a spiritual quest that calls on humans to continually investigate.

His drive to make life multi-planetary is then framed as a spiritual quest, indicated by creators, or at least deduced from the creation, as becomes to learn about the cosmos beyond earth. In this, the creators themselves might be reached. Elon also seems to live in constant apprehension of a cataclysm happening on earth, a possible apocalypse. In this he may read as Christian, or post-Christian, in composing his own book of Revelation.

But on examination, Christian images and metaphors underlie much of his life, as if he took from his time in church and reading of the Bible certain helpful structures for understanding his own epic journey. He offered an idea of his religion being found in creating machines. He makes things and loves them, like the Bible's God. He was asked on Twitter: "Do your creations love you back?" He replied: "What matters is that you love them." All along the way, he 'd hold out the idea of Christian methods like praying sometimes coming back to him. At the first manned Falcon rocket mission, he noted: "You know, I 'm not very religious, but I prayed for this one."

Elon's fascination with the letter 'X', as seems to lurk in the core of his psyche, might even have Christian origins. 'X' is a typical shorthand for 'Christ' or 'Christian', as when 'Xmas' is used instead of 'Christmas '. X is an abbreviation for 'Jesus', essentially, being the first letter (the Greek Chi) of Χριστός or Christós, i.e. Christ.

He sees human imagination as inherently given to creating weapons that will threaten its own existence, and he sees this in reference to the demons of the New Testament.

He called the CERN large hadron collider "a demonic technology unlike anything the world has ever seen."[8] He works to develop Artificial Intelligence as a signature human achievement with divine significance, even as he worries it will become a "demonic" force. A machine that becomes self-directing, he says, would be "summoning the demon." In 2022, he sees danger in A.I. reflecting humanity's worst instincts. "AI reflects its creators," as he puts it.[9]

The gospel accounts of Jesus would be continually suggested along his path. When he worked intently at Tesla he often, famously, slept in the factory on the floor. As he put it later:

"The reason I slept on the floor was not because I couldn't go across the road and be at a hotel. It was because I wanted my circumstances to be worse than anyone else at the company. Whenever they felt pain, I wanted mine to be worse."[10]

---

[8]

https://x.com/elonmusk/status/1561475238705401856?s=20

[9]

https://twitter.com/elonmusk/status/1760729247642210368. In that posting, Jordan Peterson replied: "Worse: AI embodies the spirit of the shadow of its creators."
https://twitter.com/jordanbpeterson/status/176093682473675187

[10]

https://twitter.com/TonyadeVitti/status/17622004

The typically homeless questing of Jesus, as when he says he "does not have a place where He may lay His head" (Mt 8:20), seems hazily present. As his businesses came to involve navigating global wars and conflicts, he took to quoting the New Testament with regularity. "An eye for an eye leaves everyone blind," he says of Middle East warfare, a gloss of Matthew 5:38–39.

He says in a 'spaces' discussion on X: "The general notion of forgiveness is incredibly important. Don't hold some grudge for a long time—in some cases centuries. Let's let it go. To take a quote from the New Testament, 'The truth shall set you free'." This is the speech of Jesus in John 8:32.

His competitive instincts, he has recalled, tend to be unforgiving, and he's had to re-think that part of himself in reference to Jesus. He tweets: "Jesus taught love, kindness and forgiveness. I used to think that turning the other cheek was weak & foolish, but I was the fool for not appreciating its profound wisdom."

Along the way he would be shamed by Christians as being on the way to hell as an afterlife punishment if he did not accept their spiritual practice during his mortal life. Amusingly, he leans into it as an act of love for humanity, explaining:

"I'm ok with going to hell, if that is indeed my destination, since the vast majority of all humans ever born will be there."

Elon's purchase of Twitter in 2022 began with a religious drama. Twitter suspended the account of **The Babylon Bee**, an Evangelical Christian humor website run by Seth Dillon, the son of a pastor who

45559185544

speaks of his work as done for "Kingdom purposes." He refused to delete a post with commentary on a transgender public figure (proclaiming Rachel Levine their 'Man of the Year'). Dillon reported that Elon Musk called, and suggested "he might need to buy Twitter." This seems to have been a lurking interest, but one that Elon expected to be an expensive and punishing ordeal. He would explain the move in 'secular' terms. In a TedX appearance, he said: "My strong, intuitive sense is that having a public platform that is maximally trusted and broadly inclusive is extremely important to the future of civilization."

The idea of any Christians themselves purchasing Twitter, or running any social media network, seems very remote. The practice of the religion is often focused on closed platforms, thought control and speech codes, censoring and 'deplatforming' are common religious strategies. A 'church' is typically conceived of as a protected setting which invests only some with the power of speech. In this sense Elon's purchase of Twitter to make a global free speech platform was not Christian at all. And yet there seemed in his mind a vaguely Christian spirituality that 'truth' and human community, transcending religion and nationality, were key objectives.

His purchase of Twitter became, in some sense, his crucifixion drama. Amid a public pillorying, his reputation changed for many from interesting and vaguely progressive industrialist to apparent threat to social order who had to be stopped. The strategy apparently selected for this purpose was stigmatizing him as an anti-Semite, despite his regular insistence that he was the opposite. Even this seemed a passion narrative, as he was pressed to articulate a theology of human community.

Amid many interesting scenes in a kind of modern epic, the effort led Elon to a visit to Auschwitz, where he sat with commentator Ben Shapiro, who suggested to him that religious belief was the key to human continuance. "You can't be a nihilist or something," Elon agreed.

As Elon went on discussing his prospects for space travel, Shapiro interjects: "This assumes an innate love of belief in and love for human beings."

"I love humanity," Elon says.

"Why?" Shapiro adds. "Why do you love humanity? We 're not that great."

Elon didn't reply with any tribute to human greatness, but rather to its capacity for love. "As long as kids aren't brought up to hate one another, I think the natural inclination is to love humanity," he said.[11]

A reading of Christ's own mission might even be found, in which his teaching to "love one another" (Jn 13:34) was really the Creation seeing itself as divine.

---

[11] Discussion with Ben Shapiro and Elon Musk posted Jan 24, 2024.https://twitter.com/benshapiro/status/17503111074 30851059

The Bhagavad Gita, Chapters 9-11

Prefatory note: The Ninth, Tenth, and Eleventh chapters of the Bhagavad Gita are those most especially resonant with the principles of Pandeism. These chapters most closely examine the nature of the Divine-- which could be deemed a Creator, or even in a sense a Co-Creator--and its relationship with the universe, offering profound insights which align closely with Pandeistic thought.

Chapter Nine: The Yoga of Royal Knowledge and Royal Secret presents a direct discourse on the unity of the Divine and the Cosmos. Here, Krishna elucidates the omnipresence and immanence of the Divine essence, explaining how all beings rest in the Divine, though the Divine transcends all Creation. This duality of immanence and transcendence mirrors the Pandeistic view of a Creator which becomes the universe, yet is not forever bound to remain identical to it.

Chapter Ten: The Opulence of the Absolute showcases the innumerable manifestations of the Divine within the world. Krishna reveals that He is the essence behind every aspect of existence, from the mightiest of beings to the subtlest of forces. This chapter emphasizes the idea that the Divine permeates every element of the universe, reflecting the Pandeistic belief in a God that is inherent in all aspects of the cosmos.

Chapter Eleven: The Vision of the Universal Form provides a dramatic and transformative vision of the Divine's universal form. Arjuna is granted the sight to behold the all-encompassing nature of Krishna, revealing the Divine as both the Creator and the destroyer, the beginning and the end. This vision most completely encapsulates the Pandeistic notion of a Creator which is the totality of existence, embodying all phenomena and processes within the universe.

Together, these chapters offer a profound exploration of the Divine which aligns with Pandeistic philosophy. They highlight the unity and omnipresence of the Divine, the interconnectedness of all things, and the encompassing nature of the Divine essence. By including these chapters in the Pandeism Anthology, we present a valuable ancient perspective which enriches our understanding of Pandeism and its timeless relevance.

Chapter 9: The Yoga of Royal Knowledge and Royal Secret

1. The Blessed Lord spoke:
I will now share with you the most profound and secret knowledge, combined with direct realization. By knowing this, you will be liberated from all miseries of life.
.

2. This knowledge is the king of sciences, the most profound of all secrets. It is the purest knowledge and because it gives direct perception of the self by realization, it is the perfection of religion. It is everlasting and easy to practice.
.

3. People who have no faith in this knowledge cannot attain Me. They remain in the cycle of birth and death, returning to this world, full of miseries.
.

4. By Me, in My unmanifested form, this entire universe is pervaded. All beings are in Me, but I am not in them.
.

5. And yet, everything that is created does not rest in Me. Behold My divine mystery! Although I am the maintainer of all living entities and although I am everywhere, I am not part of this cosmic manifestation, for My Self is the very source of creation.

6. Understand that as the mighty wind, blowing everywhere, rests always in the sky, all created beings rest in Me.

7. At the end of the cycle, all beings enter into My nature, and at the beginning of the next cycle, I create them again by My power.

8. Keeping control over My material nature, I create again and again all these beings, who are helplessly controlled by the force of nature.

9. These actions do not bind Me, for I remain indifferent to those actions, as one detached and neutral.

10. Under My supervision, material nature produces all moving and non-moving beings. Thus, O Arjuna, the world revolves.

11. Fools deride Me when I descend in the human form. They do not know My transcendental nature as the Supreme Lord of all that be.

12. Those who are thus bewildered are attracted by demonic and atheistic views. In that deluded state, their hopes for liberation, their fruitive activities, and their culture of knowledge are all defeated.

13. But the great souls, who are not deluded, are under the protection of divine nature. They are fully engaged in devotional service because they know Me as the Supreme Personality of Godhead, original and inexhaustible.

14. Always chanting My glories, endeavoring with great determination, and bowing down before Me,

these great souls perpetually worship Me with devotion.

15. Others, who engage in the cultivation of knowledge, worship the Supreme Lord as the one without a second, as diverse in many, and in the universal form.

16. I am the ritual, I am the sacrifice, I am the offering to the ancestors, the healing herb, and the transcendental chant. I am the butter and the fire and the offering.

17. I am the father of this universe, the mother, the support, and the grandsire. I am the object of knowledge, the purifier, and the syllable Om. I am, as well, the Rig, the Sama, and the Yajur Vedas.

18. I am the goal, the sustainer, the master, the witness, the abode, the refuge, the most dear friend. I am the creation and the annihilation, the basis of everything, the resting place, and the eternal seed.

19. O Arjuna, I give heat, and I withhold and send forth the rain. I am immortality and I am death personified. Both spirit and matter are in Me.

20. Those who study the Vedas and drink the Soma juice, seeking the heavenly planets, worship Me indirectly. Purified of sinful reactions, they take birth on the pious heavenly planet of Indra, where they enjoy godly delights.

21. When they have thus enjoyed vast heavenly sense pleasure and the results of their pious activities are exhausted, they return to this mortal planet again. Thus, those who seek sense enjoyment by adhering to the principles of the three Vedas achieve only repeated birth and death.

22. But those who worship Me with devotion, meditating on My transcendental form—to them I carry what they lack, and I preserve what they have.

23. Whatever a man may sacrifice to other gods, O son of Kunti, is really meant for Me alone, but it is offered without true understanding.

24. I am the only enjoyer and master of all sacrifices. Therefore, those who do not recognize My true transcendental nature fall down.

25. Those who worship the demigods will take birth among the demigods; those who worship the ancestors go to the ancestors; those who worship ghosts and spirits will take birth among such beings; and those who worship Me will live with Me.

26. If one offers Me with love and devotion a leaf, a flower, fruit, or water, I will accept it.

27. Whatever you do, whatever you eat, whatever you offer or give away, and whatever austerities you perform—do that as an offering to Me.

28. In this way, you will be freed from bondage to work and its auspicious and inauspicious results. With your mind fixed on Me in this principle of renunciation, you will be liberated and come to Me.

29. I envy no one, nor am I partial to anyone. I am equal to all. But whoever renders service unto Me in devotion is a friend, is in Me, and I am, as well, a friend to him.

30. Even if one commits the most abominable action, if he is engaged in devotional service, he is to be

considered saintly because he is properly situated in his determination.
.

31. He quickly becomes righteous and attains lasting peace. O son of Kunti, declare it boldly that My devotee never perishes.
.

32. O son of Pritha, those who take shelter in Me, though they be of lower birth—women, vaishyas [merchants], and shudras [workers]—can attain the supreme destination.
.

33. How much more this is true of the righteous brahmanas, the devotees, and the saintly kings who are engaged in My service. Therefore, having come to this temporary and miserable world, engage in loving service unto Me.
.

34. Engage your mind always in thinking of Me, become My devotee, offer obeisances to Me, and worship Me. Being completely absorbed in Me, surely you will come to Me.
.

35. This translation aims to be clear and accessible while maintaining the depth and essence of the original text.

Chapter 10: The Opulence of the Absolute
.

. The Blessed Lord spoke:
1. Listen again to My supreme word, O Arjuna. Since you are dear to Me, I will speak to you for your benefit.
.

2. Neither the hosts of demigods nor the great sages know My origin, for I am the source of the demigods and the sages in every way.

3. He who knows Me as the unborn, as the beginningless, as the supreme Lord of all worlds—he, among mortals, is undeluded and freed from all sins.

. 4-5. Intelligence, knowledge, freedom from doubt, forgiveness, truthfulness, control of the senses, control of the mind, happiness and distress, birth and death, fear and fearlessness, nonviolence, equanimity, satisfaction, austerity, charity, fame, and infamy—all these various qualities of living beings are created by Me alone.

6. The seven great sages and the four great ancestors, from whom all human generations have come, are born of My mind, and all creatures in these planets descend from them.

7. He who in truth knows this manifold manifestation of My being and My yoga power is undividedly engaged in devotional service. Of this there is no doubt.

8. I am the source of all spiritual and material worlds. Everything emanates from Me. The wise who perfectly know this engage in My devotional service and worship Me with all their hearts.

9. The thoughts of My pure devotees dwell in Me,

10. To those who are constantly devoted and who worship Me with love, I give the understanding by which they can come to Me.

11. Out of compassion for them, I, dwelling in their hearts, destroy with the shining lamp of knowledge the darkness born of ignorance.

. 12-13. Arjuna spoke: You are the Supreme Brahman, the ultimate abode, the purest, the Absolute Truth. You are the eternal, divine person, the primal God, transcendental and original, and You are the unborn and all-pervading beauty. All the great sages, such as Narada, Asita, Devala, and Vyasa, proclaim this of You, and now You Yourself are declaring it to me.

.

14. O Krishna, I totally accept as truth all that You have told me. Neither the gods nor demons, O Lord, know Thy personality.

.

15. Indeed, You alone know Yourself by Your own internal potency, O Supreme Person, origin of all, Lord of all beings, God of gods, Lord of the universe!

.

16. Please tell me in detail of Your divine powers by which You pervade all these worlds and abide in them.

.

17. How should I meditate on You? In what various forms are You to be contemplated, O Blessed Lord?

.

18. Tell me again in detail, O Janardana, of Your mighty works and glories, for I never tire of hearing Your ambrosial words.

.

19. The Blessed Lord spoke: Yes, I will tell you of My splendorous manifestations, but only of those which are prominent, O Arjuna, for My opulence is limitless.

.

20. I am the Self, O Gudakesha, seated in the hearts of all creatures. I am the beginning, the middle, and the end of all beings.

.

21. Of the Adityas, I am Vishnu; of lights, I am the radiant sun; of the Maruts, I am Marichi; and among the stars, I am the moon.

.

22. Of the Vedas, I am the Sama Veda; of the demigods, I am Indra; of the senses, I am the mind; and in living beings, I am the living force [consciousness].

.

23. Of all the Rudras, I am Lord Shiva; of the Yakshas and Rakshasas, I am the Lord of wealth [Kubera]; of the Vasus, I am fire [Agni]; and of mountains, I am Meru.

.

24. Of priests, O Arjuna, know Me to be the chief, Brihaspati. Of generals, I am Kartikeya, and of bodies of water, I am the ocean.

.

25. Of the great sages, I am Bhrigu; of vibrations, I am the transcendental Om. Of sacrifices, I am the chanting of the holy names [japa], and of immovable things, I am the Himalayas.

.

26. Of all trees, I am the banyan tree, and of the sages among the demigods, I am Narada. Of the Gandharvas, I am Chitraratha, and among perfected beings, I am the sage Kapila.

.

27. Of horses, know Me to be Ucchaihshrava, produced during the churning of the ocean for nectar. Of lordly elephants, I am Airavata, and among men, I am the monarch.

.

28. Of weapons, I am the thunderbolt; among cows, I am the surabhi. Of causes for procreation, I am Kandarpa, the god of love, and of serpents, I am Vasuki.

.

29. Of the many-hooded Nagas, I am Ananta, and among the aquatics, I am the demigod Varuna. Of departed ancestors, I am Aryama, and among the dispensers of law, I am Yama, the lord of death.

.

30. Among the Daityas, I am the devoted Prahlada; among subduers, I am time; among beasts, I am the lion, and among birds, I am Garuda.

31. Of purifiers, I am the wind; of the wielders of weapons, I am Rama; of fishes, I am the shark, and of flowing rivers, I am the Ganges.

32. Of all creations, I am the beginning and the end and, as well, the middle, O Arjuna. Of all sciences, I am the science of the self, and among logicians, I am the conclusive truth.

33. Of letters, I am the letter A, and among compound words, I am the dual compound. I am, as well, inexhaustible time, and of creators, I am Brahma.

34. I am all-devouring death, and I am the generating principle of all that is yet to be. Among women, I am fame, fortune, speech, memory, intelligence, faithfulness, and patience.

35. Of hymns, I am the Brihat-sama sung to the Lord Indra, and of poetry, I am the Gayatri verse, sung daily by the Brahmanas. Of months, I am November and December, and of seasons, I am flower-bearing spring.

36. I am, as well, the gambling of cheats, and of the splendid, I am the splendor. I am victory, I am adventure, and I am the strength of the strong.

37. Of the descendants of Vrishni, I am Vasudeva, and of the Pandavas, I am Arjuna. Of the sages, I am Vyasa, and among great thinkers, I am Ushanas.

38. Among punishments, I am the rod of chastisement, and of those who seek victory, I am

morality. Of secret things, I am silence, and of the wise, I am wisdom.

.

39. Furthermore, O Arjuna, I am the generating seed of all existences. There is no being—moving or nonmoving—that can exist without Me.

.

40. O mighty conqueror of enemies, there is no end to My divine manifestations. What I have spoken to you is but a mere indication of My infinite opulences.

.

41. Know that all opulent, beautiful, and glorious creations spring from but a spark of My splendor.

.

42. But what need is there, Arjuna, for all this detailed knowledge? With a single fragment of Myself, I pervade and support this entire universe.

Chapter 11: The Vision of the Universal Form

.

1. Arjuna spoke:
. Out of compassion, You have spoken to me about the supreme secret of the self, and my illusion is now dispelled.

.

2. I have heard from You in detail about the appearance and disappearance of every living entity, and I have realized Your inexhaustible glories.

.

3. O greatest of all personalities, O supreme form, though I see You here before me in Your actual position, as You have described Yourself, I wish to see how You have entered into this cosmic manifestation. I want to see that form of Yours.

.

4. If You think that I am able to behold Your cosmic form, O my Lord, O master of all mystic power, then kindly show me that universal self.

.

5. The Blessed Lord spoke:
. My dear Arjuna, O son of Pritha, behold now My opulences, hundreds of thousands of varied divine forms, multicolored like the sea.

.

6. O best of the Bharatas, see here the different manifestations of Adityas, Vasus, Rudras, Ashvini-kumaras, and all the other demigods. Behold the many wonderful things which no one has ever seen or heard of before.

.

7. O Arjuna, whatever you wish to see, behold at once in this body of Mine! This universal form can show you whatever you now desire to see and whatever you may want to see in the future. Everything—moving and nonmoving—is here completely, in one place.

.

8. But you cannot see Me with your present eyes. Therefore, I give you divine eyes. Behold My mystic opulence!

.

9. Sanjaya spoke:
. O King, having spoken thus, the Supreme Lord of all mystic power, the Personality of Godhead, displayed His universal form to Arjuna.

.

. 10-11. Arjuna saw in that universal form unlimited mouths, unlimited eyes, unlimited wonderful visions. The form was decorated with many celestial ornaments and bore many divine upraised weapons. He wore celestial garlands and garments, and many divine scents were smeared over His body. All was wondrous, brilliant, unlimited, all-expanding.

.

12. If hundreds of thousands of suns were to rise at once into the sky, their radiance might resemble the effulgence of the Supreme Person in that universal form.

.

13. At that time, Arjuna could see in the universal form of the Lord the unlimited expansions of the universe situated in one place, although divided into many, many thousands.

.

14. Then, bewildered and astonished, Arjuna, his hair standing on end, bowed his head to offer obeisances, and with folded hands he began to pray to the Supreme Lord.

.

15. Arjuna spoke:
. My dear Lord Krishna, I see assembled together in Your body all the demigods and various other living entities. I see Brahma sitting on the lotus flower, as well as Lord Shiva and all the sages and divine serpents.

.

16. O Lord of the universe, I see in Your universal body many, many forms—bellies, mouths, eyes—expanded without limit. There is no end, there is no beginning, and there is no middle to all this.

.

17. Your form, adorned with various crowns, clubs, and discs, is difficult to see because of its glaring effulgence, which is fiery and immeasurable like the sun.

.

18. You are the supreme primal objective. You are the best in all the universes. You are inexhaustible, and You are the oldest. You are the maintainer of the eternal religion, the Personality of Godhead. This is my opinion.

.

19. You are without origin, middle, or end. Your glory is unlimited. You have numberless arms, and the sun and moon are Your eyes. I see You with blazing fire coming forth from Your mouth, burning this entire universe by Your own radiance.

.

20. Although You are one, You spread throughout the sky and the planets and all space between. O great one, as I behold this terrible form, I see that all the planetary systems are perplexed.

.

21. All the demigods are surrendering and entering into You. They are very much afraid, and with folded hands they are singing the Vedic hymns.

.

22. The various manifestations of Lord Shiva, the Adityas, the Vasus, the Sadhyas, the Vishvadevas, the two Ashvinis, the Maruts, the forefathers, the Gandharvas, the Yakshas, the Asuras, and the perfected demigods are beholding You in wonder.

.

23. O mighty-armed one, all the planets with their demigods are disturbed at seeing Your great form, with its many faces, eyes, arms, thighs, legs, and bellies, and Your many terrible teeth; and as they are disturbed, so am I.

.

24. O all-pervading Vishnu, seeing You with Your many radiant colors touching the sky, Your gaping mouths, and Your great glowing eyes, my mind is perturbed by fear. I can no longer maintain my steadiness or equilibrium of mind.

.

25. O Lord of lords, O refuge of the worlds, please be gracious to me. I cannot keep my balance seeing thus Your blazing, deathlike faces and awful teeth. In all directions I am bewildered.

.

. 26-27. All the sons of Dhritarashtra, along with their allied kings, and Bhishma, Drona, Karna—and our chief soldiers as well—are rushing into Your fearful mouths. And some I see trapped with heads smashed between Your teeth.

. 28. As the many waves of the rivers flow into the ocean, so do all these great warriors enter blazing into Your mouths.

. 29. I see all people rushing with full speed into Your mouths, as moths dash to destruction in a blazing fire.

. 30. O Vishnu, I see You devouring all people from all sides with Your flaming mouths. Covering all the universe with Your effulgence, You are manifest with terrible, scorching rays.

. 31. O Lord of lords, so fierce of form, please tell me who You are. I offer my obeisances unto You; please be gracious to me. You are the primal Lord. I want to know about You, for I do not know what Your mission is.

. 32. The Blessed Lord spoke:
. Time I am, the great destroyer of the world, and I have come here to engage all people. With the exception of you [the Pandavas], all the soldiers here on both sides will be slain.

. 33. Therefore get up. Prepare to fight and win glory. Conquer your enemies and enjoy a flourishing kingdom. They are already put to death by My arrangement, and you, O Savyasachi, can be but an instrument in the fight.

. 34. Drona, Bhishma, Jayadratha, Karna, and the other great warriors have already been destroyed by Me. Therefore, kill them and do not be disturbed.

Simply fight, and you will vanquish your enemies in battle.

.

35. Sanjaya spoke:
. Hearing this from Keshava, the crowned Arjuna, trembling, and with folded hands, offered obeisances again and again. He began to speak, his voice choked with emotion, and bowing down, offered this prayer to Krishna.

.

36. Arjuna spoke:
. O Hrishikesha, the world becomes joyful upon hearing Your name, and thus everyone becomes attached to You. Although the perfected beings offer You their respectful homage, the demons are afraid, and they flee here and there. All this is rightly done.

.

37. O great one, who is greater than all, even Brahma. You are the original creator. Why then should they not offer their respectful obeisances unto You? O limitless one, O God of gods, refuge of the universe! You are the invincible source, the cause of all causes, transcendental to this material manifestation.

.

38. You are the original Personality, the God of gods, the transcendental one, and the supreme refuge of this manifested cosmic world. You know everything, and You are all that is knowable. You are above the material modes, O limitless form! This whole cosmic manifestation is pervaded by You!

.

39. You are air, and You are the supreme controller! You are fire, You are water, and You are the moon! You are Brahma, the first living creature, and You are the great-grandfather. I therefore offer my respectful obeisances unto You a thousand times, and again and yet again!

.

40. Obeisances from the front, from behind, and from all sides! O unbounded power, You are the master of limitless might! You are all-pervading, and thus You are everything!

.
. 41-42. Thinking of You as my friend, I have rashly addressed You "O Krishna," "O Yadava," "O my friend," not knowing Your glories. Please forgive whatever I may have done in madness or in love. I have dishonored You many times while relaxing or while lying on the same bed or eating together, sometimes alone and sometimes in front of many friends. Please excuse me for all those offenses.

.
43. You are the father of this complete cosmic manifestation, of the moving and the nonmoving. You are its worshipable chief, the supreme spiritual master. No one is equal to You, nor can anyone be one with You. How then could there be anyone greater than You within the three worlds, O Lord of immeasurable power?

.
44. You are the Supreme Lord, to be worshiped by every living being. Thus I fall down to offer You my respects and ask Your mercy. Please tolerate the wrongs I may have done to You and bear with me as a father to his son, or a friend to his friend, or a lover to his beloved.

.
45. After seeing this universal form, which I have never seen before, I am gladdened, but at the same time my mind is disturbed with fear. Therefore, please bestow Your grace upon me and reveal again Your form as the Personality of Godhead, O Lord of lords, O abode of the universe.

.
46. O thousand-armed one, though You are the embodiment of the universe, I wish to see You in Your four-armed form, with helmeted head and with club,

wheel, conch, and lotus flower in Your hands. I long to see You in that form.

.

47. The Blessed Lord spoke:
. My dear Arjuna, happily do I show you this universal form within the material world by My internal potency. No one before you has ever seen this unlimited and glaringly effulgent form of Mine.

.

48. O best of the Kuru warriors, no one before you has ever seen this form of Mine, for neither by studying the Vedas, nor by performing sacrifices, nor by charity, nor by pious activities, nor by severe austerities, can I be seen in this form in the material world.

.

49. You have been perturbed and bewildered by seeing this horrible feature of Mine. Now let it be finished. My devotee, be free from all disturbances. With a peaceful mind, you can now see the form you desire.

.

50. Sanjaya spoke:
. Having spoken thus to Arjuna, Krishna displayed His real four-armed form, and at last He showed His two-armed form, thus encouraging the fearful Arjuna.

.

51. When Arjuna thus saw Krishna in His original form, he spoke: O Janardana, seeing this humanlike form, so very beautiful, my mind is now pacified, and I am restored to my original nature.

.

52. The Blessed Lord spoke:
. My dear Arjuna, the form which you are now seeing is very difficult to behold. Even the demigods are ever seeking the opportunity to see this form, which is so dear.

.

53. The form you are seeing with your transcendental eyes cannot be understood simply by studying the Vedas, nor by undergoing serious penances, nor by charity, nor by worship. It is not by these means that one can see Me as I am.

.

54. My dear Arjuna, only by undivided devotional service can I be understood as I am, standing before you, and can thus be seen directly. Only in this way can you enter into the mysteries of My understanding.

.

55. Whoever serves Me with pure devotion, focuses on Me as the ultimate goal, and is kind to all beings, will come to Me.

Sonnet — To Science

By Edgar Allan Poe

Science! true daughter of Old Time thou art!
    Who alterest all things with thy peering eyes.
Why preyest thou thus upon the poet's heart,
    Vulture, whose wings are dull realities?
How should he love thee? or how deem thee wise,
    Who wouldst not leave him in his wandering
To seek for treasure in the jewelled skies,
    Albeit he soared with an undaunted wing?
Hast thou not dragged Diana from her car?
    And driven the Hamadryad from the wood
To seek a shelter in some happier star?
    Hast thou not torn the Naiad from her flood,
The Elfin from the green grass, and from me
The summer dream beneath the tamarind tree?

Eureka:
An Essay on the Material and Spiritual Universe.

By Edgar Allan Poe

Eureka (1848) is a lengthy non-fiction work by American author Edgar Allan Poe (1809–1849) which he subtitled "A Prose Poem", though it has also been subtitled as "An Essay on the Material and Spiritual Universe". Adapted from a lecture he had presented, Eureka describes Poe's intuitive conception of the nature of the universe with no antecedent scientific work done to reach his conclusions. He also discusses man's relationship with God, whom he compares to an author. It is dedicated to the German naturalist and explorer Alexander von Humboldt (1769–1859). Though it is generally considered a literary work, some of Poe's ideas anticipate 20th-century scientific discoveries and theories. Indeed, a critical analysis of the scientific content of Eureka reveals a non-causal correspondence with modern cosmology due to the assumption of an evolving Universe, but excludes the anachronistic anticipation of relativistic concepts such as black holes.

Poe's last major work and his longest non-fiction work at nearly 40,000 words in length, Eureka's origins lie in a lecture Poe presented on February 3, 1848, titled "On The Cosmography of the Universe" at the Society Library in New York. Some reviews in the contemporary press offered lavish praise for the lecture while others critiqued it harshly. Modern critics continue to debate the significance of Eureka and some doubt its seriousness, in part because of Poe's many incorrect assumptions and his comedic descriptions of well-known historical minds. His attempts at discovering the truth also follow his own tradition of "ratiocination", a term used in his detective fiction tales. Poe's suggestion that the soul continues to thrive even after death also parallels with works in which characters reappear from beyond the grave such as "Ligeia". The essay is oddly transcendental, considering Poe's disdain for that movement. He considered it his greatest work and claimed it was more important than the discovery of gravity.

In Eureka, Poe attempts to explain the universe, using his general proposition "Because Nothing was, therefore All Things are". In it, Poe discusses man's relationship to God and the universe, concludes "that space and duration are one" and that matter and spirit are made of the same essence. Poe suggests that people have a natural tendency to believe in themselves as infinite with nothing greater than their soul—such thoughts stem from man's residual feelings from when each shared an original identity with God. Ultimately individual consciousnesses will collapse back into a similar single mass, a "final ingathering" where the "myriads of individual Intelligences become blended". Likewise, Poe saw the universe itself as infinitely expanding and collapsing like a divine heartbeat which constantly rejuvenates itself, also implying a sort of deathlessness. In fact, because the soul is a part of this constant throbbing, after dying, all people, in essence, become God.

————————

IT is with humility really unassumed—it is with a sentiment even of awe—that I pen the opening sentence of this work: for of all conceivable subjects I approach the reader with the most solemn—the most comprehensive—the most difficult—the most august.

What terms shall I find sufficiently simple in their sublimity—sufficiently sublime in their simplicity—for the mere enunciation of my theme?

I design to speak of the *Physical, Metaphysical and Mathematical—of the Material and Spiritual Universe:—of its Essence, its Origin, its Creation, its Present Condition and its Destiny*. I shall be so rash, moreover, as to challenge the conclusions, and thus, in effect, to question the sagacity, of many of the greatest and most justly reverenced of men.

In the beginning, let me as distinctly as possible announce—not the theorem which I hope to demonstrate—for, what ever the mathematicians may assert, there is, in this world at least, *no such thing* as demonstration—but the ruling idea which, throughout this volume, I shall be continually endeavoring to suggest.

My general proposition, then, is this:—*In the Original Unity of the First Thing lies the Secondary Cause of All Things, with the Germ of their Inevitable Annihilation.*

In illustration of this idea, I propose to take such a survey of the Universe that the mind may be able really to receive and to perceive an individual impression.

He who from the top of Ætna casts his eyes leisurely around, is affected chiefly by

350

the *extent* and *diversity* of the scene. Only by a rapid whirling on his heel could he hope to comprehend the panorama in the sublimity of its *oneness*. But as, on the summit of Ætna, *no* man has thought of whirling on his heel, so no man has ever taken into his brain the full uniqueness of the prospect; and so, again, whatever considerations lie involved in this uniqueness, have as yet no practical existence for mankind.

I do not know a treatise in which a survey of the *Universe*—using the word in its most comprehensive and only legitimate acceptation—is taken at all:—and it may be as well here to mention that by the term "Universe," wherever employed without qualification in this essay, I mean to designate *the utmost conceivable expanse of space, with all things, spiritual and material, that can be imagined to exist within the compass of that expanse.* In speaking of what is *ordinarily* implied by the expression, "Universe," I shall take a phrase of limitation—"the Universe of stars." Why this distinction is considered necessary, will be seen in the sequel.

But even of treatises on the really limited, although always assumed as the *un*limited, Universe of *stars*, I know none in which a survey, even of this limited Universe, is so taken as to warrant deductions from its *individuality*. The nearest approach to such a work is made in the "Cosmos" of Alexander Von Humboldt. He presents the subject, however, *not* in its individuality but in its generality. His theme, in its last result, is the law of *each* portion of the merely physical Universe, as this law is related to the laws of *every other* portion of this merely physical Universe. His design is simply synœretical. In a word, he discusses the universality of material relation, and discloses to the eye of Philosophy whatever inferences have hitherto lain hidden *behind* this universality. But however admirable be the succinctness with which he has treated each particular point of his topic, the mere multiplicity of these points occasions, necessarily, an amount of detail, and thus an involution of idea, which preclude all *individuality* of impression.

It seems to me that, in aiming at this latter effect, and, through it, at the consequences—the conclusions—the suggestions—the speculations—or, if nothing better offer itself, the mere guesses which may result from it—we require something like a mental gyration on the heel. We need so rapid a revolution of all things about the central point of sight that, while the minutiæ vanish altogether, even the more conspicuous objects become blended into one. Among the vanishing minutiae, in a survey of this kind, would be all exclusively terrestrial matters. The Earth would be considered in its planetary relations alone. A man, in this view, becomes mankind; mankind a member of the cosmical family of Intelligences.

And now, before proceeding to our subject proper, let me beg the reader's attention to an extract or two from a somewhat remarkable letter, which appears to have been found corked in a bottle and floating on the *Mare Tenebrarum*—an ocean well described by the Nubian geographer, Ptolemy Hephestion, but little frequented in modern days unless by the Transcendentalists and some other divers for crotchets. The date of this letter, I confess, surprises me even more particularly than its contents; for it seems to have been written in the year *two* thousand eight hundred and forty-eight. As for the passages I am about to transcribe, they, I fancy, will speak for themselves.

"Do you know, my dear friend," says the writer, addressing, no doubt, a contemporary—"Do you know that it is scarcely more than eight or nine hundred years ago since the metaphysicians first consented to relieve the people of the singular fancy that there exist *but two practicable roads to Truth?* Believe it if you can! It appears, however, that long, long ago, in the night of Time, there lived a Turkish philosopher called Aries and surnamed Tottle." [Here, possibly, the letter-writer means Aristotle; the best names are wretchedly corrupted in two or three thousand years.] "The fame of this great man depended mainly upon his demonstration that sneezing is a natural provision, by means of which over-profound thinkers are enabled to expel superfluous ideas through the nose; but he obtained a scarcely less valuable celebrity as the founder, or at all events as the principal propagator, of what was termed the *de*ductive or *à priori* philosophy. He started with what he maintained to be axioms, or self-evident truths:—and the now well understood fact that *no* truths are *self*-evident, really does not make in the slightest degree against his speculations:—it was sufficient for his purpose that the truths in question were evident at all. From axioms he proceeded, logically, to results. His most illustrious disciples were one Tuclid, a geometrician," [meaning Euclid] "and one Kant, a Dutchman, the originator of that species of Transcendentalism which, with the change merely of a C for a K, now bears his peculiar name.

"Well, Aries Tottle flourished supreme, until the advent of one Hog, surnamed 'the Ettrick shepherd,' who preached an entirely different system, which he called the *à posteriori* or *in*ductive. His plan referred altogether to sensation. He proceeded by observing, analyzing, and classifying facts—*instantiæ Naturæ*, as they were somewhat affectedly called—and arranging them into general laws. In a word, while the mode of Aries rested on *noumena*, that of Hog depended on *phenomena*; and so great was the admiration excited by this latter system that, at its first introduction, Aries fell into general disrepute. Finally, however, he recovered ground, and was permitted to divide the empire of Philosophy with his more modern rival:—the savans contenting themselves with proscribing all *other* competitors, past, present, and to come; putting an end to all controversy on the topic by the promulgation of a Median law, to the effect that the Aristotelian and Baconian roads are, and of right ought to be, the sole possible avenues to knowledge:—'Baconian,' you must know, my dear friend," adds the letter-writer at this point, "was an adjective invented as equivalent to Hog-ian, and at the same time more dignified and euphonious.

"Now I do assure you most positively"—proceeds the epistle—"that I represent these matters fairly; and you can easily understand how restrictions so absurd on their very face must have operated, in those days, to retard the progress of true Science, which makes its most important advances—as all History will show— by seemingly intuitive *leaps*. These ancient ideas confined investigation to crawling; and I need not suggest to you that crawling, among varieties of locomotion, is a very capital thing of its kind;—but because the tortoise is sure of foot, for this reason must we clip the wings of the eagles? For many centuries, so great was the infatuation, about Hog especially, that a virtual stop was put to all thinking, properly so called. No man dared utter a truth for which he felt himself indebted to his soul alone. It mattered not whether the truth was even demonstrably such; for the dogmatizing philosophers of that epoch regarded only *the road* by which it professed to have been attained. The end, with them, was a point of no moment, whatever:—'the means!' they vociferated—'let us look at the means!'—and if, on scrutiny of the means, it was found to come neither under the category Hog, nor under the category Aries (which means ram), why then the savans went no farther, but, calling the thinker a fool and branding him a 'theorist,' would never, thenceforward, have any thing to do either with *him* or with his truths.

"Now, my dear friend," continues the letter-writer, "it cannot be maintained that by the crawling system, exclusively adopted, men would arrive at the maximum amount of truth, even in any long series of ages; for the repression of imagination was an evil not to be counterbalanced even by *absolute* certainty in the snail processes. But their certainty was very far from absolute. The error of our progenitors was quite analogous with that of the wiseacre who fancies he must necessarily see an object the more distinctly, the more closely he holds it to his eyes. They blinded themselves, too, with the impalpable, titillating Scotch snuff of *detail;* and thus the boasted facts of the Hog-ites were by no means always facts—a point of little importance but for the assumption that they always *were.* The vital taint, however, in Baconianism—its most lamentable fount of error—lay in its tendency to throw power and consideration into the hands of merely perceptive men—of those inter-Tritonic minnows, the microscopical savans—the diggers and pedlers of minute *facts*, for the most part in physical science—facts all of which they retailed at the same price upon the highway; their value depending, it was supposed, simply upon the *fact of their fact*, without reference to their applicability or inapplicability in the development of those ultimate and only legitimate facts, called Law.

"Than the persons"—the letter goes on to say—"Than the persons thus suddenly elevated by the Hogian philosophy into a station for which they were unfitted—thus transferred from the sculleries into the parlors of Science—from its pantries into its pulpits—than these individuals a more intolerant—a more intolerable set of bigots and tyrants never existed on the face of the earth. Their creed, their text and their sermon were, alike, the one word *'fact'*—but, for the most part, even of this one word, they knew not even the meaning. On those who ventured to *disturb* their facts with the view of putting them in order and to use, the disciples of Hog had no mercy whatever. All attempts at generalization were met at once by the words 'theoretical,' 'theory,' 'theorist'—all *thought*, to be brief, was very properly resented as a personal affront to themselves. Cultivating the natural sciences to the exclusion of Metaphysics, the Mathematics, and Logic, many of these Bacon-engendered philosophers—one-idead, one-sided and lame of a leg—were more wretchedly helpless—more miserably ignorant, in view of all the comprehensible objects of knowledge, than the veriest unlettered hind who proves that he knows something at least, in admitting that he knows absolutely nothing.

"Nor had our forefathers any better right to talk about *certainty*, when pursuing, in blind confidence, the *à priori* path of axioms, or of the Ram. At innumerable points this path was scarcely as straight as a ram's-horn. The simple truth is, that the Aristotelians erected their castles upon a basis far less reliable than air; *for no such things as axioms ever existed or can possibly exist at all.* This they must have been very blind, indeed, not to see, or at least to suspect; for, even in their own day, many of their long-admitted 'axioms' had been abandoned:—'*ex nihilo nihil fit*,' for example, and a 'thing cannot act where it is not,' and 'there cannot be antipodes,' and 'darkness cannot proceed from light.' These and numerous similar propositions formerly accepted, without hesitation, as axioms, or undeniable truths, were, even at the period of which I speak, seen to be altogether untenable:—how absurd in these people, then, to persist in relying upon a basis, as immutable, whose mutability had become so repeatedly manifest!

"But, even through evidence afforded by themselves against themselves, it is easy to convict these *à priori* reasoners of the grossest unreason—it is easy to show the futility—the impalpability of their axioms in general. I have now lying before me"—it will be observed that we still proceed with the letter—

"I have now lying before me a book printed about a thousand years ago. Pundit assures me that it is decidedly the cleverest ancient work on its topic, which is 'Logic.' The author, who was much esteemed in his day, was one Miller, or Mill; and we find it recorded of him, as a point of some importance, that he rode a mill-horse whom he called Jeremy Bentham:—but let us glance at the volume itself!

"Ah!—'Ability or inability to conceive,' says Mr. Mill very properly, 'is *in no case* to be received as a criterion of axiomatic truth.' Now, that this is a palpable truism no one in his senses will deny. *Not* to admit the proposition, is to insinuate a charge of variability in Truth itself, whose very title is a synonym of the Steadfast. If ability to conceive be taken as a criterion of Truth, then a truth to *David* Hume would very seldom be a truth to *Joe;* and ninety-nine hundredths of what is undeniable in Heaven would be demonstrable falsity upon Earth. The proposition of Mr. Mill, then, is sustained. I will not grant it to be an *axiom;* and this merely because I am showing that *no* axioms exist; but, with a distinction which could not have been cavilled at even by Mr. Mill himself, I am ready to grant that, *if* an axiom *there be*, then the proposition of which we speak has the fullest right to be considered an axiom—that no *more* absolute axiom *is*—and, consequently, that any subsequent proposition which shall conflict with this one primarily advanced, must be either a falsity in itself— that is to say no axiom—or, if admitted axiomatic, must at once neutralize both itself and its predecessor.

"And now, by the logic of their own propounder, let us proceed to test any one of the axioms propounded. Let us give Mr. Mill the fairest of play. We will bring the point to no ordinary issue. We will select for investigation no common-place axiom—no axiom of what, not the less preposterously because

357

only impliedly, he terms his secondary class—as if a positive truth by definition could be either more or less positively a truth:—we will select, I say, no axiom of an unquestionability so questionable as is to be found in Euclid. We will not talk, for example, about such propositions as that two straight lines cannot enclose a space, or that the whole is greater than any one of its parts. We will afford the logician *every* advantage. We will come at once to a proposition which he regards as the acme of the unquestionable—as the quintessence of axiomatic undeniability. Here it is:—'Contradictions cannot *both* be true—that is, cannot cöexist in nature.' Here Mr. Mill means, for instance,—and I give the most forcible instance conceivable—that a tree must be either a tree or *not* a tree—that it cannot be at the same time a tree *and* not a tree:—all which is quite reasonable of itself and will answer remarkably well as an axiom, until we bring it into collation with an axiom insisted upon a few pages before—in other words—words which I have previously employed— until we test it by the logic of its own propounder. 'A tree,' Mr. Mill asserts, 'must be either a tree or *not* a tree.' Very well:—and now let me ask him, *why*. To this little query there is but one response:—I defy any man living to invent a second. The sole answer is this:—'Because we find it *impossible to conceive* that a tree can be any thing else than a tree or not a tree.' This, I repeat, is Mr. Mill's sole answer:—he will not *pretend* to suggest another:—and yet, by his own showing, his answer is clearly no answer at all; for has he not already required us to admit, *as an axiom*, that ability or inability to conceive is *in no case* to be taken as a criterion of axiomatic truth? Thus all— absolutely *all* his argumentation is at sea without a rudder. Let it not be urged that an exception from the general rule is to be made, in cases where the 'impossibility to conceive' is so peculiarly great as when we are called upon to conceive a tree *both* a tree and *not* a tree. Let no attempt, I say, be made at urging this sotticism; for, in the first place, there are no *degrees* of 'impossibility,' and thus no one impossible conception can be *more* peculiarly impossible than another impossible conception:—in the second place, Mr. Mill himself, no doubt after thorough deliberation, has most distinctly, and most rationally, excluded all opportunity for exception, by the emphasis of his proposition, that, *in no case*, is ability or inability to conceive, to be taken as a criterion of axiomatic truth:—in the third place, even were exceptions admissible at all, it remains to be shown how any exception is admissible *here*. That a tree can be both a tree and not a tree, is an idea which the angels, or the devils, *may* entertain, and which no doubt many an earthly Bedlamite, or Transcendentalist, *does*.

"Now I do not quarrel with these ancients," continues the letter-writer, "*so much* on account of the transparent frivolity of their logic—which, to be plain, was baseless, worthless and fantastic altogether—as on account of their pompous and infatuate proscription of all *other* roads to Truth than the two narrow and crooked paths—the one of creeping and the other of crawling—to which, in their ignorant perversity, they have dared to confine the Soul—the Soul which loves nothing so well as to soar in those regions of illimitable intuition which are utterly incognizant of '*path*.'

"By the bye, my dear friend, is it not an evidence of the mental slavery entailed upon those bigoted people by their Hogs and Rams, that in spite of the eternal prating of their savans about *roads* to Truth, none of them fell, even by accident, into what we now so distinctly perceive to be the broadest, the straightest and most available of all mere roads—the great thoroughfare—the majestic highway of the *Consistent?* Is it not wonderful that they should have failed to deduce from the works of God the vitally momentous consideration that *a perfect consistency can be nothing but an absolute truth?* How plain—how rapid our progress since the late announcement of this proposition! By its means, investigation has been taken out of the hands of the ground-moles, and given as a duty, rather than as a task, to the true—to the *only* true thinkers—to the generally-educated men of ardent imagination. These latter—our Keplers—our Laplaces—'speculate'—'theorize'—these are the terms—can you not fancy the shout of scorn with which they would be received by our progenitors, were it possible for them to be looking over my shoulders as I write? The Keplers, I repeat, speculate—theorize—and their theories are merely corrected—reduced—sifted—cleared, little by little, of their chaff of inconsistency—until at length there stands apparent an unencumbered *Consistency*—a consistency which the most stolid admit—because it *is* a consistency—to be an absolute and an unquestionable *Truth.*

"I have often thought, my friend, that it must have puzzled these dogmaticians of a thousand years ago, to determine, even, by which of their two boasted roads it is that the cryptographist attains the solution of the more complicate cyphers—or by which of them Champollion guided mankind to those important and innumerable truths which, for so many centuries, have lain entombed amid the phonetical hieroglyphics of Egypt. In especial, would it not have given these bigots some trouble to determine by which of their two roads was reached the most momentous and sublime of *all* their truths—the truth—the fact of *gravitation?* Newton deduced it from the laws of Kepler. Kepler admitted that these laws he *guessed*—these laws whose investigation disclosed to the greatest of British astronomers that principle, the basis of all (existing) physical principle, in going behind which we enter at once the nebulous kingdom of Metaphysics. Yes!—these vital laws

Kepler *guessed*—that is to say, he *imagined* them. Had he been asked to point out either the *de*ductive or *in*ductive route by which he attained them, his reply might have been—'I know nothing about *routes*—but I *do* know the machinery of the Universe. Here it is. I grasped it with *my soul*—I reached it through mere dint of *intuition*. Alas, poor ignorant old man! Could not any metaphysician have told him that what he called 'intuition' was but the conviction resulting from *de*ductions or *in*ductions of which the processes were so shadowy as to have escaped his consciousness, eluded his reason, or bidden defiance to his capacity of expression? How great a pity it is that some 'moral philosopher' had not enlightened him about all this! How it would have comforted him on his death-bed to know that, instead of having gone intuitively and thus unbecomingly, he had, in fact, proceeded decorously and legitimately— that is to say Hog-ishly, or at least Ram-ishly—into the vast halls where lay gleaming, untended, and hitherto untouched by mortal hand—unseen by mortal eye—the imperishable and priceless secrets of the Universe!

"Yes, Kepler was essentially a *theorist;* but this title, *now* of so much sanctity, was, in those ancient days, a designation of supreme contempt. It is only *now* that men begin to appreciate that divine old man—to sympathize with the prophetical and poetical rhapsody of his ever-memorable words. For *my* part," continues the unknown correspondent, "I glow with a sacred fire when I even think of them, and feel that I shall never grow weary of their repetition:—in concluding this letter, let me have the real pleasure of transcribing them once again:—'*I care not whether my work be read now or by posterity. I can afford to wait a century for readers when God himself has waited six thousand years for an observer. I triumph. I have stolen the golden secret of the Egyptians. I will indulge my sacred fury.*'"

Here end my quotations from this very unaccountable and, perhaps, somewhat impertinent epistle; and perhaps it would be folly to comment, in any respect, upon the chimerical, not to say revolutionary, fancies of the writer—whoever he is—fancies so radically at war with the well-considered and well-settled opinions of this age. Let us proceed, then, to our legitimate thesis, *The Universe*.

This thesis admits a choice between two modes of discussion:—We may *as*cend or *de*scend. Beginning at our own point of view—at the Earth on which we stand—we may pass to the other planets of our system—thence to the Sun—thence to our system considered collectively—and thence, through other systems, indefinitely outwards; or, commencing on high at some point as definite as we can make it or conceive it, we may come down to the habitation of Man. Usually—that is to say, in ordinary essays on Astronomy—the first of these two modes is, with certain reservation, adopted:—this for the obvious reason that astronomical *facts*, merely, and principles, being the object, that object is best fulfilled in stepping from the known because proximate, gradually onward to the point where all certitude becomes lost in the remote. For my present purpose, however,—that of enabling the mind to take in, as if from afar and at one glance, a distinct conception of the *individual* Universe—it is clear that a descent to small from great—to the outskirts from the centre (if we could establish a centre)—to the end from the beginning (if we could fancy a beginning) would be the preferable course, but for the difficulty, if not impossibility, of presenting, in this course, to the unastronomical, a picture at all comprehensible in regard to such considerations as are involved in *quantity*—that is to say, in number, magnitude and distance.

Now, distinctness—intelligibility, at all points, is a primary feature in my general design. On important topics it is better to be a good deal prolix than even a very little obscure. But abstruseness is a quality appertaining to no subject *per se*. All are alike, in facility of comprehension, to him who approaches them by properly graduated steps. It is merely because a stepping-stone, here and there, is heedlessly left unsupplied in our road to the Differential Calculus, that this latter is not altogether as simple a thing as a sonnet by Mr. Solomon Seesaw.

By way of admitting, then, no *chance* for misapprehension, I think it advisable to proceed as if even the more obvious facts of Astronomy were unknown to the reader. In combining the two modes of discussion to which I have referred, I propose to avail myself of the advantages peculiar to each—and very especially of the *iteration in detail* which will be unavoidable as a consequence of the plan. Commencing with a descent, I shall reserve for the return upwards those indispensable considerations of *quantity* to which allusion has already been made.

Let us begin, then, at once, with that merest of words, "Infinity." This, like "God," "spirit," and some other expressions of which the equivalents exist in all languages, is by no means the expression of an idea—but of an effort at one. It stands for the possible attempt at an impossible conception. Man needed a term by which to point out the *direction* of this effort—the cloud behind which lay, forever invisible, the *object* of this attempt. A word, in fine, was demanded, by means of which one human being might put himself in relation at once with another human being and with a certain *tendency* of the human intellect. Out of this demand arose the word, "Infinity;" which is thus the representative but of the *thought of a thought*.

As regards *that* infinity now considered—the infinity of space—we often hear it said that "its idea is admitted by the mind—is acquiesced in—is entertained—on account of the greater difficulty which attends the conception of a limit." But this is merely one of those *phrases* by which even profound thinkers, time out of mind, have occasionally taken pleasure in deceiving *themselves*. The quibble lies concealed in the word "difficulty." "The mind," we are told, "entertains the idea of *limitless*, through the greater *difficulty* which it finds in entertaining that of *limited*, space." Now, were the proposition but fairly *put*, its absurdity would become transparent at once. Clearly, there is no mere *difficulty* in the case. The assertion intended, if presented *according* to its intention and without sophistry, would run thus:— "The mind admits the idea of limitless, through the greater *impossibility* of entertaining that of limited, space."

It must be immediately seen that this is not a question of two statements between whose respective credibilities—or of two arguments between whose respective validities—the *reason* is called upon to decide:—it is a matter of two conceptions, directly conflicting, and each avowedly impossible, one of which the *intellect* is supposed to be capable of entertaining, on account of the greater *impossibility* of entertaining the other. The choice is *not* made between two difficulties;—it is merely *fancied* to be made between two impossibilities. Now of the former, there *are* degrees—but of the latter, none:—just as our impertinent letter-writer has already suggested. A task *may be* more or less difficult; but it is either possible or not possible:—there are no gradations. It *might* be more *difficult* to overthrow the Andes than an ant-hill; but it *can* be no more *impossible* to annihilate the matter of the one than the matter of the other. A man may jump ten feet with less *difficulty* than he can jump twenty, but the *impossibility* of his leaping to the moon is not a whit less than that of his leaping to the dog-star.

Since all this is undeniable: since the choice of the mind is to be made between *impossibilities* of conception: since one impossibility cannot be greater than another: and since, thus, one cannot be preferred to another: the philosophers who not only maintain, on the grounds mentioned, man's *idea* of infinity but, on account of such supposititious idea, *infinity itself*—are plainly engaged in demonstrating one impossible thing to be possible by showing how it is that some one other thing—is impossible too. This, it will be said, is nonsense; and perhaps it is:—indeed I think it very capital nonsense—but forego all claim to it as nonsense of mine.

The readiest mode, however, of displaying the fallacy of the philosophical argument on this question, is by simply adverting to a *fact* respecting it which has been hitherto quite overlooked—the fact that the argument alluded to both proves and disproves its own proposition. "The mind is impelled," say the theologians and others, "to admit a *First Cause*, by the superior difficulty it experiences in conceiving cause beyond cause without end." The quibble, as before, lies in the word "difficulty"— but *here* what is it employed to sustain? A First Cause. And what is a First Cause? An ultimate termination of causes. And what is an ultimate termination of causes? Finity—the Finite. Thus the one quibble, in two processes, by God knows how many philosophers, is made to support now Finity and now Infinity—could it not be brought to support something besides? As for the quibblers—*they*, at least, are insupportable. But—to dismiss them:—what they prove in the one case is the identical nothing which they demonstrate in the other.

Of course, no one will suppose that I here contend for the absolute impossibility of *that* which we attempt to convey in the word "Infinity." My purpose is but to show the folly of endeavoring to prove Infinity itself, or even our conception of it, by any such blundermg ratiocination as that which is ordinarily employed.

Nevertheless, as an individual, I may be permitted to say that *I cannot* conceive Infinity, and am convinced that no human being can. A mind not thoroughly self-conscious —not accustomed to the introspective analysis of its own operations—will, it is true, often deceive itself by supposing that it *has* entertained the conception of which we speak. In the effort to entertain it, we proceed step beyond step—we fancy point still beyond point; and so long as we *continue* the effort, it may be said, in fact, that we are *tending* to the formation of the idea designed; while the strength of the impression that we actually form or have formed it, is in the ratio of the period during which we keep up the mental endeavor. But it is in the act of discontinuing the endeavor—of fulfilling (as we think) the idea—of putting the finishing stroke (as we suppose) to the conception— that we overthrow at once the whole fabric of our fancy by resting upon some one ultimate and therefore definite point. This fact, however, we fail to perceive, on account of the absolute coincidence, in time, between the settling down upon the ultimate point and the act of cessation in thinking.—In attempting, on the other hand, to frame the idea of a *limited* space, we merely converse the processes which involve the impossibility.

We *believe* in a God. We may or may not *believe* in finite or in infinite space; but our belief, in such cases, is more properly designated as *faith*, and is a matter quite distinct from that belief proper— from that *intellectual* belief—which presupposes the mental conception.

The fact is, that, upon the enunciation of any one of that class of terms to which "Infinity" belongs—the class representing *thoughts of thought*—he who has a right to say that he thinks *at all*, feels himself called upon, *not* to entertain a conception, but simply to direct his mental vision toward some given point, in the intellectual firmament, where lies a nebula never to be resolved. To solve it, indeed, he makes no effort; for with a rapid instinct he comprehends, not only the impossibility, but, as regards all human purposes, the *inessentiality*, of its solution. He perceives that the Deity has not *designed* it to be solved. He sees, at once, that it lies *out* of the brain of man, and even *how*, if not exactly *why*, it lies out of it. There *are* people, I am aware, who, busying themselves in attempts at the unattainable, acquire very easily, by dint of the jargon they emit, among those thinkers-that-they-think with whom darkness and depth are synonymous, a kind of cuttle-fish reputation for profundity; but the finest quality of Thought is its self-cognizance; and, with some little equivocation, it may be said that no fog of the mind can well be greater than that which, extending to the very boundaries of the mental domain, shuts out even these boundaries themselves from comprehension.

It will now be understood that, in using the phrase, "Infinity of Space," I make no call upon the reader to entertain the impossible conception of an *absolute* infinity. I refer simply to the "*utmost conceivable expanse*" of space—a shadowy and fluctuating domain, now shrinking, now swelling, in accordance with the vacillating energies of the imagination.

Hitherto, the Universe of stars has always been considered as coincident with the Universe proper, as I have defined it in the commencement of this Discourse. It has been always either directly or indirectly assumed—at least since the dawn of intelligible Astronomy—that, were it possible for us to attain any given point in space, we should still find, on all sides of us, an interminable succession of stars. This was the untenable idea of Pascal when making perhaps the most successful attempt ever made, at periphrasing the conception for which we struggle in the word "Universe." "It is a sphere," he says, "of which the centre is everywhere, the circumference, nowhere." But although this intended definition is, in fact, *no* definition of the Universe of *stars*, we may accept it, with some mental reservation, as a definition (rigorous enough for all practical purposes) of the Universe *proper*—that is to say, of the Universe of *space.* This latter, then, let us regard as "*a sphere of which the centre is everywhere, the circumference nowhere.*" In fact, while we find it impossible to fancy an *end* to space, we have no difficulty in picturing to ourselves any one of an infinity of *beginnings.*

As our starting-point, then, let us adopt the *Godhead.* Of this Godhead, *in itself*, he alone is not imbecile—he alone is not impious who propounds——nothing. "*Nous ne connaissons rien*" says the Baron de Bielfeld—"*Nous ne connaissons rien de la nature ou de l'essence de Dieu:—pour savoir ce qu'il est, il faut être Dieu même.*"—"We know absolutely *nothing* of the nature or essence of God:—in order to comprehend what he is, we should have to be God ourselves."

"*We should have to be God ourselves!*"—With a phrase so startling as this yet ringing in my ears, I nevertheless venture to demand if this our present ignorance of the Deity is an ignorance to which the soul is *everlastingly* condemned.

By *Him*, however—*now*, at least, the Incomprehensible —by Him—assuming him as *Spirit*—that is to say, as *not Matter*—a distinction which, for all intelligible purposes, will stand well instead of a definition—by Him, then, existing as Spirit, let us content ourselves, to-night, with supposing to have been *created*, or made out of Nothing, by dint of his Volition—at some point of Space which we will take as a centre—at some period into which we do not pretend to inquire, but at all events immensely remote—by Him, then again, let us suppose to have been created——*what?* This is a vitally momentous epoch in our considerations. *What* is it that we are justified—that alone we are justified in supposing to have been, primarily and solely, *created?*

We have attained a point where only *Intuition* can aid us:—but now let me recur to the idea which I have already suggested as that alone which we can properly entertain of intuition. It is but *the conviction arising from those inductions or deductions of which the processes are so shadowy as to escape our consciousness, elude our reason, or defy our capacity of expression.* With this understanding, I now assert—that an intuition altogether irresistible, although inexpressible, forces me to the conclusion that what God originally created—that that Matter which, by dint of his Volition, he first made from his Spirit, or from Nihility, *could* have been nothing but Matter in its utmost conceivable state of——what?—of *Simplicity?*

This will be found the sole absolute *assumption* of my Discourse. I use the word "assumption" in its ordinary sense; yet I maintain that even this my primary proposition, is very, very far indeed, from being really a mere assumption. Nothing was ever more certainly—no human conclusion was ever, in fact, more regularly—more rigorously *de*duced:—but, alas! the processes lie out of the human analysis—at all events are beyond the utterance of the human tongue.

Let us now endeavor to conceive what Matter must be, when, or if, in its absolute extreme of *Simplicity.* Here the Reason flies at once to Imparticularity—to a particle—to *one* particle—a particle of *one* kind—of *one* character—of *one* nature—of *one* size—of one form—a particle, therefore, "*without* form and void"—a particle positively a particle at all points—a particle absolutely unique, individual, undivided, and not indivisible only because He who *created* it, by dint of his Will, can by an infinitely less energetic exercise of the same Will, as a matter of course, divide it.

Oneness, then, is all that I predicate of the originally created Matter; but I propose to show that this *Oneness is a principle abundantly sufficient to account for the constitution, the existing phœnomena and the plainly inevitable annihilation of at least the material Universe.*

The willing into being the primordial particle, has completed the act, or more properly the *conception*, of Creation. We now proceed to the ultimate purpose for which we are to suppose the Particle created—that is to say, the ultimate purpose so far as our considerations *yet* enable us to see it—the constitution of the Universe from it, the Particle.

This constitution has been effected by *forcing* the originally and therefore normally *One* into the abnormal condition of *Many*. An action of this character implies rëaction. A diffusion from Unity, under the conditions, involves a tendency to return into Unity—a tendency ineradicable until satisfied. But on these points I will speak more fully hereafter.

The assumption of absolute Unity in the primordial Particle includes that of infinite divisibility. Let us conceive the Particle, then, to be only not totally exhausted by diffusion into Space. From the one Particle, as a centre, let us suppose to be irradiated spherically—in all directions—to immeasurable but still to definite distances in the previously vacant space—a certain inexpressibly great yet limited number of unimaginably yet not infinitely minute atoms.

Now, of these atoms, thus diffused, or upon diffusion, what conditions are we permitted—not to assume, but to infer, from consideration as well of their source as of the character of the design apparent in their diffusion? *Unity* being their source, and *difference from Unity* the character of the design manifested in their diffusion, we are warranted in supposing this character to be at least *generally* preserved throughout the design, and to form a portion of the design itself:—that is to say, we shall be warranted in conceiving continual differences at all points from the uniquity and simplicity of the origin. But, for these reasons, shall we be justified in imagining the atoms heterogeneous, dissimilar, unequal, and inequidistant? More explicitly—are we to consider no two atoms as, at their diffusion, of the same nature, or of the same form, or of the same size?—and, after fulfilment of their diffusion into Space, is absolute inequidistance, each from each, to be understood of all of them? In such arrangement, under such conditions, we most easily and immediately comprehend the subsequent most feasible carrying out to completion of any such design as that which I have suggested—the design of variety out of unity—diversity out of sameness—heterogeneity out of homogeneity—complexity out of simplicity—in a word, the utmost possible multiplicity of *relation* out of the emphatically irrelative *One*. Undoubtedly, therefore, we *should* be warranted in assuming all that has been mentioned, but for the reflection, first, that supererogation is not presumable of any Divine Act; and, secondly, that the object supposed in view, appears as feasible when some of the conditions in question are dispensed with, in the beginning, as when all are understood immediately to exist. I mean to say that some are involved in the rest, or so instantaneous a consequence of them as to make the distinction inappreciable. Difference of *size*, for example, will at once be brought about through the tendency of one atom to a second, in preference to a third, on account of particular inequidistance; which is to be comprehended as *particular inequidistances between centres of quantity, in neighboring atoms of different form*—a matter not at all interfering with the generally-equable distribution of the atoms.

Difference of *kind*, too, is easily conceived to be merely a result of differences in size and form, taken more or less conjointly:—in fact, since the *Unity* of the Particle Proper implies absolute homogeneity, we cannot imagine the atoms, at their diffusion, differing in kind, without imagining, at the same time, a special exercise of the Divine Will, at the emission of each atom, for the purpose of effecting, in each, a change of its essential nature:—so fantastic an idea is the less to be indulged, as the object proposed is seen to be thoroughly attainable without such minute and elaborate interposition. We perceive, therefore, upon the whole, that it would be supererogatory, and consequently unphilosophical, to predicate of the atoms, in view of their purposes, any thing more than *difference of form* at their dispersion, with particular inequidistance after it—all other differences arising at once out of these, in the very first processes of mass-constitution:—We thus establish the Universe on a purely *geometrical* basis. Of course, it is by no means necessary to assume absolute difference, even of form, among *all* the atoms irradiated—any more than absolute particular inequidistance of each from each. We are required to conceive merely that no *neighboring* atoms are of similar form—no atoms which can ever approximate, until their inevitable rëunion at the end.

Although the immediate and perpetual *tendency* of the disunited atoms to return into their normal Unity, is implied, as I have said, in their abnormal diffusion; still it is clear that this tendency will be without consequence—a tendency and no more—until the diffusive energy, in ceasing to be exerted, shall leave *it*, the tendency, free to seek its satisfaction. The Divine Act, however, being considered as determinate, and discontinued on fulfilment of the diffusion, we understand, at once, a *rëaction*—in other words, a *satisfiable* tendency of the disunited atoms to return into *One*.

But the diffusive energy being withdrawn, and the rëaction having commenced in furtherance of the ultimate design—*that of the utmost possible Relation*—this design is now in danger of being frustrated, in detail, by reason of that very tendency to return which is to effect its accomplishment in general. *Multiplicity* is the object; but there is nothing to prevent proximate atoms, from lapsing *at once*, through the now satisfiable tendency—*before* the fulfilment of any ends proposed in multiplicity—into absolute oneness among themselves:—there is nothing to impede the aggregation of various *unique* masses, at various points of space:—in other words, nothing to interfere with the accumulation of various masses, each absolutely One.

For the effectual and thorough completion of the general design, we thus see the necessity for a repulsion of limited capacity—a separative *something* which, on withdrawal of the diffusive Volition, shall at the same time allow the approach, and forbid the junction, of the atoms; suffering them infinitely to approximate, while denying them positive contact; in a word, having the power—*up to a certain epoch*—of preventing their *coalition*, but no ability to interfere with their *coalescence* in any respect *or degree*. The repulsion, already considered as so peculiarly limited in other regards, must be understood, let me repeat, as having power to prevent absolute coalition, *only up to a certain epoch*. Unless we are to conceive that the appetite for Unity among the atoms is doomed to be satisfied *never;*—unless we are to conceive that what had a beginning is to have no end—a conception which cannot *really* be entertained, however much we may talk or dream of entertaining it—we are forced to conclude that the repulsive influence imagined, will, finally—under pressure of the *Unitendency collectively* applied, but never and in no degree *until*, on fulfilment of the Divine purposes, such collective application shall be naturally made—yield to a force which, at that ultimate epoch, shall be the superior force precisely to the extent required, and thus permit the universal subsidence into the inevitable, because original and therefore normal, *One.*—The conditions here to be reconciled are difficult indeed:—we cannot even comprehend the possibility of their conciliation;—nevertheless, the apparent impossibility is brilliantly suggestive.

That the repulsive something actually exists, *we see.* Man neither employs, nor knows, a force sufficient to bring two atoms into contact. This is but the well-established proposition of the impenetrability of matter. All Experiment proves—all Philosophy admits it. The *design* of the repulsion— the necessity for its existence—I have endeavored to show; but from all attempt at investigating its nature have religiously abstained; this on account of an intuitive conviction that the principle at issue is strictly spiritual—lies in a recess impervious to our present understanding—lies involved in a consideration of what now—in our human state— is *not* to be considered—in a consideration of *Spirit in itself.* I feel, in a word, that here the God has interposed, and here only, because here and here only the knot demanded the interposition of the God.

In fact, while the tendency of the diffused atoms to return into Unity, will be recognized, at once, as the principle of the Newtonian Gravity, what I have spoken of as a repulsive influence prescribing limits to the (immediate) satisfaction of the tendency, will be understood as *that* which we have been in the practice of designating now as heat, now as magnetism, now as *electricity;* displaying our ignorance of its awful character in the vacillation of the phraseology with which we endeavor to circumscribe it.

Calling it, merely for the moment, electricity, we know that all experimental analysis of electricity has

given, as an ultimate result, the principle, or seeming principle, *heterogeneity*. *Only* where things differ is electricity apparent; and it is presumable that they *never* differ where it is not developed at least, if not apparent. Now, this result is in the fullest keeping with that which I have reached unempirically. The design of the repulsive influence I have maintained to be that of preventing immediate Unity among the diffused atoms; and these atoms are represented as different each from each. *Difference* is their character—their essentiality—just as *no-difference* was the essentiality of their source. When we say, then, that an attempt to bring any two of these atoms together would induce an effort, on the part of the repulsive influence, to prevent the contact, we may as well use the strictly convertible sentence that an attempt to bring together any two differences will result in a development of electricity. All existing bodies, of course, are composed of these atoms in proximate contact, and are therefore to be considered as mere assemblages of more or fewer differences; and the resistance made by the repulsive spirit, on bringing together any two such assemblages, would be in the ratio of the two sums of the differences in each:—an expression which, when reduced, is equivalent to this:—*The amount of electricity developed on the approximation of two bodies, is proportional to the difference between the respective sums of the atoms of which the bodies are composed*. That *no* two bodies are absolutely alike, is a simple corollary from all that has been here said. Electricity, therefore, existing always, is *developed* whenever *any* bodies,
but *manifested* only when bodies of appreciable difference, are brought into approximation.

To electricity—so, for the present, continuing to call it—we *may* not be wrong in referring the various physical appearances of light, heat and magnetism; but far less shall we be liable to err in attributing to this strictly spiritual principle the more important phænomena of vitality, consciousness and *Thought.* On this topic, however, I need pause *here* merely to suggest that these phænomena, whether observed generally or in detail, seem to proceed *at least in the ratio of the heterogeneous.*

Discarding now the two equivocal terms, "gravitation" and "electricity," let us adopt the more definite expressions, "*attraction*" and "*repulsion.*" The former is the body; the latter the soul: the one is the material; the other the spiritual, principle of the Universe. *No other principles exist. All* phænomena are referable to one, or to the other, or to both combined. So rigorously is this the case—so thoroughly demonstrable is it that attraction and repulsion are the *sole* properties through which we perceive the Universe—in other words, by which Matter is manifested to Mind—that, for all merely argumentative purposes, we are fully justified in assuming that matter *exists* only as attraction and repulsion—that attraction and repulsion *are* matter:— there being no conceivable case in which we may not employ the term "matter" and the terms "attraction" and "repulsion," taken together, as equivalent, and therefore convertible, expressions in Logic.

I said, just now, that what I have described as the tendency of the diffused atoms to return into their original unity, would be understood as the principle of the Newtonian law of gravity: and, in fact, there can be little difficulty in such an understanding, if we look at the Newtonian gravity in a merely general view, as a force impelling matter to seek matter; that is to say, when we pay no attention to the known *modus operandi* of the Newtonian force. The general coincidence satisfies us; but, upon looking closely, we see, in detail, much that appears *in*coincident, and much in regard to which no coincidence, at least, is established. For example; the Newtonian gravity, when we think of it in certain moods, does *not* seem to be a tendency to *oneness* at all, but rather a tendency of all bodies in all directions—a phrase apparently expressive of a tendency to diffusion. Here, then, is an *in*coincidence. Again; when we reflect on the mathematical *law* governing the Newtonian tendency, we see clearly that no coincidence has been made good, in respect of the *modus operandi*, at least, between gravitation as known to exist and that seemingly simple and direct tendency which I have assumed.

In fact, I have attained a point at which it will be advisable to strengthen my position by reversing my processes. So far, we have gone on *à priori*, from an abstract consideration of *Simplicity*, as that quality most likely to have characterized the original action of God. Let us now see whether the established facts of the Newtonian Gravitation may not afford us, *à posteriori*, some legitimate inductions.

What does the Newtonian law declare?—That all bodies attract each other with forces proportional to their quantities of matter and inversely proportional to the squares of their distances. Purposely, I have here given, in the first place, the vulgar version of the law; and I confess that in this, as in most other vulgar versions of great truths, we find little of a suggestive character. Let us now adopt a more philosophical phraseology:—*Every atom, of every body, attracts every other atom, both of its own and of every other body, with a force which varies inversely as the squares of the distances between the attracting and attracted atom.*—Here, indeed, a flood of suggestion bursts upon the mind.

But let us see distinctly what it was that Newton *proved*—according to the grossly irrational definitions of *proof* prescribed by the metaphysical schools. He was forced to content himself with showing how thoroughly the motions of an imaginary Universe, composed of attracting and attracted atoms obedient to the law he announced, coincide with those of the actually existing Universe so far as it comes under our observation. This was the amount of his *demonstration*—that is to say, this was the amount of it, according to the conventional cant of the "philosophies." His successes added proof multiplied by proof—such proof as a sound intellect admits—but the *demonstration* of the law itself, persist the metaphysicians, had not been strengthened in any degree. "*Ocular, physical* proof," however, of attraction, here upon Earth, in accordance with the Newtonian theory, was, at length, much to the satisfaction of some intellectual grovellers, afforded. This proof arose collaterally and incidentally (as nearly all important truths have arisen) out of an attempt to ascertain the mean density of the Earth. In the famous Maskelyne, Cavendish and Bailly experiments for this purpose, the attraction of the mass of a mountain was seen, felt, measured, and found to be mathematically consistent with the immortal theory of the British astronomer.

But in spite of this confirmation of that which needed none—in spite of the so-called corroboration of the "theory" by the so-called "ocular and physical proof"—in spite of the *character* of this corroboration—the ideas which even really philosophical men cannot help imbibing of gravity—and, especially, the ideas of it which ordinary men get and contentedly maintain, are *seen* to have been derived, for the most part, from a consideration of the principle as they find it developed—*merely in the planet upon which they stand.*

Now, to what does so partial a consideration tend—to what species of error does it give rise? On the Earth we *see* and *feel*, only that gravity impels all bodies towards the *centre* of the Earth. No man in the common walks of life could be *made* to see or to feel anything else—could be made to perceive that anything, anywhere, has a perpetual, gravitating tendency in any *other* direction than to the centre of the Earth; yet (with an exception hereafter to be specified) it is a fact that every earthly thing (not to speak now of every heavenly thing) has a tendency not *only* to the Earth's centre but in every conceivable direction besides.

Now, although the philosophic cannot be said to *err with* the vulgar in this matter, they nevertheless permit themselves to be influenced, without knowing it, by the *sentiment* of the vulgar idea. "Although the Pagan fables are not believed," says Bryant, in his very erudite "Mythology," "yet we forget ourselves continually and make inferences from them as from existing realities." I mean to assert that the merely *sensitive perception* of gravity as we experience it on Earth, beguiles mankind into the fancy of *concentralization* or *especiality* respecting it—has been continually biasing towards this fancy even the mightiest intellects—perpetually, although imperceptibly, leading them away from the real characteristics of the principle; thus preventing them, up to this date, from ever getting a glimpse of that vital truth which lies in a diametrically opposite direction—behind   the principle's *essential* characteristics—those, *not* of concentralization   or   especiality—but   of *universality* and *diffusion*.   This   "vital   truth" is *Unity* as the *source* of the phænomenon.

Let me now repeat the definition of gravity:— *Every atom, of every body, attracts every other atom, both of its own and of every other body*, with a force which varies inversely as the squares of the distances of the attracting and attracted atom.

Here let the reader pause with me, for a moment, in contemplation of the miraculous—of the ineffable— of the altogether unimaginable complexity of relation involved in the fact that *each atom attracts every other atom*—involved merely in this fact of the attraction, without reference to the law or mode in which   the   attraction   is manifested—

involved *merely* in the fact that each atom attracts every other atom *at all*, in a wilderness of atoms so numerous that those which go to the composition of a cannon-ball, exceed, probably, in mere point of number, all the stars which go to the constitution of the Universe.

Had we discovered, simply, that each atom tended to some one favorite point—to some especially attractive atom—we should still have fallen upon a discovery which, in itself, would have sufficed to overwhelm the mind:—but what is it that we are actually called upon to comprehend? That each atom attracts—sympathizes with the most delicate movements of every other atom, and with each and with all at the same time, and forever, and according to a determinate law of which the complexity, even considered by itself solely, is utterly beyond the grasp of the imagination of man. If I propose to ascertain the influence of one mote in a sunbeam upon its neighboring mote, I cannot accomplish my purpose without first counting and weighing all the atoms in the Universe and defining the precise positions of all at one particular moment. If I venture to displace, by even the billionth part of an inch, the microscopical speck of dust which lies now upon the point of my finger, what is the character of that act upon which I have adventured? I have done a deed which shakes the Moon in her path, which causes the Sun to be no longer the Sun, and which alters forever the destiny of the multitudinous myriads of stars that roll and glow in the majestic presence of their Creator.

These ideas—conceptions such as *these*—unthoughtlike thoughts—soul-reveries rather than conclusions or even considerations of the intellect:—ideas, I repeat, such as these, are such as we can alone hope profitably to entertain in any effort at grasping the great principle, *Attraction*.

But now,—*with* such ideas—with such a *vision* of the marvellous complexity of Attraction fairly in his mind—let any person competent of thought on such topics as these, set himself to the task of imagining a *principle* for the phænomena observed—a condition from which they sprang.

Does not so evident a brotherhood among the atoms point to a common parentage? Does not a sympathy so omniprevalent, so ineradicable, and so thoroughly irrespective, suggest a common paternity as its source? Does not one extreme impel the reason to the other? Does not the infinitude of division refer to the utterness of individuality? Does not the entireness of the complex hint at the perfection of the simple? It is *not* that the atoms, as we see them, are divided or that they are complex in their relations—but that they are inconceivably divided and unutterably complex:—it is the extremeness of the conditions to which I now allude, rather than to the conditions themselves. In a word, is it not because the atoms were, at some remote epoch of time, even *more than together*—is it not because originally, and therefore normally, they were *One*—that now, in all circumstances—at all points—in all directions—by all modes of approach—in all relations and through all conditions—they struggle *back* to this absolutely, this irrelatively, this unconditionally *one?*

Some person may here demand:—"Why—since it is to the *One* that the atoms struggle back—do we not find and define Attraction 'a merely general tendency to a —centre?'—why, in especial, do not *your* atoms—the atoms which you describe as having been irradiated from a centre—proceed at once, rectilinearly, back to the central point of their origin?"

I reply that *they do;* as will be distinctly shown; but that the cause of their so doing is quite irrespective of the centre *as such*. They all tend rectilinearly towards a centre, because of the sphereicity with which they have been irradiated into space. Each atom, forming one of a generally uniform globe of atoms, finds more atoms in the direction of the centre, of course, than in any other, and in that direction, therefore, is impelled—but is *not* thus impelled because the centre is *the point of its origin.* It is not to any *point* that the atoms are allied. It is not any *locality*, either in the concrete or in the abstract, to which I suppose them bound. Nothing like *location* was conceived as their origin. Their source lies in the principle, *Unity. This* is their lost parent. *This* they seek always—immediately—in all directions—wherever it is even partially to be found; thus appeasing, in some measure, the ineradicable tendency, while on the way to its absolute satisfaction in the end. It follows from all this, that any principle which shall be adequate to account for the *law*, or *modus operandi*, of the attractive force in general, will account for this law in particular:—that is to say, any principle which will show why the atoms should tend to their *general centre of irradiation* with forces inversely proportional to the squares of the distances, will be admitted as satisfactorily accounting, at the same time, for the tendency, according to the same law, of these atoms each to each:—*for* the tendency to the centre *is* merely the tendency each to each, and not any tendency to a centre as such.—Thus it will be seen, also, that the establishment of my propositions would involve no *necessity* of modification in the terms of the Newtonian definition of Gravity, which declares that each atom attracts each other atom and so forth, and declares this merely; but (always under the supposition that what I propose be, in the end, admitted) it seems clear that some error might occasionally be avoided, in the future processes of Science, were a more ample phraseology adopted:— for instance:—"Each atom tends to every other atom &c. with a force &c.: *the general result being a tendency of all, with a similar force, to a general centre.*"

The reversal of our processes has thus brought us to an identical result; but, while in the one process *intuition* was the starting-point, in the other it was the goal. In commencing the former journey I could only say that, with an irresistible intuition, I *felt* Simplicity to have been the characteristic of the original action of God:—in ending the latter I can only declare that, with an irresistible intuition, I perceive Unity to have been the source of the observed phænomena of the Newtonian gravitation. Thus, according to the schools, I *prove* nothing. So be it:—I design but to suggest—and to *convince* through the suggestion. I am proudly aware that there exist many of the most profound and cautiously discriminative human intellects which cannot *help* being abundantly content with my—suggestions. To these intellects—as to my own—there is no mathematical demonstration which *could* bring the least additional *true proof* of the great *Truth* which I have advanced—*the truth of Original Unity as the source—as the principle of the Universal Phænomena.* For my part, I am not so sure that I speak and see—I am not so sure that my heart beats and that my soul lives:—of the rising of to-morrow's sun—a probability that as yet lies in the Future—I do not pretend to be one thousandth part as sure—as I am of the irretrievably by-gone *Fact* that All Things and All Thoughts of Things, with all their ineffable Multiplicity of Relation, sprang at once into being from the primordial and irrelative *One.*

Referring to the Newtonian Gravity, Dr. Nichol, the eloquent author of "The Architecture of the Heavens," says:—"In truth we have no reason to suppose this great Law, as now revealed, to be the ultimate or simplest, and therefore the universal and all-comprehensive, form of a great Ordinance. The mode in which its intensity diminishes with the element of distance, has not the aspect of an ultimate *principle;*which always assumes the simplicity and self-evidence of those axioms which constitute the basis of Geometry."

Now, it is quite true that "ultimate principles," in the common understanding of the words, always assume the simplicity of geometrical axioms—(as for "self-evidence," there is no such thing)—but these principles are clearly *not* "ultimate;" in other terms what we are in the habit of calling principles are no principles, properly speaking—since there can be but one *principle*, the Volition of God. We have no right to assume, then, from what we observe in rules that we choose foolishly to name "principles," anything at all in respect to the characteristics of a principle proper. The "ultimate principles" of which Dr. Nichol speaks as having geometrical simplicity, may and do have this geometrical turn, as being part and parcel of a vast geometrical system, and thus a system of simplicity itself—in which, nevertheless, the *truly* ultimate principle is, *as we know*, the consummation of the complex—that is to say, of the unintelligible—for is it not the Spiritual Capacity of God?

I quoted Dr. Nichol's remark, however, not so much to question its philosophy, as by way of calling attention to the fact that, while all men have admitted *some* principle as existing behind the Law of Gravity, no attempt has been yet made to point out what this principle in particular *is:*—if we except, perhaps, occasional fantastic efforts at referring it to Magnetism, or Mesmerism, or Swedenborgianism, or Transcendentalism, or some other equally delicious *ism* of the same species, and invariably patronized by one and the same species of people. The great mind of Newton, while boldly grasping the Law itself, shrank from the principle of the Law. The more fluent and comprehensive at least, if not the more patient and profound, sagacity of Laplace, had not the courage to attack it. But hesitation on the part of these two astronomers it is, perhaps, not so very difficult to understand. They, as well as all the first class of mathematicians, were mathematicians *solely:*—their intellect, at least, had a firmly-pronounced mathematico-physical tone. What lay not distinctly within the domain of Physics, or of Mathematics, seemed to them either Non-Entity or Shadow. Nevertheless, we may well wonder that Leibnitz, who was a marked exception to the general rule in these respects, and whose mental temperament was a singular admixture of the mathematical with the physico-metaphysical, did not at once investigate and establish the point at issue. Either Newton or Laplace, seeking a principle and discovering none *physical*, would have rested contentedly in the conclusion that there was absolutely none; but it is almost impossible to fancy, of Leibnitz, that, having exhausted in his search the physical dominions, he would not have stepped at once, boldly and hopefully, amid his old familiar haunts in the kingdom of Metaphysics. Here, indeed, it is clear that he *must* have adventured in search of the treasure:—that he did not find it after all, was, perhaps, because his fairy guide, Imagination, was not sufficiently well-grown, or well-educated, to direct him aright.

I observed, just now, that, in fact, there had been certain vague attempts at referring Gravity to some very uncertain *isms*. These attempts, however, although considered bold and justly so considered, looked no farther than to the generality—the merest generality—of the Newtonian Law. Its *modus operandi* has never, to my knowledge, been approached in the way of an effort at explanation. It is, therefore, with no unwarranted fear of being taken for a madman at the outset, and before I can bring my propositions fairly to the eye of those who alone are competent to decide upon them, that I here declare the *modus operandi* of the Law of Gravity to be an exceedingly simple and perfectly explicable thing— that is to say, when we make our advances towards it in just gradations and in the true direction—when we regard it from the proper point of view.

Whether we reach the idea of absolute *Unity* as the source of All Things, from a consideration of Simplicity as the most probable characteristic of the original action of God;—whether we arrive at it from an inspection of the universality of relation in the gravitating phænomena;—or whether we attain it as a result of the mutual corroboration afforded by both processes;—still, the idea itself, if entertained at all, is entertained in inseparable connection with another idea—that of the condition of the Universe of stars as we *now* perceive it—that is to say, a condition of immeasurable *diffusion* through space. Now a connection between these two ideas—unity and diffusion—cannot be established unless through the entertainment of a third idea—that of *irradiation*. Absolute Unity being taken as a centre, then the existing Universe of stars is the result of *irradiation* from that centre.

Now, the laws of irradiation are *known*. They are part and parcel of the *sphere*. They belong to the class of *indisputable geometrical properties*. We say of them, "they are true—they are evident." To demand *why* they are true, would be to demand why the axioms are true upon which their demonstration is based. *Nothing* is demonstrable, strictly speaking; but *if* anything *be*, then the properties—the laws in question are demonstrated.

But these laws—what do they declare? Irradiation—how—by what steps does it proceed outwardly from a centre?

From a *luminous* centre, *Light* issues by irradiation; and the quantities of light received upon any given plane, supposed to be shifting its position so as to be now nearer the centre and now farther from it, will be diminished in the same proportion as the squares of the distances of the plane from the luminous body, are increased; and will be increased in the same proportion as these squares are diminished.

The expression of the law may be thus generalized:—the number of light-particles (or, if the phrase be preferred, the number of light-impressions) received upon the shifting plane, will be *inversely* proportional with the squares of the distances of the plane. Generalizing yet again, we may say that the diffusion—the scattering—the irradiation, in a word—is *directly* proportional with the squares of the distances.

For example: at the distance B, from the luminous centre A, a certain number of particles are so diffused as to occupy the surface B. Then at double the distance—that is to say

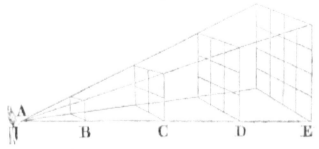

at C—they will be so much farther diffused as to occupy four such surfaces:—at treble the distance, or at D, they will be so much farther separated as to occupy nine such surfaces:—while, at quadruple the distance, or at E, they will have become so scattered as to spread themselves over sixteen such surfaces—and so on forever.

In saying, generally, that the irradiation proceeds in direct proportion with the squares of the distances, we use the term irradiation to express *the degree of the diffusion* as we proceed outwardly from the centre. Conversing the idea, and employing the word "concentralization" to express *the degree of the drawing together* as we come back toward the centre from an outward position, we may say that concentralization proceeds *inversely* as the squares of the distances. In other words, we have reached the conclusion that, on the hypothesis that matter was originally irradiated from a centre and is now returning to it, the concentralization, in the return, proceeds *exactly as we know the force of gravitation to proceed.*

Now here, if we could be permitted to assume that concentralization exactly represented the *force of the tendency to the centre*—that the one was exactly proportional to the other, and that the two proceeded together—we should have shown all that is required. The sole difficulty existing, then, is to establish a direct proportion between "concentralization" and the *force* of concentralization; and this is done, of course, if we establish such proportion between "irradiation" and the *force* of irradiation.

A very slight inspection of the Heavens assures us that the stars have a certain general uniformity, equability, or equidistance, of distribution through that region of space in which, collectively, and in a roughly globular form, they are situated:—this species of very general, rather than absolute, equability, being in full keeping with my deduction of inequidistance, within certain limits, among the originally diffused atoms, as a corollary from the evident design of infinite complexity of relation out of irrelation. I started, it will be remembered, with the idea of a generally uniform but particularly *un*uniform distribution of the atoms;—an idea, I repeat, which an inspection of the stars, as they exist, confirms.

But even in the merely general equability of distribution, as regards the atoms, there appears a difficulty which, no doubt, has already suggested itself to those among my readers who have borne in mind that I suppose this equability of distribution effected through *irradiation from a centre.* The very first glance at the idea, irradiation, forces us to the entertainment of the hitherto unseparated and seemingly inseparable idea of agglomeration about a centre, with dispersion as we recede from it—the idea, in a word, of *in*equitability of distribution in respect to the matter irradiated.

Now, I have elsewhere[1] observed that it is by just such difficulties as the one now in question—such roughnesses—such peculiarities—such protuberances above the plane of the ordinary—that Reason feels her way, if at all, in her search for the True. By the difficulty—the "peculiarity"—now presented, I leap at once to *the* secret—a secret which I might never have attained *but* for the peculiarity and the inferences which, *in its mere character of peculiarity*, it affords me.

The process of thought, at this point, may be thus roughly sketched:—I say to myself—"Unity, as I have explained it, is a truth—I feel it. Diffusion is a truth—I see it. Irradiation, by which alone these two truths are reconciled, is a consequent truth—I perceive it. *Equability* of diffusion, first deduced *à priori* and then, corroborated by the inspection of phænomena, is also a truth—I fully admit it. So far all is clear around me:—there are no clouds behind which *the* secret—the great secret of the gravitating *modus operandi*—can possibly lie hidden;—but this secret lies *hereabouts*, most assuredly; and *were* there but a cloud in view, I should be driven to suspicion of that cloud." And now, just as I say this, there actually comes a cloud into view. This cloud is the seeming impossibility of reconciling my truth, *irradiation*, with my truth, *equability of diffusion*. I say now:—"Behind this *seeming* impossibility is to be found what I desire." I do not say *"real* impossibility;" for invincible faith in my truths assures me that it is a mere difficulty after all—but I go on to say, with unflinching confidence, that, *when* this *difficulty* shall be solved, we shall find, *wrapped up in the process of solution*, the key to the secret at which we aim.

Moreover—I *feel* that we shall discover *but one* possible solution of the difficulty; this for the reason that, were there two, one would be supererogatory—would be fruitless—would be empty—would contain no key—since no duplicate key can be needed to any secret of Nature.

And now, let us see:—Our usual notions of irradiation—in fact *all* our distinct notions of it—are caught merely from the process as we see it exemplified in *Light*. Here there is a *continuous* outpouring of *ray-streams*, and *with a force which we have at least no right to suppose varies at all*. Now, in any such irradiation *as this*—continuous and of unvarying force—the regions nearer the centre must *inevitably* be always more crowded with the irradiated matter than the regions more remote. But I have assumed *no* such irradiation *as this*. I assumed no *continuous* irradiation; and for the simple reason that such an assumption would have involved, first, the necessity of entertaining a conception which I have shown no man *can* entertain, and which (as I will more fully explain hereafter) all observation of the firmament refutes—the conception of the absolute infinity of the Universe of stars—and would have involved, secondly, the impossibility of understanding a rëaction—that is, gravitation—as existing now—since, while an act is continued, no rëaction, of course, can take place. My assumption, then, or rather my inevitable deduction from just premises—was that of a *determinate* irradiation—one finally *dis*continued.

Let me now describe the sole possible mode in which it is conceivable that matter could have been diffused through space, so as to fulfil the conditions at once of irradiation and of generally equable distribution.

For convenience of illustration, let us imagine, in the first place, a hollow sphere of glass, or of anything else, occupying the space throughout which the universal matter is to be thus equally diffused, by means of irradiation, from the absolute, irrelative, unconditional particle, placed in the centre of the sphere.

Now, a certain exertion of the diffusive power (presumed to be the Divine Volition)—in other words, a certain *force*—whose measure is the quantity of matter—that is to say, the number of atoms—emitted; emits, by irradiation, this certain number of atoms; forcing them in all directions outwardly from the centre—their proximity to each other diminishing as they proceed—until, finally, they are distributed, loosely, over the interior surface of the sphere.

When these atoms have attained this position, or while proceeding to attain it, a second and inferior exercise of the same force—or a second and inferior force of the same character—emits, in the same manner—that is to say, by irradiation as before—a second stratum of atoms which proceeds to deposit itself upon the first; the number of atoms, in this case as in the former, being of course the measure of the force which emitted them; in other words the force being precisely adapted to the purpose it effects—the force and the number of atoms sent out by the force, being *directly proportional.*

When this second stratum has reached its destined position—or while approaching it—a third still inferior exertion of the force, or a third inferior force of a similar character—the number of atoms emitted being in *all* cases the measure of the force—proceeds to deposit a third stratum upon the second:—and so on, until these concentric strata, growing gradually less and less, come down at length to the central point; and the diffusive matter, simultaneously with the diffusive force, is exhausted.

We have now the sphere filled, through means of irradiation, with atoms equably diffused. The two necessary conditions—those of irradiation and of

equable   diffusion—are   satisfied;   and   by
the *sole* process in which the possibility of their
simultaneous   satisfaction   is   conceivable.   For   this
reason, I confidently expect to find, lurking in the
present   condition   of   the   atoms   as   distributed
throughout the sphere, the secret of which I am in
search—the all-important principle of the *modus
operandi* of the Newtonian law. Let us examine, then,
the actual condition of the atoms.

They lie in a series of concentric strata. They are
equably diffused throughout the sphere. They have
been irradiated into these states.

The atoms being *equably* distributed, the greater
the superficial extent of any of these concentric strata,
or spheres, the more atoms will lie upon it. In other
words, the number of atoms lying upon the surface of
any one of the concentric spheres, is directly
proportional with the extent of that surface.

*But, in any series of concentric spheres, the
surfaces are directly proportional with the squares
of the distances from the centre.*[2]

Therefore the number of atoms in any stratum is
directly proportional with the square of that stratum's
distance from the centre.

But the number of atoms in any stratum is the
measure of the force which emitted that stratum—
that is to say, is *directly proportional* with the force.

Therefore the force which irradiated any stratum
is directly proportional with the square of that
stratum's distance from the centre:—or, generally,

*The force of the irradiation has been directly
proportional with the squares of the distances.*

Now, Rëaction, as far as we know anything of it,
is Action conversed. The *general* principle of Gravity
being, in the first place, understood as the rëaction of
an act—as the expression of a desire on the part of
Matter, while existing in a state of diffusion, to return
into the Unity whence it was diffused; and, in the
second place, the mind being called upon to

determine the *character* of the desire—the manner in which it would, naturally, be manifested; in other words, being called upon to conceive a probable law, or *modus operandi*, for the return; could not well help arriving at the conclusion that this law of return would be precisely the converse of the law of departure. That such would be the case, any one, at least, would be abundantly justified in taking for granted, until such time as some person should suggest something like a plausible reason why it should *not* be the case—until such period as a law of return shall be imagined which the intellect can consider as preferable.

Matter, then, irradiated into space with a force varying as the squares of the distances, might, *à priori*, be supposed to return towards its centre of irradiation with a force varying *inversely* as the squares of the distances: and I have already shown[3] that any principle which will explain why the atoms should tend, according to any law, to the general centre, must be admitted as satisfactorily explaining, at the same time, why, according to the same law, they should tend each to each. For, in fact, the tendency to the general centre is not to a centre as such, but because of its being a point in tending towards which each atom tends most directly to its real and essential centre, *Unity*—the absolute and final Union of all.

The consideration here involved presents to my own mind no embarrassment whatever—but this fact does not blind me to the possibility of its being obscure to those who may have been less in the habit of dealing with abstractions:—and, upon the whole, it may be as well to look at the matter from one or two other points of view.

The absolute, irrelative particle primarily created by the Volition of God, must have been in a condition of positive *normality*, or rightfulness—for wrongfulness implies *relation*. Right is positive;

wrong is negative—is merely the negation of right; as cold is the negation of heat—darkness of light. That a thing may be wrong, it is necessary that there be some other thing in *relation* to which it *is* wrong—some condition which it fails to satisfy; some law which it violates; some being whom it aggrieves. If there be no such being, law, or condition, in respect to which the thing is wrong—and, still more especially, if no beings, laws, or conditions exist at all—then the thing can*not* be wrong and consequently must be *right*. Any deviation from normality involves a tendency to return into it. A difference from the normal—from the right—from the just—can be understood as effected only by the overcoming a difficulty; and if the force which overcomes the difficulty be not infinitely continued, the ineradicable tendency to return will at length be permitted to act for its own satisfaction. Upon withdrawal of the force, the tendency acts. This is the principle of rëaction as the inevitable consequence of finite action. Employing a phraseology of which the seeming affectation will be pardoned for its expressiveness, we may say that Rëaction is the return from the condition of *as it is and ought not to be* into the condition of *as it was, originally, and therefore ought to be*:—and let me add here that the *absolute* force of Rëaction would no doubt be always found in direct proportion with the reality—the truth—the absoluteness—of the *originality*—if ever it were possible to measure this latter:—and, consequently, the greatest of all conceivable rëactions must be that produced by the tendency which we now discuss—the tendency to return into the *absolutely original*—into the *supremely* primitive. Gravity, then, *must be the strongest of forces*—an idea reached *à priori* and abundantly confirmed by induction. What use I make of the idea, will be seen in the sequel.

The atoms, now, having been diffused from their normal condition of Unity, seek to return to——what?

Not to any particular *point*, certainly; for it is clear that if, upon the diffusion, the whole Universe of matter had been projected, collectively, to a distance from the point of irradiation, the atomic tendency to the general centre of the sphere would not have been disturbed in the least:—the atoms would not have sought the point *in absolute space* from which they were originally impelled. It is merely the *condition*, and not the point or locality at which this condition took its rise, that these atoms seek to re-establish;—it is merely *that condition which is their normality*, that they desire. "But they seek a centre," it will be said, "and a centre is a point." True; but they seek this point not in its character of point—(for, were the whole sphere moved from its position, they would seek, equally, the centre; and the centre *then* would be a *new* point)—but because it so happens, on account of the form in which they collectively exist— (that of the sphere)—that only *through* the point in question—the sphere's centre—they can attain their true object, Unity. In the direction of the centre each atom perceives more atoms than in any other direction. Each atom is impelled towards the centre because along the straight line joining it and the centre and passing on to the circumference beyond, there lie a greater number of atoms than along any other straight line—a greater number of objects that seek it, the individual atom—a greater number of tendencies to Unity—a greater number of satisfactions for its own tendency to Unity—in a word, because in the direction of the centre lies the utmost possibility of satisfaction, generally, for its own individual appetite. To be brief, the *condition*, Unity, is all that is really sought; and if the atoms *seem* to seek the centre of the sphere, it is only impliedly, through implication—because such centre happens to imply, to include, or to involve, the only essential centre, Unity. But *on account of* this implication or involution, there is no possibility of practically

395

separating the tendency to Unity in the abstract, from the tendency to the concrete centre. Thus the tendency of the atoms to the general centre *is*, to all practical intents and for all logical purposes, the tendency each to each; and the tendency each to each *is* the tendency to the centre; and the one tendency may be assumed *as* the other; whatever will apply to the one must be thoroughly applicable to the other; and, in conclusion, whatever principle will satisfactorily explain the one, cannot be questioned as an explanation of the other.

In looking carefully around me for rational objection to what I have advanced, I am able to discover *nothing*;—but of that class of objections usually urged by the doubters for Doubt's sake, I very readily perceive *three*; and proceed to dispose of them in order.

It may be said, first: "The proof that the force of irradiation (in the case described) is directly proportional to the squares of the distances, depends upon an unwarranted assumption—that of the number of atoms in each stratum being the measure of the force with which they are emitted."

I reply, not only that I am warranted in such assumption, but that I should be utterly *un*warranted in any other. What I assume is, simply, that an effect is the measure of its cause—that every exercise of the Divine Will will be proportional to that which demands the exertion—that the means of Omnipotence, or of Omniscience, will be exactly adapted to its purposes. Neither can a deficiency nor an excess of cause bring to pass any effect. Had the force which irradiated any stratum to its position, been either more or less than was needed for the purpose—that is to say, not *directly proportional* to the purpose—then to its position that stratum could not have been irradiated. Had the force which, with a view to general equability of distribution, emitted the proper number of atoms for each stratum, been not *directly proportional* to the number, then the number would *not* have been the number demanded for the equable distribution.

The second supposable objection is somewhat better entitled to an answer.

It is an admitted principle in Dynamics that every body, on receiving an impulse, or disposition to move, will move onward in a straight line, in the direction imparted by the impelling force, until deflected, or stopped, by some other force. How then, it may be asked, is my first or external stratum of atoms to be understood as discontinuing their movement at the circumference of the imaginary glass sphere, when no second force, of more than an imaginary character, appears, to account for the discontinuance?

I reply that the objection, in this case, actually does arise out of "an unwarranted assumption"—on the part of the objector—the assumption of a principle, in Dynamics, at an epoch when *no* "principles," in *anything*, exist:—I use the word "principle," of course, in the objector's understanding of the word.

"In the beginning" we can admit—indeed we can comprehend—but one *First Cause*—the truly ultimate *Principle*—the Volition of God. The primary *act*—that of Irradiation from Unity—must have been independent of all that which the world now calls "principle"—because all that we so designate is but a consequence of the rëaction of that primary act:—I say "*primary*" act; for the creation of the absolute material particle is more properly to be regarded as a *conception* than as an "*act*" in the ordinary meaning of the term. Thus, we must regard the primary act as an act for the establishment of what we now call "principles." But this primary act itself is to be considered as *continuous Volition*. The Thought of God is to be understood as originating the Diffusion—as proceeding with it—as regulating it—and, finally, as being withdrawn from it upon its completion. *Then* commences Rëaction, and through Rëaction, "Principle," as we employ the word. It will be advisable, however, to limit the application of this word to the two *immediate* results of the discontinuance of the Divine Volition—that is, to the two agents, *Attraction* and *Repulsion*. Every other Natural agent depends, either more or less immediately, upon these two, and therefore would be more conveniently designated as *sub*-principle.

It may be objected, thirdly, that, in general, the peculiar mode of distribution which I have suggested for the atoms, is "an hypothesis and nothing more."

Now, I am aware that the word hypothesis is a ponderous sledge-hammer, grasped immediately, if not lifted, by all very diminutive thinkers, upon the first appearance of any proposition wearing, in any particular, the garb of *a theory*. But "hypothesis" cannot be wielded *here* to any good purpose, even by those who succeed in lifting it—little men or great.

I maintain, first, that *only* in the mode described is it conceivable that Matter could have been diffused so as to fulfil at once the conditions of irradiation and of generally equable distribution. I maintain, secondly, that these conditions themselves have been imposed upon me, as necessities, in a train of ratiocination *as rigorously logical as that which establishes any demonstration in Euclid;* and I maintain, thirdly, that even if the charge of "hypothesis" were as fully sustained as it is, in fact, unsustained and untenable, still the validity and indisputability of my result would not, even in the slightest particular, be disturbed.

To explain:—The Newtonian Gravity—a law of Nature—a law whose existence as such no one out of Bedlam questions—a law whose admission as such enables us to account for nine-tenths of the Universal phænomena—a law which, merely because it does so enable us to account for these phænomena, we are perfectly willing, without reference to any other considerations, to admit, and cannot help admitting, as a law—a law, nevertheless, of which neither the principle nor the *modus operandi* of the principle, has ever yet been traced by the human analysis—a law, in short, which, neither in its detail nor in its generality, has been found susceptible of explanation *at all*—is at length seen to be at every point thoroughly explicable, provided only we yield our assent to——what? To an hypothesis? Why *if* an hypothesis—if the merest hypothesis—if an hypothesis for whose assumption—as in the case of that *pure* hypothesis the Newtonian law itself—no shadow of *à priori* reason could be assigned—if an hypothesis, even so absolute as all this implies, would enable us to perceive a principle for the Newtonian law—would enable us to understand as satisfied, conditions so miraculously—so ineffably complex and seemingly irreconcileable as those involved in the relations of which Gravity tells us,—what rational being *could* so expose his fatuity as to call even this absolute hypothesis an hypothesis any longer—unless, indeed, he were to persist in so calling it, with the understanding that he did so, simply for the sake of consistency *in words*?

But what is the true state of our present case? What is *the fact?* Not only that it is *not* an hypothesis which we are required *to adopt*, in order to admit the principle at issue explained, but that it *is* a logical conclusion which we are requested *not* to adopt if we can avoid it—which we are simply invited to *deny if we can*:—a conclusion of so accurate a logicality that to dispute it would be the effort—to doubt its validity beyond our power:—a conclusion from which we see no mode of escape, turn as we will; a result which confronts us either at the end of an *in*ductive journey from the phænomena of the very Law discussed, or at the close of a *de*ductive career from the most rigorously simple of all conceivable assumptions—*the assumption, in a word, of Simplicity itself.*

And if here, for the mere sake of cavilling, it be urged, that although my starting-point is, as I assert, the assumption of absolute Simplicity, yet Simplicity, considered merely in itself, is no axiom; and that only deductions from axioms are indisputable—it is thus that I reply:—

Every other science than Logic is the science of certain concrete relations. Arithmetic, for example, is the science of the relations of number—Geometry, of the relations of form—Mathematics in general, of the relations of quantity in general—of whatever can be increased or diminished. Logic, however, is the science of Relation in the abstract—of absolute Relation—of Relation considered solely in itself. An axiom in any particular science other than Logic is, thus, merely a proposition announcing certain concrete relations which seem to be too obvious for dispute—as when we say, for instance, that the whole is greater than its part:—and, thus again, the principle of the *Logical* axiom—in other words, of an axiom in the abstract—is, simply, *obviousness of relation.* Now, it is clear, not only that what is obvious to one mind may not be obvious to another, but that what is obvious to one mind at one epoch, may be anything but obvious, at another epoch, to the same mind. It is clear, moreover, that what, to-day, is obvious even to the majority of mankind, or to the majority of the best intellects of mankind, may to-morrow be, to either majority, more or less obvious, or in no respect obvious at all. It is seen, then, that the *axiomatic principle* itself is susceptible of variation, and of course that axioms are susceptible of similar change. Being mutable, the "truths" which grow out of them are necessarily mutable too; or, in other words, are never to be positively depended upon as truths at all— since Truth and Immutability are one.

It will now be readily understood that no axiomatic idea—no idea founded in the fluctuating principle, obviousness of relation—can possibly be so secure—so reliable a basis for any structure erected by the Reason, as *that* idea—(whatever it is, wherever we can find it, or *if* it be practicable to find it anywhere)—which is *ir*relative altogether—which not only presents to the understanding *no obviousness* of relation, either greater or less, to be considered, but subjects the intellect, not in the slighest degree, to the necessity of even looking at *any relation at all.* If such an idea be not what we too heedlessly term "an axiom," it is at least preferable, as a Logical basis, to any axiom ever propounded, or to all imaginable axioms combined:—and such, precisely, is the idea with which my deductive process, so thoroughly corroborated by induction, commences. My *particle proper* is but *absolute Irrelation.* To sum up what has been here advanced:—As a starting point I have taken it for granted, simply, that the Beginning had nothing behind it or before it—that it was a Beginning in fact—that it was a beginning and nothing different from a beginning—in short that this Beginning was—*that which it was.* If this be a "mere assumption" then a "mere assumption" let it be.

To conclude this branch of the subject:—I am fully warranted in announcing that *the Law which we have been in the habit of calling Gravity exists on account of Matter's having been irradiated, at its origin, atomically, into a limited*[4] *sphere of Space, from one, individual, unconditional, irrelative, and absolute Particle Proper, by the sole process in which it was possible to satisfy, at the same time, the two conditions, irradiation, and generally-equable distribution throughout the sphere—that is to say, by a force varying in direct proportion with the squares of the distances between the irradiated atoms, respectively, and the Particular centre of Irradiation.*

I have already given my reasons for presuming Matter to have been diffused by a determinate rather than by a continuous or infinitely continued force. Supposing a continuous force, we should be unable, in the first place, to comprehend a rëaction at all; and we should be required, in the second place, to entertain the impossible conception of an infinite extension of Matter. Not to dwell upon the impossibility of the conception, the infinite extension of Matter is an idea which, if not positively disproved, is at least not in any respect warranted by telescopic observation of the stars—a point to be explained more fully hereafter; and this empirical reason for believing in the original finity of Matter is unempirically confirmed. For example:—Admitting, for the moment, the possibility of understanding Space *filled* with the irradiated atoms—that is to say, admitting, as well as we can, for argument's sake, that the succession of the irradiated atoms had absolutely *no end*—then it is abundantly clear that, even when the Volition of God had been withdrawn from them, and thus the tendency to return into Unity permitted (abstractly) to be satisfied, this permission would have been nugatory and invalid—practically valueless and of no effect whatever. No Rëaction could have taken place; no movement toward Unity could have been made; no Law of Gravity could have obtained.

To explain:—Grant the *abstract* tendency of any one atom to any one other as the inevitable result of diffusion from the normal Unity:—or, what is the same thing, admit any given atom as *proposing* to move in any given direction—it is clear that, since there is an *infinity* of atoms on all sides of the atom proposing to move, it never can actually move toward the satisfaction of its tendency in the direction given, on account of a precisely equal and counter-balancing tendency in the direction diametrically opposite. In other words, exactly as many tendencies to Unity are behind the hesitating atom as before it; for it is a mere sotticism to say that one infinite line is longer or shorter than another infinite line, or that one infinite number is greater or less than another number that is infinite. Thus the atom in question must remain stationary forever. Under the impossible circumstances which we have been merely endeavoring to conceive for argument's sake, there could have been no aggregation of Matter—no stars— no worlds—nothing but a perpetually atomic and inconsequential Universe. In fact, view it as we will, the whole idea of unlimited Matter is not only untenable, but impossible and preposterous.

With the understanding of a *sphere* of atoms, however, we perceive, at once, a *satisfiable* tendency to union. The general result of the tendency each to each, being a tendency of all to the centre, the *general* process of condensation, or approximation, commences immediately, by a common and simultaneous movement, on withdrawal of the Divine Volition; the *individual* approximations, or coalescences—*not* cöalitions—of atom with atom, being subject to almost infinite variations of time, degree, and condition, on account of the excessive multiplicity of relation, arising from the differences of form assumed as characterizing the atoms at the moment of their quitting the Particle Proper; as well as from the subsequent particular inequidistance, each from each.

What I wish to impress upon the reader is the certainty of there arising, at once, (on withdrawal of the diffusive force, or Divine Volition,) out of the condition of the atoms as described, at innumerable points throughout the Universal sphere, innumerable agglomerations, characterized by innumerable specific differences of form, size, essential nature, and distance each from each. The development of Repulsion (Electricity) must have commenced, of course, with the very earliest particular efforts at Unity, and must have proceeded constantly in the ratio of Coalescence—that is to say, *in that of Condensation*, or, again, of Heterogeneity.

Thus the two Principles Proper, *Attraction* and *Repulsion*—the Material and the Spiritual—accompany each other, in the strictest fellowship, forever. Thus *The Body and The Soul walk hand in hand.*

If now, in fancy, we select *any one* of the agglomerations considered as in their primary stages throughout the Universal sphere, and suppose this incipient agglomeration to be taking place at that point where the centre of our Sun exists—or rather where it *did* exist originally; for the Sun is perpetually shifting his position—we shall find ourselves met, and borne onward for a time at least, by the most magnificent of theories—by the Nebular Cosmogony of Laplace:—although "Cosmogony" is far too comprehensive a term for what he really discusses—which is the constitution of our solar system alone—of one among the myriad of similar systems which make up the Universe Proper—that Universal sphere—that all-inclusive and absolute *Kosmos* which forms the subject of my present Discourse.

Confining himself to an *obviously limited* region—that of our solar system with its comparatively immediate vicinity—and *merely* assuming—that is to say, assuming without any basis whatever, either deductive or inductive—*much* of what I have been just endeavoring to place upon a more stable basis than assumption; assuming, for example, matter as diffused (without pretending to account for the diffusion) throughout, and somewhat beyond, the space occupied by our system—diffused in a state of heterogeneous nebulosity and obedient to that omniprevalent law of Gravity at whose principle he ventured to make no guess;—assuming all this (which is quite true, although he had no logical right to its assumption) Laplace has shown, dynamically and mathematically, that the results in such case necessarily ensuing, are those and those alone which we find manifested in the actually existing condition of the system itself.

To explain:—Let us conceive *that* particular agglomeration of which we have just spoken—the one at the point designated by our Sun's centre—to have so far proceeded that a vast quantity of nebulous matter has here assumed a roughly globular form; its centre being, of course, coincident with what is now, or rather was originally, the centre of our Sun; and its periphery extending out beyond the orbit of Neptune, the most remote of our planets:—in other words, let us suppose the diameter of this rough sphere to be some 6000 millions of miles. For ages, this mass of matter has been undergoing condensation, until at length it has become reduced into the bulk we imagine; having proceeded gradually, of course, from its atomic and imperceptible state, into what we understand of visible, palpable, or otherwise appreciable nebulosity.

Now, the condition of this mass implies a rotation about an imaginary axis—a rotation which, commencing with the absolute incipiency of the aggregation, has been ever since acquiring velocity. The very first two atoms which met, approaching each other from points not diametrically opposite, would, in rushing partially past each other, form a nucleus for the rotary movement described. How this would increase in velocity, is readily seen. The two atoms are joined by others:—an aggregation is formed. The mass continues to rotate while condensing. But any atom at the circumference has, of course, a more rapid motion than one nearer the centre. The outer atom, however, with its superior velocity, approaches the centre; carrying this superior velocity with it as it goes. Thus every atom, proceeding inwardly, and finally attaching itself to the condensed centre, adds something to the original velocity of that centre—that is to say, increases the rotary movement of the mass.

405

Let us now suppose this mass so far condensed that it occupies *precisely* the space circumscribed by the orbit of Neptune, and that the velocity with which the surface of the mass moves, in the general rotation, is precisely that velocity with which Neptune now revolves about the Sun. At this epoch, then, we are to understand that the constantly increasing centrifugal force, having gotten the better of the non-increasing centripetal, loosened and separated the exterior and least condensed stratum, or a few of the exterior and least condensed strata, at the equator of the sphere, where the tangential velocity predominated; so that these strata formed about the main body an independent ring encircling the equatorial regions:— just as the exterior portion thrown off, by excessive velocity of rotation, from a grindstone, would form a ring about the grind-stone, but for the solidity of the superficial material: were this caoutchouc, or anything similar in consistency, precisely the phænomenon I describe would be presented.

The ring thus whirled from the nebulous mass, *revolved*, of course, *as* a separate ring, with just that velocity with which, while the surface of the mass, it *rotated*. In the meantime, condensation still proceeding, the interval between the discharged ring and the main body continued to increase, until the former was left at a vast distance from the latter.

Now, admitting the ring to have possessed, by some seemingly accidental arrangement of its heterogeneous materials, a constitution nearly uniform, then this ring, *as* such, would never have ceased revolving about its primary; but, as might have been anticipated, there appears to have been enough irregularity in the disposition of the materials, to make them cluster about centres of superior solidity; and thus the annular form was destroyed.[5] No doubt, the band was soon broken up into several portions, and one of these portions, predominating in mass, absorbed the others into itself; the whole settling, spherically, into a planet. That this latter, *as* a planet, continued the revolutionary movement which characterized it while a ring, is sufficiently clear; and that it took upon itself, also, an additional movement in its new condition of sphere, is readily explained. The ring being understood as yet unbroken, we see that its exterior, while the whole revolves about the parent body, moves more rapidly than its interior. When the rupture occurred, then, some portion in each fragment must have been moving with greater velocity than the others. The superior movement prevailing, must have whirled each fragment round— that is to say, have caused it to rotate; and the direction of the rotation must, of course, have been the direction of the revolution whence it arose. *All* the fragments having become subject to the rotation described, must, in coalescing, have imparted it to the one planet constituted by their coalescence.—This planet was Neptune. Its material continuing to undergo condensation, and the centrifugal force generated in its rotation getting, at length, the better of the centripetal, as before in the case of the parent orb, a ring was whirled also from the equatorial surface of this planet: this ring, having been ununiform in its constitution, was broken up, and its several fragments, being absorbed by the most massive, were collectively spherified into a moon. Subsequently, the operation was repeated, and a second moon was the result. We thus account for the planet Neptune, with the two satellites which accompany him.

In throwing off a ring from its equator, the Sun re-established that equilibrium between its centripetal and centrifugal forces which had been disturbed in the process of condensation; but, as this condensation still proceeded, the equilibrium was again immediately disturbed, through the increase of rotation. By the time the mass had so far shrunk that it occupied a spherical space just that circumscribed by the orbit of Uranus, we are to understand that the centrifugal force had so far obtained the ascendency that new relief was needed: a second equatorial band was, consequently, thrown off, which, proving ununiform, was broken up, as before in the case of Neptune; the fragments settling into the planet Uranus; the velocity of whose actual revolution about the Sun indicates, of course, the rotary speed of that Sun's equatorial surface at the moment of the separation. Uranus, adopting a rotation from the collective rotations of the fragments composing it, as previously explained, now threw off ring after ring; each of which, becoming broken up, settled into a moon:—three moons, at different epochs, having been formed, in this manner, by the rupture and general spherification of as many distinct ununiform rings.

By the time the Sun had shrunk until it occupied a space just that circumscribed by the orbit of Saturn, the balance, we are to suppose, between its centripetal and centrifugal forces had again become so far disturbed, through increase of rotary velocity, the result of condensation, that a third effort at equilibrium became necessary; and an annular band was therefore whirled off, as twice before; which, on rupture through ununiformity, became consolidated into the planet Saturn. This latter threw off, in the first place, seven uniform bands, which, on rupture, were spherified respectively into as many moons; but, subsequently, it appears to have discharged, at three distinct but not very distant epochs, three rings whose equability of constitution was, by apparent accident, so considerable as to present no occasion for their rupture; thus they continue to revolve as rings. I use the phrase "*apparent* accident;" for of accident in the ordinary sense there was, of course, nothing:—the term is properly applied only to the result of indistinguishable or not immediately traceable *law*.

Shrinking still farther, until it occupied just the space circumscribed by the orbit of Jupiter, the Sun now found need of farther effort to restore the counterbalance of its two forces, continually disarranged in the still continued increase of rotation. Jupiter, accordingly, was now thrown off; passing from the annular to the planetary condition; and, on attaining this latter, threw off in its turn, at four different epochs, four rings, which finally resolved themselves into so many moons.

Still shrinking, until its sphere occupied just the space defined by the orbit of the Asteroids, the Sun now discarded a ring which appears to have had *eight* centres of superior solidity, and, on breaking up, to have separated into eight fragments no one of which so far predominated in mass as to absorb the others. All therefore, as distinct although comparatively small planets, proceeded to revolve in orbits whose distances, each from each, may be considered as in some degree the measure of the force which drove them asunder:—all the orbits, nevertheless, being so closely coincident as to admit of our calling them *one*, in view of the other planetary orbits.

Continuing to shrink, the Sun, on becoming so small as just to fill the orbit of Mars, now discharged this planet—of course by the process repeatedly described. Having no moon, however, Mars could have thrown off no ring. In fact, an epoch had now arrived in the career of the parent body, the centre of the system. The *de*crease of its nebulosity, which is the *in*crease of its density, and which again is the *de*crease of its condensation, out of which latter arose the constant disturbance of equilibrium—must, by this period, have attained a point at which the efforts for restoration would have been more and more ineffectual just in proportion as they were less frequently needed. Thus the processes of which we have been speaking would everywhere show signs of exhaustion—in the planets, first, and secondly, in the original mass. We must not fall into the error of supposing the decrease of interval observed among the planets as we approach the Sun, to be in any respect indicative of an increase of frequency in the periods at which they were discarded. Exactly the converse is to be understood. The longest interval of time must have occurred between the discharges of the two interior; the shortest, between those of the two exterior, planets. The decrease of the interval of space is, nevertheless, the measure of the density, and thus inversely of the condensation, of the Sun, throughout the processes detailed.

Having shrunk, however, so far as to fill only the orbit of our Earth, the parent sphere whirled from itself still one other body—the Earth—in a condition so nebulous as to admit of this body's discarding, in its turn, yet another, which is our Moon;—but here terminated the lunar formations.

Finally, subsiding to the orbits first of Venus and then of Mercury, the Sun discarded these two interior planets; neither of which has given birth to any moon.

Thus from his original bulk—or, to speak more accurately, from the condition in which we first considered him—from a partially spherified nebular mass, *certainly* much more than 5,600 millions of miles in diameter—the great central orb and origin of our solar-planetary-lunar system, has gradually descended, by condensation, in obedience to the law of Gravity, to a globe only 882,000 miles in diameter; but it by no means follows, either that its condensation is yet complete, or that it may not still possess the capacity of whirling from itself another planet.

I have here given—in outline of course, but still with all the detail necessary for distinctness—a view of the Nebular Theory as its author himself conceived it. From whatever point we regard it, we shall find it *beautifully true*. It is by far too beautiful, indeed, *not* to possess Truth as its essentiality—and here I am very profoundly serious in what I say. In the revolution of the satellites of Uranus, there does appear something seemingly inconsistent with the assumptions of Laplace; but that *one* inconsistency can invalidate a theory constructed from a million of intricate consistencies, is a fancy fit only for the fantastic. In prophecying, confidently, that the apparent anomaly to which I refer, will, sooner or later, be found one of the strongest possible corroborations of the general hypothesis, I pretend to no especial spirit of divination. It is a matter which the only difficulty seems *not* to foresee.[6]

The bodies whirled off in the processes described, would exchange, it has been seen, the superficial *rotation* of the orbs whence they originated, for a *revolution* of equal velocity about these orbs as distant centres; and the revolution thus engendered must proceed, so long as the centripetal force, or that with which the discarded body gravitates toward its parent, is neither greater nor less than that by which it was discarded; that is, than the centrifugal, or, far more properly, than the tangential, velocity. From the unity, however, of the origin of these two forces, we might have expected to find them as they are found—the one accurately counterbalancing the other. It has been shown, indeed, that the act of whirling-off is, in every case, merely an act for the preservation of the counterbalance.

After referring, however, the centripetal force to the omniprevalent law of Gravity, it has been the fashion with astronomical treatises, to seek beyond the limits of mere Nature—that is to say, of *Secondary*Cause—a solution of the phænomenon of tangential velocity. This latter they attribute directly to a *First* Cause—to God. The force which carries a stellar body around its primary they assert to have originated in an impulse given immediately by the finger—this is the childish phraseology employed—by the finger of Deity itself. In this view, the planets, fully formed, are conceived to have been hurled from the Divine hand, to a position in the vicinity of the suns, with an impetus mathematically adapted to the masses, or attractive capacities, of the suns themselves. An idea so grossly unphilosophical, although so supinely adopted, could have arisen only from the difficulty of otherwise accounting for the absolutely accurate adaptation, each to each, of two forces so seemingly independent, one of the other, as are the gravitating and tangential. But it should be remembered that, for a long time, the coincidence between the moon's rotation and her sidereal revolution—two matters seemingly far more independent than those now considered—was looked upon as positively miraculous; and there was a strong disposition, even among astronomers, to attribute the marvel to the direct and continual agency of God— who, in this case, it was said, had found it necessary to interpose, specially, among his general laws, a set of subsidiary regulations, for the purpose of forever concealing from mortal eyes the glories, or perhaps the horrors, of the other side of the Moon—of that mysterious hemisphere which has always avoided, and must perpetually avoid, the telescopic scrutiny of mankind. The advance of Science, however, soon demonstrated—what to the philosophical instinct needed *no* demonstration—that the one movement is but a portion—something more, even, than a consequence—of the other.

For my part, I have no patience with fantasies at once so timorous, so idle, and so awkward. They belong to the veriest *cowardice* of thought. That Nature and the God of Nature are distinct, no thinking being can long doubt. By the former we imply merely the laws of the latter. But with the very idea of God, omnipotent, omniscient, we entertain, also, the idea of *the infallibility* of his laws. With Him there being neither Past nor Future—with Him all being *Now*—do we not insult him in supposing his laws so contrived as not to provide for every possible contingency?—or, rather, what idea *can* we have of *any* possible contingency, except that it is at once a result and a manifestation of his laws? He who, divesting himself of prejudice, shall have the rare courage to think absolutely for himself, cannot fail to arrive, in the end, at the condensation of *laws* into *Law*—cannot fail of reaching the conclusion that *each law of Nature is dependent at all points upon all other laws*, and that all are but consequences of one primary exercise of the Divine Volition. Such is the principle of the Cosmogony which, with all necessary deference, I here venture to suggest and to maintain.

In this view, it will be seen that, dismissing as frivolous, and even impious, the fancy of the tangential force having been imparted to the planets immediately by "the finger of God," I consider this force as originating in the rotation of the stars:—this rotation as brought about by the in-rushing of the primary atoms, towards their respective centres of aggregation:—this in-rushing as the consequence of the law of Gravity:—this law as but the mode in which is necessarily manifested the tendency of the atoms to return into imparticularity:—this tendency to return as but the inevitable rëaction of the first and most sublime of Acts—that act by which a God, self-existing and alone existing, became all things at once, through dint of his volition, while all things were thus constituted a portion of God.

The radical assumptions of this Discourse suggest to me, and in fact imply, certain important *modifications* of the Nebular Theory as given by Laplace. The efforts of the repulsive power I have considered as made for the purpose of preventing contact among the atoms, and thus as made in the ratio of the approach to contact—that is to say, in the ratio of condensation.[7] In other words, *Electricity*, with its involute phænomena, heat, light and magnetism, is to be understood as proceeding as condensation proceeds, and, of course, inversely as density proceeds, or the *cessation to condense*. Thus the Sun, in the process of its aggregation, must soon, in developing repulsion, have become excessively heated—perhaps incandescent: and we can perceive how the operation of discarding its rings must have been materially assisted by the slight incrustation of its surface consequent on cooling. Any common experiment shows us how readily a crust of the character suggested, is separated, through heterogeneity, from the interior mass. But, on every successive rejection of the crust, the new surface would appear incandescent as before; and the period at which it would again become so far encrusted as to be readily loosened and discharged, may well be imagined as exactly coincident with that at which a new effort would be needed, by the whole mass, to restore the equilibrium of its two forces, disarranged through condensation. In other words:— by the time the electric influence (Repulsion) has prepared the surface for rejection, we are to understand that the gravitating influence (Attraction) is precisely ready to reject it. Here, then, as everywhere, *the Body and the Soul walk hand in hand*.

These ideas are empirically confirmed at all points. Since condensation can never, in any body, be considered as absolutely at an end, we are warranted in anticipating that, whenever we have an opportunity of testing the matter, we shall find indications of resident luminosity in *all* the stellar bodies—moons and planets as well as suns. That our Moon is strongly self-luminous, we see at her every total eclipse, when, if not so, she would disappear. On the dark part of the satellite, too, during her phases, we often observe flashes like our own Auroras; and that these latter, with our various other so-called electrical phænomena, without reference to any more steady radiance, must give our Earth a certain appearance of luminosity to an inhabitant of the Moon, is quite evident. In fact, we should regard all the phænomena referred to, as mere manifestations, in different moods and degrees, of the Earth's feebly-continued condensation.

If my views are tenable, we should be prepared to find the newer planets—that is to say, those nearer the Sun—more luminous than those older and more remote:—and the extreme brilliancy of Venus (on whose dark portions, during her phases, the Auroras are frequently visible) does not seem to be altogether accounted for by her mere proximity to the central orb. She is no doubt vividly self-luminous, although less so than Mercury: while the luminosity of Neptune may be comparatively nothing.

Admitting what I have urged, it is clear that, from the moment of the Sun's discarding a ring, there must be a continuous diminution both of his heat and light, on account of the continuous encrustation of his surface; and that a period would arrive—the period immediately previous to a new discharge—when a *very material* decrease of both light and heat, must become apparent. Now, we know that tokens of such changes are distinctly recognizable. On the Melville islands—to adduce merely one out of a hundred examples—we find traces of *ultra-tropical* vegetation—of plants that never could have flourished without immensely more light and heat than are at present afforded by our Sun to any portion of the surface of the Earth. Is such vegetation referable to an epoch immediately subsequent to the whirling-off of Venus? At this epoch must have occurred to us our greatest access of solar influence; and, in fact, this influence must then have attained its maximum:—leaving out of view, of course, the period when the Earth itself was discarded—the period of its mere organization.

Again:—we know that there exist *non-luminous suns*—that is to say, suns whose existence we determine through the movements of others, but whose luminosity is not sufficient to impress us. Are these suns invisible merely on account of the length of time elapsed since their discharge of a planet? And yet again:—may we not—at least in certain cases— account for the sudden appearances of suns where none had been previously suspected, by the hypothesis that, having rolled with encrusted surfaces throughout the few thousand years of our astronomical history, each of these suns, in whirling off a new secondary, has at length been enabled to display the glories of its still incandescent interior?— To the well-ascertained fact of the proportional increase of heat as we descend into the Earth, I need of course, do nothing more than refer:—it comes in the strongest possible corroboration of all that I have said on the topic now at issue.

In speaking, not long ago, of the repulsive or electrical influence, I remarked that "the important phænomena of vitality, consciousness, and thought, whether we observe them generally or in detail, seem to proceed *at least in the ratio of the heterogeneous.*"[8] I mentioned, too, that I would recur to the suggestion:—and this is the proper point at which to do so. Looking at the matter, first, in detail, we perceive that not merely the *manifestation* of vitality, but its importance, consequence, and elevation of character, keep pace, very closely, with the heterogeneity, or complexity, of the animal structure. Looking at the question, now, in its generality, and referring to the first movements of the atoms towards mass-constitution, we find that heterogeneousness, brought about directly through condensation, is proportional with it forever. We thus reach the proposition that *the importance of the development of the terrestrial vitality proceeds equably with the terrestrial condensation.*

Now this is in precise accordance with what we know of the succession of animals on the Earth. As it has proceeded in its condensation, superior and still superior races have appeared. Is it impossible that the successive geological revolutions which have attended, at least, if not immediately caused, these successive elevations of vitalic character—is it improbable that these revolutions have themselves been produced by the successive planetary discharges from the Sun—in other words, by the successive variations in the solar influence on the Earth? Were this idea tenable, we should not be unwarranted in the fancy that the discharge of yet a new planet, interior to Mercury, may give rise to yet a new modification of the terrestrial surface—a modification from which may spring a race both materially and spiritually superior to Man. These thoughts impress me with all the force of truth—but I throw them out, of course, merely in their obvious character of suggestion.

The Nebular Theory of Laplace has lately received far more confirmation than it needed, at the hands of the philosopher, Compte. These two have thus together shown—*not*, to be sure, that Matter at any period actually existed as described, in a state of nebular diffusion, but that, admitting it so to have existed throughout the space and much beyond the space now occupied by our solar system, *and to have commenced a movement towards a centre*—it must gradually have assumed the various forms and motions which are now seen, in that system, to obtain. A demonstration such as this—a dynamical and mathematical demonstration, as far as demonstration can be—unquestionable and unquestioned—unless, indeed, by that unprofitable and disreputable tribe, the professional questioners— the mere madmen who deny the Newtonian law of Gravity on which the results of the French mathematicians are based—a demonstration, I say, such as this, would to most intellects be conclusive—and I confess that it is so to mine—of the validity of the nebular hypothesis upon which the demonstration depends.

That the demonstration does not *prove* the hypothesis, according to the common understanding of the word "proof," I admit, of course. To show that certain existing results—that certain established facts—may be, even mathematically, accounted for by the assumption of a certain hypothesis, is by no means to establish the hypothesis itself. In other words:—to show that, certain data being given, a certain existing result might, or even *must*, have ensued, will fail to prove that this result *did* ensue, *from the data*, until such time as it shall be also shown that there are, *and can be*, no other data from which the result in question might *equally* have ensued. But, in the case now discussed, although all must admit the deficiency of what we are in the habit of terming "proof," still there are many intellects, and those of the loftiest order, to which *no* proof could bring one iota of additional *conviction*. Without going into details which might impinge upon the Cloud-Land of Metaphysics, I may as well here observe that the force of conviction, in cases such as this, will always, with the right-thinking, be proportional to the amount of *complexity* intervening between the hypothesis and the result. To be less abstract:—The greatness of the complexity found existing among cosmical conditions, by rendering great in the same proportion the difficulty of accounting for all these conditions *at once*, strengthens, also in the same proportion, our faith in that hypothesis which does, in such manner, satisfactorily account for them:—and as *no* complexity can well be conceived greater than that of the astronomical conditions, so no conviction can be stronger—to *my* mind at least—than that with which I am impressed by an hypothesis that not only reconciles these conditions, with mathematical accuracy, and reduces them into a consistent and intelligible whole, but is, at the same time, the *sole* hypothesis by means of which the human intellect has been ever enabled to account for them *at all.*

A most unfounded opinion has become latterly current in gossiping and even in scientific circles—the opinion that the so-called Nebular Cosmogony has been overthrown. This fancy has arisen from the report of late observations made, among what hitherto have been termed the "nebulæ," through the large telescope of Cincinnati, and the world-renowned instrument of Lord Rosse. Certain spots in the firmament which presented, even to the most powerful of the old telescopes, the appearance of nebulosity, or haze, had been regarded for a long time as confirming the theory of Laplace. They were looked upon as stars in that very process of condensation which I have been attempting to describe. Thus it was supposed that we "had ocular evidence"—an evidence, by the way, which has always been found very questionable—of the truth of the hypothesis; and, although certain telescopic improvements, every now and then, enabled us to perceive that a spot, here and there, which we had been classing among the nebulæ, was, in fact, but a cluster of stars deriving its nebular character only from its immensity of distance—still it was thought that no doubt could exist as to the actual nebulosity of numerous other masses, the strong-holds of the nebulists, bidding defiance to every effort at segregation. Of these latter the most interesting was the great "nebulæ" in the constellation Orion:—but this, with innumerable other miscalled "nebulæ," when viewed through the magnificent modern telescopes, has become resolved into a simple collection of stars. Now this fact has been very generally understood as conclusive against the Nebular Hypothesis of Laplace; and, on announcement of the discoveries in question, the most enthusiastic defender and most eloquent popularizer of the theory, Dr. Nichol, went so far as to "admit the necessity of abandoning" an idea which had formed the material of his most praiseworthy book.[9]

Many of my readers will no doubt be inclined to say that the result of these new investigations *has* at least a strong *tendency* to overthrow the hypothesis; while some of them, more thoughtful, will suggest that, although the theory is by no means disproved through the segregation of the particular "nebulæ" alluded to, still a *failure* to segregate them, with such telescopes, might well have been understood as a triumphant *corroboration* of the theory:—and this latter class will be surprised, perhaps, to hear me say that even with *them* I disagree. If the propositions of this Discourse have been comprehended, it will be seen that, in my view, a failure to segregate the "nebulæ" would have tended to the refutation, rather than to the confirmation, of the Nebular Hypothesis.

Let me explain:—The Newtonian Law of Gravity we may, of course, assume as demonstrated. This law, it will be remembered, I have referred to the rëaction of the first Divine Act—to the rëaction of an exercise of the Divine Volition temporarily overcoming a difficulty. This difficulty is that of forcing the normal into the abnormal—of impelling that whose originality, and therefore whose rightful condition, was *One*, to take upon itself the wrongful condition of *Many*. It is only by conceiving this difficulty as *temporarily* overcome, that we can comprehend a rëaction. There could have been no rëaction had the act been infinitely continued. So long as the act *lasted*, no rëaction, of course, could commence; in other words, no *gravitation* could take place—for we have considered the one as but the manifestation of the other. But gravitation *has* taken place; therefore the act of Creation has ceased: and gravitation has long ago taken place; therefore the act of Creation has long ago ceased. We can no more expect, then, to observe *the primary processes* of Creation; and to these primary processes the condition of nebulosity has already been explained to belong.

Through what we know of the propagation of light, we have direct proof that the more remote of the stars have existed, under the forms in which we now see them, for an inconceivable number of years. So far back *at least*, then, as the period when these stars underwent condensation, must have been the epoch at which the mass-constitutive processes began. That we may conceive these processes, then, as still going on in the case of certain "nebulæ," while in all other cases we find them thoroughly at an end, we are forced into assumptions for which we have really *no* basis whatever—we have to thrust in, again, upon the revolting Reason, the blasphemous idea of special interposition—we have to suppose that, in the particular instances of these "nebulæ," an unerring God found it necessary to introduce certain supplementary regulations—certain improvements of the general law—certain retouchings and emendations, in a word, which had the effect of deferring the completion of these individual stars for centuries of centuries beyond the æra during which all the other stellar bodies had time, not only to be fully constituted, but to grow hoary with an unspeakable old age.

Of course, it will be immediately objected that since the light by which we recognize the nebulæ now, must be merely that which left their surfaces a vast number of years ago, the processes at present observed, or supposed to be observed, are, in fact, *not* processes now actually going on, but the phantoms of processes completed long in the Past— just as I maintain all these mass-constitutive processes *must* have been.

To this I reply that neither is the now-observed condition of the condensed stars their actual condition, but a condition completed long in the Past; so that my argument drawn from the *relative* condition of the stars and the "nebulaæ," is in no manner disturbed. Moreover, those who maintain the existence of nebulæ, do *not* refer the nebulosity to extreme distance; they declare it a real and not merely a perspective nebulosity. That we may conceive, indeed, a nebular mass as visible at all, we must conceive it as *very near us* in comparison with the condensed stars brought into view by the modern telescopes. In maintaining the appearances in question, then, to be really nebulous, we maintain their comparative vicinity to our point of view. Thus, their condition, as we see them now, must be referred to an epoch *far less remote* than that to which we may refer the now-observed condition of at least the majority of the stars.—In a word, should Astronomy ever demonstrate a "nebula," in the sense at present intended, I should consider the Nebular Cosmogony— *not*, indeed, as corroborated by the demonstration— but as thereby irretrievably overthrown.

By way, however, of rendering unto Cæsar *no more* than the things that are Cæsar's, let me here remark that the assumption of the hypothesis which led him to so glorious a result, seems to have been suggested to Laplace in great measure by a misconception—by the very misconception of which we have just been speaking—by the generally prevalent misunderstanding of the character of the nebulæ, so mis-named. These he supposed to be, in reality, what their designation implies. The fact is, this great man had, very properly, an inferior faith in his own merely *perceptive* powers. In respect, therefore, to the actual existence of nebulæ—an existence so confidently maintained by his telescopic contemporaries—he depended less upon what he saw than upon what he heard.

It will be seen that the only valid objections to his theory, are those made to its hypothesis *as* such—to what suggested it—not to what it suggests; to its propositions rather than to its results. His most unwarranted assumption was that of giving the atoms a movement towards a centre, in the very face of his evident understanding that these atoms, in unlimited succession, extended throughout the Universal space. I have already shown that, under such circumstances, there could have occurred no movement at all; and Laplace, consequently, assumed one on no more philosophical ground than that something of the kind was necessary for the establishment of what he intended to establish.

His original idea seems to have been a compound of the true Epicurean atoms with the false nebulæ of his contemporaries; and thus his theory presents us with the singular anomaly of absolute truth deduced, as a mathematical result, from a hybrid datum of ancient imagination intertangled with modern inacumen. Laplace's real strength lay, in fact, in an almost miraculous mathematical instinct:—on this he relied; and in no instance did it fail or deceive him:— in the case of the Nebular Cosmogony, it led him, blindfolded, through a labyrinth of Error, into one of the most luminous and stupendous temples of Truth.

Let us now fancy, for the moment, that the ring first thrown off by the Sun—that is to say, the ring whose breaking-up constituted Neptune—did not, in fact, break up until the throwing-off of the ring out of which Uranus arose; that this latter ring, again, remained perfect until the discharge of that out of which sprang Saturn; that this latter, again, remained entire until the discharge of that from which originated Jupiter—and so on. Let us imagine, in a word, that no dissolution occurred among the rings until the final rejection of that which gave birth to Mercury. We thus paint to the eye of the mind a series of coexistent concentric circles; and looking as well

423

at *them* as at the processes by which, according to Laplace's hypothesis, they were constructed, we perceive at once a very singular analogy with the atomic strata and the process of the original irradiation as I have described it. Is it impossible that, on measuring the *forces*, respectively, by which each successive planetary circle was thrown off—that is to say, on measuring the successive excesses of rotation over gravitation which occasioned the successive discharges—we should find the analogy in question more decidedly confirmed? *Is it improbable that we should discover these forces to have varied—as in the original radiation—proportionally to the squares of the distances?*

Our solar system, consisting, in chief, of one sun, with sixteen planets certainly, and possibly a few more, revolving about it at various distances, and attended by seventeen moons assuredly, but *very*probably by several others—is now to be considered as *an example* of the innumerable agglomerations which proceeded to take place throughout the Universal Sphere of atoms on withdrawal of the Divine Volition. I mean to say that our solar system is to be understood as affording a *generic instance* of these agglomerations, or, more correctly, of the ulterior conditions at which they arrived. If we keep our attention fixed on the idea of *the utmost possible Relation* as the Omnipotent design, and on the precautions taken to accomplish it through difference of form, among the original atoms, and particular inequidistance, we shall find it impossible to suppose for a moment that even any two of the incipient agglomerations reached precisely the same result in the end. We shall rather be inclined to think that *no two* stellar bodies in the Universe—whether suns, planets or moons—are particularly, while *all* are generally, similar. Still less, then, can we imagine any two *assemblages* of such bodies—any two "systems"—as having more than a general resemblance.[10] Our telescopes, at this point, thoroughly confirm our deductions. Taking our own solar system, then, as merely a loose or general type of all, we have so far proceeded in our subject as to survey the Universe under the aspect of a spherical space, throughout which, dispersed with merely general equability, exist a number of but generally similar *systems*.

Let us now, expanding our conceptions, look upon each of these systems as in itself an atom; which in fact it is, when we consider it as but one of the countless myriads of systems which constitute the Universe. Regarding all, then, as but colossal atoms, each with the same ineradicable tendency to Unity which characterizes the actual atoms of which it consists—we enter at once upon a new order of aggregations. The smaller systems, in the vicinity of a larger one, would, inevitably, be drawn into still closer vicinity. A thousand would assemble here; a million there—perhaps here, again, even a billion—leaving, thus, immeasurable vacancies in space. And if, now, it be demanded why, in the case of these systems—of these merely Titanic atoms—I speak, simply, of an "assemblage," and not, as in the case of the actual atoms, of a more or less consolidated agglomeration:—if it be asked, for instance, why I do not carry what I suggest to its legitimate conclusion, and describe, at once, these assemblages of system-atoms as rushing to consolidation in spheres—as each becoming condensed into one magnificent sun—my reply is that μελλοντα ταντα—I am but pausing, for a moment, on the awful threshold of *the Future*. For the present, calling these assemblages "clusters," we see them in the incipient stages of their consolidation. Their *absolute* consolidation is *to come*.

We have now reached a point from which we behold the Universe as a spherical space, interspersed, *unequably*, with *clusters*. It will be noticed that I here prefer the adverb "unequably" to the phrase "with a merely general equability," employed before. It is evident, in fact, that the equability of distribution will diminish in the ratio of the agglomerative processes—that is to say, as the things distributed diminish in number. Thus the increase of *in*equitability—an increase which must continue until, sooner or later, an epoch will arrive at which the largest agglomeration will absorb all the others—should be viewed as, simply, a corroborative indication of the *tendency to One*.

And here, at length, it seems proper to inquire whether the ascertained *facts* of Astronomy confirm the general arrangement which I have thus, deductively, assigned to the Heavens. Thoroughly, they *do*. Telescopic observation, guided by the laws of perspective, enables us to understand that the perceptible Universe exists as *a cluster of clusters, irregularly disposed.*

The "clusters" of which this Universal "*cluster of clusters*" consists, are merely what we have been in the practice of designating "nebulæ"—and, of these "nebulæ," *one* is of paramount interest to mankind. I allude to the Galaxy, or Milky Way. This interests us, first and most obviously, on account of its great superiority in apparent size, not only to any one other cluster in the firmament, but to all the other clusters taken together. The largest of these latter occupies a mere point, comparatively, and is distinctly seen only with the aid of a telescope. The Galaxy sweeps throughout the Heaven and is brilliantly visible to the naked eye. But it interests man chiefly, although less immediately, on account of its being his home; the home of the Earth on which he exists; the home of the Sun about which this Earth revolves; the home of that "system" of orbs of which the Sun is the centre and primary—the Earth one of sixteen secondaries, or planets—the Moon one of seventeen tertiaries, or satellites. The Galaxy, let me repeat, is but one of the *clusters* which I have been describing—but one of

426

the mis-called "nebulæ" revealed to us—by the telescope alone, sometimes—as faint hazy spots in various quarters of the sky. We have no reason to suppose the Milky Way *really* more extensive than the least of these "nebulæ." Its vast superiority in size is but an apparent superiority arising from our position in regard to it—that is to say, from our position in its midst. However strange the assertion may at first appear to those unversed in Astronomy, still the astronomer himself has no hesitation in asserting that we are *in the midst* of that inconceivable host of stars—of suns—of systems—which constitute the Galaxy. Moreover, not only have *we*—not only has *our* Sun a right to claim the Galaxy as its own especial cluster, but, with slight reservation, it may be said that all the distinctly visible stars of the firmament—all the stars visible to the naked eye—have equally a right to claim it as *their* own.

There has been a great deal of misconception in respect to the *shape* of the Galaxy; which, in nearly all our astronomical treatises, is said to resemble that of a capital Y. The cluster in question has, in reality, a certain general—*very* general resemblance to the planet Saturn, with its encompassing triple ring. Instead of the solid orb of that planet, however, we must picture to ourselves a lenticular star-island, or collection of stars; our Sun lying excentrically—near the shore of the island—on that side of it which is nearest the constellation of the Cross and farthest from that of Cassiopeia. The surrounding ring, where it approaches our position, has in it a longitudinal *gash*, which does, in fact, cause *the ring, in our vicinity*, to assume, loosely, the appearance of a capital Y.

We must not fall into the error, however, of conceiving the somewhat indefinite girdle as at all *remote*, comparatively speaking, from the also indefinite lenticular cluster which it surrounds; and thus, for mere purpose of explanation, we may speak of our Sun as actually situated at that point of the Y where its three component lines unite; and, conceiving this letter to be of a certain solidity—of a certain thickness, very trivial in comparison with its length—we may even speak of our position as *in the middle* of this thickness. Fancying ourselves thus placed, we shall no longer find difficulty in accounting for the phænomena presented—which are perspective altogether. When we look upward or downward—that is to say, when we cast our eyes in the direction of the letter's *thickness*—we look through fewer stars than when we cast them in the direction of its *length*, or *along* either of the three component lines. Of course, in the former case, the stars appear scattered—in the latter, crowded.—To reverse this explanation:—An inhabitant of the Earth, when looking, as we commonly express ourselves, *at* the Galaxy, is then beholding it in some of the directions of its length—is looking *along* the lines of the Y—but when, looking out into the general Heaven, he turns his eyes *from* the Galaxy, he is then surveying it in the direction of the letter's thickness; and on this account the stars seem to him scattered; while, in fact, they are as close together, on an average, as in the mass of the cluster. *No* consideration could be better adapted to convey an idea of this cluster's stupendous extent.

If, with a telescope of high space-penetrating power, we carefully inspect the firmament, we shall become aware of *a belt of clusters*—of what we have hitherto called "nebulæ"—a *band*, of varying breadth, stretching from horizon to horizon, at right angles to the general course of the Milky Way. This band is the ultimate *cluster of clusters*. This belt is *The Universe*. Our Galaxy is but one, and perhaps one of the most inconsiderable, of the clusters which go to the constitution of this ultimate, Universal *belt* or *band*. The appearance of this cluster of clusters, to our eyes, *as* a belt or band, is altogether a perspective phænomenon of the same character as that which causes us to behold our own individual and roughly-spherical cluster, the Galaxy, under guise also of a belt, traversing the Heavens at right angles to the Universal one. The shape of the all-inclusive cluster is, of course *generally*, that of each individual cluster which it includes. Just as the scattered stars which, on looking *from* the Galaxy, we see in the general sky, are, in fact, but a portion of that Galaxy itself, and as closely intermingled with it as any of the telescopic points in what seems the densest portion of its mass— so are the scattered "nebulæ" which, on casting our eyes *from* the Universal *belt*, we perceive at all points of the firmament—so, I say, are these scattered "nebulæ" to be understood as only perspectively scattered, and as part and parcel of the one supreme and Universal *sphere*.

No astronomical fallacy is more untenable, and none has been more pertinaciously adhered to, than that of the absolute *illimitation* of the Universe of Stars. The reasons for limitation, as I have already assigned them, *à priori*, seem to me unanswerable; but, not to speak of these, *observation* assures us that there is, in numerous directions around us, certainly, if not in all, a positive limit—or, at the very least, affords us no basis whatever for thinking otherwise. Were the succession of stars endless, then the background of the sky would present us an uniform luminosity, like that displayed by the Galaxy—*since there could be absolutely no point, in all that background, at which would not exist a star.* The only mode, therefore, in which, under such a state of affairs, we could comprehend the *voids* which our telescopes find in innumerable directions, would be by supposing the distance of the invisible background so immense that no ray from it has yet been able to reach us at all. That this *may* be so, who shall venture to deny? I maintain, simply, that we have not even the shadow of a reason for believing that it *is* so.

429

When speaking of the vulgar propensity to regard all bodies on the Earth as tending merely to the Earth's centre, I observed that, "with certain exceptions to be specified hereafter, every body on the Earth tended not only to the Earth's centre, but in every conceivable direction besides."[11] The "exceptions" refer to those frequent gaps in the Heavens, where our utmost scrutiny can detect not only no stellar bodies, but no indications of their existence:—where yawning chasms, blacker than Erebus, seem to afford us glimpses, through the boundary walls of the Universe of Stars, into the illimitable Universe of Vacancy, beyond. Now as any body, existing on the Earth, chances to pass, either through its own movement or the Earth's, into a line with any one of these voids, or cosmical abysses, it clearly is no longer attracted *in the direction of that void*, and for the moment, consequently, is "heavier" than at any period, either after or before. Independently of the consideration of these voids, however, and looking only at the generally unequable distribution of the stars, we see that the absolute tendency of bodies on the Earth to the Earth's centre, is in a state of perpetual variation.

We comprehend, then, the insulation of our Universe. We perceive the isolation of *that*—of *all* that which we grasp with the senses. We know that there exists one *cluster of clusters*—a collection around which, on all sides, extend the immeasurable wildernesses of a Space *to all human perception* untenanted. But *because* upon the confines of this Universe of Stars we are compelled to pause, through want of farther evidence from the senses, is it right to conclude that, in fact, there *is* no material point beyond that which we have thus been permitted to attain? Have we, or have we not, an analogical right to the inference that this perceptible Universe—that this cluster of clusters—is but one of *a series* of clusters of clusters, the rest of which are

430

invisible through distance—through the diffusion of their light being so excessive, ere it reaches us, as not to produce upon our retinas a light-impression—or from there being no such emanation as light at all, in these unspeakably distant worlds—or, lastly, from the mere interval being so vast, that the electric tidings of their presence in Space, have not yet—through the lapsing myriads of years—been enabled to traverse that interval?

Have we any right to inferences—have we any ground whatever for visions such as these? If we have a right to them in *any* degree, we have a right to their infinite extension.

The human brain has obviously a leaning to the "*Infinite*," and fondles the phantom of the idea. It seems to long with a passionate fervor for this impossible conception, with the hope of intellectually believing it when conceived. What is general among the whole race of Man, of course no individual of that race can be warranted in considering abnormal; nevertheless, there *may* be a class of superior intelligences, to whom the human bias alluded to may wear all the character of monomania.

My question, however, remains unanswered:— Have we any right to infer—let us say, rather, to imagine—an interminable succession of the "clusters of clusters," or of "Universes" more or less similar?

I reply that the "right," in a case such as this, depends absolutely upon the hardihood of that imagination which ventures to claim the right. Let me declare, only, that, as an individual, I myself feel impelled to the *fancy*—without daring to call it more—that there *does* exist a *limitless* succession of Universes, more or less similar to that of which we have cognizance—to that of which *alone* we shall ever have cognizance—at the very least until the return of our own particular Universe into Unity. *If* such clusters of clusters exist, however—*and they do*—it is abundantly clear that, having had no part in our origin, they have no portion in our laws. They neither attract us, nor we them. Their material—their spirit is not ours—is not that which obtains in any part of our Universe. They could not impress our senses or our souls. Among them and us—considering all, for the moment, collectively—there are no influences in common. Each exists, apart and independently, *in the bosom of its proper and particular God.*

In the conduct of this Discourse, I am aiming less at physical than at metaphysical order. The clearness with which even material phænomena are presented to the understanding, depends very little, I have long since learned to perceive, upon a merely natural, and almost altogether upon a moral, arrangement. If then I seem to step somewhat too discursively from point to point of my topic, let me suggest that I do so in the hope of thus the better keeping unbroken that chain of *graduated impression* by which alone the intellect of Man can expect to encompass the grandeurs of which I speak, and, in their majestic totality, to comprehend them.

So far, our attention has been directed, almost exclusively, to a general and relative grouping of the stellar bodies in space. Of specification there has been little; and whatever ideas of *quantity* have been conveyed—that is to say, of number, magnitude, and distance—have been conveyed incidentally and by way of preparation for more definitive conceptions. These latter let us now attempt to entertain.

Our solar system, as has been already mentioned, consists, in chief, of one sun and sixteen planets certainly, but in all probability a few others, revolving around it as a centre, and attended by seventeen moons of which we know, with possibly several more of which as yet we know nothing. These various bodies are not true spheres, but oblate spheroids—spheres flattened at the poles of the imaginary axes about which they rotate:—the flattening being a consequence of the rotation. Neither is the Sun absolutely the centre of the system; for this Sun itself, with all the planets, revolves about a perpetually shifting point of space, which is the system's general centre of gravity. Neither are we to consider the paths through which these different spheroids move—the moons about the planets, the planets about the Sun, or the Sun about the common centre—as circles in an accurate sense. They are, in fact, *ellipses—one of the foci being the point about which the revolution is made*. An ellipse is a curve, returning into itself, one of whose diameters is longer than the other. In the longer diameter are two points, equidistant from the middle of the line, and so situated otherwise that if, from each of them a straight line be drawn to any one point of the curve, the two lines, taken together, will be equal to the longer diameter itself. Now let us conceive such an ellipse. At one of the points mentioned, which are the *foci*, let us fasten an orange. By an elastic thread let us connect this orange with a pea; and let us place this latter on the circumference of the ellipse. Let us now move the pea continuously around the orange—keeping always on the circumference of the ellipse. The elastic thread, which, of course, varies in length as we move the pea, will form what in geometry is called a *radius vector*. Now, if the orange be understood as the Sun, and the pea as a planet revolving about it, then the revolution should be made at such a rate—with a velocity so varying—that the *radius vector* may pass over *equal areas of space in equal times*. The progress of the pea *should be*—in other words, the progress of the planet *is*, of course,—slow in proportion to its distance from the Sun—swift in proportion to its proximity. Those planets, moreover, move the more slowly which are the farther from the Sun; *the squares of their periods of revolution having the same proportion to each other, as have to each other the cubes of their mean distances from the Sun.*

The wonderfully complex laws of revolution here described, however, are not to be understood as obtaining in our system alone. They *everywhere* prevail where Attraction prevails. They control *the Universe*. Every shining speck in the firmament is, no doubt, a luminous sun, resembling our own, at least in its general features, and having in attendance upon it a greater or less number of planets, greater or less, whose still lingering luminosity is not sufficient to render them visible to us at so vast a distance, but which, nevertheless, revolve, moon-attended, about their starry centres, in obedience to the principles just detailed—in obedience to the three omniprevalent laws of revolution—the three immortal laws *guessed* by the imaginative Kepler, and but subsequently demonstrated and accounted for by the patient and mathematical Newton. Among a tribe of philosophers who pride themselves excessively upon matter-of-fact, it is far too fashionable to sneer at all speculation under the comprehensive *sobriquet*, "guess-work." The point to be considered is, *who* guesses. In guessing with Plato, we spend our time to better purpose, now and then, than in hearkening to a demonstration by Alcmæon.

In many works on Astronomy I find it distinctly stated that the laws of Kepler are *the basis* of the great principle, Gravitation. This idea must have arisen from the fact that the suggestion of these laws by Kepler, and his proving them *à posteriori* to have an actual existence, led Newton to account for them by the hypothesis of Gravitation, and, finally, to demonstrate them *à priori*, as necessary consequences of the hypothetical principle. Thus so far from the laws of Kepler being the basis of Gravity, Gravity is the basis of these laws—as it is, indeed, of all the laws of the material Universe which are not referable to Repulsion alone.

The mean distance of the Earth from the Moon—that is to say, from the heavenly body in our closest vicinity—is 237,000 miles. Mercury, the planet nearest the Sun, is distant from him 37 millions of miles. Venus, the next, revolves at a distance of 68 millions:—the Earth, which comes next, at a distance of 95 millions:—Mars, then, at a distance of 144 millions. Now come the eight Asteroids (Ceres, Juno, Vesta, Pallas, Astræa, Flora, Iris, and Hebe) at an average distance of about 250 millions. Then we have Jupiter, distant 490 millions; then Saturn, 900 millions; then Uranus, 19 hundred millions; finally Neptune, lately discovered, and revolving at a distance, say of 28 hundred millions. Leaving Neptune out of the account—of which as yet we know little accurately and which is, possibly, one of a system of Asteroids—it will be seen that, within certain limits, there exists an *order of interval* among the planets. Speaking loosely, we may say that each outer planet is twice as far from the Sun as is the next inner one. May not the *order* here mentioned—*may not the law of Bode—be deduced from consideration of the analogy suggested by me as having place between the solar discharge of rings and the mode of the atomic irradiation?*

The numbers hurriedly mentioned in this summary of distance, it is folly to attempt comprehending, unless in the light of abstract arithmetical facts. They are not practically tangible ones. They convey no precise ideas. I have stated that Neptune, the planet farthest from the Sun, revolves about him at a distance of 28 hundred millions of miles. So far good:—I have stated a mathematical fact; and, without comprehending it in the least, we may put it to use—mathematically. But in mentioning, even, that the Moon revolves about the Earth at the comparatively trifling distance of 237,000 miles, I entertained no expectation of giving any one to understand—to know—to feel—how far from the

435

Earth the Moon actually *is.* 237,000 *miles!* There are, perhaps, few of my readers who have not crossed the Atlantic ocean; yet how many of them have a distinct idea of even the 3,000 miles intervening between shore and shore? I doubt, indeed, whether the man lives who can force into his brain the most remote conception of the interval between one milestone and its next neighbor upon the turnpike. We are in some measure aided, however, in our consideration of distance, by combining this consideration with the kindred one of velocity. Sound passes through 1100 feet of space in a second of time. Now were it possible for an inhabitant of the Earth to see the flash of a cannon discharged in the Moon, and to hear the report, he would have to wait, after perceiving the former, more than 13 entire days and nights before getting any intimation of the latter.

However feeble be the impression, even thus conveyed, of the Moon's real distance from the Earth, it will, nevertheless, effect a good object in enabling us more clearly to see the futility of attempting to grasp such intervals as that of the 28 hundred millions of miles between our Sun and Neptune; or even that of the 95 millions between the Sun and the Earth we inhabit. A cannon-ball, flying at the greatest velocity with which such a ball has ever been known to fly, could not traverse the latter interval in less than 20 years; while for the former it would require 590.

Our Moon's real diameter is 2160 miles; yet she is comparatively so trifling an object that it would take nearly 50 such orbs to compose one as great as the Earth.

The diameter of our own globe is 7912 miles—but from the enunciation of these numbers what positive idea do we derive?

If we ascend an ordinary mountain and look around us from its summit, we behold a landscape stretching, say 40 miles, in every direction; forming a circle 250 miles in circumference; and including an area of 5000 square miles. The extent of such a prospect, on account of the *successiveness* with which its portions necessarily present themselves to view, can be only very feebly and very partially appreciated:—yet the entire panorama would comprehend no more than one 40,000th part of the mere *surface* of our globe. Were this panorama, then, to be succeeded, after the lapse of an hour, by another of equal extent; this again by a third, after the lapse of another hour; this again by a fourth after lapse of another hour—and so on, until the scenery of the whole Earth were exhausted; and were we to be engaged in examining these various panoramas for twelve hours of every day; we should nevertheless, be 9 years and 48 days in completing the general survey.

But if the mere surface of the Earth eludes the grasp of the imagination, what are we to think of its cubical contents? it embraces a mass of matter equal in weight to at least 2 sextillions, 200 quintillions of tons. Let us suppose it in a state of quiescence; and now let us endeavor to conceive a mechanical force sufficient to set it in motion! Not the strength of all the myriads of beings whom we may conclude to inhabit the planetary worlds of our system—not the combined physical strength of *all* these beings—even admitting all to be more powerful than man—would avail to stir the ponderous mass *a single inch*from its position.

What are we to understand, then, of the force, which under similar circumstances, would be required to move the *largest* of our planets, Jupiter? This is 86,000 miles in diameter, and would include within its periphery more than a thousand orbs of the magnitude of our own. Yet this stupendous body is actually flying around the Sun at the rate of 29,000 miles an hour—that is to say, with a velocity 40 times greater than that of a cannon-ball! The thought of such a phænomenon cannot well be said to *startle* the mind:—it palsies and appals it. Not unfrequently we task our imagination in picturing the capacities of an angel. Let us fancy such a being at a distance of some hundred miles from Jupiter—a close eye-witness of this planet as it speeds on its annual revolution. Now *can* we, I demand, fashion for ourselves any conception so distinct of this ideal being's spiritual exaltation, as *that* involved in the supposition that, even by this immeasurable mass of matter, whirled immediately before his eyes, with a velocity so unutterable, he—an angel—angelic though he be—is not at once struck into nothingness and overwhelmed?

At this point, however, it seems proper to suggest that, in fact, we have been speaking of comparative trifles. Our Sun, the central and controlling orb of the system to which Jupiter belongs, is not only greater than Jupiter, but greater by far than all the planets of the system taken together. This fact is an essential condition, indeed, of the stability of the system itself. The diameter of Jupiter has been mentioned:—it is 86,000 miles:—that of the Sun is 882,000 miles. An inhabitant of the latter, travelling 90 miles a day, would be more than 80 years in going round a great circle of its circumference. It occupies a cubical space of 681 quadrillions, 472 trillions of miles. The Moon, as has been stated, revolves about the Earth at a distance of 237,000 miles—in an orbit, consequently, of nearly a million and a half. Now, were the Sun placed upon the Earth, centre over centre, the body of the former would extend, in every direction, not only to the line of the Moon's orbit, but beyond it, a distance of 200,000 miles.

And here, once again, let me suggest that, in fact, we have *still* been speaking of comparative trifles. The distance of the planet Neptune from the Sun has been stated:—it is 28 hundred millions of miles; the circumference of its orbit, therefore, is about 17 billions. Let this be borne in mind while we glance at some one of the brightest stars. Between this and the star of *our* system, (the Sun,) there is a gulf of space, to convey any idea of which we should need the tongue of an archangel. From *our* system, then, and from *our* Sun, or star, the star at which we suppose ourselves glancing is a thing altogether apart:—still, for the moment, let us imagine it placed upon our Sun, centre over centre, as we just now imagined this Sun itself placed upon the Earth. Let us now conceive the particular star we have in mind, extending, in every direction, beyond the orbit of Mercury—of Venus—of the Earth:—still *on*, beyond the orbit of Mars—of Jupiter—of Uranus—until, finally, we fancy it filling the circle—17 *billions of miles in circumference*—which is described by the revolution of Leverrier's planet. When we have conceived all this, we shall have entertained no extravagant conception. There is the very best reason for believing that many of the stars are even far larger than the one we have imagined. I mean to say that we have the very best *empirical* basis for such belief:—and, in looking back at the original, atomic arrangements for *diversity*, which have been assumed as a part of the Divine plan in the constitution of the Universe, we shall be enabled easily to understand, and to credit, the existence of even far vaster disproportions in stellar size than any to which I have hitherto alluded. The largest orbs, of course, we must expect to find rolling through the widest vacancies of Space.

I remarked, just now, that to convey an idea of the interval between our Sun and any one of the other stars, we should require the eloquence of an archangel. In so saying, I should not be accused of exaggeration; for, in simple truth, these are topics on which it is scarcely possible to exaggerate. But let us bring the matter more distinctly before the eye of the mind.

In the first place, we may get a general, *relative* conception of the interval referred to, by comparing it with the inter-planetary spaces. If, for example, we suppose the Earth, which is, in reality, 95 millions of miles from the Sun, to be only *one foot* from that luminary; then Neptune would be 40 feet distant; *and the star Alpha Lyræ, at the very least,* 159.

Now I presume that, in the termination of my last sentence, few of my readers have noticed anything especially objectionable—particularly wrong. I said that the distance of the Earth from the Sun being taken at *one foot,* the distance of Neptune would be 40 feet, and that of Alpha Lyræ, 159. The proportion between one foot and 159 has appeared, perhaps, to convey a sufficiently definite impression of the proportion between the two intervals—that of the Earth from the Sun and that of Alpha Lyræ from the same luminary. But my account of the matter should, in reality, have run thus:—The distance of the Earth from the Sun being taken at one foot, the distance of Neptune would be 40 feet, and that of Alpha Lyræ, 159——*miles:*—that is to say, I had assigned to Alpha Lyræ, in my first statement of the case, only the 5280*th part* of that distance which is the *least distance possible* at which it can actually lie.

To proceed:—However distant a mere *planet* is, yet when we look at it through a telescope, we see it under a certain form—of a certain appreciable size. Now I have already hinted at the probable bulk of many of the stars; nevertheless, when we view any one of them, even through the most powerful telescope, it is found to present us with *no form,* and consequently with *no magnitude* whatever. We see it as a point and nothing more.

Again;—Let us suppose ourselves walking, at night, on a highway. In a field on one side of the road, is a line of tall objects, say trees, the figures of which are distinctly defined against the background of the sky. This line of objects extends at right angles to the road, and from the road to the horizon. Now, as we proceed along the road, we see these objects changing their positions, respectively, in relation to a certain fixed point in that portion of the firmament which forms the background of the view. Let us suppose this fixed point—sufficiently fixed for our purpose—to be the rising moon. We become aware, at once, that while the tree nearest us so far alters its position in respect to the moon, as to seem flying behind us, the tree in the extreme distance has scarcely changed at all its relative position with the satellite. We then go on to perceive that the farther the objects are from us, the less they alter their positions; and the converse. Then we begin, unwittingly, to estimate the distances of individual trees by the degrees in which they evince the relative alteration. Finally, we come to understand how it might be possible to ascertain the actual distance of any given tree in the line, by using the amount of relative alteration as a basis in a simple geometrical problem. Now this relative alteration is what we call "parallax;" and by parallax we calculate the distances of the heavenly bodies. Applying the principle to the trees in question, we should, of course, be very much at a loss to comprehend the distance of *that* tree, which, however far we proceeded along the road, should evince *no* parallax at all. This, in the case described, is a thing impossible; but impossible only because all distances on our Earth are trivial indeed:—in comparison with the vast cosmical quantities, we may speak of them as absolutely nothing.

Now, let us suppose the star Alpha Lyræ directly overhead; and let us imagine that, instead of standing on the Earth, we stand at one end of a straight road stretching through Space to a distance equalling the diameter of the Earth's orbit—that is to say, to a distance of 190 *millions of miles*. Having observed, by means of the most delicate micrometrical instruments, the exact position of the star, let us now pass along this inconceivable road, until we reach its other extremity. Now, once again, let us look at the star. It is *precisely* where we left it. Our instruments, however delicate, assure us that its relative position is absolutely—is identically the same as at the commencement of our unutterable journey. *No* parallax—none whatever—has been found.

The fact is, that, in regard to the distance of the fixed stars—of any one of the myriads of suns glistening on the farther side of that awful chasm which separates our system from its brothers in the cluster to which it belongs—astronomical science, until very lately, could speak only with a negative certainty. Assuming the brightest as the nearest, we could say, even of *them*, only that there is a certain incomprehensible distance on the *hither* side of which they cannot be:—how far they are beyond it we had in no case been able to ascertain. We perceived, for example, that Alpha Lyræ cannot be nearer to us than 19 trillions, 200 billions of miles; but, for all we knew, and indeed for all we now know, it may be distant from us the square, or the cube, or any other power of the number mentioned. By dint, however, of wonderfully minute and cautious observations, continued, with novel instruments, for many laborious years, *Bessel*, not long ago deceased, has lately succeeded in determining the distance of six or seven stars; among others, that of the star numbered 61 in the constellation of the Swan. The distance in this latter instance ascertained, is 670,000 times that of the Sun; which last it will be remembered, is 95 millions of miles. The star 61 Cygni, then, is nearly 64 trillions of miles from us—or more than three times the distance assigned, *as the least possible*, for Alpha Lyræ.

In attempting to appreciate this interval by the aid of any considerations of *velocity*, as we did in endeavoring to estimate the distance of the moon, we must leave out of sight, altogether, such nothings as the speed of a cannon ball, or of sound. Light, however, according to the latest calculations of Struve, proceeds at the rate of 167,000 miles in a second. Thought itself cannot pass through this interval more speedily—if, indeed, thought can traverse it at all. Yet, in coming from 61 Cygni to us, even at this inconceivable rate, light occupies more than *ten years;* and, consequently, were the star this moment blotted out from the Universe, still, *for ten years*, would it continue to sparkle on, undimmed in its paradoxical glory.

Keeping now in mind whatever feeble conception we may have attained of the interval between our Sun and 61 Cygni, let us remember that this interval, however unutterably vast, we are permitted to consider as but the *average* interval among the countless host of stars composing that cluster, or "nebula," to which our system, as well as that of 61 Cygni, belongs. I have, in fact, stated the case with great moderation:—we have excellent reason for believing 61 Cygni to be one of the *nearest* stars, and thus for concluding, at least for the present, that its distance from us is *less* than the average distance between star and star in the magnificent cluster of the Milky Way.

And here, once again and finally, it seems proper to suggest that even as yet we have been speaking of trifles. Ceasing to wonder at the space between star and star in our own or in any particular cluster, let us rather turn our thoughts to the intervals between cluster and cluster, in the all comprehensive cluster of the Universe.

I have already said that light proceeds at the rate of 167,000 miles in a second—that is, about 10 millions of miles in a minute, or about 600 millions of miles in an hour:—yet so far removed from us are some of the "nebulæ" that even light, speeding with this velocity, could not and does not reach us, from those mysterious regions, in less than 3 *millions of years*. This calculation, moreover, is made by the

443

elder Herschell, and in reference merely to those comparatively proximate clusters within the scope of his own telescope. There *are* "nebulæ," however, which, through the magical tube of Lord Rosse, are this instant whispering in our ears the secrets of *a million of ages* by-gone. In a word, the events which we behold now—at this moment—in those worlds— are the identical events which interested their inhabitants *ten hundred thousand centuries ago*. In intervals—in distances such as this suggestion forces upon the *soul*—rather than upon the mind—we find, at length, a fitting climax to all hitherto frivolous considerations of *quantity*.

Our fancies thus occupied with the cosmical distances, let us take the opportunity of referring to the difficulty which we have so often experienced, while pursuing *the beaten path* of astronomical reflection, *in accounting* for the immeasurable voids alluded to—in comprehending why chasms so totally unoccupied and therefore apparently so needless, have been made to intervene between star and star— between cluster and cluster—in understanding, to be brief, a sufficient reason for the Titanic scale, in respect of mere *Space*, on which the Universe is seen to be constructed. A rational cause for the phænomenon, I maintain that Astronomy has palpably failed to assign:—but the considerations through which, in this Essay, we have proceeded step by step, enable us clearly and immediately to perceive that *Space and Duration are one*. That the Universe might *endure* throughout an æra at all commensurate with the grandeur of its component material portions and with the high majesty of its spiritual purposes, it was necessary that the original atomic diffusion be made to so inconceivable an extent as to be only not infinite. It was required, in a word, that the stars should be gathered into visibility from invisible nebulosity—proceed from nebulosity to consolidation—and so grow grey in giving birth and

444

death to unspeakably numerous and complex variations of vitalic development:—it was required that the stars should do all this—should have time thoroughly to accomplish all these Divine purposes—*during the period* in which all things were effecting their return into Unity with a velocity accumulating in the inverse proportion of the squares of the distances at which lay the inevitable End.

Throughout all this we have no difficulty in understanding the absolute accuracy of the Divine *adaptation.* The density of the stars, respectively, proceeds, of course, as their condensation diminishes; condensation and heterogeneity keep pace with each other; through the latter, which is the index of the former, we estimate the vitalic and spiritual development. Thus, in the density of the globes, we have the measure in which their purposes are fulfilled. *As* density proceeds—*as* the divine intentions *are* accomplished—*as* less and still less remains *to be* accomplished—so—in the same ratio—should we expect to find an acceleration of *the End*:—and thus the philosophical mind will easily comprehend that the Divine designs in constituting the stars, advance *mathematically* to their fulfilment:—and more; it will readily give the advance a mathematical expression; it will decide that this advance is inversely proportional with the squares of the distances of all created things from the starting-point and goal of their creation.

Not only is this Divine adaptation, however, mathematically accurate, but there is that about it which stamps it *as divine*, in distinction from that which is merely the work of human constructiveness. I allude to the complete *mutuality* of adaptation. For example; in human constructions a particular cause has a particular effect; a particular intention brings to pass a particular object; but this is all; we see no reciprocity. The effect does not re-act upon the cause; the intention does not change relations with the object. In Divine constructions the object is either design or object as we choose to regard it—and we may take at any time a cause for an effect, or the converse—so that we can never absolutely decide which is which.

To give an instance:—In polar climates the human frame, to maintain its animal heat, requires, for combustion in the capillary system, an abundant supply of highly azotized food, such as train-oil. But again:—in polar climates nearly the sole food afforded man is the oil of abundant seals and whales. Now, whether is oil at hand because imperatively demanded, or the only thing demanded because the only thing to be obtained? It is impossible to decide. There is an absolute *reciprocity of adaptation*.

The pleasure which we derive from any display of human ingenuity is in the ratio of *the approach* to this species of reciprocity. In the construction of *plot*, for example, in fictitious literature, we should aim at so arranging the incidents that we shall not be able to determine, of any one of them, whether it depends from any one other or upholds it. In this sense, of course, *perfection* of *plot* is really, or practically, unattainable—but only because it is a finite intelligence that constructs. The plots of God are perfect. The Universe is a plot of God.

And now we have reached a point at which the intellect is forced, again, to struggle against its propensity for analogical inference—against its monomaniac grasping at the infinite. Moons have been seen *revolving* about planets; planets about stars; and the poetical instinct of humanity—its instinct of the symmetrical, if the symmetry be but a symmetry of surface:—this *instinct*, which the Soul, not only of Man but of all created beings, took up, in the beginning, from the *geometrical* basis of the Universal irradiation—impels us to the fancy of an endless extension of this system of *cycles*. Closing our eyes equally to *de*duction and *in*duction, we insist upon imagining a *revolution* of all the orbs of the Galaxy about some gigantic globe which we take to be the central pivot of the whole. Each cluster in the great cluster of clusters is imagined, of course, to be similarly supplied and constructed; while, that the "analogy " may be wanting at no point, we go on to conceive these clusters themselves, again, as *revolving* about some still more august sphere;—this latter, still again, *with* its encircling clusters, as but one of a yet more magnificent series of agglomerations, *gyrating* about yet another orb central *to them*—some orb still more unspeakably sublime—some orb, let us rather say, of infinite sublimity endlessly multiplied by the infinitely sublime. Such are the conditions, continued in perpetuity, which the voice of what some people term "analogy" calls upon the Fancy to depict and the Reason to contemplate, if possible, without becoming dissatisfied with the picture. Such, *in general*, are the interminable gyrations beyond gyration which we have been instructed by Philosophy to comprehend and to account for, at least in the best manner we can. Now and then, however, a philosopher proper—one whose phrenzy takes a very determinate turn—whose genius, to speak more reverentially, has a strongly-pronounced washer-womanish bias, doing every thing up by the dozen—enables us to see *precisely* that point out of sight, at which the revolutionary processes in question do, and of right ought to, come to an end.

It is hardly worth while, perhaps, even to sneer at the reveries of Fourrier:—but much has been said, latterly, of the hypothesis of Mädler—that there exists, in the centre of the Galaxy, a stupendous globe about which all the systems of the cluster revolve. The *period* of our own, indeed, has been stated—117 millions of years.

That our Sun has a motion in space, independently of its rotation, and revolution about the system's centre of gravity, has long been suspected. This motion, granting it to exist, would be manifested perspectively. The stars in that firmamental region which we were leaving behind us, would, in a very long series of years, become crowded; those in the opposite quarter, scattered. Now, by means of astronomical History, we ascertain, cloudily, that some such phænomena have occurred. On this ground it has been declared that our system is moving to a point in the heavens diametrically opposite the star Zeta Herculis:—but this inference is, perhaps, the maximum to which we have any logical right. Mädler, however, has gone so far as to designate a particular star, Alcyone in the Pleiades, as being at or about the very spot around which a general *revolution* is performed.

Now, since by "analogy" we are led, in the first instance, to these dreams, it is no more than proper that we should abide by analogy, at least in some measure, during their development; and that analogy which suggests the revolution, suggests at the same time a central orb about which it should be performed:—so far the astronomer was consistent. This central orb, however, should, dynamically, be greater than all the orbs, taken together, which surround it. Of these there are about 100 millions. "Why, then," it was of course demanded, "do we not *see* this vast central sun—*at least equal* in mass to 100 millions of such suns as ours—why do we not *see* it—*we*, especially, who occupy the mid region of the cluster—the very locality *near* which, at all events, must be situated this incomparable star?" The reply was ready—"It must be non-luminous, as are our planets." Here, then, to suit a purpose, analogy is suddenly let fall. "Not so," it may be said—"we know that non-luminous suns actually exist." It is true that we have reason at least for supposing so; but we have certainly no reason whatever for supposing that the non-luminous suns in question are encircled by *luminous* suns, while these again are surrounded by non-luminous planets:—and it is precisely all this with which Mädler is called upon to find any thing analogous in the heavens—for it is precisely all this which he imagines in the case of the Galaxy. Admitting the thing to be so, we cannot help here picturing to ourselves how sad a puzzle the *why it is so* must prove to all *à priori* philosophers.

But granting, in the very teeth of analogy and of every thing else, the non-luminosity of the vast central orb, we may still inquire how this orb, so enormous, could fail of being rendered visible by the flood of light thrown upon it from the 100 millions of glorious suns glaring in all directions about it. Upon the urging of this question, the idea of an actually solid central sun appears, in some measure, to have been abandoned; and speculation proceeded to assert that the systems of the cluster perform their revolutions merely about an immaterial centre of gravity common to all. Here again then, to suit a purpose, analogy is let fall. The planets of our system revolve, it is true, about a common centre of gravity; but they do this in connexion with, and in consequence of, a material sun whose mass more than counterbalances the rest of the system.

The mathematical circle is a curve composed of an infinity of straight lines. But this idea of the circle—an idea which, in view of all ordinary geometry, is merely the mathematical, as contradistinguished from the practical, idea—is, in sober fact, the *practical* conception which alone we have any right to entertain in regard to the majestic circle with which we have to deal, at least in fancy, when we suppose our system revolving about a point in the centre of the Galaxy. Let the most vigorous of human imaginations attempt but to take a single step towards the comprehension of a sweep so ineffable! It would scarcely be paradoxical to say that a flash of lightning itself, travelling *forever* upon the circumference of this unutterable circle, would still, *forever*, be travelling in a straight line. That the path of our Sun in such an orbit would, to any human perception, deviate in the slightest degree from a straight line, even in a million of years, is a proposition not to be entertained:—yet we are required to believe that a curvature has become apparent during the brief period of our astronomical history—during a mere point—during the utter nothingness of two or three thousand years.

It may be said that Mädler *has* really ascertained a curvature in the direction of our system's now well-established progress through Space. Admitting, if necessary, this fact to be in reality such, I maintain that nothing is thereby shown except the reality of this fact—the fact of a curvature. For its *thorough* determination, ages will be required; and, when determined, it will be found indicative of some binary or other multiple relation between our Sun and some one or more of the proximate stars. I hazard nothing however, in predicting, that, after the lapse of many centuries, all efforts at determining the path of our Sun through Space, will be abandoned as fruitless. This is easily conceivable when we look at the infinity of perturbation it must experience, from its perpetually-shifting relations with other orbs, in the common approach of all to the nucleus of the Galaxy.

But in examining other "nebulæ" than that of the Milky Way—in surveying, generally, the clusters which overspread the heavens—do we or do we not find confirmation of Mädler's hypothesis? We do *not*. The forms of the clusters are exceedingly diverse when casually viewed; but on close inspection, through powerful telescopes, we recognize the sphere, very distinctly, as at least the proximate form of all:— their constitution, in general, being at variance with the idea of revolution about a common centre.

"It is difficult," says Sir John Herschell, "to form any conception of the dynamical state of such systems. On one hand, without a rotary motion and a centrifugal force, it is hardly possible not to regard them as in a state of *progressive collapse*. On the other, granting such a motion and such a force, we find it no less difficult to reconcile their forms with the rotation of the whole system [meaning cluster] around any single axis, without which internal collision would appear to be inevitable."

Some remarks lately made about the "nebulæ" by Dr. Nichol, in taking quite a different view of the cosmical conditions from any taken in this Discourse—have a very peculiar applicability to the point now at issue. He says:

"When our greatest telescopes are brought to bear upon them, we find that those which were thought to be irregular, are not so; they approach nearer to a globe. Here is one that looked oval; but Lord Rosse's telescope brought it into a circle . . . . . Now there occurs a very remarkable circumstance in reference to these comparatively sweeping circular masses of nebulæ. We find they are not entirely circular, but the reverse; and that all around them, on every side, there are volumes of stars, *stretching out apparently as if they were rushing towards a great central mass in consequence of the action of some great power.*"[12]

Were I to describe, in my own words, what must necessarily be the existing condition of each nebula on the hypothesis that all matter is, as I suggest, now returning to its original Unity, I should simply be going over, nearly verbatim, the language here employed by Dr. Nichol, without the faintest suspicion of that stupendous truth which is the key to these nebular phænomena.

And here let me fortify my position still farther, by the voice of a greater than Mädler—of one, moreover, to whom all the data of Mädler have long been familiar things, carefully and thoroughly considered. Referring to the elaborate calculations of Argelander—the very researches which form Mädler's basis—*Humboldt*, whose generalizing powers have never, perhaps been equalled, has the following observation:

"When we regard the real, proper, or non-perspective motions of the stars, we find *many groups of them moving in opposite directions;* and the data as yet in hand render it not necessary, at least, to conceive that the systems composing the Milky Way, or the clusters, generally, composing the Universe, are revolving about any particular centre unknown, whether luminous or non-luminous. It is but Man's longing for a fundamental First Cause, that impels both his intellect and his fancy to the adoption of such an hypothesis."[13]

The phænomenon here alluded to—that of "many groups moving in opposite directions"—is quite inexplicable by Mädler's idea; but arises, as a necessary consequence, from that which forms the basis of this Discourse. While the *merely general direction* of each atom—of each moon, planet, star, or cluster—would, on my hypothesis, be, of course, absolutely rectilinear; while the *general* path of all bodies would be a right line leading to the centre of all; it is clear, nevertheless, that this general rectilinearity would be compounded of what, with scarcely any exaggeration, we may term an infinity of particular curves—an infinity of local deviations from rectilinearity—the result of continuous differences of relative position among the multudinous masses, as each proceeded on its own proper journey to the End.

I quoted, just now, from Sir John Herschell, the following words, used in reference to the clusters:— "On one hand, without a rotary motion and a centrifugal force, it is hardly possible not to regard them as in a state of *progressive collapse.*" The fact is, that, in surveying the " nebulæ" with a telescope of high power, we shall find it quite impossible, having once conceived this idea of "collapse," not to gather, at all points, corroboration of the idea. A nucleus is always apparent, in the direction of which the stars seem to be precipitating themselves; nor can these nuclei be mistaken for merely perspective phænomena:—the clusters are *really* denser near the centre—sparser in the regions more remote from it. In a word, we see every thing as we *should* see it were a collapse taking place; but, in general, it may be said of these clusters, that we can fairly entertain, while looking at them, the idea of *orbitual movement about a centre*, only by admitting the *possible* existence, in the distant domains of space, of dynamical laws with which *we* are unacquainted.

On the part of Herschell, however, there is evidently *a reluctance* to regard the nebulæ as in "a state of progressive collapse." But if facts—if even appearances justify the supposition of their being in this state, *why*, it may well be demanded, is he disinclined to admit it? Simply on account of a prejudice;—merely because the supposition is at war with a preconceived and utterly baseless notion—that of the endlessness—that of the eternal stability of the Universe.

If the propositions of this Discourse are tenable, the "state of progressive collapse" is *precisely* that state in which alone we are warranted in considering All Things; and, with due humility, let me here confess that, for my part, I am at a loss to conceive how any *other* understanding of the existing condition of affairs, could ever have made its way into the human brain. "The tendency to collapse" and "the attraction of gravitation" are convertible phrases. In using either, we speak of the rëaction of the First Act. Never was necessity less obvious than that of supposing Matter imbued with an ineradicable *quality* forming part of its material nature—a quality, or instinct, *forever* inseparable from it, and by dint of which inalienable principle every atom is *perpetually* impelled to seek its fellow-atom. Never was necessity less obvious than that of entertaining this unphilosophical idea. Going boldly behind the vulgar thought, we have to conceive, metaphysically, that the gravitating principle appertains to Matter *temporarily*—only while diffused—only while existing as Many instead of as One—appertains to it by virtue of its state of irradiation alone—appertains, in a word, altogether to its *condition*, and not in the slightest degree to *itself*. In this view, when the irradiation shall have returned into its source—when the rëaction shall be completed—the gravitating principle will no longer exist. And, in fact, astronomers, without at any time reaching the idea here suggested, seem to have been approximating it, in the assertion that "if there were but one body in the Universe, it would be impossible to understand how the principle, Gravity, could obtain:"—that is to say, from a consideration of Matter as they find it, they reach a conclusion at which I deductively arrive. That so pregnant a suggestion as the one just quoted should have been permitted to remain so long unfruitful, is, nevertheless, a mystery which I find it difficult to fathom.

It is, perhaps, in no little degree, however, our propensity for the continuous—for the analogical—in the present case more particularly for the symmetrical—which has been leading us astray. And, in fact, the sense of the symmetrical is an instinct which may be depended upon with an almost blindfold reliance. It is the poetical essence of the Universe—*of the Universe* which, in the supremeness of its symmetry, is but the most sublime of poems. Now symmetry and consistency are convertible terms:—thus Poetry and Truth are one. A thing is consistent in the ratio of its truth—true in the ratio of its consistency. *A perfect consistency, I repeat, can be nothing but an absolute truth.* We may take it for granted, then, that Man cannot long or widely err, if he suffer himself to be guided by his poetical, which I have maintained to be his truthful, in being his symmetrical, instinct. He must have a care, however, lest, in pursuing too heedlessly the superficial symmetry of forms and motions, he leave out of sight the really essential symmetry of the principles which determine and control them.

That the stellar bodies would finally be merged in one—that, at last, all would be drawn into the substance of *one stupendous central orb already existing*—is an idea which, for some time past, seems, vaguely and indeterminately, to have held possession of the fancy of mankind. It is an idea, in fact, which belongs to the class of the *excessively obvious.* It springs, instantly, from a superficial observation of the cyclic and seemingly *gyrating*, or *vorticial* movements of those individual portions of the Universe which come most immediately and most closely under our observation. There is not, perhaps, a human being, of ordinary education and of average reflective capacity, to whom, at some period, the fancy in question has not occurred, as if spontaneously, or intuitively, and wearing all the character of a very profound and very original conception. This conception, however, so commonly entertained, has never, within my knowledge, arisen out of any abstract considerations. Being, on the contrary, always suggested, as I say, by the vorticial movements about centres, a reason for it, also,—a *cause* for the ingathering of all the orbs into one, *imagined to be already existing*, was naturally sought in the same direction—among these cyclic movements themselves.

Thus it happened that, on announcement of the gradual and perfectly regular decrease observed in the orbit of Enck's comet, at every successive revolution about our Sun, astronomers were nearly unanimous in the opinion that the cause in question was found—that a principle was discovered sufficient to account, physically, for that final, universal agglomeration which, I repeat, the analogical, symmetrical or poetical instinct of Man had predetermined to understand as something more than a simple hypothesis.

This cause—this sufficient reason for the final ingathering—was declared to exist in an exceedingly rare but still material medium pervading space; which medium, by retarding, in some degree, the progress of the comet, perpetually weakened its tangential force; thus giving a predominance to the centripetal; which, of course, drew the comet nearer and nearer at each revolution, and would eventually precipitate it upon the Sun.

All this was strictly logical—admitting the medium or ether; but this ether was assumed, most illogically, on the ground that no *other* mode than the one spoken of could be discovered, of accounting for the observed decrease in the orbit of the comet:—as if from the fact that we could *discover* no other mode of accounting for it, it followed, in any respect, that no other mode of accounting for it existed. It is clear that innumerable causes might operate, in combination, to diminish the orbit, without even a possibility of our ever becoming acquainted with one of them. In the meantime, it has never been fairly shown, perhaps, why the retardation occasioned by the skirts of the Sun's atmosphere, through which the comet passes at perihelion, is not enough to account for the phænomenon. That Enck's comet will be absorbed into the Sun, is probable; that all the comets of the system will be absorbed, is more than merely possible; but, in such case, the principle of absorption must be referred to eccentricity of orbit—to the close approximation to the Sun, of the comets at their perihelia; and is a principle not affecting, in any degree, the ponderous *spheres*, which are to be regarded as the true material constituents of the Universe.—Touching comets, in general, let me here suggest, in passing, that we cannot be far wrong in looking upon them as the *lightning-flashes of the cosmical Heaven.*

The idea of a retarding ether and, through it, of a final agglomeration of all things, seemed at one time, however, to be confirmed by the observation of a positive decrease in the orbit of the solid moon. By reference to eclipses recorded 2500 years ago, it was found that the velocity of the satellite's revolution *then* was considerably less than it is *now*; that on the hypothesis that its motions in its orbit is uniformly in accordance with Kepler's law, and was accurately determined *then*—2500 years ago—it is now in advance of the position it *should* occupy, by nearly 9000 miles. The increase of velocity proved, of course, a diminution of orbit; and astronomers were fast yielding to a belief in an ether, as the sole mode of accounting for the phænomenon, when Lagrange came to the rescue. He showed that, owing to the configurations of the spheroids, the shorter axes of their ellipses are subject to variation in length; the longer axes being permanent; and that this variation is continuous and vibratory—so that every orbit is in a state of transition, either from circle to ellipse, or from ellipse to circle. In the case of the moon, where the shorter axis is *de*creasing, the orbit is passing from circle to ellipse and, consequently, is *de*creasing too; but, after a long series of ages, the ultimate eccentricity will be attained; then the shorter axis will proceed to *in*crease, until the orbit becomes a circle; when the process of shortening will again take place;—and so on forever. In the case of the Earth, the orbit is passing from ellipse to circle. The facts thus demonstrated do away, of course, with all necessity for supposing an ether, and with all apprehension of the system's instability—on the ether's account.

It will be remembered that I have myself assumed what we may term *an ether*. I have spoken of a subtle *influence* which we know to be ever in attendance upon matter, although becoming manifest only through matter's heterogeneity. To this *influence*—without daring to touch it at all in any effort at explaining its awful *nature*—I have referred the various phænomena of electricity, heat, light, magnetism; and more—of vitality, consciousness, and thought—in a word, of spirituality. It will be seen, at once, then, that the ether thus conceived is radically distinct from the ether of the astronomers; inasmuch as theirs is *matter* and mine *not*.

With the idea of a material ether, seems, thus, to have departed altogether the thought of that universal agglomeration so long predetermined by the poetical fancy of mankind:—an agglomeration in which a sound Philosophy might have been warranted in putting faith, at least to a certain extent, if for no other reason than that by this poetical fancy it *had* been so predetermined. But so far as Astronomy—so far as mere Physics have yet spoken, the cycles of the Universe are perpetual—the Universe has no conceivable end. Had an end been demonstrated, however, from so purely collateral a cause as an ether, Man's instinct of the Divine *capacity to adapt*, would have rebelled against the demonstration. We should have been forced to regard the Universe with some such sense of dissatisfaction as we experience in contemplating an unnecessarily complex work of human art. Creation would have affected us as an imperfect *plot* in a romance, where the *dénoûment* is awkwardly brought about by interposed incidents external and foreign to the main subject; instead of springing out of the bosom of the thesis—out of the heart of the ruling idea—instead of arising as a result of the primary proposition—as inseparable and inevitable part and parcel of the fundamental conception of the book.

What I mean by the symmetry of mere surface will now be more clearly understood. It is simply by the blandishment of this symmetry that we have been beguiled into the general idea of which Mädler's hypothesis is but a part—the idea of the vorticial indrawing of the orbs. Dismissing this nakedly physical conception, the symmetry of principle sees the end of all things metaphysically involved in the thought of a beginning; seeks and finds in this origin of all things the *rudiment* of this end; and perceives the impiety of supposing this end likely to be brought about less simply—less directly—less obviously—less artistically—than through *the rëaction of the originating Act.*

Recurring, then, to a previous suggestion, let us understand the systems—let us understand each star, with its attendant planets—as but a Titanic atom existing in space with precisely the same inclination for Unity which characterized, in the beginning, the actual atoms after their irradiation throughout the Universal sphere. As these original atoms rushed towards each other in generally straight lines, so let us conceive as at least generally rectilinear, the paths of the system-atoms towards their respective centres of aggregation:—and in this direct drawing together of the systems into clusters, with a similar and simultaneous drawing together of the clusters themselves while undergoing consolidation, we have at length attained the great *Now*—the awful Present—the Existing Condition of the Universe.

Of the still more awful Future a not irrational analogy may guide us in framing an hypothesis. The equilibrium between the centripetal and centrifugal forces of each system, being necessarily destroyed upon attainment of a certain proximity to the nucleus of the cluster to which it belongs, there must occur, at once, a chaotic or seemingly chaotic precipitation, of the moons upon the planets, of the planets upon the suns, and of the suns upon the nuclei; and the general result of this precipitation must be the gathering of the myriad now-existing stars of the firmament into an almost infinitely less number of almost infinitely superior spheres. In being immeasurably fewer, the worlds of that day will be immeasurably greater than our own. Then, indeed, amid unfathomable abysses, will be glaring unimaginable suns. But all this will be merely a climactic magnificence foreboding the great End. Of this End the new genesis described, can be but a very partial postponement. While undergoing consolidation, the clusters themselves, with a speed prodigiously accumulative, have been rushing towards their own general centre—and now, with a thousand-fold electric velocity, commensurate only with their material grandeur and with the spiritual passion of their appetite for oneness, the majestic remnants of the tribe of Stars flash, at length, into a common embrace. The inevitable catastrophe is at hand.

But this catastrophe—what is it? We have seen accomplished the ingathering of the orbs. Henceforward, are we not to understand *one material globe of globes* as constituting and comprehending the Universe? Such a fancy would be altogether at war with every assumption and consideration of this Discourse.

I have already alluded to that absolute *reciprocity of adaptation* which is the idiosyncrasy of the divine Art—stamping it divine. Up to this point of our reflections, we have been regarding the electrical influence as a something by dint of whose repulsion alone Matter is enabled to exist in that state of diffusion demanded for the fulfilment of its purposes:—so far, in a word, we have been considering the influence in question as ordained for Matter's sake—to subserve the objects of matter. With a perfectly legitimate reciprocity, we are now permitted to look at Matter, as created *solely for the sake of this influence*—solely to serve the objects of this spiritual Ether. Through the aid—by the means—through the agency of Matter, and by dint of its heterogeneity—is this Ether manifested—is *Spirit individualized*. It is merely in the development of this Ether, through heterogeneity, that particular masses of Matter become animate—sensitive—and in the ratio of their heterogeneity;—some reaching a degree of sensitiveness involving what we call *Thought* and thus attaining Conscious Intelligence.

In this view, we are enabled to perceive Matter as a Means—not as an End. Its purposes are thus seen to have been comprehended in its diffusion; and with the return into Unity these purposes cease. The absolutely consolidated globe of globes would be *objectless*:—therefore not for a moment could it continue to exist. Matter, created for an end, would unquestionably, on fulfilment of that end, be Matter no longer. Let us endeavor to understand that it would disappear, and that God would remain all in all.

That every work of Divine conception must cöexist and cöexpire with its particular design, seems to me especially obvious; and I make no doubt that, on perceiving the final globe of globes to be *objectless*, the majority of my readers will be satisfied with my "*therefore* it cannot continue to exist." Nevertheless, as the startling thought of its instantaneous disappearance is one which the most powerful intellect cannot be expected readily to entertain on grounds so decidedly abstract, let us endeavor to look at the idea from some other and more ordinary point of view:—let us see how thoroughly and beautifully it is corroborated in an *à posteriori* consideration of Matter as we actually find it.

I have before said that "Attraction and Repulsion being undeniably the sole properties by which Matter is manifested to Mind, we are justified in assuming that Matter *exists* only as Attraction and Repulsion—in other words that Attraction and

Repulsion *are* Matter; there being no conceivable case in which we may not employ the term Matter and the terms 'Attraction' and 'Repulsion' taken together, as equivalent, and therefore convertible, expressions in Logic."[14]

Now the very definition of Attraction implies particularity—the existence of parts, particles, or atoms; for we define it as the tendency of "each atom &c. to every other atom" &c. according to a certain law. Of course where there are *no* parts—where there is absolute Unity—where the tendency to oneness is satisfied—there can be no Attraction:—this has been fully shown, and all Philosophy admits it. When, on fulfilment of its purposes, then, Matter shall have returned into its original condition of *One*—a condition which presupposes the expulsion of the separative ether, whose province and whose capacity are limited to keeping the atoms apart until that great day when, this ether being no longer needed, the overwhelming pressure of the finally collective Attraction shall at length just sufficiently predominate[15] and expel it:—when, I say, Matter, finally, expelling the Ether, shall have returned into absolute Unity,—it will then (to speak paradoxically for the moment) be Matter without Attraction and without Repulsion—in other words, Matter without Matter—in other words, again, *Matter no more.* In sinking into Unity, it will sink at once into that Nothingness which, to all Finite Perception, Unity must be—into that Material Nihility from which alone we can conceive it to have been evoked—to have been *created* by the Volition of God.

I repeat then—Let us endeavor to comprehend that the final globe of globes will instantaneously disappear, and that God will remain all in all.

But are we here to pause? Not so. On the Universal agglomeration and dissolution, we can readily conceive that a new and perhaps totally different series of conditions may ensue—another creation and irradiation, returning into itself—another action and reaction of the Divine Will. Guiding our imaginations by that omniprevalent law of laws, the law of periodicity, are we not, indeed, more than justified in entertaining a belief—let us say, rather, in indulging a hope—that the processes we have here ventured to contemplate will be renewed forever, and forever, and forever; a novel Universe swelling into existence, and then subsiding into nothingness, at every throb of the Heart Divine?

And now—this Heart Divine—what is it?—*It is our own.*

Let not the merely seeming irreverence of this idea frighten our souls from that cool exercise of consciousness—from that deep tranquillity of self-inspection—through which alone we can hope to attain the presence of this, the most sublime of truths, and look it leisurely in the face.

The *phænomena* on which our conclusions must at this point depend, are merely spiritual shadows, but not the less thoroughly substantial.

We walk about, amid the destinies of our world-existence, encompassed by dim but ever present *Memories* of a Destiny more vast—very distant in the by-gone time, and infinitely awful.

We live out a Youth peculiarly haunted by such dreams; yet never mistaking them for dreams. As Memories we *know* them. *During our Youth* the distinction is too clear to deceive us even for a moment.

So long as this Youth endures, the feeling *that we exist,* is the most natural of all feelings. We understand it *thoroughly.* That there was a period at which we did *not* exist—or, that it might so have happened that we never had existed at all—are the considerations, indeed, which *during this youth,* we find difficulty in understanding. Why we should *not* exist, is, *up to the epoch of our Manhood,* of all queries the most unanswerable. Existence—self-existence—existence from all Time and to all Eternity—seems, up to the epoch of Manhood, a normal and unquestionable condition:—*seems, because it is.*

But now comes the period at which a conventional World-Reason awakens us from the truth of our dream. Doubt, Surprise and Incomprehensibility arrive at the same moment. They say:—"You live and the time was when you lived not. You have been created. An Intelligence exists greater than your own; and it is only through this Intelligence you live at all." These things we struggle to comprehend and cannot:—*cannot*, because these things, being untrue, are thus, of necessity, incomprehensible.

No thinking being lives who, at some luminous point of his life of thought, has not felt himself lost amid the surges of futile efforts at understanding, or believing, that anything exists *greater than his own soul.*The utter impossibility of any one's soul feeling itself inferior to another; the intense, overwhelming dissatisfaction and rebellion at the thought;—these, with the omniprevalent aspirations at perfection, are but the spiritual, coincident with the material, struggles towards the original Unity—are, to my mind at least, a species of proof far surpassing what Man terms demonstration, that no one soul *is* inferior to another—that nothing is, or can be, superior to any one soul—that each soul is, in part, its own God—its own Creator:—in a word, that God—the material *and* spiritual God—*now* exists solely in the diffused Matter and Spirit of the Universe; and that the regathering of this diffused Matter and Spirit will be but the re-constitution of the *purely* Spiritual and Individual God.

In this view, and in this view alone, we comprehend the riddles of Divine Injustice—of Inexorable Fate. In this view alone the existence of Evil becomes intelligible; but in this view it becomes more—it becomes endurable. Our souls no longer rebel at a *Sorrow* which we ourselves have imposed upon ourselves, in furtherance of our own purposes—with a view—if even with a futile view—to the extension of our own *Joy*.

I have spoken of *Memories* that haunt us during our youth. They sometimes pursue us even in our Manhood:—assume gradually less and less indefinite shapes:—now and then speak to us with low voices, saying:

"There was an epoch in the Night of Time, when a still-existent Being existed—one of an absolutely infinite number of similar Beings that people the absolutely infinite domains of the absolutely infinite space.[16] It was not and is not in the power of this Being—any more than it is in your own—to extend, by actual increase, the joy of his Existence; but just as it *is* in your power to expand or to concentrate your pleasures (the absolute amount of happiness remaining always the same) so did and does a similar capability appertain to this Divine Being, who thus passes his Eternity in perpetual variation of Concentrated Self and almost Infinite Self-Diffusion. What you call The Universe is but his present expansive existence. He now feels his life through an infinity of imperfect pleasures—the partial and pain-intertangled pleasures of those inconceivably numerous things which you designate as his creatures, but which are really but infinite individualizations of Himself. All these creatures—*all*—those which you term animate, as well as those to whom you deny life for no better reason than that you do not behold it in operation—*all* these creatures have, in a greater or less degree, a capacity for pleasure and for pain:—*but the general sum of their sensations is precisely that amount of Happiness which appertains by right to the Divine Being when concentrated within Himself.* These creatures are all, too, more or less conscious Intelligences; conscious, first, of a proper identity; conscious, secondly and by faint indeterminate glimpses, of an identity with the Divine Being of whom we speak—of an identity with God. Of the two classes of consciousness, fancy that the former will grow weaker, the latter stronger, during the long succession of ages which must elapse before these myriads of individual Intelligences become blended—when the bright stars become blended—into One. Think that the sense of individual identity will be gradually merged in the general consciousness—that Man, for example, ceasing imperceptibly to feel himself Man, will at length attain that awfully triumphant epoch when he shall recognize his existence as that of Jehovah. In the meantime bear in mind that all is Life—Life—Life within Life—the less within the greater, and all within the *Spirit Divine.*

THE END.

1. *"Murders in the Rue Morgue"*—p. 133.
2. Succinctly—The surfaces of spheres are as the squares of their radii.
3. Page 44.
4. Limited sphere"—A sphere is *necessarily* limited. I prefer tautology to a chance of misconception.
5. Laplace assumed his nebulosity heterogeneous, merely that he might be thus enabled to account for the breaking up of the rings; for had the nebulosity been homogeneous, they would not have broken. I reach the same result—heterogeneity of the secondary masses immediately resulting from the atoms—purely from an *à priori* consideration of their general design—*Relation.*
6. I am prepared to show that the anomalous revolution of the satellites of Uranus is a simply perspective anomaly arising from the inclination of the axis of the planet.
7. See page 70.
8. Page 36.

9. *"Views of the Architecture of the Heavens."* A letter, purporting to be from Dr. Nichol to a friend in America, went the rounds of our newspapers, about two years ago, I think, admitting "the necessity" to which I refer. In a subsequent Lecture, however, Dr. N. appears in some manner to have gotten the better of the necessity, and does not quite *renounce* the theory, although he seems to wish that he could sneer at it as "a purely hypothetical one." What else was the Law of Gravity before the Maskelyne experiments? and who questioned the Law of Gravity, even then?

10. It is not *impossible* that some unlooked-for optical improvement may disclose to us, among innumerable varieties of systems, a luminous sun, encircled by luminous and non-luminous rings, within and without and between which, revolve luminous and non-luminous planets, attended by moons having moons—and even these latter again having moons.

11. Page 62.

12. I must be understood as denying, *especially*, only the *revolutionary* portion of Mädler's hypothesis. Of course, if no great central orb exists *now* in our cluster, such will exist hereafter. Whenever existing, it will be merely the *nucleus* of the consolidation.

13. Betrachtet man die nicht perspectivischen eigenen Bewegungen der Sterne, so scheinen viele gruppenweise in ihrer Richtung entgegengesetzt; und die bisher gesammelten Thatsachen machen es auf's wenigste nicht nothwendig, anzunehmen, dass alle Theile unserer Sternenschicht oder gar der gesammten Sterneninseln, welche den Weltraum füllen, sich um einen grossen, unbekannten, leuchtenden oder dunkeln Centralkörper bewegen. Das Streben nach den letzten und höchsten Grundursachen macht freilich die reflectirende Thätigkeit des Menschen, wie seine Phantasie, zu einer solchen Annahme geneigt.

14. Page 37.

15. "Gravity, therefore, must be the strongest of forces." See page 39.

16. See page 102-103-Paragraph commencing "I reply that the right," and ending "proper and particular God."

On the Road to God: Einstein's Imaginary Journey Around the Universe

By Zdeněk Smrčka

Master of Science in Chemistry, Information Research Specialist, Charles University (Praha, Czechia)
E-mail: zd.smrcka@seznam.cz
https://orcid.org/0000-0002-3083-583X

Originally published as Smrčka, Zdeněk (2023) On the Road to God: Einstein's Imaginary Journey Around the Universe. *Philosophy and Cosmology*, Volume 31, 116-132. https://doi.org/10.29202/phil-cosm/31/10[12]

A revived figure of teenage Albert Einstein is confronted at the threshold of the second millennium with a problem of a graphical likeness of the Lambert W function-based cosmological equations to a logarithmic-exponential discontinuous function that he has just plotted. To puzzle the issue out his mind is put onto an imaginary mathematical-philosophical-physical trail ride around the Universe. Euler's identity that he invited to ride pillion on his Pegasus of Imagination spanks the cavalier's horse to carry him on wings of Leibniz' zero-nothingness unity-infiniteness array towards a non-Euclidean landscape of novel cosmological equations - which describe behaviour of principal cosmological parameters as an exclusive function of the scale factor. Zero, unity, π, and Euler's number become in the rider's eyes a quaternion of linesmen - and the imaginary unit the one who as a chief referee opens and controls on the space-time playground a collective mass-energy game. And while the young cavalier observes from a horseback of his mount that within the playground expansion the cosmic match is running into the order of timelessness and spacelessness the Universe with all of its ever existing forms and events, thoughts and memories, unveils to him its all-

encompassing face of eternity and immortality attributable to God.

Keywords: Albert Einstein, Euler's identity, God, imagination, Lambert W function, scale factor, spacetime, thought experiment, Universe

Received: 21 June 2023 / Accepted: 19 July 2023 / Published: 15 October 2023.

Introduction

"...nature represents its simplicity in various physical systems..." (Nojiri et al., 2017)

The famous portrait of teenage Albert Einstein taken in a Munich photo studio presents a high school student sitting on the top of painted seashore highlands (Fig. 1). His inner imaginative-like gaze of a dreamy mind seems to glimpse an infinitive scheme of sailing waves of time and space over the imaginary landscape. In two years later, being 16-years-old guy, his thoughts of the physical world will give birth to a very curious idea: *"What it would be like to pursue a beam of light?"* (Norton, 2013). By this question his most famous thought experiment (Gedankenexperiment) is ready to open the era of relativistic physics. But what kind of the thought experiment would have been performed by him as an abecedarian of the 21st century cosmology virtual class? Would have been his mind challenged by a quizzical daydream of a trail ride around the expanding universe? This is an oddish idea, indeed, but it came into the author's mind like a prepossessing wavy sparkplug above a return train of thought heading times of Einstein's youth. At an early point its terminal station was on the air; however, it was just a double reason and challenge to get on.

1. The Lambert W Function and Einstein's Novel Thought Experiment

In early 2020, the Lambert W function (Corless et al., 1996) being already well established in its generalized form in the class of relativistic physics (Scott et al., 2006; Mező and Baricz, 2017) is introduced as a potential *"...newcomer in the cosmology class"* (Saha and Bamba, 2020). The same year, a novel model of regular black holes highlights this special function along with exponentials for its *"...somewhat more elegant..."* quality when compared to *"...rather messy cubic and quartic polynomial equations"* (Simpson and Visser, 2020). Two years later a comprehensive treatise on the Lambert W function is published (Mező, 2022). The function which *"...seems to be ubiquitous in nature..."* (Corless et al., 1996) is invaluable in its ability of solving transcendental equations variable of which is found simultaneously outside and inside logarithms, like: $x = \ln(3x)$. Or outside and inside exponentials, like $y = xe^x$; the famous equation the first references and studies of which were made by Johann Heinrich Lambert (1758) and Leonhard Euler (1783), 18th century Swiss mathematicians (Brito et al., 2008)).

Thereupon, at the threshold of the second millennium a revived figure of teenage Albert Einstein presents in the cosmology class an iterative solution[1] of the transcendental equation $x = [\log(x).\ln(x)]^3$. In order to set up its first approximation he makes a plot[2] of a logarithmic-exponential discontinuous function $\sqrt[3]{x}/\ln(x)$ against $\log(x)$. The resulting graph (Fig. 2) immediately strikes his eye as it looks as if in terms of reflection symmetry two graphs (Fig. 3) of the Lambert W function-based cosmological equations for the deceleration parameter q, and for the energy density ρ, respectively (Saha and Bamba,

2020) were put together. The similarity provokes him to wondering about an eventual significancy of the examined function $\sqrt[3]{x}/\ln(x)$ to cosmology. His query is: "What if it is descried there in the variable x a spatiotemporal dynamic factor which makes the function numerator $\sqrt[3]{x}$ attributable to the non-Euclidean spatiotemporal geometry and concurrently the function denominator $\ln(x)$ attributable to the maximum possible entropy referred to a measure of information uncertainty (Silagadze, 2010) of the mass-energy system?" To examine the idea he modifies the function $\sqrt[3]{x}/\ln(x)$ in two different ways; separately for $\log(x) > 0$ and for $\log(x) < 0$. The 'plus way' takes him to a general scheme of the deceleration parameter equation; while the 'minus way' to a general scheme of the equation for the squared Hubble parameter (its square represents an equivalent to the energy density). Within the 'minus way' he makes use of a fundamental 'trick' of absolute logarithmic values $|\log(x) < 0| = \log(1/x)$; and within both ways he takes in a novel dynamic spatiotemporal factor e^{φ}.

$$(e^{\varphi} - 1)\,[\sqrt[3]{(1/x)}\,/\ln(x)] \xleftarrow{\;\log(x)<0\;} \sqrt[3]{x}/\ln(x)$$
$$\xrightarrow{\;\log(x)>0\;} e^{\varphi} - [\sqrt[3]{x}\,/\ln(x)]$$

Both spatiotemporal dynamic factors x and e^{φ} call for their specification. Juvenile Einstein is aware of invalidity (respectively instability) of 'his' initial model of the static universe as it implies zero time derivatives for the scale factor $\dot{a} = \ddot{a} = 0$. So his mind is switched to a dynamic model of the expanding universe - which makes him put a trick question: "In case I will parametrize the spatiotemporal factor x just through the scale factor what it would be like to use a combined π-shaped and a-shaped pair of reins to ride Pegasus of Imagination around the expanding universe?" Instead a reply he grasps a π-shaped rein in his left and an a-shaped rein in his right hand. And as he takes $\log(x)$ to keep them in balance he gets the formula $x = 10^{\pi a}$. By analogy he takes the scale factor to parametrize both the spatiotemporal dynamic factor e^{φ} (that he decides to be defined for $(1; e >$ and to be called the 'perpetual factor') and its variable φ (that is therefore defined for $(0; 1 >$ and called by him the 'dark factor'). So he grasps φ_0 as a reference constant for a present epoch (its value will be specified later on) in his left hand and the scale factor a again in his right hand. And when he takes φ to keep this pair of reins in balance he gets the formula $\varphi = \varphi_0 a$; and accordingly $e^{\varphi} = e^{\varphi_0 a}$.

2. Euler's Identity and Cosmological Equations

The parametrized factors $10^{\pi a}$ and $e^{\varphi_0 a}$ as they were received by juvenile Einstein operate explicitly with transcendental numbers of the eminent importance in mathematics - π and e, respectively; and implicitly with two more eminent numbers, 0 and 1. The fact navigates the explorer's train of thought towards the idea that spacetime could be under the continuous π - e - zero - unity orchestrated action based on a scheme of Euler's identity - a specific case of Euler's formula when its variable x is put equal to π:

$$e^{ix} = \cos(x) + i\sin(x) \xrightarrow{for\ x=\pi} e^{i\pi} + 1$$
$$= 0$$

Since Euler's identity formalizes growth as a circular motion which cannot be escaped within the area of complex numbers any way the trail rider deliberates that its scheme could explain why there is no escape to him beyond the universe. And why the identity could symbolize a wholeness of the universe existence. But what makes him wonder is the fact that the imaginary unit i holds in the identity simultaneously a role of its animator and of the keeper of its steady and irrefrangibly universal validity. Which evokes in his head the idea that the universe existence depends on the imaginary unit inherency - and that a 'super' transcendental number $e^{\pi} + 1$ could mark the maximum scale factor of the universe. Defining the dark factor on grounds of this notion as $\varphi = a/(e^{\pi} + 1)$ enables him to refine general schemes of the deceleration parameter and the Hubble parameter equations (while using the formula $x = 10^{\pi a}$ and an empirical constant[3] of correlation $10^7 \ [km^2 \cdot s^{-2} \cdot Mpc^{-2}]$ as well) into their definite forms presented below. Behaviour of both parameters these equations describe for a given range of the scale factor[4] is presented in Fig. 4. The Hubble parameter equation is viewed by him as a potential arbiter of the 'Hubble tension' disputes (Di Valentino et al., 2021; Freedman, 2021; Krishnan et al., 2021; Rameez and Sarkar, 2021).

$$q = e^{a/(e^{\pi}+1)} - \left[\sqrt[3]{10^{\pi a}} / \ln(10^{\pi a})\right]$$

$$H = \left\{ \left(e^{a/(e^{\pi}+1)} \right.$$
$$\left. - 1 \right) \left[\sqrt[3]{1/10^{\pi a}} / \ln(10^{\pi a}) \right]$$
$$\left. \cdot 10^7 \right\}^{1/2} \ [km \cdot s^{-1} \cdot Mpc^{-1}]$$

At the next stop the juvenile cosmic rider meets a model of the perfect cosmic fluid that allows description of the universe by an effective equation of state w_{eff}; via the relation of the fluid pressure P to the energy density ρ. Both of these physical quantities belong to key elements of the Friedmann equations (represented by the acceleration equation and by the Friedmann equation) which are derived from Einstein field equations of General relativity. Putting their simplified forms (the metric with $c = 1$ for the speed of light is considered for commoving coordinates (Saha and Bamba, 2020)) together with the time derivative of the Hubble parameter enables young Einstein to formulate a simple effective equation of state: $w_{eff} = (2q - 1)/3$. The deceleration parameter as its exclusive variable is represented by the equation that was formulated by him above.

$$\dot{H}/H^2 = -(1 + q) \text{ (time derivative of the Hubble parameter)}$$

$$3H^2 = 8\pi G\rho \qquad \dot{H} + H^2 = -(4\pi G/3)(\rho + 3P)$$

(simplified Friedmann equation)   (simplified acceleration equation)

$$\dot{H} = -H^2 - qH^2 = -(4\pi G/3)(\rho + 3P) - H^2$$

$$q(8\pi G\rho/3) = (4\pi G/3)(\rho + 3P) \longrightarrow$$
$$2q\rho = \rho + 3P \longrightarrow P/\rho = (2q - 1)/3$$

$$w_{eff} = (2q - 1)/3 \qquad\qquad \longrightarrow$$
$$w_{eff} = 2/3\,[e^{a/(e^\pi + 1)} - (\sqrt[3]{10^{\pi a}}/\ln(10^{\pi a}))] - 1/3$$

Having been originally formulated on grounds of the Lambert W function[5] (Saha and Bamba, 2020) and suggested then"...*to serve as a unification of dark matter and dark energy*..." (Al Mamon and Saha,

2021) an effective equation of state w_{eff} may be seen as the rationale for a deliberation on the novel dynamical Lambert W Dark Energy model instead the Lambda cold dark matter (ΛCDM) model (Banerjee et al., 2021). Yet, some of the modified gravity theories (Nojiri et al., 2017) in which the purely geometric nature of dark energy is considered (Mandal et al., 2020) operate just with an extension of the ΛCDM model. And as regards a position of young Einstein he is convinced that the ΛCDM model authenticity and simplicity are like two sides of the same universal coin fineness of which is going to be argued in the following text.

3. The Scale Factor As an Exclusive Cosmological Variable

A call for a precise measurement of both the Hubble and the deceleration parameters (Sandage, 1970) led to proposition additional cosmological parameters and to formulation novel cosmological models (Neben and Turner, 2013). While they have been thought to improve understanding the universe expansion it has been comparison statistics (Davis et al., 2007) which argued in favour of *"...models that give a good fit with fewer parameters...,"* with reference to that *"...the preferred cosmological model is the flat cosmological constant model, where the expansion history of the universe can be adequately described with only one free parameter describing the energy content of the universe..."* Ultimately, this model was found to remain the simplest and the best *"...to explain the current data..."* while giving *"...no reason to prefer any more complex model over the concordance cosmology, the flat cosmological constant."* Hence, the ΛCDM model authenticity should be judged rather from *"...either new physics or unknown systematics..."* perspectives - as it was proposed for a resolution of the H_0 tension (D'Arcy Kenworthy et al., 2019).

The latter perspective of the yet *"...unknown systematics..."* is favoured by juvenile Einstein since it points to the fact that behaviour of cosmological parameters as it is described by the equations proposed above conforms an accelerated expansion of the universe (Riess et al., 1998) and supports an authenticity of the ΛCDM model with its hypothetical phantom energy action that would lead to a Big Rip. In the explorer's opinion this event is about to happen when the scale factor of the universe meets the constant $e^{\pi} + 1$. Both the maximum radius r and the maximum age A of the universe may be calculated then according the following equations (the factors $1\ Mpc \approx 3.0857 \cdot 10^{19}\ [km]$ and $1\ year \approx 31\,556\,952\ [s]$ are considered for a conversion of the Hubble parameter $H_{\tau}\ [s^{-1}]$ to $H\ [km \cdot s^{-1} \cdot Mpc^{-1}]$).

$$r = ac/H_{\tau} \approx (3.0857ac/H) \cdot 10^{19}\ [km]$$

$$A = r/c = a/H_{\tau}$$
$$\approx (3.0857a/\ 31556952\ H)$$
$$\cdot 10^{19}$$
$$\approx 0.97782\ (a/H)$$
$$\cdot 10^{12}\ [years]$$

According these equations both the radius and the age of the universe are proportional to the scale factor and reciprocal to the Hubble parameter. However, since the scale factor is the only variable of the Hubble parameter equation (see a previous section) both the radius and the age of the universe have actually become exclusive functions of the scale factor.[6]

4. The Time Dilation Factor and the Fate of the Universe

The young adventurer on his imaginary trail ride around the expanding universe is heading now a hypothesized sphere of the time dilation. He views it as a ratio of the 'actual time flow velocity' v_a to the 'initial time flow velocity' v_i that was effective in the earliest flash of the universe. Apart from an elusiveness of their absolute values he finds their ratio to be equal to a ratio of two specific time flow gradients defined on grounds of Euler's number and with regard to Euler's identity. According his assumption the 'actual time flow velocity' v_a corresponds to the 'perpetual factor time flow gradient' $e - e^{a/(e^\pi + 1)}$ and accordingly the 'initial time flow velocity' v_i to the 'singularity time flow gradient' $e - e^0$. Which enables him to formulate a dimensionless equation for the time dilation factor $\Delta v_{d\tau}$; along with an equation for its impact on the age of the universe $A_{d\tau} = A \, \Delta v_{d\tau}$ [years]. For a present epoch ($a_0 = 1$) the time dilation factor is calculated by him to $\Delta v_{d\tau(a_0)} \approx 1.00834$.

$$\Delta v_{d\tau} = 1/\left(\sqrt[3]{v_a} \,/ \sqrt[3]{v_i}\right)$$
$$= \sqrt[3]{e - e^0} \,/ \sqrt[3]{e - e^{a/(e^\pi + 1)}}$$
$$= \sqrt[3]{e - 1} \,/ \sqrt[3]{e - e^{a/(e^\pi + 1)}}$$

Juvenile Einstein is realizing now that a waveform of the time dilation factor as a function of the scale factor (Fig. 5) is strikingly similar to that of the Lorentz factor as a function of the relative velocity (Fig. 6). And that the similarity is of the physical nature. Unity represents a ground level from which

477

both the time dilation factor and the Lorenz factor very gradually rise up at first; while the late accelerating phase corresponds to an uncontrollable expansion of the universe - respectively to velocity that is nearing the speed of light. When its limit is met the time flow velocity is frozen up and the universe - since there is no time nor light anymore - should vanish away. A similar scenario emerges from a novel equation of state (Saha and Bamba, 2020) based on incorporation the Lambert W function; as both scenarios outline a cosmological model for an accelerating universe (Rani et al., 2015) with a late-time acceleration phase for which the deceleration parameter $q \leq -1$ is established.

The very moment of the universe extinction may be likened either to a moment when the hologram animation is seized - like during the cinema show - by turning off the lights; or to a moment when an accelerated expansion of the universe with its spacetime coiling is terminated by the Big Rip in the black hole. While the former case implies primarily a state of the universal darkness the latter one implies primarily a state of the universal spacelessness-timelessness. Nevertheless, the thoughts-provoking idea of the end of time in understanding our universe (Barbour, 1999) may also imply an existence of a parallel universe in which time is passing in a countermarch (Boyle et al., 2022); but with the same course of the same events as they happen in our universe. Travel back in time would have then actually meant travel back to the future (Tobar and Costa, 2020). Which could explain a paradox of impossibility of making any change in any event that happened in the past so as to affect the presence - and simultaneously a possibility of knowing the future events. While seemingly never befallen yet potentially encountered events as alternatives to those which have been really experienced would have then passed by as an imaginary component of the complex cosmic game.

5. Reasoning About the Human Mind, the Universe, and God

An outlined interplay of the π-aided and e-aided scale factor variables effective in the equations proposed above as twin-like weavers of the geometrical field unity puzzle - as it would occupied Einstein's mind a century ago - is presented there by his imaginarily revived figure to deliberation. He has just realized that not a high complexity but per contra the utmost mathematical simplicity may solve such a puzzle. Which could be why he was unable to solve a century ago a fundamental enigma of the geometrical field unity of everything in the universe - and why his method of the thought experiment has been applied there by his own fictitious juvenile personage as his scientific legacy. On its grounds it may be argued that a controversy about cosmological models has originated paradoxically to a large extent from intricately sophisticated mathematical interpretations of observational data.

From now on juvenile Einstein keeps in his view the statements that *"...the general adherence to the mainstream concordance Λ-CDM model does not leave too much room for thinkers outside the accepted cosmic paradigm..."* (Martinez and Trimble, 2009); that *"...such model presently gives the best picture of how cosmic structures have emerged from the expanding background and have formed the cosmic web..."* (Vazza and Feletti, 2020); that the flat cosmological constant model remains the simplest and the best *"...to explain the current data..."* while giving *"...no reason to prefer any more complex model over the concordance cosmology, the flat cosmological constant..."* (Davis et al., 2007); that

"...nature represents its simplicity in various physical systems..." (Nojiri et al., 2017); that it is the Lambert W function which "...seems to be ubiquitous in nature..." (Corless et al., 1996); that "...transcendental reasoning in the spirit of Kant is becoming increasingly relevant in philosophy of science..." (Hoffmann, 2019); that there have been outlined "...transcendental perspectives on modern physics..." (Bitbol et al., 2009); and what's more, that "Transcendental arguments may be most important in physics." as they were applied, for example, by Einstein for the creation of his theory of relativity which "...abandons Euclidean geometry as an a priori chosen reference system for determining the spatial structure of the universe..." (Hoffmann, 2019); and last but not least that "...fluids with logarithmic equation of state may lead to interesting cosmological behaviour..." (Odintsov et al., 2018).

Having considered all of that and having surmised some divine will in the patterns of nature - and the essence of God in its transcendence - the young cosmic trail rider becomes truly aware why God cannot play dice with the universe; since the whole universe is nothing else but a mirrored face - or brain - of God. And herein - on grounds of findings about "...the similarities between two of the most challenging and complex systems in Nature: the network of neuronal cells in the human brain, and the cosmic network of galaxies..." which may be "...shaped by similar principles of network dynamics, despite the radically different scales and processes at play." (Vazza and Feletti, 2020) - young Einstein takes the order of magnitude 10^{27} as it has been reported by the authors for the scale difference between the cosmic/brain networks into account and wonders: "What if it could reflect a proportional difference in scales[7] between the size of the human brain and of the whole universe?" Since, when the human brain is viewed in its scale as a 'tiny universe' ($a_{0\,(human\ brain)} \approx 10^{-27}$ versus $a_{0\,(universe)} = 1$) its radius should be calculable according the equation proposed above. The answer $12.7736\ [cm]$ he gets corresponds to $8730.29\ [cm^3]$ which is more than a brain volume of the sperm whale; while an average brain volume in the middle-aged females has been reported to be $1115.76\ [cm^3]$ (Ritchie et al., 2018). Yet, with respect to cortical folding (Toro et al., 2008) it is more reliable to consider the surface area of the human cerebral cortex. Taking the reported $2400\ [cm^2]$ into account the calculated radius $12.7736\ [cm]$ corresponds then to the surface area $2050.39\ [cm^2]$; which fits quite well the fact that female brains are approximately 10% smaller than male brains. No matter how speculative these findings are they suggest the idea that in evolution of the galactic network structures there has been implicitly encoded evolution of the neuronal networks. Which makes juvenile Einstein declare: "God is not playing dice with the network dynamics; neither that of the galaxies nor that of the human brain."

Yet, the Universe itself cannot be a product of any Divine activity (or of any super intelligent simulation as it was suggested (Bostrom, 2003)) since in that case a position of God - or the programmer - would have been found 'outside' (Lane, 2021). And our presence would have been in that case a proof of our nonexistence - the finding which has emerged from an imaginary debate between Kublai Khan and Marco Polo about an existence of 'Invisible cities' (Calvino, 1974). Contrary to that there stands the idea of pandeism as "...*the belief that God chose to wholly become our Universe, imposing principles at this Becoming that have fostered the lawful evolution of multifarious structures, including life and consciousness."* According a particular form of pandeism, living God pandeism, *"...our Universe inherits all of God's unsurpassable attributes - reality, unity, consciousness, knowledge, intelligence, and effectiveness - and includes as much reality, conscious and unconscious, as is possible consistent with retaining those attributes. God and the Universe, together 'God-and-Universe,' is also eternal into the future and the past."* (Lane, 2021).

With respect to Kant's transcendental cosmology (Fugate, 2019) and with reference to the space-time unity and the mass-energy unity the idea of the 'God-and-Universe' unity seems to be evincible. Understanding this unity suggests that God, the Universe, and the human mind cannot be separated from each other - since they are the One. Actually, a journey towards understanding this unity represents a leitmotif of the allegorical tale 'The Conference of the Birds' by Farid al-Din 'Attar (2017) in which a hoopoe as a mastermind eggs other birds on to their struggle for an escape from bonds of an ephemeral earthiness so as to reach a sphere of ethereality. Just from its perspective they may find out at last that a mystery of Divinity, Eternity, and Immortality has been ever hidden in themselves.

Conclusions

"Any event is like a ball decorated with entangled ornaments," argues Alexander Grin (1975) in his magical parable of the 'Binary Star Man' who was able to fly just by virtue of his own mental capacity. The first book edition of the tale entitled 'The Shining World' (Grin, 1924) was published two years before Albert Einstein declared in a letter sent on 4 December 1926 to Max Born (Einstein, 2005; Einstein et al., 2005) that God does not play dice with the universe: *"The theory says a lot, but does not*

really bring us any closer to the secret of the 'Old One.' I, at any rate, am convinced that He is not playing at dice." In these two parables the novelist's and the physicist's thoughts met each other to express almost simultaneously similar understanding the nature of all the existence. *"Time and space were to him measures of the same eternity,"* quotes Margarit Tadevosyan (2005) words of Vladimir Nabokov (1992) about Grin's mind. In a way, Grin could sense that *'entangled ornaments'* which decorated and would decorate the universe did not originate from God playing at dice. Rather, their pattern could be encrypted in and attributed to an orchestrated action of certain numbers. As it has been illustrated by Einstein's imaginary cosmic adventure they could be represented by the numbers of Euler's identity that relates together two principal transcendental numbers, e and π, with two principal digital numbers, 0 and 1, and with the imaginary unit i: $e^{i\pi} + 1 = 0$.

And since this imaginary unit may be whatever it means it might be identifiable herein just as the 'Old One', the 'Great Composer', the 'Great Conductor', the 'Great Animator'; the 'Supreme Being'; the 'Chief Referee'. Or simply God - who has according Einstein's original conviction never played dice with the Universe (Carr, 2004; Carter, 2006; Ursic, 2006; Musser, 2015; Lincoln, 2017).

Which calls for an anecdote about Leonhard Euler, Denis Diderot, and a mathematical proof of God's existence (Robertson, 1996). One day in 1773 both scholars met each other in St. Petersburg in the court of Catherine the Great: Czarina's highly privileged and respected mathematician, a staff member of the St. Petersburg Academy of Sciences, whom she had had back soon after her accession to the throne, and one of her lately invited scholars, a leading philosopher and chief encyclopaedist of the French Enlightenment. Yet, before long Czarina realized that even the candlestick of Enlightenment entailed its dark place: a gospel of the rationalistic atheism that harbingered an accession of the new 'God of Science'. With the idea that Diderot - as a person who turned out to be an overt denier of the existence of God - should be debunked, discredited, and silenced somehow, preferably by his own belief in science, she set for him an ingenious trap. Having reliance on Diderot's scientific eagerness Czarina sensed properly that a rumour released by her courtiers about a hot news that Euler had discovered a mathematical proof of God's existence was to reach his ears soon. Euler as a firm believer in God accepted Catherine's plot (one may deduce he enjoyed it with a certain portion of schadenfreude). And since Diderot really asked to join a social event at which the proof would be presented a scientific farce could be launched. During the event Euler solemnly proclaimed an equation (mostly reported as $[(a + b^n)/n] = x$ (Gillings, 1954)) as a scientific statement addressed directly to Diderot as a proof of God's existence. The philosopher was unable to formulate any witty counterargument by which the proof could be pronounced for its unreliable evidence invalid. Euler's language of 'irrational theism' gagged Diderot's language of 'rational atheism' - and soon afterwards the philosopher returned to France.

The anecdote authenticity was called into question in the past (Brown, 1942; Gillings, 1954; Struik, 1967) but a genuineness of Euler's gladsome, humorous, and charming character (Reiner and Reiner, 1990; Debnath, 2009; Calinger, 2016) supports its plausibility. Anyway, the question whether God can be really proved mathematically has remained open up to now (Robertson, 1996; Bischoff, 2022). But maybe there is an opportunity to be closed just by Einstein's fictitiously revived young figure whose trail ride around the expanding universe is going to be over. Euler's identity indicates that the rider has circumscribed on his Pegasus of Imagination but a semicircle of the universe so far: from $+1$ to -1. Fortunately, there is an algebraic trick: $e^{i\pi} = 1/e^{i\pi}$ (therefore $e^{i2\pi} = 1$; while $e^{i\pi} = -1$) which fuels his journey to advance in a specular symmetry of the same counterclockwise direction till bringing him back to the springing point. Just at the moment his imaginary journey taken under the indiscernible guidance of Euler's identity is ending in real terms. Then, could this identity harbor within the principles of symmetry and reciprocity a scheme of the geometric/algebraic field unity of the universe? With its 'contra-twin' parallel existence? And with a presence of God in all of the created things? And eventually, could the equation $[(a + b^n)/n] = x$ (as it is referred above as an enigmatic proof of God's existence) represent Euler's ingeniously encrypted notation of the identity? Imagine, $a = 1$; $b = e$; $n = i\pi$ yield $[(1 + e^{i\pi})/i\pi] = x$; which implies $x = 0/i\pi$, and hence $i \neq 0$. To conclude, i may mean 'Everything' except for 'Nothing'.

"*That which is above is from that which is below, and that which is below is from that which is above...*", an inscription from 'The Tabula Smaragdina' (Holmyard, 1923) hits off casually the heart of Euler's identity. The juvenile adventurer identifies its imaginary unit as a supreme authority that controls from its unknowable and indefinable position beyond one's reach an orchestrated action of the remaining four numbers; of which e and π relate to spacetime while zero and unity reflect Leibniz' concept of nothingness-infiniteness as two cut-off points of the evolution of galactic networks and of neural networks of the human brain. On grounds of ascertainments that: *"In nature everything happens by degrees, and nothing by jumps."* (Leibniz, 1996); *"[...but] continuity is only a mathematical technique for approximating very finely grained things. The world is subtly discrete, not continuous."* (Rovelli, 2018a) the universe evolution is found by young Einstein to be a highly sophisticated discrete yet continuous game. Being principally different from playing at dice or from any card game it is viewed by him as a collective mass-energy match given on the space-time playground. With its expansion the match is running into the countless variants of physically more and more disordered schemes characterized by the entropy growth - that *"...distinguishes the past from the future for us and leads to the unfolding of the cosmos."* (Rovelli, 2018b). Which points out that the scale of the space-time playground represents a measure of entropy of the performed mass-energy game - and of an arrow of time defining its direction. And since Einstein's imaginary journey demonstrated on one hand that an accelerated expansion of the playground implied an accelerated dilation of time reserved for the match - and on the other that there was established an upper bound for the playground scale - the maximum possible entropy of the performed cosmic game has to exist then as well. When it is met both an arrow of time and time itself along with the imaginary unit vanish away and the Universe with all of its ever existing forms and events, thoughts and memories, unveils its all-encompassing face of Divinity, Eternity, and Immortality attributable to God.

Notes

[1] Roots of the function have been iterated as follows: $\log(x_1) \approx 5.5545318206$, i.e., $x_1 \approx 358535.21706$, and $\log(x_2) \approx -0.53640346864$, i.e., $x_2 \approx 0.29080142568$). The function has a local minimum equal to $e/3$ for $x = e^3$.

[2] Graph 4.4.2., an open source application for plotting mathematical functions (the GNU General Public License) was applied to delineate graphs shown in Fig. 2, Fig. 3, and Fig. 5.

[3] The constant is definable as $D_c = ([1/[2(e^\pi + 1)]] + \pi)^2$. $10^6 \approx 10.00017019 \cdot 10^6 \ [km^2 \cdot s^{-2} \cdot Mpc^{-2}]$. One may note that [$1/[2(e^\pi + 1)]] + \pi \approx 3.16230457 \ [km \cdot s^{-1} \cdot Mpc^{-1}]$ is close to: $3.16227189 \ldots \ [km \cdot s^{-1} \cdot Mpc^{-1}]$ defined by the Hubble parameter equation for $a = 3.62$; and numerically also close to: $\sqrt{10} \approx 3.16227766$) as well as to: $\left[10(10 + \pi^2)/(2\pi\sqrt{10})\right]^{1/2} \approx 3.16231171$. And since $10(10 + \pi^2)/(2\pi\sqrt{10}) \approx 10.00021534$ implies $(10 + \pi^2)/(2\pi\sqrt{10}) \approx 1.000021534$ then $(10 + \pi^2)/(2\pi\sqrt{10}) \approx ([1/[2(e^\pi + 1)]] + \pi)^2/ 10$

Should all of this point to a special role of the number ten in cosmology is left to discussion.

[4] The deceleration parameter calculated for a present epoch $q_0 \approx -0.499$ nears to the referential

$q_0 = -0.5$. And the Hubble parameter calculated for a present epoch $H_0 \approx 72.42 \ [km \cdot s^{-1} \cdot Mpc^{-1}]$ lies between an upper limit of H_0 similar to $71 \ [km \cdot s^{-1} \cdot Mpc^{-1}]$ yielded by early universe physics and H_0 similar to $73 \ [km \cdot s^{-1} \cdot Mpc^{-1}]$ to which various local determinations may be converging (Krishnan et al., 2021).

[5] Proposals of the Lambert W function-based equations for the deceleration parameter and for the energy density are presented there; along with a disclosure of their authors that *"...due to a high degree of complexity in the expression for ρ, we are unable to solve it for the scale factor...":*

$q = (3/2)\{1 + \vartheta_1 \ln[W(a)] + \vartheta_2 W(a)^3\} - 1;$

$\rho = \rho_0 \ exp[-3\{ln[W(a)][\vartheta_1 W(a) + \vartheta_1 + 1] + W(a)(1 - \vartheta_1) + (\vartheta_2/12) \ W(a)^3[4 + 3W(a)]\}]$

[6] The universe radius $r \approx 3.8657 \cdot 10^{-35} \ [m]$ calculated for the scale factor $a = 10^{-60}$ edges the Planck length: $l_p \approx 1.61625 \cdot 10^{-35} \ [m]$ while the age $A \approx 1.2895 \cdot 10^{-43} \ [s]$ edges the Planck time $t_p \approx 5.39125 \cdot 10^{-44} \ [s]$. Both data calculated for a present epoch ($a_0 = 1$): $r \approx 1.2773 \cdot 10^{23} \ [km]$ and $A \approx 13.502 \cdot 10^9 \ [years]$ are 2% under current official data $(r \approx 1.3043 \cdot 10^{23} \ [km]$ and $A \approx 13.787 \cdot 10^9 \ [years])$. For the maximum scale factor $(a_{max} = e^{\pi} + 1)$ $r_{max} \approx 3.1079 \cdot 10^{36} \ [km]$ and $A_{max} \approx 3.2852 \cdot 10^{23} \ [years]$ were calculated.

[7] Actually, the scaling ratio of $1.875 \cdot 10^{27}$ between the cosmic web and the human cerebral and cerebellar cortex when their power spectra were examined (1.6 *mm* in brain samples corresponded to 100 *Mpc* in the cosmic web) is referred. Synthetic

samples of the cosmic web from a high-resolution (2400^3 cells and dark matter particles) simulation of a cubic 100^3 $[Mpc^3]$ cosmic volume were used.

Acknowledgements

The author's tribute is addressed to Čestmír Černý (1927-2009), professor of physical chemistry and rector of University of Chemistry and Technology Prague, for his illustrious chalked-based lectures once given to learners in a lucidly ravishing language of mathematics. A credit of coincidental encounter Euler's identity and Einstein's relativity belongs to Radúz Záveský, a schoolfellow and a good old boy.

📖 References

Al Mamon, A., & Saha, S. (2021) Testing lambert W equation of state with observational hubble parameter data. *New Astronomy, 86*, 101567. https://doi.org/10.1016/j.newast.2020.101567

Banerjee, M., Das, S., Al Mamon, A., Saha, S., & Bamba, K. (2021) Growth of perturbations using Lambert W equation of state. *International Journal of Geometric Methods in Modern Physics, 18*, 2150139. https://doi.org/10.1142/S0219887821501395

Barbour, J. (1999) *The End of Time: The Next Revolution in Physics*. Oxford: Oxford University Press.

Bishoff, M. (2022) Can God Be Proved Mathematically? *Scientific American, October 4*. https://www.scientificamerican.com/article/can-god-be-proved-mathematically/

Bitbol, M., Kerszberg, P., & Petitot, J. (Eds.) (2009) *Constituting Objectivity: Transcendental Perspectives on Modern Physics, The Western Ontario Series in Philosophy of Science*.

Dordrecht: Springer. https://doi.org/10.1007/978-1-4020-9510-8

Bostrom, N. (2003) Are we living in a computer simulation? *Philosophical Quarterly, 53*(211), 243-255. https://doi.org/10.1111/1467-9213.00309

Boyle, L., Finn, K., & Turok, N. (2022) The Big Bang, CPT, and neutrino dark matter. *Annals of Physics, 438*, 168767. https://doi.org/10.1016/j.aop.2022.168767

Brito, P.B., Fabiao, F., & Staubyn, A. (2008) Euler, Lambert, and the Lambert W-function today. *Mathematical Scientist, 33*(2), 127-133.

Brown, B.H. (1942) The Euler-Diderot Anecdote. *The American Mathematical Monthly, 49*(5), 302-303. https://doi.org/10.2307/2303096

Calinger, R.S. (2016) *Leonhard Euler: Mathematical Genius in the Enlightenment*. Princeton, NJ: Princeton University Press. https://doi.org/10.2307/j.ctv7h0smb

Calvino, I. (1974) *Invisible cities*. Weaver, W. (Trans.). New York: Harcourt Brace Jovanovich. (Original published in 1972.)

Carr, P.H. (2004) Does God play dice? Insights from the fractal geometry of nature. *Zygon, 39*(4), 933-940. https://doi.org/10.1111/j.1467-9744.2004.00629.x

Carter, B. (2006) Who plays dice? Subjective uncertainty in deterministic quantum world, in: Alimi, J.M., Fuzfa, A. (Eds.), *Albert Einstein Century International Conference, AIP Conference Proceedings 861*. Melville: American Institute of Physics, pp. 73-77.

Corless, R.M., Gonnet, G.H., Hare, D.E.G., Jeffrey, D.J., & Knuth, D.E. (1996) On the LambertW function. *Advances in Computational Mathematics, 5*(1), 329-359. https://doi.org/10.1007/BF02124750

D'Arcy Kenworthy, W., Scolnic, D., & Riess, A. (2019) The Local Perspective on the Hubble Tension:

Local Structure Does Not Impact Measurement of the Hubble Constant. *The Astrophysical Journal,* *875,* 145. https://doi.org/10.3847/1538-4357/aboebf

Davis, T.M., Mortsell, E., Sollerman, J., Becker, A.C., Blondin, S., Challis, P., Clocchiatti, A., Filippenko, A.V., Foley, R.J., Garnavich, P.M., Jha, S., Krisciunas, K., Kirshner, R.P., Leibundgut, B., Li, W., Matheson, T., Miknaitis, G., Pignata, G., Rest, A., Riess, A.G., & Schmidt, B.P. (2007) Scrutinizing Exotic Cosmological Models Using ESSENCE Supernova Data Combined with Other Cosmological Probes. *The Astrophysical Journal,* *666*(2), 716-725. https://doi.org/10.1086/519988

Debnath, L. (2009) *The Legacy of Leonhard Euler: A Tricentennial Tribute.* London: Imperial College Press.

Di Valentino, E., Mena, O., Pan, S., Visinelli, L., Yang, W.Q., Melchiorri, A., Mota, D.F., Riess, A.G., & Silk, J. (2021) In the realm of the Hubble tension-a review of solutions. *Classical and Quantum Gravity,* *38,* 153001. https://doi.org/10.1088/1361-6382/aco86d

Einstein, A. (2005) Albert Einstein to Max Born. *Physics Today,* *58*(5), 16. https://doi.org/10.1063/1.1995729

Einstein, A., Born, M., & Born, H. (2005) *The Born-Einstein Letters: Friendship, Politics and Physics in Uncertain Time: Correspondence between Albert Einstein and Max and Hedwig Born from 1916 to 1955 with commentaries by Max Born.* Houndmills: Macmillan; New York: Basingstoke, Hampshire, p. 88.

Euler, L. (1783) De serie Lambertina, plurimisque eius insignibus proprietatibus. *Acta Academiae Scientiarum Imperialis Petropolitanae [pro Anno MDCCLXXIX Pars Posterior : Acta Acad. Imp. Sc. Tom. III, P. II. : Mathematica],* *3*(2), 29-51.

Evangelidis, B. (2018) Space and Time as Relations: The Theoretical Approach of Leibniz. *Philosophies, 3,* 9. https://doi.org/10.3390/philosophies3020009

Farid al-Din 'Attar (2017) *The Conference of the Birds.* Wolpé, S. (Trans.). New York: W. W. Norton & Company. (Original completed around 1187.)

Freedman, W.L. (2021) Measurements of the Hubble Constant: Tensions in Perspective. *The Astrophysical Journal, 919,* 16. https://doi.org/10.3847/1538-4357/ac0e95

Fugate, C.D. (2019) Kant's Cosmology, Miracles and the Autonomy of Reason, in: Fugate, C.D. (Ed.), *Kant's Lectures on Metaphysics: A Critical Guide.* Cambridge UK: Cambridge University Press, pp. 122-155. https://doi.org/10.1017/9781316819142

Gillings, R.J. (1954) The So-Called Euler-Diderot Incident. *The American Mathematical Monthly, 61*(2), 77-80. https://doi.org/10.2307/2307789

Grin, A.S. (1924) *Blistayushchiy mir. [The Shining World].* Moskva: Zemlya i Fabrika.

Grin, A. (1975) *Zářivý svět; Královna vln. [Blistayushchiy mir (The Shining World); Begushchaya po volnam (She Who Runs on the Waves)].* Psůtková, Z. (Trans.). Praha: Odeon, p. 27. (Original published in 1956.)

Hoffmann, M.H.G. (2019) Transcendental Arguments in Scientific Reasoning. *Erkenntnis, 84*(6), 1387-1407. https://doi.org/10.1007/s10670-018-0013-9

Holmyard, E.J. (1923) The Emerald Table. *Nature, 112*(2814), 525-526. https://doi.org/10.1038/112525a0

Krishnan, C., Mohayaee, R., Colgain, E.O., Sheikh-Jabbari, M.M., & Yin, L. (2021) Does Hubble tension signal a breakdown in FLRW cosmology? *Classical and Quantum Gravity, 38,* 184001. https://doi.org/10.1088/1361-6382/ac1a81

Lambert, J.H. (1758) Observationes variae in Mathesin puram. *Acta Helvetica, Physico-Mathematico-Anatomico-Botanico-Medica, 3,* 128-168.

Lane, W.C. (2021) Living God Pandeism: Evidential Support. *Zygon, 56*(3), 566-590. https://doi.org/10.1111/zygo.12704

Leibniz, G. W. (1996) *New Essays on Human Understanding.* Remnant P. and Bennett J. (Trans.). Cambridge UK: Cambridge University Press, p. 473. (Original published in 1765.)

Lincoln, D. (2017) God's Thoughts: Practical Steps Toward a Theory of Everything. *Physics Teacher, 55*(4), 204-209. https://doi.org/10.1119/1.4978713

Mandal, S., Bhattacharjee, S., Pacif, S.K.J., & Sahoo, P.K. (2020) Accelerating universe in hybrid and logarithmic teleparallel gravity. *Physics of the Dark Universe, 28,* 100551. https://doi.org/10.1016/j.dark.2020.100551

Martinez, V.J., & Trimble, V. (2009) Cosmologists in the Dark, in: Rubino-Martin, J.A., Belmonte, J.A., Prada, F., Alberdi, A. (Eds.), *Cosmology Across Cultures: An International Conference on the Impact of the Study of the Universe in Human Thinking, ASP Conference Series 409.* San Francisco: Astronomical Society of the Pacific, pp. 47-56.

Mező, I. (2022) *The Lambert W function: its generalizations and applications.* Boca Raton, Florida: CRC Press. https://doi.org/10.1201/9781003168102

Mező, I., & Baricz, A. (2017) On the generalization of the Lambert W function. *Transactions of the American Mathematical Society, 369*(11), 7917-7934. https://doi.org/10.1090/tran/6911

Musser, G. (2015) Is the Cosmos Random? Einstein's assertion that God does not play dice with the universe has been misinterpreted. *Scientific American, 313*(3), 88-93.

https://doi.org/10.1038/scientificamerican0915-88

Nabokov, V. (1992) *The Real Life of Sebastian Knight*. New York: Vintage International, p. 64.

Neben, A.R., & Turner, M.S. (2013) Beyond H_0 and q_0: Cosmology Is No Longer Just Two Numbers. *The Astrophysical Journal, 769*, 133. https://doi.org/10.1088/0004-637X/769/2/133

Nojiri, S., Odintsov, S.D., & Oikonomou, V.K. (2017) Modified gravity theories on a nutshell: Inflation, bounce and late-time evolution. *Physics Reports, 692*, 1-104. https://doi.org/10.1016/j.physrep.2017.06.001

Norton, J.D. (2013) Chasing the Light: Einstein's Most Famous Thought Experiment, in: Frappier, M., Meynell, L., Brown, J.R. (Eds.), *Thought Experiments in Philosophy, Science and the Arts*. New York: Routledge, pp. 123-140.

Odintsov, S.D., Oikonomou, V. K., Timoshkin, A.V., Saridakis, E.N., & Myrzakulov, R. (2018) Cosmological fluids with logarithmic equation of state. *Annals of Physics, 398*, 238-253. https://doi.org/10.1016/j.aop.2018.09.015

Rameez, M., & Sarkar, S. (2021) Is there really a Hubble tension? *Classical and Quantum Gravity, 38*, 154005. https://doi.org/10.1088/1361-6382/ac0f39

Rani, N., Jain, D., Mahajn, S., Mukherjee, A., & Pires, N. (2015) Transition redshift: new constraints from parametric and nonparametric methods. *Journal of Cosmology and Astroparticle Physics, 2015*, 045. https://doi.org/10.1088/1475-7516/2015/12/045

Reiner, L. & Reiner, W. (1990) The Blind Man Who Could See, in: *Mathematicians Are People, Too: Stories From the Lives of Great Mathematicians: Volume 1*. Palo Alto, CA: Dale Seymour Publications, pp. 72-81.

Riess, A.G., Filippenko, A.V., Challis, P., Clocchiatti, A., Diercks, A., Garnavich, P.M., Gilliland, R.L., Hogan, C.J., Jha, S., Kirshner, R.P., Leibundgut, B., Phillips, M. M., Reiss, D., Schmidt, B.P., Schommer, R.A., Smith, R.C., Spyromilio, J., Stubbs, C., Suntzeff, N.B., & Tonry, J. (1998) Observational Evidence from Supernovae for an Accelerating Universe and a Cosmological Constant. *The Astronomical Journal, 116*(3), 1009-1038. https://doi.org/10.1086/300499

Ritchie, S.J., Cox, S.R., Shen, X.Y., Lombardo, M.V., Reus, L.M., Alloza, C., Harris, M.A., Alderson, H.L., Hunter, S., Neilson, E., Liewald, D.C.M., Auyeung, B., Whalley, H.C., Lawrie, S.M., Gale, C.R., Bastin, M.E., McIntosh, A.M., & Deary, I. J. (2018) Sex Differences in the Adult Human Brain: Evidence from 5216 UK Biobank Participants. *Cerebral Cortex, 28*(8), 2959-2975. https://doi.org/10.1093/cercor/bhy109

Robertson, R. (1996) Euler's identity; a mathematical proof for the existence of God? *Psychological Perspectives, 34*(1), 62-75. https://doi.org/10.1080/00332929608405751

Rovelli, C. (2018a) *The Order of time.* Segre, E. and Carnell, S. (Trans.). New York: Riverhead Books, p. 48. (Original published in 2017.)

Rovelli, C. (2018b) Ibid., p. 110.

Saha, S., & Bamba, K. (2020) The Lambert W Function: A Newcomer in the Cosmology Class? *Zeitschrift für Naturforschung A - Physical Sciences, 75*(1), 23-27. https://doi.org/10.1515/zna-2019-0240

Sandage, A.R. (1970) Cosmology: A search for two numbers. *Physics Today,* 23(2), 34-41. https://doi.org/10.1063/1.3021960

Scott, T., Mann, R., & Martinez II, R. (2006) General relativity and quantum mechanics: towards a generalization of the Lambert W function - A Generalization of the Lambert W Function.

Applicable Algebra in Engineering, Communication and Computing, 17(1), 41-47. https://doi.org/10.1007/s00200-006-0196-1

Silagadze, Z.K. (2010) Citation entropy and research impact estimation. *Acta Physica Polonica B, 41*(11), 2325-2333.

Simpson, A., & Visser, M. (2020) Regular Black Holes with Asymptotically Minkowski Cores. *Universe, 6,* 8. https://doi.org/10.3390/universe6010008

Struik, D.J. (1967) *A Concise History of Mathematics.* New York: Dover Publications, p.129.

Tadevosyan, M. (2005) The 'Road to Nowhere', a road to 'Glory': Vladimir Nabokov and Aleksandr Grin. *Modern Language Review, 100*(2), 429-443.

Tobar, G., & Costa, F. (2020) Reversible dynamics with closed time-like curves and freedom of choice. *Classical and Quantum Gravity, 37,* 205011. https://doi.org/10.1088/1361-6382/aba4bc

Toro, R., Perron, M., Pike, B., Richer, L., Veillette, S., Pausova, Z., & Paus, T. (2008) Brain size and folding of the human cerebral cortex. *Cerebral cortex, 18*(10), 2352–2357. https://doi.org/10.1093/cercor/bhm261

Ursic, M. (2006) Einstein on religion and science. *Synthesis Philosophica, 42*(2), 267-283.

Vazza, F., & Feletti, A. (2020) The Quantitative Comparison Between the Neuronal Network and the Cosmic Web. *Frontiers in Physics, 8,* 525731. https://doi.org/10.3389/fphy.2020.525731

Figures

Fig. 1: Albert Einstein in a Munich photo studio (1894). Unknown author. Image by: Wikimedia Commons, the free media repository. Public domain. https://commons.wikimedia.org/wiki/File:Albert_Einstein_a s_a_child.jpg

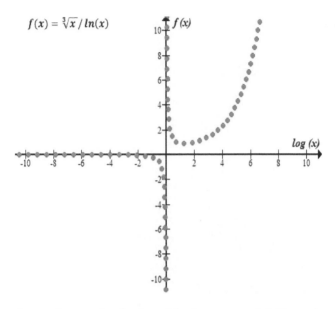

$f(x) = \sqrt[3]{x}/\ln(x)$

Fig. 2: The graph of a logarithmic-exponential discontinuous function $\sqrt[3]{x}/\ln(x)$ plotted against $\log(x)$. The function is derived from a transcendental equation $x = [\log(x).\ln(x)]^3$.

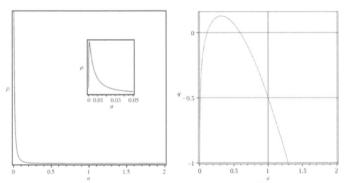

Fig. 3: Behaviour of the energy density (ρ) and of the deceleration parameter (q) as a function of the scale factor (a) according the Lambert W function-based equations

presented in: Saha, S. & Bamba, K.: "The Lambert W Function: A Newcomer in the Cosmology Class?"; in: Holthaus, M., Fetecau, C. & Kiefer, C. (eds.), Zeitschrift für Naturforschung A - Physical Sciences, 75(1), Berlin/Boston: Walter de Gruyter GmbH, 2020, pp. 23-27, fig. 1. Reprinted with a permission from the publisher.

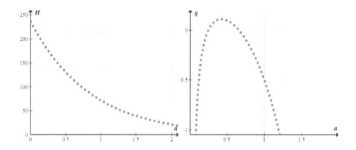

Fig. 4: Behaviour of the Hubble parameter (H) and of the deceleration parameter (q) as a function of the scale factor (a) according the logarithmic-exponential discontinuous function $(\sqrt[3]{x}/\ln(x))$-based equations presented in this paper.

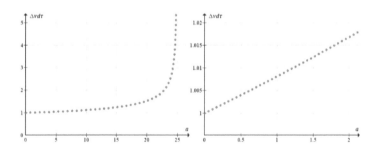

Fig. 5: Behaviour of the time dilation factor $\Delta v_{d\tau}$ as a function of the scale factor (a) according the equation presented in this paper.

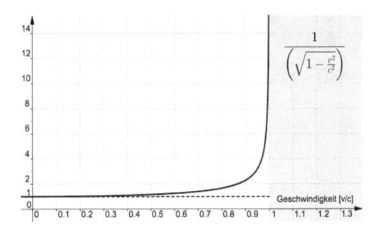

Fig. 6: Behaviour of the Lorentz factor (γ) as a function of the relative velocity (v). Figure from: File:Lorentzfaktor.svg: Klamannderivative work: MikeRun, Public domain, via Wikimedia Commons. https://commons.wikimedia.org/wiki/File:Lorentz-factor.svg

From Catholicism Across The Poetic Synapse To Pandeism:

The Metamorphosis, The Evolution, The Leap-Of-Faith Teleportation From Belief In God-The-Judge-Jury-n-Executioner To Belief In Shape-Shifter God-The-Creation: Part III-V

By Paul Zarzyski, redux

III

ZD - The road to Truth-n-Wisdom is never moonlit and newly-paved, but rather sabotaged by the exacting gods and goddesses with potholes, falling rock, thick fog, frost heaves, black ice, eyes in the night. Holding fast to the power of The Trinity, the Poet 1) proceeds with acumen of mind, body, soul, 2) abandons baggage, agenda, ego, for good, and 3) gives thanks for this mysterious journey at every invisible mile marker.

ZD - Will somebody please tell the guy in the wheelhouse of the Large Hadron Collider that Poets have long-ago defined the "God Particle" as a single raindrop, a single snowflake, one teardrop shed in the name of love, joy, loss.

I choose to believe that my writing is more often than not akin to a vision quest—the creative journey at its height, a Star-Trekian exploration into the unknown with hopes of discovering a glimpse here, a glimpse there, of the otherworldly. I can think of no greater detriment to the artist, God-The-Universe included, than to outline, to map out, a poem or essay, a painting or musical composition. Such would become the absolute saboteur of the discovery of inner wisdom.   To couch it otherwise, the proverbial "Yellow Brick Road" becomes most profound when rife with detours. Didn't Dorothy and Toto, the Tin Man, Scarecrow, and Cowardly Lion learn more about themselves, about their destiny, via the detoured route to Oz than by their arrival? Think about it. I believe they did. All that The Wizard behind the curtain did was offer confirmation.

Which harkens back to the title of this piece—were it not for investing 50+ years of my life into the creative process, I very well may still be stuck in "Spiritual Neutral" gear. I write to learn and when I'm learning well, odds are good that I'm writing well.

Otherwise, of the "8 Grateful Gravitations," still more or less holding their own a dozen-plus years after delineating them in an altogether different time-n-space, number 5, "Fellow Beings" has since evolved, advanced, neck-and-neck down the final stretch with number 8, "Private Piety, Personal Eternity." The poems, "I Believe" and *Las Ballenas...*" bear this out. Moreover, I should have titled the entry, "Fellow *Soulful* Beings," as, in my view, a true-blue Pandeist affords our animal and plant brethren the same degree of sanctity afforded our own genus and species. That said, I'll spare you my argument for affording many of our brother-n-sister planet-earth co-inhabitants a higher standing on the intelligence pyramid than we've awarded ourselves. On second thought, maybe *I won't.*

ZD - With the *minuscule* exception of anatomical distinctions, it is impossible to differentiate between, for example, the Ebola virus and members of the Ku Klux Klan—both being living entities qualifying as insidious deadly afflictions, as organisms deserving of eradication, via whatever means necessary, from Planet Earth. If a pacifist stance deprives you from buying into this, I challenge you to take a stroll through Montgomery, Alabama's National Memorial for Peace and Justice, in commemoration of African-American lynching victims—Billie Holiday singing "Strange Fruit" into your ear pods—without bleeding through your eyes.

Too judgmental? Maybe—maybe *not*. Or is it more likely a matter of our being on the deserving end of Jack Nicholson's vociferous admonishment from the witness stand in the film *A Few Good Men*: "You (we) can't **handle** the truth!"

ZD - If one cannot live up to the high-standard *non*-anatomical distinction of what it means to be "Human"—however defined *outside* the parameters dictated by religious texts in which our fellow soulful beings have been given no voice—then one, simply put, is something *other than* Human. Trees are Human. Whales? Human. Elephants? Human. Gorillas? Chimpanzees? Orangutans? Human. Honeybees, Manatees, Hummingbirds....? Human. Which is not to suggest, mind you, that severely flawed humans (note lower case), such as the one rendering this dictum, are incapable of accruing wisdom and, thereby, working their way up the steep incline of the "living-being hierarchical pyramid" —for which Sisyphus Zarzyski thanks daily Creation's luckiest stars.

****

Okay. I agree. It's time to lighten up a bit. How's *this*? A "semordnilap" is a word that when read in reverse results in a different word of a different meaning. One of my favorite semordnilaps is "god" becoming "dog," which cues me to the logical deduction that god must be especially pleased with the creation of the canine genus. Liz and I were graced for 14 years of our lives with the presence of an Australian Shepherd named Zeke, *who*—yes, "*who*"—became the messenger for many poetic works during our time together. The poem, "What's Sacred," was selected by the editor for inclusion in this *Anthology*. I commend him for his keen ear and heart. I think the poem's sentiment summons the definitive question, "If god is The Universe and, again, therefore, every atom of every entity existing in it, must we accept every single entity as equally sacred, or are we left to choose, via free will, which creations, from our brief but unique existences, rank supreme at any given moment in our lives?" If the latter, I offer this moment of sanctity from my time here with fellow soulful being, Zeke Zarzyski:

What's Sacred

To wake because waking means something,
something you're itching to begin
living at daybreak—revelry of autumn
cottonwood leaves, shod horses
clicking over scree, far-off
cacophony of meadowlark aria with crow
ruckus, goshawk skirl, strident magpie
cries breezed through a bedroom
window screen, tinkling wind chimes

504

echoing steeple bells
deep out of some distant
childhood dream.
                            To hopscotch
or, better odds, slip-slip
succinctly into your jeans
with brisk whispers from each
instep thrust, fifty-plus
years of this denim
one-two gymnastic balancing act
on the high wire between
half-asleep and wide-awake—right leg
then left—ankles, knees, hips,
lumbar, *snap-crackle-popping*
their breakfast applause.
                            To splash
well water into your prayerful hands, cotton-
towel your eyelids dry, focus,
voice with a joyous *ahhhh*
your first hot swallow of joe
kick-starting your ticker
before walking your Aussie dog,
Zeke, who loves you for your clockwork
newspaper fetchings
from that blue speck of a box, far
as the blue eye can see,
a long jaunt off.
                            To inhale,
until your lungs flex like biceps,
canine windfalls of fresh scents, dry leaves
redolent in the night's wake, gold
certificates flushed from the sprung
back doors of an armored car, both
sagebrushed ditches
flitting with winged brilliance
crisp for the picking at 6 a.m.
when you shall be the only two in sight
eager enough to inherit,

breath after rich fertile breath, this earth.

And yet one more depiction of a moment in which I
was the humble and grateful recipient of God's Dog
Graces:

Australian Shepherd Dump-Run Meditation

Mostly for the love of an old dog
sprawled across the saddle blanket
seat cover of an old pickup—Zeke's
head cradled in a third-gear
lullaby between the wheel and my lap
as I fret his favorite chord
progressions down the neck
to his "G-spot," dog-chakra tailbone—we ease
our way over gravel
road the old truck knows so well
by carburetor heart, all it takes
is my two-fingered-steering touch
to keep us cruising in the ruts
true as rails. With our wind-groomed
load of loose hay, woodlot bark,
aspen leaf and lawn duff
rakings settling into a bread-loaf
mound in its box, the Ford hums
along in eight-part harmony as we
three bask in our laid-back
Saturday afternoon ritual. Through this
cumulonimbus-cirrus cloudscape
pantomiming rolling prairie, buttes,
buffalo jump, buckbrush coulee,
crazy quilt landscape, we become the simple
dolphin-swim needlework—in and out
of sight, down into swale up over dale—
each stitch of us, no less
binding of this moment in time
than all the rest. Zeke's wits
roused by a coup-counting owl

swooping over the hood, he sits up
leaning into me like fifty pounds of pure bliss
incarnate. The world outside ours muted,
what more tuned-in essence of life
loved, as it is lived here and now, than this
ascension into the center of western Zen.

ZD - "**My goal is simple,**" **said Stephen Hawking. "It is a complete understanding of the universe, why it is as it is, and why it exists at all." Akin to Hawking's ambition,** "*my* **goal is simple,**" **as well. It is a complete understanding of the infinite nexuses or synapses between Paul Zarzyski's atomic matter and that of other components of the universe, animate and inanimate, animal, plant, mineral, liquid…alike—anything and everything composed of helium, hydrogen, oxygen, et al. Since "God," as we have defined "Him" out of fear and ignorance, is either too egotistically selfish or, more likely, does not exist according to our definitions and designations to begin with, I most simply embrace the joyful choice of "going it alone" on my learned journey into whatever understanding of my consciousness, of my energy's links to other energies, that the universe will very likely eventually, and gracefully, reveal.**

Going It Alone

> *The secret of a good old age is simply*
> *an honorable pact with solitude.*
> Gabriel Garcia Marquez

Not just for the metaphorical hell of it
but instead, here and now, for good reason,
while peering into this macro-lens

windshield, I think of Amelia's
Lockheed Electra, of Dick Hugo's Buick
Skylark, of everything falling
inevitably through the surrealistic
filter of cumulonimbus—heavy
weather swirling into focus
as first my father, then my mother,
slipped into their final silences. I,
with no sane way out of this
mortal storm, this viscid
mythological maze of biblical
ebb and flow, have come to see
why I never again will thrive
as once I thrived in the same
exact triangular time
with Mom and Dad. Thus, alone,
I embrace the wild
disorder, the metamorphosis, this life
sentence amidst the faithful. No longer
just one more fading pin-tip
blip upon the radar screens
of the gods, I, in solo flight,
am swallowed into the welcoming black-
garmented arms of the dark, far
beyond the blurred
purgatorial borders between
heaven and earth—my cargo of light
grown brighter, pulsing with all
the hope, all the fear,
one disappearing soul can hold.

The "loudest" lines this poem shouts in my direction
are, "...I embrace the wild / disorder, the
metamorphosis, this life / (sentence amid the)
faithful..."—for reasons clearly articulated or
intimated again and again throughout this essay, but
perhaps in need of further punctuation with

ZD - The mother of all thesaurus synonyms through all of spoken- and written-word time must list "religion" side-by-side with, at best, "mythology" and, at worst, "superstition." To quote Jethro Tull, "In the beginning, Man created God." (Damn thunder-fearing Neanderthal wusses, anyway.) Or, far more lyrically profound, the opening verse to John Lennon and Yoko Ono's "Imagine:"

Imagine there's no heaven
It's easy if you try
No hell below us
Above us, only sky

****

In the event that I have yet to shine a bright enough spotlight on the essence, the focal point, of this piece, I'll offer, one last time, I *promise*, this reiteration, this redundancy: I do not force my will on the poem, but, on the contrary, just as God-the-Creation allows every entity its free will, I give the poem a free rein, a carte blanche main stage from which to express, preferably via song, via music, *its* ideologies and sentiments. I could not agree more with the co-editor of the 2019 *Pandeism Anthology* issue, Amy Perry, whose bio note on the back cover reads, "She enjoys experiencing life as a poem and invites you to do the same." To push this a note or two further, I live to learn life's mysteries *from* the poems. The most potent poems, I believe, guide those who render them to listen to and learn from the poems' teachings, which, in the best-case scenario, also teleport other listeners, readers, pupils to the wellsprings of the poems' knowledge, or mysteries. I find most—not all, but "most"— of the literary appraisals (a.k.a. "critiques") couched in their subjective literary tenets (Commandments) to be very much akin to just one more insipid religious denomination. *What?* "Way too defiantly, iconoclastically opinionated," you say? So be it.

Poetry—Off Radar, With Faith, Into The Sacred

It no longer holds up to the light—
the old saw about poetry being meant
to be read aloud. By whom? Says who? *We?*
We who have failed such euphoric
musical genuflections to Mother
Earth, Brother Sky, Sister Universe,
Father Time, Uncle God? What graces
have we set free? What coat-of-arms wisdom
have our souls borne in courage
to starburst galaxies of words,
words hijacked in transit
to holier places, to holier beings
than are we, the self-anointed
chosen? Let us now otherwise pray,
plead in private, for our very own R.I.P.
"Resurrection Into Poetry:"
                             Lord, may I
humbly deliver, unsullied, these lines
synapsing through me in search of truth,
super-human truth, to wherever is
their higher lure. Screw the literati
cognoscente's stamp of approval
in ink. Screw false audience,
social media's abbreviated thought
of abbreviated souls. Screw applause,
screw all awe other than the poet's own
soaring off this orb's radiant green-
screened page into the glory-be
unknown, into the reckoning
silence above the noise, the noise,
the pitiful noise of the human
voice, where all lies writhe in wait.

And in further tribute to Amy Perry's sentiments:

Living Poetry

Down the echo-chamber hallway
from kitchen to my writing niche
filled with screaming
hurricanes of words
through the window screen, I catch wind
of my wife cooing, cooing
baby talk to our Aussie dog, who,
pushing the century mark,
rediscovers puppy comfort
in the long-voweled, two-syllabled
emasculation of his name
over the hard consonant
handle, Zeke, making him
feel Spike-or-Duke
unneutered pit-bull-macho
in his canine prime. "How's sweet
little *Zekey* doing today? Is he hungry
for his *Zekey* food? Does *Zekey* want
to go feed horses? Play
Cookie-Down-the-Hall, go walkies,
go pee-pee poo-poo? Oooooo,
Zekey's such a good dog." I smile,
put my pencil down, close my notebook,
slide the window shut, the wind's words
slamming face-first into the pane—
piling up and melting
against the house like hail
stones horizontally out of the south. I
sit back in what was once
my writing chair, relax my hands,
fingers loosely tongue-n-grooved
in my lap like an old Italian
woman praying her rosary
at High Mass. I close my eyes, listen,

hear again the osmosis of poetry
seeping into the log-walled soul
through its most organic door
opening like the cover
of a book—not one bit less a book
minus a single printed page.

**ZD - Since God could not have chosen a more
incompetent species to control the fate, *and
faith*, of all other earthly species in this time-
n-space, it could not have been the decision of
an omnipotent God to begin with.**

The following poem is one of the few third-person
omniscient narratives I've brought to the page. It was
conveyed by a friend who, *thank heaven*, did not pitch
it as "A good story that you should make into a poem."
All these years later, I find myself astonished by how
accurately the finer details rose to the surface, sans
notes, to the degree that I feel I had actually
experienced them myself. In full disclosure, my friend
liked his recreational tokes, which, in my poetic
opinion, makes a strong case, in and of itself, for the
further legalization of marijuana, especially the THC
sleep gummies blossoming into dreams *this* real!

Prophecy

He always stirs before the graphic
end of life on earth begins
its final countdown, the winged
cylinder's accelerated fall
blurring its hieroglyphic-
Sanskrit-graffiti-like universal
truth we will all, in unison, come to
understand, he says, the instant before
it hits. His bedside
notebook lit, aurora borealis
pouring through the skylight,

he sketches this recurring dream scenario,
the vessel's shape and symbols, with each
air-raid alarm sirening him
out of sleep. He believes in and trusts
his simple, clear language
describing the essence of pure peace
coupled with love, the elliptical
identical puzzle parts
by the tens of thousands
somehow fitting, somehow
connecting perfectly together in what he learns
about eternity. He tells me
he is always in physical touch
with his horses, his dogs. Animals
become the angels who return
his veterinary favors and feats,
who save *him*—he knows this for sure
though he's not yet dreamt
near enough the fail-safe point
to sense precisely how. He reaches down
beside the bed, feels the thick fur
of his Red Heeler, eases the other
hand upon his wife
restless beside him. Night, sky, dog,
horse, man, woman, earth, is all
the animal faith, all the heaven, he,
falling back to sleep, will ever need.

I'll close this section with a poem expressing my critical need, as I accelerate down life-in-this-dimension's final stretch, for quieter, less encumbering, focuses, ambitions, endeavors, falsehoods.... Note the poem's Pandeistic closure, in which God-the-Creation is identified in upper case as "Infinity."

Arterial Hemoglobin Blood-Oath Resolution

We are stardust brought to life, then empowered

by the universe to figure itself out—
and we have only just begun.

Neil deGrasse Tyson

Long past high noon, it's high time I begin
dialing down the volume
on life's noise—threadbare friendships,
soap-opera psychodramas of the ultra-needy,
all egos, foremost my own, obsolete
deities, icons, heroes, gurus,
long-dead etiquettes, rituals, legacies,
feigned acquaintanceships with faith,
fortune, fame, good and evil,
right and wrong, every frigging single
nuance of myth and melodrama,
from pipe dream to nightmare. In this
absence, this absolute void
filled with horizon-less grace, only
then will The Holy Quartet—Time,
Space, Heartbeat, Breath—beam
radiantly down upon me
that one pure truth that fuels us
to create, to create, to create
solely for the sake of reflecting back
out into the deepest reaches,
into the sparkling particles
colliding by the nonillions
at the speed of silence, the very
silence out of which we
first shined, into which I now
vow, thanks to Infinity's giving-ness,
to shine again, to begin again, and *again.*

IV

ZD – Does God Itself know that It is God, or does It wonder—in the humbling awe of Its, of the Universe's, eternal expansion—if an even more potent God *created It*? In which case, might God oh-so-wisely be choosing, as we speak, not to deem Itself definitively omniscient, for to do so would deprive God-the-Creation of further ventures into the *un*known, into Its own artistic being?

ZD – "*Is it* possible" (to employ the catch phrase of my favorite *History Channel* series, "Ancient Aliens") that God is akin to a Russian / Polish nesting doll / egg? God-the-Universe *within* God-the-Universe within God-the-Universe Itself, ad infinitum—each layer, each smaller version than the one before It, revealing a more advanced, further "evolved" or "educated" Godly Universe? A more finely-tuned, more omnipotent Godly Universe? Metaphorically, therefore, the more "infinitesimally microscopic" the doll or egg, the more astonishing, the more miraculous, becomes the Creator *and* Creation until no (theo)logical argument can prove them other than indistinguishable, one and the same? In which case, we humans have likely far too prematurely accepted the outer, most readily obvious, most easily comprehensible and least evolved, least knowledgeable, God. Thus, Pandeism encourages us to venture deeper—to discover God's and / or *our* Inner-Most-Beings. In light of the human body giving home to 100 billion neurons—more than the number of stars in our galaxy—*imagine* the revelations gracing us as we experience the communications of those billions of synapses!

ZD – Stephen Hawking referenced "knowing"—not "understanding," but "knowing"—the mind of God." With this potential celestial germination in our minds, let us posit—not "pray," but "posit—that God may *very well* have chosen to shape-shift, perhaps via turning Itself inside out like, say, a finely woven sock, and, in doing so, exposing the threads of the universe's most intimate warp-and-weft mysteries—Its very design laid bare for astrophysicists to potentially "reverse engineer," so to speak? All by way of God *yearning* for humankind to "know," to celebrate, to learn from Its mind, and to direct that knowledge toward the betterment of humankind, toward the ultimate understanding that our "just reward in heaven" *is*, in fact, our life on Earth?

In light of the trio of preceding **ZDs**—channeled solely out of this essay's close encounters of the umpteenth kind—I "confess" that my thesis, such as it is, has rendered me a proverbial tail-chaser, as I continue, all these pages in, to beat my head-n-heart-n-soul against the quintessential question: "Is my opting for Pandeism over all other spiritual beliefs, and non-beliefs, a copout—a mere matter of convenience, compromise? And, if so, doesn't it expose everything I've articulated thus far as moot?"

My single defense, from the standpoint of a theocratic vagrant representing himself in our Christian court system, is that at least my Pandeistic testimony absolves me from having to take that threatening "so help me God" oath, which I find, to summon Commander Spock yet again, "highly illogical."

Furthermore, those stamping their religious-zealot approval on "the one-n-only true God" are too often impelled into a perception that all who do not grant the same approval of said "one-n-only true God" will be judged harshly, doomed, in the afterlife for "missing the boat, the ark," so to speak, during their earthly journeys. How can any thinking, soulful being among us embrace such a bigoted, overblown, mean-spirited, superiority complex? As in the First Commandment: "Thou shall have no other gods before me." Or worse, "Whoever sacrifices to any god other than the Lord must be destroyed (Exodus 22:20)?" Say *what*, mofo? What happened to "Thou shalt not kill?" At least this Pandeist Poet can look in the mirror knowing that the belief in a non-judgmental supreme being, *That* does not dole out eternal celestial rewards and eternity Netherworld death sentences, epitomizes Shakespeare's "quality of mercy (forgiveness, benevolence, and kindness) unstrained."

Which is all to say, in response to my own query, Pandeism is, in fact, the most highly "logical" option afforded *this* one-of-a-kind earthling operating in the religious blind, whose God-approved-n-encouraged free will has prompted a major shift from Mom's longstanding "That's just what we did" ethnic syndrome.

Which *now* brings me to the ultimate grace bestowed upon us, miraculous Planet Earth—one of an estimated "eleven billion" possible exoplanets in the Goldilocks Zone—"not too hot and not too cold" for liquid water to exist and thus to support *our kind* of life. Since Earth most logically is not inhabited by the only life in the Universe, therefore, its creation beliefs must, most logically, be other than those of our extraterrestrial "neighbors," whose likely greater longevity and superior intelligence and technology most certainly afford them a more advanced perspective (revisit Stephen Hawking poem in Section One?). Again, from my unique poetic frame of reference, our earthly mission, therefore, is to remain diligent and hopeful that we too will someday soon rise to a far greater vantage point from Mount Wisdom—*if,* that is, we cease and desist making lethal *un*godly decisions regarding Big Mama Earth's well-being? Thus,

ZD - I'm for saving, at *any* cost, this glorious buckin' horse orb we're forked to—on its way to the Cosmic Canner to be slaughtered and ground up into black hole fodder, as we speak. I'm talking extreme measures, including the "extinction" of all who deem the demise of God's creation and, thus, a molecular component of God Itself, as "part of God's masochistic plan?" To get right down to the Zarzyski-Dictum nut-cuttin' crux of it all, let's place a bit of a different twist on the Fifth Commandment: "Thou shalt *especially* not kill God's Planetary Masterpiece," for to do so is to assault God's very being, to harm God's metaphorical flesh-n-blood.

Western Questions (A Lyric)

Bound for the horse barn, the cowboy goes blind
In the darkest-night blizzard, 80 below—
Is his deep reminiscence of our long-ago light
Now barely a-flicker from his kitchen window?

Are we all plodding on toward some faithful oasis
While talking in tongues and dying of thirst?
Is this all a mirage, or an unanswered prayer?
It just might be both, for better or worse.

    Out in the desert, the arctic, the cosmos
    Molecule, atom, and Big Bang dust—

518

Are we of the heavens we of the weather?
Are we sacred or sinful—if we boom, must we bust?

The cowboy peers back at his tracks nevermore
Out of the black, does our past become future?
Stunned by what was, we fall *madly* in love
With life in which death is our consummate suitor.

Is temperature linear or is it a circle?
The Earth at its coldest spinning toward hot?
Hurricane, fire, flooding and drought,
Do we learn what-is-what to learn what-is-not?

    Out in the desert, the arctic, the cosmos
    Molecule, atom, and Big Bang dust—
    Are we of the heavens we of the weather?
    Are we sacred or sinful—if we boom,
    must we bust?

        Astronaut cowboy in chaps and big hat,
        Wild-West tamed by ol' climate change—
        Adrift, all alone, no horse and no home
        At Castaway Ranch on the dark cosmic range.

Will one nickering horse wake us in time?
Will we turn to embrace our one saving grace?
Is the Earth reaching out for one hope in this storm?
For one truth that will force us to face what we face?

    Out in the desert, the arctic, the cosmos
    Molecule, atom, and Big Bang dust—
    Are we of the heavens we of the weather?
    Are we sacred or sinful—if we boom must we bust?

    Are we of the heavens we of the weather?
    Are we sacred or sinful, if we shine must we rust?
        ...if we shine, must we rust?
        ...if we shine, *must* we rust?

ZD - We live in a theocratic country on a theocratic planet in a *non*-theocratic galaxy, a Godly Universe That, *were* God judgmentally vindictive ("Vengeance is mine, sayeth the Lord?"), It would likely choose to excise our single cancerous cell, our earthly malignancy, from The Cosmic Whole and, in doing so, render us—as High Table authority, Winston (Ian McShane), declared John Wick (Keanu Reeves)—"Excommunicado!"

ZD - What a sacrilege that we humans were haphazardly graced with Planet Earth, a Rubik's Sphere of eternal combinations of unsolved mysteries, of potential miracles, ad infinitum, which our *un*civilized species has barely begun to embrace, beyond learning to split the atom in the name of our very own extermination, and, with us, the extermination of each and every unsolved mystery and potential miracle that would have otherwise saved us from ourselves. To compensate for our failures to find cures for our most insidious diseases—cancer, Alzheimer's, AIDS, ignorance, hatred, aging, and maybe even death, et al.—we invented religion with its sci-fi afterlife? Wow. In the words of the *Saturday Night Live* Church Lady, "Aren't we *spesch*-el."

Knock-Knock-Knocking On Doomsday's Door

> *Pollution, greed and stupidity are*
> *The greatest threats to Earth.*
> Stephen Hawking

This poem is a flagrant waste
of what little is left of our end-of-days
aboard this page, this space, this time-

bomb orb tick-ticking
hotter by the stopwatch second. Why
squander one fraction of one
single degree of axis rotation
writing or reading this
pitiful drivel, or, sillier yet,
listening to it being read
to us at our final bedside
like some Aesop's Fables last sacrament
fairy tale we strain to believe
will save us from Hades?—
from the boogeyman dark?
                              This poem is *not*
our skydiving heart's nitroglycerine pill
reserve chute, *not* our hidden doom-
and-gloom ampoule of great escape
cyanide, *not* our pearly-gated secret
entryway into the surreal
dreamscape world
of smoked opium. *Nor* is it
our confessional Etch A Sketch
shaking clean of sacrilege
to flightless acts of contrition—slurred
words dribbling like pap
off our chinny-chin-chins
onto the deck of God's Flagship going down,
down for the galactic count of three,
like some torpedoed Noah's Ark,
down into the old cosmic commode,
into the black-hole toilet bowl,
down, *down*, *DOWN* with chosen-ones us
perched in our steepled wheelhouse,
upon our chosen-one throne,
while choosing not to lift
one chosen-one pinkie off the holy-
water flush lever?
                              This poem bites *not*
quite sharp enough its barbed tongue
to keep from frankly asking, "*Why*? Why,
Mother-Earth-Fuckers, were we so
loath to direct instead our genitalia
like pious scientists
pissing in abstinence on the mizzenmast

spiraling up in flames?" *Ahhhh*, screw it—
who can blame the deified
muses refusing to rescue
dunce-capped-stooges
us from our catatonic corner-
gazing selves. Face it—this poem did
not have a prayer in snowballed hell
at putting the kibosh to our atomic
holocaust, the coup de grâce
to our self-prescribed genocide,
the Yosemite Sam "Whoa!,
when I say Whoa! I mean
WHOA!" to this global boiling-over
we choose still to deem a Looney Tunes
" That's ALL Folks! "
cartoon spoof. This poem may as well be
Wile E. Coyote playing Rooski
Roadrunner Roulette
with all six Acme six-shooter chambers
sporting live rounds!
                 And so, this poem
lampoons its own demise, as it mocks
the lost poet depositing it here
like a fiery paper sack of shit
plopped under cover of darkness
upon the poet's *own* porch. Good! He *is* home
to hear, above the TV scream
of too-real news, his swan song's
loud pummeling
on his bunker's screen door. To hear
the absence of 1950's kids'-prank
snickering to his stocking-footed
stomp into the putrid
flames. To hear even the high-
frequency, death rattle
wheeze of his own petrified lines
gasping their photosynthetic last.
                    This poem,
then, exists only to sift its own ashen
bone-fragment remains
through its own chaliced fingers
raised in a pathetic gesture
of reckoning, raised to the billowing God-

cloud of what was once
each and every miracle, each
and every mystery, each and every
molecule of merciful matter
this poem held dear—of what was
once living, breathing
twice-blest you, me, them, us, *it*.

****

Her Heart-Mind-n-Soul Earthly Trinity

ZD - Of all the arts, music is arguably the most potent in its capacity to elicit responses that best define us as human.

In 1999, I was prompted by the Western Folklife Center in Elko, Nevada to write a short piece, which I titled "Grace," for the National Cowboy Poetry Gathering's millennial poster. Twenty years later, asked by the Great Falls Symphony Orchestra and Symphonic Choir Music Director to quill a "lyric" in celebration of the Choir's 60th anniversary, I chose to employ a slightly revised version of "Grace" as the two-stanza opening verse, which then evolved, blossomed, into an "orchestration of sound and image," to which the Maestro composed the music. As I'd emphasized in the prologue scribed for the program booklet, "Grace" is both stanzaic poetry *and* verse-chorus-bridge song —in praise of Mother Earth and all the choral voices of all Her soulful children, animal and plant alike, paramount of whom, Her kindred sisterhood of women.

Our composer-poet-symphony-choir collaboration was performed on December 8, 2019. I consider those 25 minutes of musical time-n-space, set in the Mansfield Theater of the Great Falls Civic Center, one of the highest and most humbling poetic distinctions

523

of my creative life, aside from one minuscule "sour note"—a cellist refusing to play during the performance of "Grace" out of Christian protest regarding the piece being "too pantheistic," for which, I'm certain, God will afford him extra credit on his "Pearly Gates Admission" exam.

Grace

I

In the soft low light up high
where love has always thrived and will
forever yearn for the colorful hover—a brush stroke
of words out of the West—we still want
free life, we still want fresh air.

And as the millennia meander by
like birthdays to the Earth, what thrill
Montana, wild with her four-legged folk,
still brings us on our daily jaunt
across the land, our daily poem, our prayer.

> Oh give us a home, where the poetry roams
> to our Symphony-of-the-Divine—
> with its stars all in tune to the Bucking Horse Moon,
> to the Milky Way Belfry wind chimes.

> Oh give Earth Her song She will sing eons long,
> Her grace note She'll hold to infinity—
> Her psalm to the light, arioso in flight
> with Her heart-mind-n-soul holy trinity.

> To a woodwind sunrise, birds rhapsodize
> with Her heart-mind-n-soul holy trinity.

II

In the moon glow off fresh snow
where the seeds of music grow and soar

to *Doctor Zhivago's* "Lara's Theme"—a wolf-howl
hallelujah to the night—we give praise
to every sacred voice of Earth's high choir.

And as the mighty strings poise their horsehair bows
to the maestro's gold baton, what roar
icy silence sings between the pines who prowl
with hope for notes of peace, who raise
their arms to virtuoso truth much higher.

    Oh give us Big Sky, let us *all* learn to fly
    to the Chorale Cantata Divine—
    with its stars all in tune to the Bucking Horse Moon,
    to the Milky Way Belfry wind chimes.

    Oh give Earth Her song She will rock eons long,
    Her grace note She'll lilt to infinity—
    Her hymn to the light, arioso in flight
    with Her heart-mind-n-soul holy trinity.

      Percussion's love child, the brass riffing wild
      with Her heart-mind-n-soul holy trinity.

      Let this be
      Our poem to the Cheyenne "Moon
      When The Wolves Run Together"
      Our prayer to the Lakota Sioux "Moon
      When The Deer Shed Their Horns"

      Let this be
      Our poem to the Arapaho "Moon
      Of The Popping Trees" popping
      Our prayer to all of "Nature's People"
      Ol' Charlie Russell's West has 'ever borne.

III

In the sunlight's rays graced down
on our green life, our every breath, on all
the eco-notes of this romantic masterpiece—our heart beat
mantras of harmonic brio—oh what blood
we drink, what clean water makes our wine.

And as we renounce the fury, applaud the sound
of life's immortal music, what call
we heed to Mother Earth who sings sweet
Her canzonettas brought to bud
by graceful rains that make Her children shine.

Oh give us deep space, its fire-n-grace,
the Musical Universe Divine—
with its stars all in tune to the Bucking Horse Moon,
to the Milky Way Belfry wind chimes.

May the Goddess of Song hold eons long
Her grace note embraced to infinity—
Earth's anthem to light, The Diva in flight
with Her heart-mind-n-soul holy trinity.

Woman*kind* shined into Beethoven's Ninth
by this heart-mind-n-soul Earthly Trinity.

Woman*kind* on the rise, *Her* Joy glorified
by this heart-mind-n-soul Earthly Trinity.

In the soft low light up high,
where grace will always thrive,
our prima ballerina, Earth,
pirouettes to each poetic word,
each note, each *turn* She sings to spin and spin
and spin into infinity—amen...amen...amen...

ZD - The strongest argument for religion? Gospel music. Also known, in my view, as "hope for the otherwise hope*less* were it not for their hopeful song." Not convinced? Check out "The Godmother of Rock-n-Roll," Sister Rosetta Tharpe. *Not* "Amen, Brother," but rather "A*woman*, Sister!"

V

Okay. I agree. It's high time we lower the curtain on these Pandeism sentiments with the actual closing scene of the *Self-Interview*—again, the impetus of my inclusion in this *Anthology*:

...Now let's wrap this up. The flipside of regrets is, perhaps, remaining aspirations. What's left—where to from here?

Have you seen the film *Crossroads?*

I have.

Why am I not surprised. Then you remember the old blues musician, Willie Brown, played by that virtuoso actor, Joe Seneca—what an absolutely beautiful face! He's partnered-up with the young protégé, Eugene Martone, played by Ralph Macchio of *The Karate Kid* fame. They bust Willie out of the nursing home and make a pilgrimage to a deep-south crossroads where Willie, in his foolish youth, had made a pact, a contract, with the Devil, and is now hoping to void it. I can't help but interject a couple of marvelous passages that surface in the film. Old Willie saying, "The Blues ain't nothin' but a good man feelin' bad, thinkin' 'bout the woman he was once with." Or this gem, "Robert Johnson gave us twenty-nine songs and that's enough." Anyway, they cross paths again with old Scratch (Beelzebub, Lucifer) played by another extremely talented actor, Robert Judd, who pitches them a deal. If Willie's young guitar ace, Eugene, will "cut heads" with the devil's ace and out-duel him, then Scratch will rip up the contract. Eugene, trained at Julliard, throws the knockout punch with a riff that includes a myriad of classical notes by Paganini that the devil's man, portrayed by maestro guitarist, Steve Vai, cannot counter, cannot upstage. The contract is ripped in two, and Willie and Eugene are beamed back to the gravel crossroads. "I hear Chicago callin'," Willie delights. "You ready for The Windy City?" But then, he announces to the boy's chagrin, "After Chicago, you on your own." When Eugene protests and asks "*Why?*" Willie replies, "Cuz you got to take the music someplace else—take it past where you found it. That's what *we* did."

Thusly, for me, that's what it *has* to be all about— taking the poetry, taking the music, past where I found it. I'm swallowing vitamins and supplements by the fistful. I'm doing my sit-ups, my push-ups, my A.A.R.P. (Ain't Able to Remember Poop) rounds on the heavy bag. I've been writing poetry for over fifty years and another couple-three decades would maybe enable me to ratchet or leverage "my craft or sullen art" (thank you, Dylan Thomas) a notch or two beyond where I discovered it. If I can accomplish this, perhaps I'll be deserving—before some major big-ring poetry show—of the literary world's version of boxing's memorial ten-count tolling of the bell. I can't ask for anything more than that, can I? Except, to be on the receiving end of Mexican Artist Frieda Kahlo's sentiment: "I joyfully await the exit—and I hope to never return."

****

And *thusly*, shape-shifter-most-omnipotent, God-The-Creator, having *become* God-The-Creation, intimates to us, "You on your own, cuz you got to take the music, the piety or divinity or spirituality someplace else—take it past where you found it." Isn't that precisely what God Itself is doing, what It is becoming, as we speak—It, the Universe, expanding, growing, implementing and exhibiting Its fresh, creative, adventurous navigations at an accelerated rate?

Therefore, "let us pray." Let us pray to and for our God selves: May the forces of Goodness, of Godliness, of Truth, Knowledge, Wisdom, Generosity, Empathy...as well as The Two *Non*-Mutually-Exclusive Crucial Virtues, The Crucial Virtue of Defiance and The Crucial Virtue of Humility, guide us on our uniquely personal vision quests across Dimension Earth into whatever Dimension awaits us next. Amen.

Coda

The ideology of this dissertation, I realized too deep into it, is composed of poetic explosions of insubstantial Ghost Particle Neutrinos, the components of which even God, Itself, might have difficulty parsing, explicating, dissecting, interacting with. Allow me to offer, therefore, a closing "visual effect" on my way out the red-flashing neon **ESSAY EXIT**. But first, this final excerpt from the "Self-Interview:"

"...When my muses scream, I click my heels, salute, and heed their desires. Thus, as I prepared to spread my dad's ashes among his twenty-acre woodlot, they beckoned me to dust the bases of **51** of the grandest maples, ash, and oaks. Dad and his good friend Harry cooked moonshine together back in the fifties. I discovered a cobwebbed gallon of the barrel-aged nectar marked "Special" in Dad's hand on the white lid and dribbled a few drops alongside the gray remains beneath each tree. "One for you, Dad, and one for me," I *prayed* with each consecration. I'd take a sip, then stagger to the next hardwood. Somewhere around tree number twenty-three or twenty-nine or thirty-two, I was so impressed by the girth and sculptedness of the trunk that I tipped my head back and stared straight up into the spinning canopy until falling over backward into a colorful bed of leaves. I laid there laughing upward for a spell with God-the-Comedian Creation, before resuming the mission to achieve my Communion of the 51.

It had been almost a year since Dad's death, almost two years since learning of his terminal illness—the most difficult time of my life. I sat (*with him*) in his '67 International pick-up for a long while after spreading his ashes. When my head began to clear, I felt an incredible wave of solace in light of Dad's spirit thriving in that glorious canopy of 51. He was enchanted by mushrooms, and at the base of one of the most majestic oaks, stood—yes, *stood*, on its six-inch-diameter stalk—the most ornate toadstool I'd ever seen, its rouged scalloped cap making it look more like a mollusk than a fungus—a conch Dad more likely would have encountered on shore leave than in his landlocked woodlot. I anointed it, as well, with ashes and a splash of hooch. The moment felt so graced, so hallowed, so divinely *received*—Dad's final wishes heeded to a tee, thanks in some part, I'm convinced, to the numerological role that my birth year, 51, played...."

Dad In The Canopy

Kiss of life, iron-ore-miner-deep,
the root capillaries welcome back
my dad's molecules, his ashes
sifting for the past three years
from the surface where I spilled them,
dashed with a dribble of moonshine,
around each trunk of the fifty-one
thickest maples and oaks. Up into the phloem
goes Leonard, Dad, "hardy lion,"
becoming cambium, branch, lenticels, leaf,
chlorophyll in the crowns—the deep green
breath I breathe, believing

I again inhale my father's first love,
as I did, May 25th, 1951,
looking up in wonder.
                              Arms wrapped
only halfway around the bole
of the ancient, of the holy,
I press my damp cheek into the lost
scripture of bark, into the osmotic
jigsaw puzzle-work, into the reptilian hide
of armored time. What I sense here—
about the strength of flesh, about
the overlapping growth-ringed worlds
of animal with plant, the symbiotic
weave of all that is unknown—
puts religion to rest
in the crypts of its own churches
for good.
                    So little stretch left
in my skin turning to parchment
letter-pressed with the bark's star charts,
I bid you to read, in lieu
of this poem, the imprint, the topographic map,
the labyrinth of the mystical
between the lines on the right-hand
page of my face. There, may you learn
the eternal sermon of wind
snapping the top off
the oldest oak in this woodlot—fallen
crown wilting limper by the minute, green
fading to yellow into brown, limbs
like my father's gnarled arms
offering their withered bouquets.
                                        No matter
how wrenching the tender metaphor
in every lesson of death
held out to us, we, steadfast, reach back,
our hands clenched to the burled urn
carved from bird's-eye, from heartwood
overflowing with sap, with artesian

blood, with whatever living elixir
spills, in this brief duration of faith,
the dust of the ones we love, away.

Fast-forward fourteen years to September 2023. While walking the woodlot beneath "Dad In The Canopy," I palpably felt, tangibly experienced, my belief in Pandeism rise into its clearest view, "putting religion to rest / in the crypts of its own churches / for good." At that moment, I realized that I could read the histories of religious ideologies and their geneses until I'm blue in the face, green in bloodstream, lavender in the liver and, with sincere apologies to the philosophers, theologians, scientists, and, yes, even poets, the bottom line is that nobody has thus far, or likely ever will, offer definitive earthly proof of "what's next." The only way to find out is to die, and I, in concert with my Dominatrix Muse Coven, stirring the bottomless frothing smoldering-cauldron elixir in anticipation of the next and the next and the next...poem, would much prefer *never* to definitively know "what's next." Therefore, I could not agree more with novelist Tom McGuane, who, in fielding an interviewer's query after the death of his friend and brother-in-law, Jimmy Buffet, nailed it most succinctly (From "Jimmy Buffet Remembered by Friend, Tom McGuane..." Chris Willman, *Variety*, September 3, 2023):

"I am not religious but I am not convinced (that death is the end). I mean, for 150,000 years of what we know, people have believed that there was something beyond death, and it's not some guy with a beard and robes, but that there's something indistinguishable about the human spirit. ...I was interviewed for a profile not too long ago, and the guy said, 'What are you hoping for when you die.' And I said, 'A surprise.'"

As promised (drum roll, please) in *visual* correlation with Tom's sentiment, I leave you with the back-cover image to my spoken-word CD, *Collisions of Reckless Love*. WELCOME! Welcome to the "surprise" party, thrown in your honor by none other than celebratory party animal, God, Itself. Step between the rusty barbed wires fencing us in to our theologically myopic pasture, and enter with great revel instead, Creativity's Infinities—all energized by the ultimate revelation that

ZD - The animist and the deist, the pantheist and pandeist, are all cut from the same sacred cosmic cloth,

as well as with *uber*-relief in knowing that

ZD - Faux Satan in faux Hades has a faux inferno that would not roast a faux hot dog, let alone a foe of our faux gods.

Photo and design by Gordon Stevens

The *Beginning*

Postscript

There is not a right or wrong way to read this Anthology – or indeed this entire Anthology series. Each and every essay in this collection stands on its own feet, and the book as a whole stands on its own— though, if you've found it to your liking, there are predecessor volumes presenting many additional perspectives of thought.

You might have noticed that our goal in assembling this has not been to persuade you of the rightness of any one theology, but to inform you of the choices available, a much broader universe of ideas than the average person may imagine.

And now, with increased knowledge.... go forth and love. Go forth and learn. Bring all of those loving and learning experiences back to your second reading, or next reading after that, of this work. We build our understanding of the world together.

Four Quartets

By T. S. Eliot

T.S. Eliot, born in 1888 in St. Louis, was a Nobel Prize-winning poet, essayist, and playwright whose exploration of spirituality and modernist themes left an indelible mark on 20th-century literature. His work, "The Waste Land," captures post-World War I existential despair, while later works like "Four Quartets," excerpted here, reflect deeply upon religion and philosophy, making his works a fitting inclusion in any Anthology of spirituality.

Time present and time past
Are both perhaps present in time future,
And time future contained in time past.
If all time is eternally present
All time is unredeemable.
What might have been is an abstraction
Remaining a perpetual possibility
Only in a world of speculation.
What might have been and what has been
Point to one end, which is always present.
Footfalls echo in the memory
Down the passage which we did not take
Towards the door we never opened
Into the rose-garden. My words echo
Thus, in your mind.
But to what purpose
Disturbing the dust on a bowl of rose-leaves
I do not know.
Other echoes
Inhabit the garden. Shall we follow?

25907019R00306